Kidnapped

PAULA S. FASS

Harvard University Press
Cambridge, Massachusetts
London, England

First Harvard University Press paperback edition
published in 1999 by arrangement with
Oxford University Press

Library of Congress Cataloging-in-Publication Data
Fass, Paula S.
Kidnapped : child abduction in America / Paula S. Fass.
p.   cm.   Includes bibliographical references and index.
ISBN 0-674-00082-X (pbk.)
1. Kidnapping—United States—History—Case studies.
2. Abduction—United States—History—Case studies.
1. Missing children—United States—History—Case studies.
I. Title.
HV6598.F37   1997   364.15′4′0830973—dc21   97-27674

Parts of Chapter 2 were published as "Making and Remaking an Event:
The Leopold and Loeb Case," *Journal of American History*,
80 (December 1993), 919-51.

For Bluma and Charles

CONTENTS

ACKNOWLEDGMENTS

Throughout the research and writing of this book, I have had the good fortune to receive support from a variety of institutions and many friends and colleagues. It is a pleasure to acknowledge them here. Twice, in the summer of 1990 and in 1994–95, the National Endowment for the Humanities provided me with fellowships for independent study. I am very grateful to that wonderful American institution. In 1991–92, together with a group of other delighted scholars, I benefited from the hospitality of the Center for Advanced Study in the Behavioral Sciences in Stanford, California. That marvelous year of study and fellowship was made possible by the Andrew W. Mellon Foundation and the National Endowment for the Humanities (#RA-20037-88), which financed the center's activities on my behalf, and by a Humanities Research Fellowship from the University of California at Berkeley. In various ways over the past eight years, the University of California Committee for Research in the Humanities has assisted my work, especially in its generous funding of research assistance. Without the work of a group of talented and dedicated research assistants this book could never have been completed. I want to thank especially Eric Weisbard and Jesse Berrett, whose skills and resourcefulness (not to speak of patience) were without parallel, and Tracy Oliver, Sara Nichel, Kelly Evans-Pfeifer, and Laura Mihailoff, who made extremely important contributions. Carol Baxter taught me to use the computer, for which I will always be grateful.

Various organizations and people who are actively engaged in finding kidnapped children have been very kind to me. I want to thank the staff of the National Center for Missing and Exploited Children in Arlington, Virginia, and especially Julia Cartwright, for their assistance. Amidst their many tasks, they found the time to meet with me, introduce me to their work, provide me with important materials, and encourage my historical inquiries. David Collins, whose son tragically disappeared almost twenty years ago, has worked tirelessly on behalf of missing children. He shared some of his experiences with me, and I thank him for his generosity. I also appreciate the assistance of the staff at the Polly Klaas Foundation, who supplied me with information and photographs.

Several friends and colleagues read the manuscript at strategic points and provided me with important guidance. Sissela Bok was extraordinary in her kindness and vigorous advice, and her thorough reading was invaluable to my revisions. Lizabeth Cohen read with her usual sharp insight. Sheila Rothman, long a friend and mentor, helped me with the manuscript in many ways. Paul Rock, a visitor from London, read the manuscript of a stranger with great discernment. I only wish we had met earlier so that I could have responded more fully to his suggestions. My colleague and friend Robert Middlekauff has been inestimably important to me for a long time. In reading this book in manuscript he gave me the kind of support that made it possible for me to make it better. Other people read parts of the manuscript during its evolution. I would especially like to thank Daniel Rodgers, Gert Brieger, Louise Tilly, Richard Watson, Mary Ann Mason, David Thelen, and Nathan Hale, Jr. I have been shameless in using colleagues in many places for information and bibliography, among them Peter Sahlins, Andrew Barshay, Susanna Elm, Thomas Barnes, Irv Scheiner, Aron Rodrigue, Peter Novick, James Leiby, Roger Lane, Michael Schudson, Theodore Hamm, and Brian Horrigan, who introduced me to the Wetterling case. I also profited from lively exchanges at the Wesleyan Center for the Humanities, the Rutgers Historical Seminar, the Berkeley Family Seminar, and the Townsend Center for the Humanities at Berkeley.

The excellent staff at Oxford University Press have worked hard to make this book. I wish to thank Joellyn Ausanka, Brandon Trissler, and Catherine Clements, a copy editor with both a sense of style and a sense of humor. Above all, I want to thank Sheldon Meyer, who has been my editor at Oxford for twenty years. He has chaperoned me through the writing of three books and any number of wonderful meals. He is an exemplary editor—supportive, smart, and kind. My agent, Cullen Stanley, miraculously appreciates both literature and business.

My husband, Jack, has been there for me always. This book would not exist without him. While I was trying to figure out what happened to any one of my many Charleys he was there figuring it out with me and being as deeply affected. He knows how much I depend on his good judgment, good humor, and good heart.

I come from a family from which many children were taken, among them brothers and sisters I never knew. I dedicate this book to my own children, whom I have around me to treasure and adore, but I have not forgotten (and never will) the children lost to others.

Kidnapped

Introduction

During winter break in 1994, my family and I took a short and much-needed vacation in Santa Barbara, California. By then I had been at work on this book for five years, and I thought I knew a lot about it, emotionally as well as intellectually. In fact, I had started investigating child kidnapping precisely because I am what many would no doubt describe as an overanxious mother, fearful to let my children out of my sight in public places. The thought that someone might be lurking to take my child was one of the horrors with which I had early become acquainted as a mother. By December 1994, however, I thought I had gotten many of my fears under control, as my studies had suggested that child kidnappings, while a serious and revealing part of our society and its history, were uncommon, and I had come to believe that my worries were not good for my children and terrible for me. I now had an "intellectual handle" on the problem, I thought.

Then on the afternoon of December 28, my husband, Jack, thirteen-year-old daughter, Bibi, and seven-year-old son, Charlie, were strolling down State Street, Santa Barbara's main drag. It was warm and sunny, and we were all relaxed. My son, playing a common childhood game of avoiding the cracks on the sidewalks, was focused on his feet and therefore a few yards behind the rest of us. I would occasionally glance back to make sure he was all right. I had promised him an ice cream cone, and the store was in one of those shallow malls just off the street that have come to characterize new retail spaces in many of California's older, picturesque cities. I was now at the front of our troop, leading the way to the ice cream store, when I asked my husband to check on Charlie. Only seconds before Charlie had been just behind us. Now he was gone. We ran back to State Street, thinking he must be there. He was not. We searched frantically for a couple of minutes, each of us going in a different direction. People began to ask us what was wrong; the police came. Charlie was nowhere to be seen. Then I dropped into a black hole. I was literally inside a nightmare, my ears seemed disconnected from the outside world and humming, my eyes were staring into a tunnel, all my senses were focused on one excruciating fact— Charlie was gone. I would never see him again. I began to scream my son's name and ran frantically down the middle of the street (the sidewalks were full of people). I felt the complete anguish of certain loss. That afternoon, as about one hundred people joined us in our search and as I devoted myself to shouting Charlie's name, I understood something about child kidnapping that had previously eluded me.

Fortunately, the experience (but not the understanding) lasted only ten minutes, ten minutes I cannot adequately describe, despite an academic's usual facility for words, and for which there is no analogy. Charlie had heard me screaming, but his own seven-year-old response could not be heard above the din of a lively public place. When a concerned woman (one of the multitude now actively seeking him—the warm and helpful response of these "strangers" was amazing) saw a boy alone at the end of the street, as if frozen at the corner, she asked if his name was Charlie. He was initially reluctant to give out this precious personal information to a stranger (he had been well taught at home) but finally decided that she looked safe and that she knew where I (still screaming) was. My son returned and the incident became, like other previous ones where my children hid in department store racks or were not exactly where I expected them to be when I went to get them at school, little pieces of mother-trauma now safely in the past. Immediately after I was reunited with Charlie, many mothers on State Street shared their similar experiences with me. Each joined her anxiety to mine, and we reassured each other with this miraculous recovery. Some of them recalled losses lasting five minutes; for others the experiences lasted as much as an hour. Like mine, theirs were also history now, behind them while the children they love, and for whom they carry kidnap fears like live coals, are still very much with them. Their experiences, like mine, have become only stories.

But other mothers and fathers have not been so lucky. And other stories have not been similarly and wonderfully resolved. For these other mothers and fathers, the black hole of loss is a permanent condition, or it lasts a long time, long enough to re-create their lives with the emptiness at the center. This book is about these stories (and tangentially also about brief losses like mine). I have opened it with my own little story because losing Charlie in Santa Barbara taught me as much about the people whose stories I tell as all the thousands of hours of reading, thinking, and writing that I have put into this book. It taught me about the intensity, and the boundlessness, of the pain that comes with the realization that your child has vanished.

The stories I tell in this book are about children who vanish from their parents lives, in many cases forever, in all cases because they have been willfully abducted in a crime that we call kidnapping. The book is about the way we have come socially and culturally to define, understand, deal with, and imagine this crime. It is about the intersection between personal pain and social meaning. When Charlie disappeared in Santa Barbara, I was in shock because I believed that some terrible fate had befallen him. I imagined the worst. I did not think that he might have just wandered down the street or that some kind stranger had bought him an ice cream or joined his game. After all, the strangers in Santa Barbara were very kind to me. My fear and the pain of my personal loss grew from a specific social interpretation that has spread like a deadly cancer. And it is this public interpretation about what it means for a child to just disappear that this book is about.

That interpretation has been shaped by and through stories about real kidnappings, and our fears have developed over time as a result of particular historical experiences and the ways in which actual kidnappings have been publicaly represented. This book is about those historical experiences and the stories they have left in their wake. Each of the stories I tell was culturally resonant, capturing and embodying problems and concerns that appeared urgent in their time, especially relating to family life, gender roles, sexuality, crime, and public order. Because these stories absorbed so many cultural flavors, they became especially pungent to contemporaries, and they are instructive to us by revealing how our own stories relate to contemporary issues. But the kidnappings also influenced each other historically as each left a residue of expectations about the crime; patterns of behavior by parents, police, and criminals; laws and organizations dedicated to children; and distinct ways to understand childhood danger. The experiences of the victims of today's kidnappers, and the broad fears about kidnapping that afflict millions of parents, can only be fully understood in this historical context because the history of the crime has created our personal expectations and institutional responses. The crime today is a product of its past.

Child kidnapping became a serious public problem during this period because Americans developed strong beliefs about and emotional attachments to childhood. Emerging powerfully in the nineteenth century, these beliefs have ever since defined our common views of the characteristics of childhood and the nature of parental sentiments. The fears about child loss that emerged in this context helped to direct the social commitment to children in very specific ways. Instead of a broad drive toward child welfare and well-being and a community's common obligation to all children, kidnap fears directed this heightened sensitivity toward the safety of one's own children. It thus helped to create a wider and wider divide between the family's protectiveness to its own and the public spaces inhabited by strangers. As these stories were orginally framed, kidnapping exposed the children of the middle class to the new dangers of city life and urban vice. But the kidnapping stories, like many malleable and evolving forms, moved in new directions in the twentieth century: first to expose how pervasive the dangers to children was since even well-educated and well-placed boys could become kidnappers, and then how it could threaten even the most powerful. Eventually, as kidnapping rang louder and louder cultural alarms about childhood danger, no child was safe. By the mid-twentieth century, the kidnapping threat, which always hid the possibility of sexual danger (stolen by who knows who for who knows what purpose?), was thoroughly democratized in the form of the sexual predator.

Child kidnapping became an incubus to our warmest beliefs and feelings for children, a crime that both exploited the ideals and bedeviled the emotions that surrounded them. Part of this development naturally grew from the emotions themselves as love and fear of loss developed side by side. But a good part was the result of the means by which kidnapping fears were created and managed in the press and the evolving twentieth-century media.

Indeed, since the nineteenth century, parents have depended on publicity to retrieve their stolen children. That very dependence has helped to turn kidnapping from a minor criminal problem into a public preoccupation. In transforming kidnapping into a public concern, cultural publicity has preyed on our tenderest sentiments about children and the very drive created by these sentiments to protect and defend them. These positive emotions were insistently invoked in the stories of child endangerment—the kidnap tales—that I retell in this book. The stories confirmed the appropriate emotions, values, and commitments of the middle-class sentimentalization of childhood; but instead of turning them in social directions, toward child protection, the stories about child kidnapping exploited the emotions themselves. Thus, historically, the means by which we have represented our commitments to our children's welfare have attached titillations to their exploitation. This is part of the paradox of child kidnapping, and it helps to explain our growing alarm over the crime and, probably, its growing incidence as well: the very stories we have used to signal our cultural commitment to children have defined those children's loss as part of their appeal.

The more we know about the crime and the more fearsome it becomes, the more addicted we seem to be to the dangers it poses for the children we love. The crime has been so sensationally presented that the despoilation of innocence, which provides the emotional charge of these stories, has become a major source of cultural thrill. We see this all around us today, as stories of child kidnappings and abuse fill the schedule of television programs like *America's Most Wanted*, *Law and Order*, *The X-Files*, and *Prime Suspect*, and the many made-for-television movies that include both real and made-up stories. The nightly news is full of children threatened by abduction and children lost to abductors. Child victimization has also become a prominent part of the mystery fiction genre. As a society, we are haunted everywhere by pictures of abducted children in police stations, in newspapers, on television and posters, and on more homey objects like milk cartons. We have literally surrounded ourselves with reminders of our lost children, which serve both as cautions and come-ons, provoking anxiety and defining a cultural indulgence that exploits the very children we seek to protect. This seeming contradiction is, in fact, the result of how child kidnapping has been framed and has evolved historically. By exploiting our fears and indulging our most extreme (and brutal) fantasies, our public representations do not channel our warm concern for children toward genuine protection and advocacy of their many needs; they substitute thrill for social commitment. Of course, people do care, as the people in Santa Barbara cared about Charlie and as the many who turn out to search for missing children all over the country care. But as a society we have not expressed real care for our children—whose various needs at home, in school, in the community are manifested every day—only a fearful pity. We have become so engrossed by the crime of child abduction that parental kidnapping, which has been a social problem since the nineteenth century but was until quite recently kept distinct from stranger abduction, has now been added to the count and the drama of stranger kidnappings. By inflating the numbers, we have added a complex social problem (parental abduction) to a heinous crime to portray child kidnapping as an even more common and therefore more terrifying occurrence. Child kidnapping has become like a ride at an amusement park, frightening and entertaining us at the same time.

A variety of contradictions have become attached to child kidnapping, riveting the attention of the enormous number of people fascinated by the stories (both real and fictional) and tormenting the much smaller number of victims. Many of these contradictions revolve around the role of publicity and the media, which are essential to any hope for the recovery of a child while they are instrumental in the exploitative hysteria that has periodically and increasingly beset the problem. Contradications also beset the ambiguous relationship between the parents of victims and the police, who are looked to for help and restitution. Issues related to responsible publicity and effective police behavior have been part of the problem of child abduction since 1874, where this book begins, with the first public instance of child kidnapping—the notorious ransom abduction of Charley Ross, probably the most famous American child in the late nineteenth century, whose story was known for generations as the archetypical tale of child kidnapping.

It is important to remember that while 1874 marks the historical beginning of child kidnapping in the United States, children had disappeared long before, and child theft is probably an ancient occurrence, familiar to many societies. Even the Old Testament contains instances of this, most notably in the story of Joseph, who was captured and sold by his own brothers. His disappearance caused his father, Jacob, great anguish. But before 1874, in the United States at least, the disappearance of children or their abduction was not defined as a social problem. It had no public existence. Child kidnapping emerged at a specific historical moment because it was embedded in the instruments of modern society and culture, both within a specific context of attitudes toward children and toward the obligations of parents, and molded by evolving political institutions like laws and the police and by cultural institutions like psychiatry and the media. Before 1874 there was no expectation that children would be kidnapped. There was no need for the kind of psychological analysis, social interpretation, or legal breast-beating that has accompanied it ever since and certainly no need for a history of the problem. And there could be no anxiety like that which I share with millions of mothers and fathers all over the United States. This anxiety has been shaped and directed into its current form because at a certain historical point the kidnapping of children became a public issue, one that developed over time into what we perceive to be a widespread problem.

The issue of child kidnapping first emerged into public consciousness as the story of the loss of a particular child, and it has remained ever since most vividly represented in stories of specific lost and missing children. I have chosen to retell it that way because it is most true to our experience of the problem. In the course of my retellings, I show how each story's plot and details were heavily weighted with the social issues of its time and how they were connected with each other so that knowledge of previous kidnappings affected beliefs and responses to future kidnappings. Today we make certain assumptions about the nature of a kidnappping—its cause, consequence, and probable outcome—because of past experience, but these earlier kidnappings were often differently explained and understood. In other words, our definition of the crime (even, indeed, the courts' definition) has been historically derived.[1]

It is my hope that the reader will come to see how the stories I tell shaped the crime of child kidnapping over the past hundred and twenty years so that the various elements of our present-day experiences and anxieties, as well as our cultural fixations, can be better understood. As I learned in Santa Barbara, to understand is not to conquer. But we need to understand, nevertheless, and a history of this problem is essential to our understanding of how we have come by our problems and how the very nature of our culture has created the problem of child kidnapping and brought it into each of our homes and our lives.

回||回

Even though child kidnapping in the United States became a fully constructed public issue only in 1874 and had no history before then, it did have
a variety of antecedents. It is not my intention to explore these in detail, but
a brief introduction to these helps us more fully to understand the manner
in which the modern crime of kidnapping drew on earlier experiences, as
well as more fully to appreciate how it was new.

The term kidnapping, which came originally from "kidnapper"—a cant
term for thief—originated in the late seventeenth century (1682 according
to the *Oxford English Dictionary*). The term itself is a compound of "kid" and
"nap," both slang terms, meaning respectively "child" and "seize." As if in
anticipation of contemporary American obsessions, it was early associated
with the New World since it referred to stealing and carrying off usually
children, but others as well, for service on American plantations. The great
English legal commentator, Sir William Blackstone, maintained the ex-
traterritorial connection in his definition, "the forcible abduction or stealing
away of a man, woman or child from their own country and sending them
into another." Since labor in the New World was scarce and providing it
profitable, carrying off a person for mercenary reasons became the basis for
the definition of the word, and the illegal seizure and carrying of a person
became the definition of the crime (a misdemeanor) in Anglo-American
common law. When Robert Louis Stevenson wrote his famous book, *Kidnapped* in 1886, he retained the full original reference of the word. The story
was set in 1751, and his young Scottish hero, seventeen-year-old David Bal-
four, was denied his inheritance when his wicked and malicious uncle had
him falsely lured onto and then bound on a vessel headed for the Carolinas.
"In those days," the narrator observed, "men were still sold into slavery on
the plantations." [2]

Of course, seventeenth-century England was not the first or only society
in which the practice of forcibly capturing and holding people (for labor or
ransom) occurred. The Latin word *plagiarius* originally meant a torturer or
plunderer and included the kidnapper as a variant. Somewhat later it took
on its familiar modern meaning, the stealing of what Montaigne in the sixteenth century referred to as the children of one's soul—one's writings. [3]
Many societies and cultures have experienced forms of snatching and abduction. Starting in medieval times, probably in the ninth century in Is-

lamic countries and some centuries later in Europe, Jews (because of their geographic mobility as merchants) were often captured on their travels, and their ransoming became a conventional and obligatory part of Jewish community life in the Middle Ages. In Europe, Jews were often also captured and accused of various profanations against Christian practice. For Jews to pay into a fund for the ransom of captured brethren was a good deed, required even above the need to give charity to the poor (a revered Jewish tradition). During the same period, kings and royal heirs were also vulnerable to captivity and to the political extortion to which this subjected them, as were young noblewomen whose inheritance was sought by suitors whom they could be forced thereby to marry. But these individuals or groups were either so vulnerable or outcast or so rich and powerful that they were set apart, subject to experiences unrelated to that of the general population.[4]

The new seventeenth-century term "kidnap," however, suggests the inception of a broadly threatening phenomenon. In fact, a substantial part of the population in the English North American colonies of the seventeenth and early eighteenth centuries (outside of New England) was composed of indentured servants, who were recruited by means fair and foul from among the newly dislocated populations of an England on the brink of industrialization. The recruitment of workers was a profitable enterprise, and it spawned practices that were terrifying. One of the most frightening characters of English folklore of the time was the "spirit," a shadowy figure who recruited or kidnapped adults to board America-bound ships. These agents often abducted those who were hardly fully conscious— drunkards and the simpleminded. They were also known to lure children with sweets. A similar kind of enterprise soon affected the European continent in the early eighteenth century as it became another source of immigration. The peopling of America had thus from the beginning involved methods of recruitment that included both outright kidnapping and other means that, while short of explicit thievery, employed various deceits and immoral inducements to encourage transportation. Though long forgotten by the late nineteenth century, this experience was in many ways at the root of our society.[5]

This same need for labor in the new American lands had also reawakened the ancient African and Middle Eastern trade in slaves, another form of human theft and entrapment. By the late seventeenth century, what was to become one of the largest forced population dislocations was strongly under way, and by the eighteenth century, the massive African slave trade was at its peak. In the seventeenth and eighteenth centuries, European traders tended not to think of the African slave trade in terms of theft, but as part of the newly internationalized trade in merchandise. However, by the lights of the more humanitarian sensibilities of the nineteenth century and in the context of the abolitionist campaigns against slavery and especially books like Harriet Beecher Stowe's sensational *Uncle Tom's Cabin*, the forced sale of Africans, including children (from Africa and within the United States), had left a troubling residue in the American imagination.[6]

The Anglo-American experience with kidnapping had thus been substantial, and most of it had distinct mercenary connections. It was in France that a significant and chilling variant on the idea of child disappearance emerged in the fifteenth century. As historian George Bataille has shown, the horrible crimes of Gilles de Rais, an extraordinarily rich and powerful Breton nobleman, have often been interwoven with the notorious fable of Bluebeard. Nevertheless, the Lord de Rais (a marshal of France who fought alongside Joan of Arc) was very much a real historical monster, who kidnapped innumerable children, sodomized them, sadistically killed and then mutilated them for his own libertine (and possibly demon-worshipping) pleasures. In his confession, Gilles de Rais admitted: "because of his passion and sensual delight, he took and had others take so many children that he could not determine with certitude the number whom he'd killed and caused to be killed, with whom he committed the vice and sin of sodomy; and he said and confessed that he had ejaculated spermatic seed in the most culpable fashion on the bellies of the said children, as much after their deaths as during; on which children, he and sometimes his accomplices . . . inflicted various types and manner of torment. . . . Which children dead, he embraced them, and he gave way to contemplating those who had the most beautiful heads and members, and he had their bodies cruelly opened and delighted at the sight of their internal organs."[7]

With the Lord de Rais we are in the presence of the kind of sadistic tormenter of children who haunts the contemporary imagination. It is no wonder that for a long time he was relegated to the realm of scary fairy tales, among the goblins, witches, and trolls who were believed to spirit away children, and it was assumed that he was more a fable than a historical figure. Whether real or invented, Gilles de Rais defined the outer possibilities of human depredation and of imaginable crimes. This was the case in 1460 when he was publicly executed, and it remains so today. We do well to remind ourselves that this kind of behavior, and other such horrible acts inflicted on children, have had a recurrent historical presence. According to Bataille, de Rais was a kind of sacred monster, an individual so set apart from the rest of humanity, so self-sufficient and so self-defined, that he could operate by his own rules, apart from the ordinary confines of normality. Monsters of this kind define the norm by transcending it. Today, these unthinkable crimes are once again on our social horizon, and as they express the most heinous reaches of human depravity, they also help to set clear boundaries on acceptable behavior.

Thus the theft and torture of children for nonmonetary gain, a theme of special significance in contemporary America, has a history in the West at least as old as the capture of children for economic exploitation. In France the two themes came together in the eighteenth century on the eve of the French Revolution. At that point, as large numbers of "street children" (really the children of the Paris poor) seemed to simply vanish or were observed being abducted by the police (usually for labor in the colonies), rumor spread that they were being sacrificed by the "mad" king for therapeutic purposes because the blood of innocent children was believed to have curative properties. The therapeutic or cultic use of children's blood has had a tenacious hold on the European imagination for centuries. This accusation against the Jews, "the blood libel," had initially served various kinds of psychological and sociological purposes specific to its time and was resurrected when the campaigns against the Jews were recurrently renewed. Today, the belief that children are sacrificed for cultic purpose recurs in popular beliefs about satanic cults and rings. That children could serve to cure or were needed in rituals (usually devoted to anti-Christian objectives) has been associated with the misuse or sacrifice of their very innocence and purity. In fact, there was never any evidence against the king of France and none against the Jews of the Middle Ages (and there is none to substantiate extensive satanic practices today), but this oft-imagined crime allowed the projection of extreme hostility, anxiety, and suspicions. It ejected those accused of such monstrous behavior from the fellowship of humankind. Indeed, the theft of children by those assumed to be less than fully human, even without the supposed torture or sacrifice of blood remained an important residue in beliefs about gypsies. All over modern Europe (and to a lesser degree in the United States), the belief that gypsies stole children as they passed through towns and villages on their endless wandering was part of this process of ejection since gypsies were defined as utterly apart from and outside of the community.[8]

For centuries in Europe children had thus been used both as symbols of their abductor's loathsome behavior or lack of humanity and as objects of mercenary exploitation. Each of these fundamental manipulations of childhood would become important in the modern history of child kidnapping.

But the most direct antecedents of the modern experience of child kidnapping were closer to home. For two centuries, the most vivid crimes in North America were associated with the taking of white captives by Indians. The many and varied accounts of these experiences by the redeemed or the escaped were an indigenous form of American literature and a fundamental aspect of American self-representation. These accounts, written by adult captives and adults originally captured as children, were published and republished in English beginning in 1676, when the narrative of the captivity of Mrs. Mary Rowlandson first appeared. And they remained a dependably popular form of literature and a vital part of the American imagination until just after the Civil War, when the genre died out. It is worth examining certain features of this genre here both because it so often featured tortured and abducted children and because it had become an exhausted form at just the point when the modern problem of child kidnapping began.[9]

Although historians have paid much attention to the internal transformations of the captivity narratives, from exercises in religious faith in the late seventeenth century to romantic adventures in the nineteenth, our own needs are best served by observing them as a single important form, a type of literature that familiarized readers with a terrible experience of loss and prepared them for certain kinds of painful intrafamilial emotions. From that perspective, three features are most significant. All the narratives involved violent abductions from home. They very frequently featured the forced separation of family members, often of children from parents, and sometimes the death and violation of children in the presence of their mothers (especially in women's narratives). Often this separation is accompanied by a helpless lack of knowledge about the location and fate of children or a numbing inability to act on their behalf. Finally, the Indian marauders are portrayed as strangers to the white community. Even when some of the native Americans are individually known to white settlers, the Indians are ultimately cultural strangers, their habits, rituals, and behavior defined as savage and barbaric. They are "strange" because they are not within the community and "strange" because they are so profoundly different in behavior, appearance, and human sensibility.

A brief passage from the Rachel Plummer narrative of 1839 gives a sense of how these elements operate together: "I must call my readers to bear with me in rehearsing the continued barbarous treatment of the Indians. My child kept crying, and almost continually calling for 'Mother,' though I was not allowed even to speak to it. At the time they took off my fetters, they brought my child to me, supposing that I gave suck. As soon as it saw me, it, trembling with weakness, hastened to my embraces. Oh, with what feelings of love and sorrow did I embrace the mutilated body of my darling little James Pratt. I now felt that my case was much bettered, as I thought they would let me have my child; but oh, mistaken, indeed, was I; for as soon as they found that I had weaned him, they, in spite of all my efforts, tore him from my embrace. He reached out his hands toward me, which were covered with blood, and cried, 'Mother, Mother, oh, Mother!' I looked after him as he was borne from me, and I sobbed aloud. This was the last I ever heard of my little Pratt. Where he is, I know not." Lavinia Eastlock employed similar themes in 1862: "During the day I heard the children crying most of the time; sometimes I heard them screaming and crying. . . . No one can imagine my feelings. . . . I thought then and I think now, that they were torturing the children. . . . About 4 o'clock in the afternoon I heard three guns fired. The children then ceased crying. Poor innocent ones!—they were now at rest."[10]

These nineteenth-century narratives clearly draw upon the expectation of the sentimental attachment between mother and child, the brutality of forced separation, and the abuse of innocence. These were certainly all Victorian themes, but they were not exclusively Victorian. In fact, earlier narratives had drawn on similar images, and the captivity literature generally tended to have a solid undercurrent that emphasized the forced separation of children from their mothers and the heartless savagery of Indians who felt no compunction about mutilating children. Thus, Mary Rowlandson wrote in 1676, "I went to see my daughter Mary, who was at this same Indian Town. . . . She was about ten years old. . . . When I came in sight, she would fall a weeping; at which they were provoked and would not let me come near her, but bade me be gone; which was a heart-cutting word to me. I had one Child dead, another in the Wilderness, I knew not where, the third they would not let me come near to. . . . Heart-aking thoughts here I had about my poor children, who were scattered up and down among the wild beasts of the forest." "The Infidels," declared Rowlandson, "haling Mothers one way, and Children another, and some wallowing in their blood." Indeed, Indians were often portrayed as sadistic in the destruction of infants and children. Rachel Plummer, among others, described horrify-ing scenes. Of her seven-week-old infant, Plummer recalled, "one of them caught hold of the child by the throat; and with his whole strength, and like an enraged lion actuated by its devouring nature, held on like the hungry vulture, until my child was to all appearance entirely dead. . . . As soon as they found it had recovered a little, they again tore it from my embrace. . . . They tied a platted rope round the child's neck, and threw its naked body into the large ledges of prickly pears. . . . They would then pull it down through the pears. This they repeated several times. One of them then got on a horse, and tying the rope to his saddle, rode round a circuit of a few hundred yards, until my little innocent was not only dead, but literally torn to pieces."[11] The narratives about Indian captivity and cruelty accustomed Americans to several themes that would recur in the creation of a new threat, the crime of child kidnapping. Among these were the pain of family separation, the helpless lack of knowledge about the whereabouts of chil-dren, the fear of strange and violent marauders, and child mutilation.

A related aspect of Indian abduction was also available to American fears from the beginning: the issue of identity. The idea of a threatening change in the identity of one's child had long been a familar part of the European folklore (and available in, among others, Shakespeare's plays) about the changeling, the stolen child who had been replaced by malicious fairies with another, usually strange spirit. As historian John Demos has recently reminded us, capture by the Indians was feared not only because it might result in death or torture, but because it could portend an alteration in iden-tity. Many young captives became firmly part of the Indian culture into which they were absorbed and did not "return" to their old homes and lives. This possibility was often as horrifying to white Americans as the outright loss of the child since it raised profound questions about the absorption into savagery and loss of civilized behavior for the missing child.[12] For the vic-tims of child kidnapping this theme often arises, as parents who no longer know their child's whereabouts or with whom he or she is associating an-guish about the effects on the child's character and identity of these new associations or about new behaviors required for survival. In 1874, Christian Ross worried that his son's new criminal associates would spoil his respectable and good-natured son. More than one hundred years later, Etan Patz's father was horrified by the thought that his son might be altogether changed after being for several years forced to live in a pedophilic relationship with his abductor, and he wondered if he would even be the same child he had once known. Many parents whose children have been abducted by spouses fear that their children will no longer be known to them, not only because they have been so long gone but because of the loss by the victimized parents of control over the child's nurture and future. As with folkloric fears about changelings or the concern about children abducted by Indians, modern child kidnapping calls up disturbing questions about the lost connection between child and parents as well as more immediate questions about the child's welfare. And this concern is a key to the pain that child kidnapping provokes in the culture. The child is precious as an extension of our nurture and of ourselves.

While the Indian capture of white women and children was an expression of warfare and a terrifying confrontation in the wilderness between cultures that propelled white Americans to define themselves through the contrast, *kidnapping became a crime*. As a crime, it forced Americans to confront the possibility of villainy within their own culture and ultimately within their own breasts. Initially, Americans hoped to lay the blame for the new crime of child kidnapping on outsiders, but that ploy proved untenable in the face of the evidence. And the evidence pointed to a new kind of terror, a form of rapacity that attacked the most vulnerable members of society precisely because they were increasingly the most precious. As Americans confronted the first case of ransom kidnapping in 1874, they could draw on certain sensibilities about separation and depredation familiar from Indian captivity narratives as well as even more ancient memories and traditions. But the explicit emphasis on the theft of the child in order to extort money introduced them to a very new consequence of having invested their children with the sentimental values of love and devotion. If the Indians had threatened to forestall the future of white conquest in the American wilderness by stealing (or killing) their children, kidnappers threatened a much more intimate kind of future and tore at the family bond.[13]

◙ III ▣

For the purposes of this book, I have defined as children those from infancy to their mid-teens; they are the subjects of most kidnap stories and their helplessness is usually essential to the power of these stories. In the following chapter, I will describe how kidnapping became a notorious crime when little Charley Ross was kidnapped from his home in 1874, how Charley's father learned to respond to this crime, and what it meant to Americans. The case of Charley Ross was a defining social experience, which created not just a new crime, but became a fixture of the popular imagination. By the early twentieth century, the crime became a familiar feature of the landscape. It was then recast as a new threat by the kidnappings of the 1920s, especially the notorious case of Leopold and Loeb, which raised questions about what kinds of people were capable of inflicting horrible crimes on children. In the new psychologically sensitive environment of the time, these questions moved the crime into thoroughly modern channels, away from theft for money, to emotionally even more wrenching possibilities. By the 1930s, America's kidnapping problem became an international event with the abduction of Charles A. Lindbergh, Jr. That event broadcast the vulnerability of even the most powerful to the criminality, which now seemed omnipresent in America, a vulnerability symbolized by the kidnapping of a child. After the extraordinary attention paid to the Lindbergh case, the crime of kidnapping became not only a very serious federal offense, but the subject of sensationalized media attention.[14]

The evolving media, in new and evermore pervasive guises, helped to transform the crime from a social problem to a national fixation. In the 1950s, some of the psychological currents stirred up in the 1920s were attached to a general uneasiness about sexuality and gender and a recharged familialism. Babies and adolescent girls seemed to be especially vulnerable victims, as the two San Francisco Bay Area cases I examine will show. In the past, media attention had focused on the rich and the celebrated, although all children could be victimized. After World War II, the infatuation with the bizarre experiences of ordinary people, which would culminate in a modern media reigned over by the Donahues and the Oprahs, began to focus on new kinds of abductions. Indeed, although ransomings still made news, sex made bigger news. The emphasis on children as victims of sexual crimes and the focus on ordinary families peaked in the 1980s in a social redefinition of the crime, now focused on parental kidnappings and sexual abductions. A crime that had once evoked horror because it was rare now evoked horror because it was so common. In the very recent past, the growing number of children who have been described as brutally abducted has made the crime of child kidnapping an almost daily phenomenon and a staple of the local news. Easy victims of a seemingly chaotic society, abducted children have been exploited as a source for daily sensationalism.

In the past 120 years, Americans have made and remade the crime of child kidnapping. Whatever the human proclivities for sadistic abuse of children (and the tale of Gilles de Rais suggests that this may appear at any time), the modern problem of child abduction is historically specific, part of how our culture views children, parenthood, and sexuality and how it defines strangers, community, and crime. The stories that we tell ourselves about these crimes against children help us to define these issues. The stories that I tell here have played key roles in the evolution of the modern crime of child kidnapping, but they are not the only ones I could tell; other stories were important, and every one was a wrenching abomination to the victim's family and to the child, whether it made history or not. In telling these stories, I hope I can show why we have surrendered to the fear of kidnappers in our culture perhaps more than to any other fear.

CHAPTER ONE

"The Lost Boy"

The Abduction of Charley Ross

The world, from of old to our day, is full of stories of stolen children. They are stories of bereavements sharper than death. Among the saddest of these touching stories, among the most deeply veiled in mysteries, is the story and mystery of Charles Brewster Ross. The story is already familiar in various degrees of fullness and accuracy to millions of sympathetic hearts.[1]

Sometime on the afternoon of July 1, 1874, Charles Brewster Ross and his brother, Walter, disappeared from the front lawn of their comfortable upper-middle-class home on Washington Lane in Germantown, Pennsylvania. In the early evening of the same day, Walter came home, escorted by a man who had found him crying outside a store in Kensington, another Philadelphia district, about eight miles away. Four-year-old Charles— always known as Charley—was the younger of the two brothers and the youngest son in the Ross household of seven children. Charley did not return.

According to Walter, two men took them away in their horse and buggy that Wednesday afternoon. These men were not entirely strangers. On the Saturday before they had come by the house and given the boys candy. When the boys told their father about this, Christian Ross issued the standard warnings about taking candy from strangers. But since Saturday the men had twice returned to chat with the boys, and Walter and Charley were apparently relaxed and amenable to the offers of candy on that fateful Wednesday. More portentiously, they were friendly to the suggestion that they all go off to buy firecrackers for the approaching July Fourth celebration. Walter, a sharp observer, remembered the streets and bridges the four then traversed as they fled the Ross house, and the fact that the older of the two men had a deformed nose and drank occasionally from a "dark bottle" lying on the bottom of the wagon. Despite the time of year, the men put the wagon cover over the boys. Walter also told his father that after a while Charley began to cry and wanted to go home. Charley was still weepy when they came to a store at Palmer and Richmond Streets, where Walter was given twenty-five cents to buy firecrackers. When he came out loaded down with his purchases, the men, the wagon, and Charley were gone.

The tale of little Charley's disappearance and the attempts to recover him became one of the most poignant and well-known stories of childhood in the late nineteenth century. And it defined the public perception of the crime of child kidnapping for generations to come. Indeed, the memory of Charley's mystery lingered well into the twentieth century, where it remained the essential abduction tale until it was displaced by the kidnapping of another Charles in 1932. The story of the Lindbergh baby, which we today assume to be the archetypical kidnapping and certainly the most notorious, in fact occupied psychological and cultural space that had been delineated almost sixty years earlier.

Throughout the late nineteenth century and well into the twentieth, Charley Ross's abduction was thoroughly familiar in American culture, where it served as a touchstone for victim's families, and was specifically alluded to by subsequent kidnappers and in the courts whenever major child kidnappings took place. And the Ross case was known as both "the crime of the century" and as the first ransom kidnapping in America.[2] Whether it was either of these matters less than the extraordinary and dramatic part it played in defining the act of child kidnapping and in demarcating the psychological terrain that child abduction would occupy thereafter for parents and for the culture. As a significant public story, the disappearance of Charley Ross is the beginning of the history of child kidnapping in the United States.

回|回

Our knowledge of Charley Ross's abduction and of his parents' attempts to bring him home was sharply etched by the memoir that Christian Ross published in 1876: *The Father's Story of Charley Ross, the Kidnapped Child Con-*

taining a Full and Complete Account of the Abduction of Charles Brewster Ross From the Home of His Parents in Germantown, with the Pursuit of the Abductors and Their Tragic Death; The Various Incidents Connected with the Search for the Lost Boy; The Discovery of Other Lost Children, Etc, Etc. With Facsimiles of Letters from the Abductors. In the usual manner of Victorian titles, this one speaks volumes, not only in its own length, but in highlighting the themes that dominate the story. Most notable is the image of "the lost boy," which from very early in the case became the the most often used term[3] and interchangeable with Charley himself, just as it is in this title. As the "lost boy," Charley's undefined whereabouts, his unknown identity, and the excruciating uncertainty about whether he was still alive (by this point, Charley had been missing for two years) emphasized the tragedy of Charley's fate. Christian experienced the pain of these mysteries as a "bereavement sharper than death" and proposed that knowledge of his son's sure death would be much preferred. Charley as the kidnapped child would have had a finite identity since there were no others known to be kidnapped at the time, but as the lost child his identity merged with that of the many lost children of the period as the title suggests. It was just this merging between Charley Ross's specific identity as "the lost boy" and the fact that the description "lost child" was a more general nineteenth-century theme (remember the "lost boys" in Barrie's *Peter Pan*) that captures some of the power the story had at the time and its ability to evoke broader social issues. Indeed, many children were lost in nineteenth-century cities, and the image of the lost or displaced child had become a staple of Victorian literature, most memorably perhaps in Charles Dickens's *Oliver Twist*.[4] Christian was able to draw deeply on the resonances, both real and fictional, that his son's disappearance and displacement could evoke.

The title also proclaims itself "a Full and Complete Account." Christian Ross was here responding to three issues that bedeviled the case from its beginning: The limited information that was officially made available to the public through the newspapers as part of the pursuit of the kidnappers; Ross's refusal to release the content of the ransom notes, both because he feared copycats and because he hoped to shield his wife from knowledge of some of the more coldblooded threats made against Charley; and finally, the fact that within weeks of the abduction ugly stories began to circulate that either Ross or his wife was involved in the abduction. These allegations were published in the newspapers, especially the *New York Herald*, and were the basis of a popular New York play. In other words, the initial facts about Charley's disappearance lacked transparency and their meaning was not self-explanatory. Instead, the story was mysterious and suspicious because unfamiliar. And it energetically generated a variety of well-known explanations, some of these deeply harmful to the Ross family. Christian lays claim in the title to clearing up these mysteries (though not the mystery of Charley's whereabouts) and to telling the whole and full truth about Charley's disappearance. And while his own story, as we shall see, is far from transparent, his version has become the definitive one and has served as the basis for all subsequent retellings.[5]

Finally, Ross's title glancingly refers to the dominant theme of his story: the redemption through suffering that resulted from the tragedy of the lost child. For while Christian Ross failed to find *his own child*, Charley's abduction, the publicity and public outcry it created, and Christian's devoted search for Charley led to the recovery of other children and their reconciliation with parents. Thus Charley, who after July 1 was fatherless, was always portrayed as a sadly beautiful, uncommonly sweet, curly-haired innocent, beloved by all. With his sorrowful brown eyes, Charley became a kind of *"ecce juvenile,"* who transcended his own particular set of family relations to allow other family relations to be saved and healed. Christian symbolism is quite consciously part of Ross's portrayal and his memoir is prefaced by a long introduction by the Norton Professor of Theology at the Lutheran Theological Seminary.[6] In fact, as we shall see, this overt Christian symbolism was being publicly replaced by a set of secular domestic meanings centered on personal identity and parental emotion in the very act of telling Charley's story. Although Christian could draw upon the deep resonances of the Christ story, his tale of "the lost boy" had father-son implications of a very different kind.

Christian's story is fundamental to our knowledge of Charley, but Charley was not kidnapped alone and it is only because Walter (aged six) was also taken and subsequently released that we know some of the details of the actual abduction. Walter and Christian's stories are therefore integral parts of Charley's. But, certain members of the large Ross household are hardly there and are certainly not vehicles of translation and interpretation. These include two of Charley's sisters (Marian Kimball and Anne Christine Ross), who were in the house at the time of the abduction and figure not at all in the story; several house servants, including the two nursemaids

responsible for the children (Bridget and Sarah Kerr); and, most significantly, Charley's mother, Sarah Ann Lewis. Mrs. Ross is not a transmitter of
Charley's story. She was not even at home at the time he was taken, but recovering from some unknown ailment in Atlantic City. Indeed, Sarah Ross
was not told about the abduction until July 6, almost a week after Charley
had disappeared. Christian claims to have tried to shield Sarah from the fact
and the details of the abduction because he hoped to recover the child before
she returned. In so doing, and later in trying to keep her away from his negotiations with the kidnappers, Christian essentially excluded Sarah from
Charley's story. He and he alone became the negotiator, arbitrator, and de-
finer of his son's future and of his story. Even Sarah's grief was transmitted
through her husband's memoir. This could sometimes be moving ("the anguish of my wife I could not undertake to assuage. . . . Tears afford an outlet
for grief, but with her the fountain was dry"), but secondhand, nevertheless.
In newspaper accounts, too, Sarah is a shadowy figure, described in the
clichés of grief: "the poor mother," "the stricken lady." She was almost
never interviewed in the press. The *New York Herald* described Sarah's sad-
ness as "something so noble, so hopeful, so womanly." Indeed, both Christian and the newspapers freely speak on behalf of women, usually in the
most abstract terms. The *New York Times*, for example, noted that "the
name of Charley Ross has become a household word throughout the country and many a mother's heart has bled."[7] In fact, it was paternal roles that
were being publicly defined through the story of Charley Ross's kidnapping, while identifiable women's voices were silent and the mother's presence obscured by cliché.

At some point then, in response to the rumors and innuendos generated
by an as yet incomprehensible crime, Christian realized the need for an "official story," a story that would reestablish his authority and possibly even
return his son. For Christian claims to have written his book to "assist someone, perhaps even Charley to identify himself" and to help obtain "the
means to enable me to continue a search that cannot be abandoned until the
child is found alive, or his death is certainly proven to us."[8] The continuing
uncertainties about Charley's whereabouts and fate brings his story most
fully to life in this the most fundamental document of his existence.

In fact, however, Christian's story is only one of the three stories that con-
stituted the story of the Lost Boy, captivated the public imagination, and defined the act of kidnapping for generations. The second story is about the

police's attempt to capture the abductors, and the third is of the multiple sightings (resurrections) of Charley as his story became part of popular culture. In this last, most public story, "Charley Ross" was found again and again all over the United States and abroad. This final story involved thousands of people actively searching for Charley and, in the process, making "the lost boy" a national figure. In this way, the story of Charley that Christian tried to define in order to repossess his son moved far beyond Christian's control, becoming firmly embedded in American culture. In the process, the new crime of kidnapping was introduced into every part of the American landscape.

Christian's personal search for Charley continued relentlessly until his death in 1897, when it was taken up by his wife, Sarah. And even after her death in 1912, grown men would come forward in all parts of the United States to identify themselves as "the lost child." Fifty years after his disappearance, Charley's abduction had become the "classic kidnapping" case and so well known that it remained a natural for newspapers. As journalist Edward H. Smith observed in 1927, "Any kind of an item suggesting the discovery of Charlie [sic] Ross is always good copy and will be telegraphed about the country from end to end, and printed at greater or lesser length." As late as 1939, Gustav Blair, a carpenter, had himself adjudged Charley Ross in an Arizona court, and just after Walter Ross died in 1943, a Germantown paper announced that "Philadelphia police this week, for the thousandth time, were given a tip which may turn out to be a valuable clue in the search for Charley Ross," no longer "little" but still *lost*.[9] By then, of course, Charley's story had been absorbed into legend.

𝗮||𝗯

After Walter returned home without Charley, Christian Ross tried frantically to retrace the path taken by the abductors and to enlist the assistance of the Germantown police in that quest. When they were initially informed by Christian in the early evening, the police were hardly alarmed about the child's well-being, describing it as the result of some prank, "a drunken frolic." They became more concerned after Walter returned without his brother. In Christian's words, "The detectives declared there must have been some motive for the act, and were utterly at a loss to even surmise what it could be." Then with the advice of the police, Charley made his first public appearance in a newspaper want ad in the *Philadelphia Ledger* on July 3, 1874: "Lost, on the first instant, a small boy about 4 years of age, light complexion, and light curly hair."[10] Given Charley's subsequent fame, it was an inconspicuous debut, but one that already framed the problem by noting that he was "lost." It is perhaps significant that his initial appearance was as a nameless child.

In the late nineteenth century, the phenomenon of lost children was not at all uncommon, and notices of this kind, inconspicuous personals (not news), were a feature of many newspapers. In San Francisco, for example, one child was listed in the Lost and Found column of the *San Francisco Chronicle* just one week after Charley was listed in Philadelphia, simply as "Lost—at noon, July 10th, a LITTLE GIRL two and a half years old, wore a red shawl and brown dress trimmed with green." Then as now, children were lost for many reasons, from casually wandering off or running away from abuse to being stolen or murdered. Very few of them became stories as Charley did; most did not even make it into the papers. Most stray children were eventually located when they were turned into local police stations. In Boston, for example, in the year 1887, the police recorded 1,572 lost children. Thus, it was not surprising that in the ad for Charley readers who knew of his whereabouts were asked to return him to the central police station in Philadelphia, "corner 5th and Chestnut Streets." The ad for Charley, like many others, also promised an unspecified "reward." [11]

While waiting for a positive response, Christian and his brother-in-law Joseph Lewis (Sarah's brother and a Philadelphia neighbor) together with the police conducted searches of the local area. These searches were to go on for some time and would eventually spread to large areas of Pennsylvania, New York, and New Jersey as the police enlisted the help of neighboring districts and cities. Knowing only that Charley had been taken but not why, the police acted on customary assumptions and tried to find Charley and his abductors by making inquiries at such places as ferry stops, taverns, livery stables. As word of mouth spread, the news about Charley began to generate an assortment of rumors. In one of the first of these, a child had been spotted in a gypsy wagon "crying bitterly" who it was "suspected did not belong to them." In all, the police in Philadelphia and elsewhere reportedly searched 200 gypsy caravans within a year and one-half after Charley disappeared.[12]

As they became more desperate, the police moved well beyond gypsy wagons and began unwarranted door-to-door searches of Italian neighborhoods (Italians were associated with "brigandage" and seen as disreputable and exotic), gambling dens, and houses of ill-fame. In other words, confronted with a new situation, the police pursued their usual hunches, associating Charley's disappearance with the unsavory and disreputable, with gypsies, Italians, and the underworld. [13]

On Independence Day 1874, three days after the abduction, some of the mystery of Charley's disappearance was cleared up when the Ross household received its first letter from the abductors, with a demand for an (as yet unspecified) ransom in exchange for the safe return of the child. The letter was brought to Christian, who was at the police station in Philadelphia, by his brother. "So overwhelming was the astonishment and indignation that for a time every one was silent. Then followed varied expressions of horror, as each one realized that there existed a human being capable of committing an act so cruel, so full of unspeakable torment to its victims as that of child stealing. The disguised writing, the evident effort at bad spelling, the absence of any signature, and the revelation of the fact that my child had been taken away for money, indicated that the wretch who designed the plot had carefully prepared to guard himself and his vile accomplices from detection." The danger with which Charley was threatened was very much emphasized by such a "foreign" and malignant form of writing ("any aproch is maid to his hidin place that is the signil for his instant anihilation"). The writing sought to hide the identity of the perpetrators and to incite fear and loathing. When the facts leaked to the press (despite police restrictions on publication of the details), the horror moved outside the Ross household. The *New York World* asked, "If there is a crime viler, baser, more anti-social than . . . blackmailing, . . . it is the crime that has been committed in Philadelphia . . . blood-mailing."[14] Indeed, kidnapping shared with blackmailing both the manipulation of fear and the violation of privacy, the careful screen around the self and the family that had been erected in nineteenth-century society and sensibility.

For Ross, the sense of revulsion and horror was soon followed by a sense of "relief" that Charley was still alive. Christian would subsequently have many opportunities to repeat this particular pattern of emotions (disgust, horror, and relief) because his negotiations with the kidnappers would span *five months* and involve *twenty-three ransom notes* in all, and several attempts at direct contact. "Savages," Ross wrote, "before dispatching their *enemies* frequently torture them by tearing the flesh piecemeal from the quivering limbs of their victims; but these men remorselessly, in hope of gain, increased by every stroke of the pen the torture which they had inflicted, not upon *enemies*, but upon those who had never injured them." Since at various points Ross was informed that his son was being kept in a very small, uninhabitable place, that he had not urinated for 24 to 30 hours because of an infection, and always that he remained precariously close to being "anihilated," Ross's sense that he was being slowly tortured is understandable. Indeed, Ross's long, drawn-out experience with the abductors of his son became an object lesson for subsequent victim's families. Sometimes, as in the cases of John Conway (1897) and Eddie Cudahy (1900), Ross was specifically recalled in the kidnap note.

In Ross's memoir, each ransom note is carefully and fully reprinted (with facsimiles of the original), preserving for posterity the literary remains of which after July 1 Charley's life is constructed and the source of Christian's suffering. The notes were often long, very explicit, and highly charged emotionally as the kidnappers become in turn impatient with, angry at, or forgiving of Christian's response or lack of response to their demands. "If you love money more than child yu be its murderer not us for the money we will have if we dont from yu we be sure to git it from some one els for we will mak examples of your child that others may be wiser. . . . Yu money or his lif we wil have—so consider wel wat yu be duing." Ross was repeatedly reminded that "yu wil hav two pay us befor yu git him from us."[15]

Despite the long and elaborate communications, Charley was not returned, and much of the power and energy generated by Charley's abduction comes from the mystery at the heart of Christian's story—the mystery of the unpaid ransom. The kidnappers asked for $20,000. While it is likely that Christian did *not* have that sum personally available (he had suffered reversals in the panic of 1873), he had access to the people and institutions who could make it available to him. Christian Ross was in fact so well connected in Philadelphia that his friends and cronies (including the mayor) raised $20,000 on his behalf. Rather than a ransom, however, it was raised as a "reward" for the capture of the kidnappers *and* the safe return of the child. This proviso, of course, restricted how the money could be used since it necessarily involved setting a trap for the kidnappers, a trap the cagey kidnappers foresaw and effectively avoided by refusing to make a direct, simultaneous child-for-money exchange. The kidnappers were adamant about those terms. Whenever Christian tried to alter them, he was reminded: "Ros, it is our place to dictate, yues to comply." The kidnappers often implied that it was fruitless to seek Charley in hopes of finding him with his abductors because the child was already elsewhere, in the care of an unknowing accomplice (making Charley's whereabouts in the event of the abductors' death completely inaccessible). They insisted time and again that a period of time elapse between the receipt of the ransom (unmarked, low denomination bills) and the return of the child (through an unknowing intermediary).[16]

But Ross's inability to raise an acceptable no-strings ransom could not have been the whole reason for Christian's refusal to pay for his son's return. Two weeks after the first demand, one wealthy Philadelphian offered to pay the entire ransom in order to relieve his wife of the agony she felt about Charley's by-then long-term absence. According to the *Philadelphia Inquirer*, the man's "invalid wife" was "growing insane over the Ross abduction." But Christian refused this extraordinary act of generosity. Even earlier, it was reported that his brother-in-law offered him $10,000 to get the child back. Indeed, Ross's refusal to pay the ransom very soon generated a large number of extremely ingenious theories, some of them published in the New York and Pennsylvania newspapers. These slanderous charges in fact led Christian to institute libel proceedings. (The charge was publicly withdrawn.) Most of the theories implicated Ross in the theft of his own child; some portrayed Christian as eager to benefit from the anticipated subscriptions and rewards. In others, Charley was not Christian's child at all, but a by-product of an illicit liaison by Mrs. Ross. Indeed, these melodramatic Victorian explanations (she an adultress; he a bankrupt con man) resulted in a play, *Pique*, by John Daly, which had a long run on Broadway. The *New York Times* openly suggested that the play was based on Charley's story since "truth is stranger than fiction."[17]

Such Victorian projections suggest the degree to which the Ross case was being enveloped in popular explanations as it increasingly stimulated the public's imagination. And they demonstrate how the newness of ransom kidnapping was being adapted to cultural prefigurations. Indeed, as Christian noted, "Few persons were prepared to believe that a child could or would be stolen in this country for the sole object of a ransom. The crime was so atrocious that they could not realize that the helplessness and innocence of childhood could be taken advantage of to rend the heart-strings of parents for the sake of gain." Ross also observed that American institutions were unprepared. "A new crime was attempted to be inaugurated in our country. . . . No laws are found in the books of any State which anticipated the commission of so unnatural an offense, nor was any punishment provided commensurate with its heinousness."[18]

While the attempt to understand the new crime in older terms helped to bridge the need for explanation and meaning, they hardly explain Ross's failure to pay the ransom. He subsequently spent the rest of his life and all his money searching for his son (and clearing his reputation). And these transgressive, antifamilial fantasies were unlikely explanations for Ross's behavior because after three months of the now compounded ordeal (his son's abduction, the tortured relations with the kidnappers, and the assaults on his honor), he suffered a complete physical and mental collapse and retreated to his own ancestral home (and, one imagines, his mother's arms). Indeed, it is hard not to be moved by Christian's description of his experience as a man overcome by circumstance: "The incessant strain upon mind and body for the past three months—the alternation of hope and fear—the anxious pursuit—the weary labor by day, and the sleepless nights—were surely a heavy burden to carry, without the heartless slanders and calumnies which were coined and circulated about Mrs. Ross and myself. . . . For several weeks I had felt my strength yielding to the excessive tax upon my system, and for days was kept up only by force of will, strung to the greatest tension by longing for our lost darling. When the break came it was sudden and overwhelming; both body and mind succumbed at the same time."[19]

Christian's own explanation for his failure to pay the ransom is compact and estimable—the police told him not to and he wished to protect the public from a repetition of his experience. His reported response to the offer by the rich Philadelphia gentleman was "I thank you, sir, I cannot accept your generous offer; for having taken the position that I would not compound the felony, I prefer continuing to make efforts to find the criminals, hoping, if successful in getting them that I will recover my child, and probably prevent a repetition of child-stealing for ransom." Extremely sensitive about the ransom issue, Ross practically began his memoir in self defense about his refusal to pay: "Fully appreciating the danger which might result to society should the brigands prove successful in their infamous experiment, the case was placed in the hands of police authorities of the city . . . with the understanding that I would never consent to compound the crime, preferring to wait and suffer in the hope of securing the criminals with the child. The terrible anguish caused by this long suspense, to which the knowledge of the child's death would be a relief, it is impossible to describe."[20] Here as else-where, Ross describes the child's death as preferable to the suspense of not knowing what had become of him. Ross, like many subsequent parents of kidnap victims, suffered as much from the excruciating uncertainty and from anxiety about what had happened to the child's identity as from fears about his death.

In listening to the police, Ross subordinated his own goals to theirs. The police's objective, then and since, has been to capture criminals. If Ross paid the ransom in the ways offered by Charley's captors, the police knew that the kidnappers were unlikely to be caught, thus challenging the usual morality about the fruits of criminal behavior. Christian and his defenders also argued that civic-mindedness required that the ransom not be paid since a successful exchange (from the point of view of the kidnappers) would set an ugly precedent. Any new form of extortion (airplane hijack-ings are a good modern example) is resisted for this reason. As Charles Krauth explained in the introduction to Christian's book, "one such prize, so promptly drawn in such a lottery, would have awakened the cupidity and sharpened the cunning of that large class, who are always on the alert to dis-cover new and hopeful openings for their unscrupulous villainy." Charley's abduction seemed to provide a whole new set of possibilities to the criminal classes, one whose example needed to be quickly extirpated. Thus, George Washington Walling, chief of the New York police, wrote Ross that "any arrangements made with the kidnappers for the restoration of the child would be a public calamity; no child would be safe hereafter if it had parents or friends who could raise money. " Waller was firmly defining Christian's obligation as a defense of a certain class of citizens. But in becoming a kind of hero to the law, Christian was also rather pitiable, and even so august an authority on honor as the *New York Times* could see how the anguish of the heart might reasonably lead to the payment of ransom money. Chiding those who believed that paying the ransom would be "an act of weakness" and urging such to "try to imagine what he would do himself if his own child were in the hands of these unknown scoundrels," the *Times* asked, "How few men would have the firmness—say rather the stoicism—to re-sist the pleadings of their own hearts, enforced by the cry of a frantic mother bereaved of her child?"[21] Here as throughout the case, while a "frantic mother" clung to the background, it was masculine behavior that was primarily at issue, with the *Times* clearing a wide path for the simple pleadings of a father's heart.

Christian initially cooperated with the police in the hope that this would not require the sacrifice of his child, and he publicly defended the police's handling of the case. But Christian's growing anxiety about his course of action cost him dearly: "The public was clamorous for the arrest and punishment of the kidnappers at any cost, yet were ignorant of the risk to the life of my child and subsequent terror to which I was subjected. *It is comparatively easy to sacrifice another man's child for the public good,* and my anxious suspense is easier conceived than borne." As the case dragged on, he became less optimistic and, it seems, eventually was ready to accept the kidnappers' terms. I say seems because this is one of the areas in which Christian's memoirs are most opaque. Whether Christian relented and agreed that the kidnappers' demands be met despite the advice of his friends, or the matter was taken out of his hands when he collapsed, or he collapsed because the matter was removed from his control is not clear. What is certain is that the last negotiations that might have struck a simple ransom-for-child deal were conducted by Mrs. Ross's family, with Sarah Ross probably somewhere in the picture (though Christian hardly acknowledges a place for her). By then, however, it was too late since the attempt at exchange, made by the Lewises (Mrs. Ross's brother and nephew) at the Fifth Avenue Hotel in New York on November 17 was marred by the palpable presence of the police, not authorized by the Lewises but all too obvious to the kidnappers. The ransom demands stopped. So did the news about Charley. "Thus ended a correspondence characterized by a heartlessness and brutality unsurpassed in the annals of crime. . . . Five long months a constant dread possessed us that the threats they contained would be literally executed; and though our hearts yearned to hear something of our suffering stolen one, yet each letter was opened with fear and trembling . . . none but ourselves can ever know how bitter the draught in the chalice."[22]

As the kidnappers had shrewdly foretold ("we will mak examples of your child that others may be wiser"), the consequences of Ross's failure to meet the kidnapper's demands became an object lesson for subsequent victims' families. This was conspicuously the case in the ransom kidnapping of Eddie Cudahy in Omaha, Nebraska, on December 19, 1900. Eddie's father was the largest meatpacker in Nebraska, and when he received the ransom note, it included a reminder: "If you remember, some twenty years ago, Charley Ross was kidnapped in New York City [sic] and $20,000 ransom asked. Old man Ross was willing to give up the money, but Byrnes, the great [New York] detective, with others, persuaded the old man not to give up the money, assuring him that the thieves would be captured. Ross died of a broken heart, sorry that he allowed the detectives to dictate to him." While he got some of the facts wrong, Eddie's kidnapper got the gist of the story right. Cudahy probably needed little reminding of Charley's fate or that of his father since Charley's story was well and widely known. Cudahy's response was quick and emphatic. "I am determined to punish the people connected with the affair, but, of course, my first consideration is to get the boy back." Cudahy kept the police away while he paid the ransom. "What's $25,000 compared to my boy," Mrs. Cudahy is reported to have said. Eddie returned within hours. By then, the memory of Charley's story was part of collective history, and the Cudahys could act firmly and effectively.[23]

While Ross never complied with the kidnappers' demands, he did participate in the first of the classic kidnap capers—the money drop from a moving train, brilliantly encoded by Akira Kurasawa in his kidnap movie *High and Low*. This scene would be replayed or attempted repeatedly after Charley's kidnapping, most strikingly in the Blakely Coughlin case (1920) and in the planned ransom escapade by Leopold and Loeb (1924). In the Ross case, the ploy was new and ultimately unsuccessful because the kidnappers never met the train. Accustomed to following Ross's moves in the newspapers (where Christian's pursuit of the repeated Charley sightings were steadily reported), the kidnappers believed that he had gone instead to another town to follow up a lead on his son. If they had made their rendezvous, however, they would have found a letter rather than the required cash in the suitcase that Ross planned to drop from the train. By this point, Christian was being advised by a whole passel of people, including his wealthy and influential Philadelphia subscribers and the New York police (the police had been reliably informed that the kidnappers were in New York), all playing for more time. "I am compelled to tell you," Christian advised his son's kidnappers in the note contained in the suitcase, "that I cannot throw away twenty thousand dollars on the wild plan you suggest. It is impossible for me to give you twenty thousand dollars and trust to you to bring me my child at some subsequent time. I desire to act with you in good faith. . . . I must insist upon having some positive, tangible proof that you have the child."[24] The best that can be said for this note is that Ross was not yet in a kidnap mode. He wanted the kidnappers to play by his rules, to give him proof, to accept his good faith, to understand that he could not literally "throw away" that much money out of the train. Unfortunately the kidnappers had Charley, and the rules of this new game were theirs to define.

For the kidnappers that game was as clear as Charley's value was simple: a very precise $20,000. This was an enormous sum of money for its time and provides some sense of the value the kidnappers could expect to be attached to a child of a family like the Rosses, not rich but distinctly middle class in values and tastes. But this equivalence that the kidnappers hoped to impose was in the sensibilities of the late nineteenth century both absurd and horrifying. Ross was evidently not prepared to think in these terms. Nor had he learned to think as Charley's kidnappers expected him to think—as a father whose own identity is defined by his fatherly actions and his son's welfare. Ross was still too much the public man, citizen, businessman, a man of honor and religion, his wife's protector. After Christian's ordeal, a kidnapping would almost immediately peel away these other roles and reify fatherhood in the form of the devoted parent; as Eddie Cudahy's father said, "my first consideration is to get the boy back." Indeed, starting with the Ross case, kidnapping defined the emotional costs and expectations of a newly emotional fatherhood. Christian, we can all agree, acted nobly, but looking back we cannot help knowing that he was wrong and careless of his son's life. His dilemma, the pull between noble civic behavior and fulfillment of responsible fatherhood, would disappear as a public problem for subsequent kidnap victims because the story of Charley's perpetual lostness would eliminate the choice. After Christian's experience, families confronted by a ransom demand would try to foreshorten their children's stories by acceding to ransom demands; many would keep the case entirely a private matter. But Christian, in failing to act only as a father, forced Charley to become more than a son—he became a public story, limited neither by his kidnapper's $20,000 price tag nor by his former physical existence.[25]

⊡ ||| ⊡

Although Charley would remain forever lost, it is ironic that those believed to be his kidnappers would be caught. Where the father failed, the police succeeded, but in a perverse and gothic fashion. From the outset, their behavior in the Ross case was disgraceful, in this as in so many other ways, setting the pattern for future kidnappings. The police received well-deserved criticism because they seemed unable to deal with the situation; indeed, some of the early suspicions about Ross's role resulted from the widespread inability to believe that the police could be so ineffectual. "That not the slightest clew has been obtained of the whereabouts of the child is the most remarkable fact in the criminal annals of the country." The *New York Times* added its voice to the condemnation of police ineptitude. "The machinery of the law, which was thought sufficient to have effected the rescue of the child long before now has proved itself to be absolutely worthless, and it is folly to place reliance upon it any longer." Christian, as an upstanding citizen of Philadelphia, believed that the police would act on his behalf since it was for people like him—middle class, respectable, property-owning family men—that the urban police were created. And Philadelphia had one of the first urban police forces. When the site of the action moved to New York City, which had a famous police chief, George Washington Walling, the situation was hardly better. There were points during the Ross case when the police were themselves accused of engaging in criminal activities.[26]

In the preprofessional police force of the mid nineteenth century, the institution was politically defined and individual officers were usually driven by expectations of private reward rather than by the values of fulfilling professional duties. Indeed, most child thefts did not involve the police at all since most families affected were poor and could not raise a reward sufficient to stimulate police action. Even the great Walling was accused in the course of the Ross case court proceedings of having delayed action in order to receive the outstanding reward money. In many cases, the police refused to acknowledge that a child had actually been taken or assured poor parents that it would no doubt soon return (just as they had initially reassured Ross). In the case of Maria Hoyle, who witnessed her child being seized in the street as she stood at the window, the police were reported to be simply "unable to aid her in the recovery of the child." Maria Hoyle, then "in a state of mental agony," vainly wandered through the streets and "visited the different precincts in the hopes of finding the little one." In another case, a young child who was found in one upstate New York county (Saratoga), "kept by a woman in a backwoods place," had never been reported missing by his father, William B. Brink, a ferry collector, in Brooklyn. Whether Brink had learned from Christian's experience to expect a simple money for child exchange and not to befuddle the issue by involving the police or whether he distrusted the police for other good reasons is not clear.[27] What is clear is that the police rarely succeeded in kidnap cases and that wealthy victims after the publicity surrounding the Ross case often worked hard to keep the police from interfering in the early stages of ransom negotiations.

In Charley's case, with a huge reward at stake, both the Philadelphia and New York police were actively hunting for the kidnappers, and they scoured the neighborhoods and enlisted the assistance of police forces throughout the area. But while they seemed to search for Charley, that was really a secondary goal. (Indeed, Christian with the help of his friends was pursuing Charley in other ways and with the assistance of a private Pinkerton force.) The police were really after the criminals. By early fall, the New York police, on the basis of tips from informants, were pretty certain they knew who these were—a couple of thieves named William Mosher and Joseph Douglass who had been in trouble with the law before. They lamely sought to capture these two with the assistance of Mosher's brother-in-law, William Westervelt, a crooked former policeman. They thought that Westervelt could be induced to cooperate in the hopes of being reinstated on the force. In fact, according to evidence presented at Westervelt's trial, he was all the while providing Mosher and Douglass with inside information on police moves. At his trial (where he maintained his complete innocence), Westervelt was accused by state's witnesses of repeatedly deceiving the police. It was never clear, however, how much Westervelt knew about the actual kidnapping. He almost certainly did not know Charley's whereabouts or if he was still alive since he could have bought his own freedom with that information.

When the police finally caught up with Mosher and Douglass, it was a scene worthy of the best Victorian melodrama and was depicted in just such terms. The story, with its requisite dark and rainy night and references to light "flickering through the blinds," occupied the *entire front page* of the *New York Times* for December 15, 1874, and was captioned "Crime and its Expiation." The two thieves had been caught, not by the police but by a layman, in the midst of a simple robbery attempt at the home of Judge Van Brunt on the eastern shore of Long Island, in Bay Ridge (Brooklyn). Both were shot. Mosher died instantly. Douglass followed a few hours later, but only after making a deathbed confession: "It's no use lying now, I helped to steal Charlie [sic] Ross. . . . Mosher knows all about it." Told that Mosher was dead, Douglass could not give Charley's whereabouts, but said that "the boy will get home all right." By December, everyone knew who Charley was, and the police whom the thieves had managed to elude for more than five months were quickly summoned. Walter was brought in to identify the bodies. His positive identification meant that six months after Charley's abduction, his captors were known and dead.[28]

The police initially hesitated to arrest Westervelt, who, they hoped, would lead them to the child, but on April 13, 1875, Westervelt traveled to Philadelphia where the police arrested him ("kidnapped" according to Westervelt's attorney), and he was subsequently put on trial as an accessory to kidnapping. In the meantime, the Pennsylvania legislature had passed a new kidnapping statute, transforming a previously defined misdemeanor (punishable by a maximum of seven years) into a felony with imprisonment of up to twenty-five years. The law was passed unanimously by both houses of the Pennsylvania legislature on February 25, 1875. Attached to it was a special provision that gave immunity to those now concealing a child. The provision, to expire on March 25, 1875, was quite specifically intended to protect Charley by offering an amnesty to those holding him. To these provisions, Christian added his own: a reward of up to $5,000 "for expenses or otherwise in bringing about his [Charley's] restoration" and a proclamation that he believed that Mosher and Douglass were the sole kidnappers. The last would indemnify anyone who helped to return the child.[29]

Westervelt's trial started on August 30, 1875, and lasted almost three weeks, during which time Charley was very much on the front pages of American newspapers. In Philadelphia the trial dominated the news. The daily space devoted to the trial in the *Philadelphia Inquirer* ranged from a low of 17 inches on a slow day to over 258 inches of newsprint. Three or four column spreads were very common. The coverage of the trial and its denouement suggested the degree to which the new crime of kidnapping needed an ending that vindicated the law, much as Charles Krauth's introduction to Christian's memoirs suggested that his story was a good way to introduce the young to the evils of crime and to lure them away from those "sensational" stories that invest criminals with romance to "dazzle and lure the young with examples of crime."[30]

In summing up, Judge Elcock said that the abduction of Charley, "has been widely regarded as *the worst crime of the century*. The assassin's knife has created no such widespread horror. It has made every father and mother in the land tremble lest the grasp of some fiend in human shape . . . should carry away to *a fate worse than death* one of the children of their hearts. A father's broken spirit, a mother, true to a mother's love, looking with hope into the darkness of the future, yet doubting hope, still crying for the return of her son, the whole people indignant at the weakness of police authority, a child of freedom restrained of his liberty, perhaps deprived of his life, are some of the results of the abduction. This continent confines not the anxious hearts looking for the return of little Charley Ross, for his wrongs have traveled the seas to foreign lands, and yet the mystery of his whereabout is, to this hour, with shame be it said, unsolved." Alcock's words summed up the horror to family and society of the fear and loss entailed in Charley's abduction.[31]

On October 9, Westervelt was sentenced for conspiring to kidnap, harbor, and conceal Charles Brewster Ross to seven years, the maximum sentence allowable under the old law. Judge Elcock reminded Westervelt of "the enormity of the offense" and that "justice calls for your severe punishment." In an earlier day, Elcock recalled, justice would have subjected the defendent to "burning in the hand, cutting off of the ears, nailing the ear or ears to a pillory, placing in and upon the pillory, whipping and imprisonment for life," thus evoking the full potential retributative horror of what he had done. He also observed that "I had hoped ere this I would have been appealed to for a light sentence by some merciful cry revealing something of the fate of Charlie [sic] Ross, but I have heard not even a whisper, nor beheld a ray of hope, and if the knowledge of his fate rests with you, you have become your own executioner." Westervelt's eye's were reported to have welled with tears as he plucked at his beard. In his summons to the jury, Elcock had taken note of the fact that "for one year and two months the voice of Charley Ross has been lost to his home, and that, while the prisoner has his children in life around him, another father mourns his son through this terrible crime." Fathers, innocent and guilty, were before the bench. Charley had not returned, but the law had been vindicated, with the two presumed kidnappers dead and an accomplice sentenced to the maximum legal penalty. George Washington Walling declared himself entirely satisfied: "No case . . . gave me greater solicitude." One part of Charley's story had come to a conventional close.[32]

⊡ IV ⊟

Neither the pursuit and capture of Mosher and Douglass nor Westervelt's trial had uncovered Charley's whereabouts. This third story, the search for Charley, the longest and cruelest of the stories created by Charley's abduction, became a genuine part of American popular culture. As Judge Elcock noted, Charley was known far and wide, even beyond American borders. In fact, Ross often received letters and tips from Europeans who thought they spotted the child or expressed their outrage at the abduction and sympathy for the parents. In the process of searching for and finding Charley, everywhere and nowhere, thousands of people made Charley into America's lost child and much more. And Douglass, by declaring that Charley would return, had set off a renewed hunt, conducted this time not by the police but by thousands, perhaps hundreds of thousands, of people in America and beyond, intent on returning Charley to his father.

Charley's status as *the lost child* and the avidity with which Americans devoted themselves to his search requires that we examine in some detail the problem of lost children in the late-nineteenth-century world in which Charley's story grew, and where it was transformed from a personal misfortune into a public event. Lost children were not uncommon in the United States in the years after the the Civil War, although how they became lost varied greatly. Some lost children had been discarded by their parents, while others had wandered away or been stolen. What bound them together and to Charley was their disconnection from their families. One article in 1882 claimed that in New York alone about 300 children were lost each month. In fact, this figure probably underestimates the extent of the problem. The annual reports of the New York Society for the Prevention of Cruelty to Children (begun the same year Charley was stolen) showed that the police and the society together returned as many as 6,000 New York children in 1877 alone. Many children, of course, were lost (or found) and never returned. Although Charley was known as the first child stolen for ransom, other child stealings were recorded in the years surrounding Charley's disappearance. In 1869, a *New York Times* article expressed the view that child stealing was rare in America, though common in Europe, but by 1874, and in the wake of the Ross case, the same paper noted that "of late years child stealing in this country has been largely on the increase."[33] In my own research, I have encountered scattered notices about child thefts covering a wide variety of types, though the coverage of these cases is usually brief, sometimes even informal. Most probably never came to public attention at all.

By 1874 all manner of abductions were already known, ranging from simple parental child snatching to cruel stranger abuse. In one case, Kate Bowen simply took the daughter of Susan Brown, aged five, with her when she left the New York City neighborhood she shared with the Browns. When she was caught and arrested, she received the maximum allowable sentence for a misdemeanor, seven years' imprisonment. In response to the case, the *New York Times* noted enigmatically that the recorder who issued the sentence "was influenced by the fact that numerous cases of child-stealing had occurred for some months previous, and he desired to set an example before this class of criminals which would deter them from being guilty of such inhuman outrages." The *Times* reporter may or may not have had Charley specifically in mind but there was certainly an increased tendency for newspapers to report child thefts after Charley disappeared and papers gave frequent updates or roundups of such cases in the wake of the news about Charley. As Ross observed, "Children never seemed half so precious as now. A new cause of anxiety and a new apprehension was carried by men to their daily business. A new reason for thankfulness was found that the kidnapper had not invaded the family circle during their absence."[34] Charley's case brought others to public attention. More significantly, it turned what were once merely curiosities into a social problem.

In one extraordinary summary a few weeks after Charley's disappearance, the *Times* described the full panoply of abduction forms by giving recent examples. "During the past ten years the cases of child stealing in this country have been very numerous, although those of the class to which that of little Charlie [sic] Ross belongs have been rather rare. Kidnappers hitherto have chiefly devoted their attention to the children of poor parents from motives of safety, the probabilities not being at all in favor of a hot pursuit by the police where there was no reward to be had save the thanks of grief-stricken fathers and mothers." The article included descriptions of two cases of parental abduction; in both of which the father kidnapped a child or children given into the custody of the mother in a divorce proceeding. Another, quite bizarre case of parental abduction had taken place in 1871 when a women who had given her child to the Shakers because she could not support it, tried to take her child back eight years later, but failed and was charged with kidnapping.[35]

Other cases of child theft involved physical abuse and brutality. One girl stolen in New Orleans was used as the object of abuse by both a husband and wife named Burgess who "having long been in the habit of quarreling and beating each other, appear to have finally concluded that it would be better to find a third person upon whom they might shower their blows." The child was put to sleep on a bare floor, without cover, severely beaten by the man and "hung by her toes from a nail." "A favorite amusement of both Burgesses was to take their poor little prisoner and bind the tresses of her hair to a crook in the wall and allow her body to extend from it until its weight pulled it from the roots. They fed her on moldy crusts and occasional scraps." The *Times* was not known for its sensationalization and usually refrained from such descriptions, common in places like the *National Police Gazette*, but this case clearly aroused the disgust (and interest) of the usually sedate paper. Some girls were stolen for what must have been purposes of sexual exploitation or even prostitution, although the newspapers usually provided very little to go on beyond brief descriptions that fit neatly into patterns of classic sexual abduction. Some children appear to have been abducted and put to work as beggers, street musicians, or circus entertainers, occupations that aroused the special ire of child protectors in the late nineteenth century. Often these children were abducted for a day and then left alone to be returned to the nearest police station, where they were found by their parents.[36]

There was another, quite different, kind of child disappearance, rarely described as such by newspapers but increasingly part of urban childhood at the time of Charley's disappearance. These were children removed by official and semiofficial child-saving agencies like the various Societies for the Prevention of Cruelty to Children or the New York based Children's Aid Society. At the height of their activities these child-protection organizations removed thousands of children from their homes or streets and placed them in shelters, residential schools, or on farms out West. The story of these organizations and their activities has been told elsewhere, but their part in creating the phenomenon of "lost children" is directly part of Charley's story. For as Christian Ross asserted, "Our experience has taught us that it is the easiest possible thing to be mistaken in identity," and Charley's story is haunted by concerns about mistaken identity, changed identity, and lost identities. These children's protective societies helped to raise the issue of identity as a profound urban issue in the late nineteenth century as they responded to some of the very problems that Ross encountered as he tried to follow up the thousands of leads given to him and discovered that there were legions of children in America either with no homes or in homes other than their parents'. Many of the "children we have traced," Christian reported, "and whose history we could find out, have been abandoned by their parents. Sometimes the father, at other times the mother, would leave a child at a place or house, either to board or to be temporarily cared for, and never return for him."[37] Since some of these children were turned in as Charley, or identified themselves as Charley, Charley's status as a lost boy became quickly fused with that of other lost (including abandoned) children, only a small number of whom had been stolen or abducted. Often Christian, whose memoirs enshrine him as a devoted father to a lost child, discovered children abandoned by fathers who could not or would not act the proper part. Sometimes he helped to reunite these children with their parents, thus reawakening paternal devotion and rekindling the required family commitment. Charley's story thus became a sharp reminder of parental responsibility, something also raised in the activities of newly formed child protective associations.

In New York City from 1869 to 1870, 9,000 boys spent one or more nights in the Children's Aid Society lodging houses. The total number of children "placed out" in the semiofficial adoptions sponsored by the society (but which were often forms of child labor recruitment) was many times this number. Many, but not all, were taken to western states and territories. At the height of these placements, between 1853 and 1893, 91,536 children were disposed of in this fashion. In most of these cases, agencies like the Children's Aid Society dealt with genuine orphans or abused children and castaways, children whose helplessness was called to their attention. But, almost 30 percent of the children placed by the society in 1873 had both parents living and another 12 percent had one live parent.[38] These usually impoverished children were removed from their homes in quite different ways than Charley, but like him they were displaced, some were reidentified and "lost." From their inception these agencies had tried to redefine and reidentify these children, most of them immigrants, usually Catholic, and replace former identities with more acceptable ones. The Children's Aid Society came in for considerable criticism on this basis as a child-stealing agency. Numerous rumors surrounded its work "to the effect that the Society renamed the children in the West so that 'even brothers and sisters might marry.' The rumor that children 'were sold as slaves and that the agents enriched themselves from the transactions' had, according to Charles Loring Brace (the founder and guiding light of the Children's Aid Society) a wide circulation." In New York City, the Children's Aid Society was a semiofficial state agency with police powers, authorized to take possession of what we would call "children at risk" and at least partly paid from public coffers. A former agent of the society began an investigation by the state legislature in 1871 into the charge that "the Society was proselytizing the children sent out, changing their names, or leaving them without proper care out West." And the *Catholic World* was actively involved in warning people against what it considered the legalized abduction perpetrated by the society. The Catholic Church was, of course, deeply concerned about the possibility that members of its communion would have their identities altered, although in Italy, the church was itself held responsible for the abduction and forced Christianization of Jewish children.[39]

In an article published in 1896, Jacob Riis provided a moving reminder that for those whose children were taken by the legal action of the state the experience of loss might be little different than when children were taken by strangers through ransom abductions. In this "true" story, called (of course) "Lost Children," Riis tells about a peddler and recent immigrant, Max Lubinsky, "poor and friendless in a strange land," who was a pious Jew. Lubinsky's daughter, Yetta, disappeared one day while on her way to her father's street cart with his supper. Picked up by the Society for the Prevention of Cruelty to Children as "a lost child," she disappeared without a trace. The parents kept up a search and vigil for more than a year, keeping faith that the child would return. With Riis's help they "searched the police records, the hospital, the morgue, and the long register of the river's dead. She was not there. Having made sure of this, we turned to the children's asylums." But the organizations provided no response to initial inquiries and descriptions of little Yetta. "A year passed, and we were compelled at last to give over the search."

Riis was deeply moved by the Lubinskys' quiet dignity and "the strength of domestic affection that burned with anguished faith in the dark tenement after the many months of weary failure." Then by a fluke of good fortune, Yetta was found. "Two long years had passed, and the memory of her and hers had long since faded out of Mulberry Street, when, in the overhauling of one of the children's homes we thought we had canvassed thoroughly, the child turned up, as unaccountably as she had been lost. . . . Not knowing her name . . . they had given her one of their own choosing; and *thus disguised*, she might have stayed there forever, but for the fortunate chance that cast her up to the surface once more, and gave the *clue to her identity* at last. Even then her father had nearly as much trouble in proving *his title* to his child as he had had in looking for her."[40] While losing identity was easy and part of "the way of the city," establishing "title" to a child with one of the city agencies was very difficult indeed, and it is more than likely that the Lubinskys would not have succeeded without Riis's help.

Others were not so lucky. Children who were lost or temporarily placed with the agencies could disappear forever or the agencies could refuse to return them. One such was the family of Thomas Glennon, who had lived, like the Lubinskys, on Mulberry Street, in the heart of the East Side slum. Glennon had three children, Lizzie, aged sixteen, Ellen, aged ten, and Hugh, aged eight. The two youngest frequently received aid from the Children's Aid Society in the form of outdoor relief. As the father's health declined, the society took the two youngest into their shelter. When he died (he was a widower), an aunt of the children's, Mrs. Rainey, came to claim the children, saying that "their relatives were both willing and able to educate them" and reunite them with their sister, Lizzie. But the matron in charge refused and claimed that the children were not there. When the aunt went to court and obtained a writ of habeus corpus, the judge of the state supreme court "dismissed the writ on the application of Mr. D. R. Jacques, counsel for the Children's Aid Society." "A statement was made in court . . . that the children have been sent out West, and that they were given to Miss Stephens [the matron of the home] by their father because he wished them to be brought up in the Protestant faith and away from the influence of their relatives."[41] Apparently, neither the rights of the aunt nor of the sister could carry the day, and the children were lost to them and to their former identities.

Children who disappeared in the late nineteenth century might have been abducted by strangers, neighbors, divorced parents, beggers, seducers, or the state. They could also have been murdered. The *National Police Gazette*, which specialized in the gruesome and brutal, sometimes carried these stories ("An Appalling Outrage: Unprecedented Barbarity—Murder and Mutilation"), but most newspapers shied away from such lurid tales. Even respectable papers like the *Philadelphia Inquirer* and the *San Francisco Chronicle*—indeed, the *New York Times* (although it sharply limited coverage)—were forced to report the horrible serial murders purportedly committed by Jesse Pomeroy, who was arrested in the same year Charley was lost. Pomeroy, a fourteen-year-old at the time of his arrest but supposedly a murderer for some years before, was convicted of brutally slaughtering Katie Curran and Horace Millen, his acts anticipating the murderous child abductions of the 1920s. Unlike these latter criminals, who framed their murders as kidnappings, Pomeroy had not yet learned about this new crime.[42]

In discussing the disappearance of the children later found murdered, the newspapers almost always referred to them as "lost," as indeed they were until their corpses were discovered. In the case of Katie Curran, the city had raised a $500 reward for the detection of the abductor. "Days, weeks, and months . . . passed on, but nothing was heard of the missing child." When finally found, "Her body had been lacerated and mangled in the most frightful manner, and in the way that has characterized all the previous crimes of the young fiend, being indeed literally torn asunder." Well-known in his own day, Pomeroy prefigured the famous boy murderers of the 1920s; as if anticipating their cold-blooded attitude, "Young Pomeroy, soon after his arrest, made a cool and detailed confession of his guilt to the chief of police," a confession he subsequently retracted. Pomeroy was found guilty and was sentenced to hang. After his death sentence was commuted, Pomeroy remained in prison, where he died in 1932 at the age of sixty-nine. The police, according to the *Philadelphia Inquirer*, "came in for a merited share of the abuse" for the "indifferent manner in which the case [Katie's disappearance] had been treated by officers in South Boston." Boston, like New York and Philadelphia, had another old, established, but still quite unprofessional police force.[43]

Only in extreme cases like Jesse Pomeroy's would respectable papers engage in elaborate discussions of the horrible or frightening, especially in relationship to children, which were staples of the cheap press. In that sense, Charley's story was an acceptable way to discuss the much wider phenomenon of lost children and the terrible dangers to which children were exposed—and to encourage the attendant sensational emotions. Charley could evoke the poignancy of these lost children without their anonymity and insignificance. When Charley became "the lost boy," he highlighted all these other abductions, abandonments, and disappearances, and he transformed the phenomenon of lost children from the realm of the private and sentimental into a vigorous and meaningful public story. Charley's story resonated with these others but with a difference. The extraordinarily long search that his father mounted for him gave Charley a public existence denied to most of these others. And the fact that the Rosses were exceptionally well connected gave Christian the public access largely denied to the poor and anonymous. But Mosher and Douglas also helped to make Charley into a much larger story than any previous disappearance since they had not only stolen him, but sought to return him to his family—for a price. In creating the new crime of ransom kidnapping, the abductors created outrage about the apparent vulnerability of the rich and powerful to the possible loss of *their* children. This new threat was both connected to an awareness of other lost children in the society and a threat much closer to home for those respectable folks who read the *New York Times* or the *Philadelphia Inquirer*. To this were added the huge rewards that were posted at various times, making it profitable for many (police and laymen alike) to seek to find Charley. As a result, unlike the absence, loss, disappearance, and dangers experienced by other children, Charley's story was a public issue, a story of childhood that was well and actively known.

Charley thus became the first lost child with a coast-to-coast existence. Indeed, we can still encounter Charley today, as I did recently, when I walked into a small general store in Woodside, California (preserved as a historic site) and found an 8-by-11 poster of Charley hanging near the entrance. This was one of the hundreds of thousands distributed by the Pinkerton agency. The poster reproduces an artist's rendering of an old photo of Charley (of when he was two since the family had nothing more recent), contains a brief physical description, and offers a large reward for his return. News about Charley's abduction made its way in many forms throughout the country and, in a period before so-called mass communications, to a truly amazing degree penetrated the landscape. Woodside was then, as its name implied, barely an outpost of civilization, on the map because of its giant trees. Christian's hunt for his son had by the time of the Westervelt arrest taken on epic proportions, including $20,000 spent on detectives and $8,000 on printing and photographing; and 700,000 circulars were distributed throughout the land, even to a then very isolated California lumber town. Five hundred thousand people were reportedly engaged in the search. By that point, 600 Charley Rosses had been reported, and Christian was spending all his time and would eventually spend the rest of his life pursuing the endless leads.[44]

ꇞ√ꇞ

The search for Charley had begun by word of mouth, starting in the Germantown neighborhood at the beginning of July and radiating to larger and larger areas of New Jersey, New York, and Pennsylvania as family, friends, neighbors, and the police sought the child. It was accelerated during the summer of 1874 by newspaper reports, hints of scandal, and the combined notice given to the case by the police and the Pinkertons. As Ross began to follow up leads, the news about Charley spread with each sighting and with each visit by Ross (often to quite distant places) to determine whether a suspected child was in fact his son. Eventually, and especially after the death of Mosher and Douglass, posters saturated the country as Ross attempted to bring Charley out from whatever hole he might have been hidden should he have been boarded in some unsuspecting farm or tenement.

In his memoirs, Ross reported that Charley had become so well known and sympathy for his family's agony so widely shared that the Western Union Company provided Ross with his own line free of charge in order to facilitate the pursuit of leads, which early began to pour in. Charley was being "discovered" in so many places that Ross was forced to vet the sightings by extensive use of the cable since he could not possibly physically follow up every lead. Apparently, some of the sightings were the result of the fact that the name Charley or Charley Ross was being given as a proper name or a nickname to children throughout the land. "Among the most difficult to trace satisfactorily, are children who have assumed, or to whom has been given, the name of Charley Ross. Many instances of this kind have occurred, not only in the large cities, but in far distant places. Singular as it may seem, even little children in our city have heard so much about Charley Ross, that whenever they see another child resembling the picture which they so well know, they are ready to call out, 'There is Charley Ross.'" The *Ladies' Home Journal*, in commemorating the fiftieth anniversary of Charley's abduction, told the story of a Norwegian couple visiting Philadelphia for the first time who were interested in neither Independence Hall nor the Liberty Bell, but only in visiting Charley's old house in Germantown. "He was the one Philadelphian of whom they had heard, amid their mountains and fiords." The author continues, "Still the tale of this Germantown lad's abduction remains the great and tragic and moving tale of child stealing. After the story of Joseph and his brethren, no story of a *lost* boy has so powerfully touched the chords of the human heart."[45]

It was not just Charley's name that became widely recognized. Everyone it seemed, knew about the sweetly serious face and the golden ringlets. And every mother with a child even vaguely resembling the lost child became hostage to the good intentions of strangers hoping to be helpful (or to win the reward). Ross had purposely withheld the information that his son had brown not blue eyes, hoping thereby to stop just such precipitous misidentifications, but that seemed to help very little; somehow even obviously blue-eyed children were soon reported to be brown-eyed. After a while Ross gave people certificates of inspection to warrant that a particular child had already been examined (because of a resemblance and the possibility of repeated misidentification), and the child was not Charley. So ubiquitous had knowledge of Charley's loss become that other lost children brought to police stations identified themselves as Charley Ross, "Whether these children supposed all lost children must be called 'Charley Ross,' or whether they thought that by assuming the name, they would secure kind treatment," Christian acknowledged, "I do not know."[46]

This incorporation of the name, face, and story of Charley into child life was indeed astonishing, but it was not just children who were affected by Charley's stories. It was usually adults who pursued leads and excitedly informed Christian of their discoveries. Indeed, Ross was deluged with offers of assistance, many of them unwanted, including attempts to locate the child with mesmerism, witchcraft, spiritualism, and other psychic keys. "Astrologers, fortune-tellers, dreamers, somnambulists—in fact there can scarcely be named a secret profession, from some of whose believers I have not received communications, asking me to test its power." Some wrote, others just appeared on his doorstep. Ross put the best face on it all. "Is the fate of Charley Ross to be despaired of? Not by the help of God, if every parent who loves his child, if the whole motherhood everywhere, is silently pledged to join in and renew the search."[47] Ross had enlisted all the parents of America in his search and in the process confirmed that searching for Charley was a demonstration of the love for one's own child. Indeed, Charley's story soon became a story of dedication to one's own child as Christian created his self-portrait as the good father who left behind career and public life in the endless pursuit of his son.

In addition to helpful or helpfully intended actions, the search for

Charley also led to those that were cruel and exploitative. These, too, helped to keep Charley's story alive. As the "name of Charley Ross [became] a household word throughout the country and many a mother's heart has bled," Christian received misleading notes and became the subject of wild hoaxes that sent him on fruitless searches. Entrepreneurs also took advantage of the Charley phenomenon. One Philadelphia street ventriloquist tricked people into believing that Charley was inside a box screaming, "Let me out, I'm dying," until the gathering crowd turned into an ugly mob, ready to lynch the perpetrator. In another instance, a traveling circus company in New England displayed a wax replica of the Ross family. It was the most popular attraction. When Ross went himself to investigate, he discovered enormous crowds around the attraction and the fact that there was not the least resemblance between the figure of Charley and that of his son. Accusing the owner of misrepresentation and of impeding his search, Ross learned that the same figures had been used at an earlier time to represent the "temperate family" in a dyptytch of temperate and intemperate families. That contrasting display had now become the "Intemperate Family" and "The Ross Family," the latter symbolically becoming the social ideal and the object of moral sympathy. The owner vowed to do all he could to help find Charley and took with him on his travels the correct information and a sheaf of posters. But nothing could reverse the fact that the man had now completely diffused Charley's identity. The figure of Charley not only did not look like Christian's son; he had come to represent something quite other than himself.[48]

So great was Charley as an American attraction that the greatest popular culture entrepreneur of all, P. T. Barnum, became involved in the search for him. Barnum sent Christian a telegram and an offer: "If you will meet me at my home here before Monday I will pay your expenses both ways. I will pay a large reward, and I think I can get Charley, if alive." When Ross met him, Barnum offered to advertise a $10,000 reward for Charley that would strategically follow him all over the country. His only demand was that Charley become for a time part of his traveling exhibit as reimbursement for his expenses. "I am known to everybody," Barnum told Ross, "even to the lowest criminal classes." Ross accepted on condition that if the child were found the family would have the option of reimbursing Barnum rather than placing the child in the circus. The ad for $10,000 reward was prepared by Barnum and placed widely in papers throughout the country.

This was now the third of the large reward notices that had been placed; the first offered $20,000, the second $5,000, and the third $10,000, and Charley had by this time, the spring of 1877, become, in his father's words, "public property." So public had little Charley's identity become that one inmate of an insane asylum outside Baltimore was discovered screaming, "I am Charley Ross! I am Charley Ross! take me! take me!"[49]

回∨|回

Once it was so widely advertised, Charley's abduction set off alarm bells in the minds of parents across the nation. A brutal crime, a violation of privacy and the sanctity of the family, it needed "no shadow of darkness" as Christan warned. "Well may parents be struck with terror in realizing this peril, and in feeling that their children are no longer safe upon the lawns or lanes which were once thought as safe as the nursery or school-room. Well may they shudder at the bare possibility of one of their offspring being snatched from them by miscreants for vile traffic." Vile traffic, Ross's well-chosen words, evoked all the horror associated with the barbarous slave trade, the lurid trade in women's bodies, and blackmail.

The newspapers reported and reflected upon the panic that Charley's abduction caused, trying at once to calm parents' fears (less likely than "being struck by lightning") and to search out the causes for this new plague. Immigration, increased wealth, the anonymity of city life—all these and more were at the base of the problem. But it was Christian Ross who captured the Victorian mood best with its special soupçon of gothic titillation that even attached Charley's innocence to the strange wax figures in the traveling circus. "When it became known to the public that the object of the kidnappers in stealing the child was to extract a large sum of money from the parents before giving him up, a thrill of horror ran through the nation." If Americans were horrified by the invention of a new crime, they were also thrilled by its possibilities in depicting the range of evil and depravity available in the unknown haunts of the city. "These men," Christian later reflected, "had no bowels of mercy; in them the eclipse of goodness was complete; their depravity black as Egyptian night, and total. Dragging their innocent prey from his own sweet home into their polluted den, they contrived to guard themselves at every point, and traffic on parental anguish." Christian had found both the moral explanation and the very basis for the the public interest—the Victorians had found a new titillation, a new crime, "black as Egyptian night," a crime so foul it destroyed innocence. At another point in his memoir, Christian spoke of the "cold chill of horror that accompanied reading the kidnap note." It was this exposure to a new and mysterious evil, one that preyed on innocence that made the story so irresistible. At a time when childhood was increasingly sentimentalized, and children portrayed as innocent and vulnerable, that very process made them subject to sensationalization. While this fit into earlier, well-known images of child exploitation and spoilation, like that in *Oliver Twist*, it moved beyond them to reveal new levels of sinfulness and ghastly depravity.[50]

Having invented a new crime, however, there was now a very large price to pay because it came, in Christian's words, at the cost of "parental anguish." The Charley Ross case was fundamental to the history of American child kidnapping not only because it set the terms of subsequent kidnappings in the motifs of train drops, ransom notes, and police bungling, but because it made clear that the parent-child bond (not just the clichéd weeping mother) was the most important and resolute of obligations and the most necessary (if vulnerable) source of personal identity. Indeed, early in the case, the *Philadelphia Inquirer* suggested that "In his unremitting efforts in search of his child, Mr. Ross is . . . bearing the cares of every parent in the land." When Ross encouraged all parents to join him in his search, he also urged them to identify with his plight. The case thus carved out a peculiar psychological terrain in which emotional attachments to children and the maintenance of clear family identifications was bound up with the terrible fears about spoiled innocence and loss at the hands of strangers. "In some respects," Christian declared, "this crime is worse than murder, being not only torture to the child, who by terror and confinement must necessarily suffer greatly," but because of "the anguish of the parents." "Who is safe? What parent can trust his child out of his sight, if kidnapping is so simple?" Charley's abduction caused the *New York Times* similarly to reflect on a new social vulnerability. "Must it, then, be accepted that any of us are liable to have our children stolen from the public streets and in open day?" Although highly unlikely to happen to any one reader, the Ross case revealed, even pried open, a new social helplessness. "This Philadelphia business shows that any one of us is liable to such a loss."[51]

The *Times* argued that the source of the new problem was the looseness of cities with their accompanying loss of moral fiber, proliferation of wealth, and the attractions these offered to extorters. The cities had also become the site for the development of a new class of "desperate adventurers," "human vermin," previously unknown in America, but long familiar in the "capitals of Europe." Americans were still naive, not yet aware of their new condition. Like children themselves in a newly sophisticated world, they were ripe for exploitation, "too free, too unsuspicious of strangers. We forget that things are not with us now as they were with our fathers."[52] The *Times* had exposed the vulnerability of a new set of fathers who, as they looked upon their sons with increasingly loving eyes, would become much more suspicious of strangers who threatened their identity and their safety.

In emphasizing the obligations of fathers to their offspring above all other male roles, Charley's story had reinvented the family circle. One of the costs of the refashioned family bond would be the sense of community trust, of faith in neighborliness and a commitment to the open exchange between family and community. "Formerly when a small child was missed from home no one imagined that any worse fate had befallen it than that of accidental drowning in some convenient stream," the *New York Times* assured parents. This meant, of course, the death of the child, but the *Times* seemed not troubled by such a simple loss, not associated as was kidnapping with the possibilities of lost identity and the threat of strangers. "Now," fifteen months after Charley disappeared, "every tramp is looked upon as a probable child-stealer and every wandering gypsy woman is suspected of having three or four surreptitious children concealed upon her person. It has actually become dangerous for a stranger to speak to a stray infant on the street, or to offer a propitiatory candy to a squalling baby on a ferry boat. Such advances are likely to be mistaken for the preliminary steps of a bold attempt at kidnapping. . . . If the fear of child-stealing continues to spread, it will be equally hazardous for a charitable person to give temporary shelter to a lost child."[53] That was the crux of the matter. In confirming parental sentiment, the Ross case had made such gestures of neighborliness and friendliness suspect. In the new life of the city, crossing the boundary between family and stranger had become dangerous. In the midst of a society in which identities could be lost along with one's children, the act of shielding one's children meant turning one's back on the stranger. Of course, Charley's story did not initiate these moves. It was, after all, left to an impersonal agency and not neighbors to offer shelter to the lost boys of New York, the 9,000 who sought lodging for the night in the years 1869 to 1870. But Charley's story confirmed them, legitimized them, and became a foundation story for modern American childlife.

Charley's story suggested that behind the new fear of kidnapping was something even more haunting than the death of the child. With the child's disappearance came the torment of his unknown fate and parent's fears about his unwholesome experiences and malign companions. Kidnapping was an extreme and terrifying manifestation of their lack of control over the child's future in a city rife with dangerous evils. Christian put the matter well: "With whom is he? Are they kind to him? Do his childish eyes which knew nothing but home and home kindness see sights revolting? . . . Does he hear brutal language? Are the scenes about him so strange that his memory of us gradually fails, and his recollections of love, home and friends will all be swept away? . . . Stolen by thieves, will he be taught to be a thief? Will he grow to love crime? . . . Stern death would be far kinder than the rude arms that snatched away our little boy." [54] With the stranger came the robber of children's identity, the thief who threatened who they were. Christian's portrayal of the bitter anguish of not knowing the end of the story carries all the discomforts that a lack of narrative closure always brings. But Christian also evokes the painful fears of any loving parent worried about his child's future self ("will he become a thief?"), here very much compounded because that future lies in an unknown stranger's hands. Fear of the criminal classes haunted late-nineteenth-century society. How much more fearsome had they now become when they threatened the lives and destinies of the children of the respectable citizens of the city?

When State's Attorney Robert E. Crowe would make his final arguments in the kidnap case against Leopold and Loeb in 1924, he included Charley in his summation: "Fifty years ago Charlie [sic] Ross was kidnapped. . . . He was never found, and yet we all, even those of us born many years after, still talk about the case of Charlie Ross. There is something in the nature of the crime itself that arrests the attention of every person in the land. . . . The heart of every father, the heart of every mother, the heart of every man who has a heart, goes out to *the parents of the child."* Charley's story had always been Christian's story, the story of parents (fathers primarily) who now feared for their children's vulnerability (and their own) in a world made strange by the new dangers of anonymity and urban complexity. By 1924, the case of Charley Ross had become part of kidnap legend and American culture. It had "assumed a national character, and really affect[ed] every household," as Christian had predicted, because it had come to represent the problem of parents in a modern age.[55]

Charley's story had redefined the image of the lost child so that it meant not any helpless child or the child of others—all those lost children of the poor and the immigrant—but the perils that awaited one's own children. In confirming the paternal bond and paternal emotion, it thus constricted the very extension of self—the outpouring of empathy for the lost child— which made the search for Charley such a large social enterprise. While each new story of kidnapping, as we shall see, allowed a tentative breaking down of those barriers—rebinding family, neighbors, and strangers in a renewed commitment to childhood innocence—each confirmed the fears for one's own children and their precedence over all others. Christian, whose book did so much to create Charley's story, had initially attached a different moral to Charley's story, painting him as the redeemer whose loss had led to the discovery and return of other children to their parents. He became the "child of the people," released from his former self. In 1874, however, Christian's imagery was not what was finally absorbed culturally. Instead, as Christian was himself aware, Charley's disappearance had precipitated a self-protective response. "Children never seemed half so precious as now. . . . A new reason for thankfulness was found that the kidnappers had not invaded the family circle during their absence. *Men* awoke to the existence of a danger to which their children were exposed, of which before they had had no suspicion."[56]

Christian had not secured the return of his son; subsequently every father would do whatever was required to get his own child back. Fatherly sentiment, love for one's own, eclipsed the obligation to all others. In this context, fathers could even indulge in public displays of emotion. "The publication of private griefs is rarely admissible," Christian told his readers, "but the loss of our child in so atrocious a way has taken such hold upon public sympathy that there seems to be a necessity for violating the sanctity of home, and giving to the world that which otherwise would have been kept sacred within our own hearts." The sanctity of the home could be breached for a new sanctification of parental obligation. A private pain had become a public story. This great fatherly moment of a new dedication to the love of children had come in the context of a great loss, and it would be the loss or a sense of potential loss that would thereafter haunt the love of children. If an earlier time had been haunted by a real fear about child death, represented by the image of a mother's love tinged with sorrow, kidnapping confirmed that love and grief were still profoundly part of parenthood, now captured in the image of a father's love haunted by anxiety.[57]

Christian's book about Charley became a best seller in its day.[58] In its story of the loss of a child, it summed up a psychological moment when love for children and fear for their public safety would become inseparable parts of modern sentimental attachments. Charley's story has bequeathed to the future a powerful mix of parental love and anxiety. But Christian had also sensed the "thrill of horror" that made the case popular, and that thrill left a particular residue in the culture. The Ross case had drawn upon and surrounded child abduction with a certain Victorian exploitation of sensation, attaching a titillation that has survived to this day. In the story of Charley Ross, the Victorians created a new crime to which we remain addicted. With the crime came the sensationalization of parental anguish and the exploitation of children for our own pleasures of projection. The abduction of Charley set the pattern for subsequent abductions. It not only provided specific precedents and cautionary advice about proper kidnap etiquette, but also opened up a cultural territory in the public exploitation of children, fed by the imaginings of the horrible abuse suffered by other people's children and the emotional dread of losing our own.

CHAPTER TWO

"The Most Amazing Crime in the History of Chicago—and of the United States"

Leopold and Loeb

Richard Loeb and Nathan Leopold plotted every detail of their planned abduction (a plot deeply informed by their knowledge of actual cases and detective fiction)—everything except the identity of the victim. This they left to chance and opportunity. Even the ransom notes, which were painstakingly cast in advance, left the name of the victim's family deliberately blank, to be filled in only after the crime had been committed. On the day of the kidnapping, Leopold and Loeb had considered several children (all boys) who caught their attention in the school yard of the elite Harvard School in Chicago where they went in search of a victim. But only Robert (Bobby) Franks, a neighbor of Loeb's and a distant cousin, presented just the combination of accessibility and opportunity that would pay off. It was therefore fourteen-year-old Bobby who, in the late afternoon of May 21, 1924, was lured into the Willys-Knight automobile that Leopold rented especially for the occasion.[1]

The almost lackadaisical manner in which Bobby was chosen was an apt reflection of the bizarre nature of the crime: the plotting and execution of the criminal act had always been far more significant to Leopold and Loeb than the victim or the ransom. This inversion in the usual motive for kidnapping fueled the public's experience of the case. The pair had taken the (by then) well-worn etiquettes of kidnapping established by the Ross case and confirmed by other cases, and turned them on their head. Instead of a concerned father negotiating for his son's return with an anonymous and shadowy criminal, theirs would become the story of master criminals using the common expectations about paternal behavior first to play a sadistic game and then to grab the limelight. The year 1924 was the fiftieth anniversary of Charley Ross's disappearance. While the *New York Times* and the *Ladies' Home Journal* featured commemorative articles on the "Lost Boy," Leopold and Loeb changed the ground rules, introduced a new form of the kidnap story, and sensationally altered the public fears on which it preyed.[2]

The case of the two kidnap-murderers ignited several new matches in the growing conflagration of child kidnapping. Whereas the police had previously defined the arena of expertise (such as it was), attention now shifted to psychiatry. And to the horror felt about motives, once confined to the equation of child and ransom money, were added the perverse possibilities that lay in sexuality. In their crime, Leopold and Loeb not only ended the dominance of a single pattern, but lit a very long fuse that illuminated twentieth-century preoccupations.

Initially, however, in the absence of knowledge about the criminals or their motives, the press expected the usual and paid trite homage to the brutally murdered child and to the ill-fated father and mother ("Mrs. Franks was beautiful in her grief"). Very quickly the sensation provided by pathetic pictures of young Bobby and clichéd images of the weeping and distracted mother (still portrayed in the same stereotypical terms as Sarah Ross) gave way to the hunt for the slayers, followed by the magnetic imagery of the confessed kidnappers. As the British *New Statesman* observed about the case, "The great Chicago murder case . . . stands alone in the records of crime. Sensational murders are common enough. . . . But no crime that the modern world knows of can be set beside the killing of the boy Robert Franks by Nathan Leopold and Richard Loeb." Noting the insatiable public attention directed at the case, it went on shrewdly to remark that the drama became even more riveting after the question of the identity of the perpetrators was apparently solved: "When the mystery was at an end there began the exploitation of Leopold and Loeb on a scale and with a recklessness going beyond anything hitherto known." In fact, in many ways the mystery had only begun.[3]

凹[回

Kidnapping had always held the child's death as a possible outcome, and this threat was poised like a knife at the throat of parents in all successful ransom negotiations, such as that of John Conway (1897), Eddie Cudahy (1900), or Willie Whitla (1909). It was the final anguish for those who were not successful. When thirteen-month-old Blakely Coughlin was kidnapped from his nursery in Norristown, Pennsylvania, there was no initial ransom demanded; only a ladder and footprints were left behind. After a week of anxiety and a number of false extortion notes, the Coughlins finally received what seemed like the real thing. "We kill nobody. Just leave them to starve. The price is $6,000." The case dragged on for weeks as the Coughlin's sought proof that this extortioner really had the child. They made a number of attempts at an exchange, including a train drop, all with the police in close range. When the suspected kidnapper was finally captured, he confessed and admitted that in stifling baby Blakely's cry on the night of the abduction, he had silenced the baby forever. But the child's death had been an unhappy outcome, not the intended goal of the kidnapping. The story was still about the child. The convicted criminal, August Pascal, was hardly known then and has long since been forgotten.[4] But when Leopold and Loeb decided on the spur of the moment to make Bobby Franks their victim, when they killed him and proceeded with their plot, they substituted their own psyches for the face of their victim in the public's imagination.

They were certainly extraordinary boys. Both were intellectually precocious. At nineteen, Nathan was already a University of Chicago graduate and considered a young prodigy. His knowledge of fourteen languages, spectacular memory, years of experience as an amateur (but already published) ornithographer,[5] and imminent matriculation at the Harvard Law School spoke of his fine mind and grand future. Leopold was unstinting in his own praise and did not shy away from the dazzle that his credentials could provoke. Richard, eighteen, had graduated the year before from the University of Michigan, at seventeen the youngest graduate in the school's history. More personable, but equally self-absorbed, Richard was the more superficially attractive and beguiling. Both were very rich and came from families prominent among the Jewish social elite of Chicago, which included among others the family of Julius Rosenwald (whose grandson was among those Leopold and Loeb had considered kidnapping). Richard's father was a vice president in Rosenwald's Chicago-based Sears Roebuck and Company. The Leopolds had made their money in shipping. Both lived in the exclusive Hyde Park section of Chicago in imposing mansions where servants (including valets and governesses) saw to their needs. Young Leopold and Loeb were up-to-date and modern in the 1920s' sense of the term—both smoked conspicuously, drank regularly, and were sexually outspoken. Leopold was impeccably dressed and groomed. Loeb, far handsomer than his partner, was debonair, socially popular, an athlete and fraternity man, and very attractive to women.[6] These were boys with every natural and social advantage, golden boys of the American dream.

Robert Franks, too, might have been such a boy, although at fourteen he had had less chance either to show his natural talents or to enjoy his social advantages. His parents came from the same wealthy Hyde Park milieu, and, while his family was probably as rich as the Leopolds, it was less socially prominent since his father had begun as a pawnbroker before establishing himself in real estate. The Franks had converted to the Christian Science faith.

When Bobby did not return for dinner on the afternoon of May 21, Jacob Franks began a frantic and unsuccessful search for his child. Franks learned that evening that Bobby had been kidnapped and was being held for ransom when his wife answered a phone call from a stranger. The next morning he received a carefully cast ransom note signed by "George Johnson." That name (as Richard Loeb almost certainly knew) had been used as an alias in the kidnapping of John Conway in 1897. In the best, now fifty-year-old, kidnap tradition, Franks prepared to turn over the required $10,000 in unmarked, old, small denomination bills and to follow the "kidnappers' instructions to the letter." The police, as instructed, had not been brought in. But before he could proceed through the maze of chain letter instructions that had been part of the elaborate plot (these included train drops), the unexpected early discovery of Bobby's body stifled Leopold and Loeb's fun in enacting a kidnap caper. Instead, Jacob Franks learned that the body of an unidentified child had been found stuffed in a culvert by a workman crossing the Hegewisch swamp on the outskirts of the city. The child was clean and well kept, "no homeless waif." Thus, although the child had been found with a pair of eyeglasses (which Bobby did not wear), Franks sent his brother-in-law to check out the possibilities. With his own identification of the body, the ransom and the kidnap plot were swallowed up in the inexplicable murder.[7]

Like other victims, Jacob had feared this outcome ("Should you, however, disobey any of our instructions, even slightly, death will be the penalty") but hoped to forstall it. While previous kidnappings had sometimes resulted in death, they had always held out the promise, as did the note Jacob had received, that "your son will be safely returned to you within . . . hours of our receipt of the money."[8] Only this time that bargain was never meant to be kept because Bobby Franks had been killed well before his father could possibly have paid the ransom, indeed, well before the ransom note had been delivered. Franks knew this immediately, and soon so did the American public.

This deliberate murder (as the subsequent confessions would confirm) altered the delicate chemistry of kidnap expectations and introduced a new terror for those who feared for their children. In the long week between the discovery of Bobby's body and the confessions of his abductors, as the police and the press pursued all possible leads and concentrated on the two pieces of physical evidence, the glasses found at the scene and the ransom note, the public had time to contemplate what this meant for the children of America and for their parents. Bobby's body was unclothed when it was discovered and had various suspicious marks and discolorations (including on the genitals). As part of their investigation, therefore, the police rounded up various sex offenders for questioning—"morons" they were called at the time—and thus the public, with the help of the press, could also ponder the sexual possibilities.[9]

During the week of investigations, suspicion began to gather around the unlikely figure of Nathan Leopold, Jr. Boastful and cold, the brilliant young Leopold was skillfully identified as the owner of the glasses found with Bobby's body through systematic detective work. While Nathan talked his way out of that connection (he was after all a bird expert who held classes at Hegewisch), he had a harder time with the evidence of the ransom note. This had been linked by a young reporter, Alvin Goldstein, to the law group study notes that Leopold regularly typed (Goldstein would share a Pulitzer Prize for his work on the case). Leopold was then forced to produce his long rehearsed alibi, in which he and his good friend, Richard Loeb, were occupied by a sexual rendezvous with two "chippies," whose names Leopold could not fully recall but whose favors had kept them very much occupied at the time of the murder. On May 31, Loeb was brought to police headquarters to corroborate the alibi. Then quickly Loeb, and as a result Leopold also, confessed to the kidnap-murder of Robert Franks. These stunning confessions transformed the case from a troubling and disturbing crime into an "amazing" story "without parallel"; one that, like the loss of Charley, so captured the imagination of its day that it was frequently called "the crime of the century."[10]

Loeb's and Leopold's confessions left the framework created by the Charley Ross case behind by relocating attention from the crime victim to the criminals and by removing from kidnapping the by then customary motive, money. Intially at least, Leopold and Loeb were the most unlikely murderers. But each confession corroborated the essentials of the other, except in minor details and the fact that each accused the other of administering the fatal blow. And on the very long day between their early morning confessions and the time they were allowed to see the attorneys their parents had engaged on their behalf, they physically led the police through the maze of notes they had constructed and along the detailed route of their elaborate kidnap-murder plot. In the process, they gathered together the various pieces of Bobby's clothing and the bloodstained rug in which he had been wrapped. Leopold and Loeb also revealed that they had plans to kill their victim from the outset and as part of their plot. Their confessions and their attitude conveyed a sense of glee, the strange satisfaction that came from committing an apparently motiveless crime. The confessions confirmed the insignificance of Bobby's identity, making everyone's children more vulnerable than before, when kidnapping had some clear objective, and rendering parents more helpless than ever. Altogether, the young Leopold and Loeb had given the state a "hanging case."[11]

▣ ‖ ▣

Leopold and Loeb created a new association between kidnapping and murder. But why? The state argued that the young millionaires' sons were like every other set of kidnapppers, interested in the expected $10,000 ransom which, in their materialistic abandon, they hoped to squander. They killed Bobby to hide their own identities. For the prosecution the case was simple and traditional. But most people, inspired by the elaborate newspaper coverage, perceived that the case was new and its motives much murkier. In one interpretation, the one that long prevailed in the popular press and especially in the fiction that spilled forth from the case, the kidnapping was an excuse for the murder—a kind of theatrical frame, reinforced by readings in previous real-life kidnappings and the detective genre. The boys were thrilled by the killing itself. And the plotting and murder were meant to cement the boys' (probably erotic) friendship and express their sense of Nietzchean superiority.[12] In this view, the kidnapping was merely a joke and entirely secondary.

Another, no less likely explanation, was offered by Dr. H. S. Hulbert, who served on the defense team: "In early childhood [Loeb] was strongly impressed by a story of kidnapping in a book which he had read and the crime of kidnapping seemed to him to be *the maximum crime* and there had been growing . . . an ambition to commit kidnapping and make it a perfect mysterious crime and the carrying out of this ambition which had been fostered in his contemplations was the motive of the crime." In this view, kidnapping was both the source of inspiration and the ideal vehicle of expression for someone bent on criminality. In other words, kidnapping had by the 1920s, fifty years after Charley's disappearance, become so firmly part of public imagination that it became an ideal criminal form, ready to be brought to a kind of aesthetic consummation by the two master criminals. The kidnapping was the objective. The victim was killed to cover traces of the kidnappers, because he could identify them. Certainly, the extensive lengths to which Leopold and Loeb went in their drawn-out preparations and in perfecting their elaborate plans over the course of eight months lends support for this view. In Loeb's case, it was a historical case that first caught his fancy. "This boy early in life conceived the idea that there could be a crime that nobody could ever detect; that there could be one where the detective did not land his game. He had been interested in the story of Charley Ross."[13] Charley had receded from the public stage only to reappear, still inextricably bound to the crime of kidnapping, as an active ingredient in private fantasies.

If the deliberate intention to sacrifice a child to some ideal of criminality was not horrifying enough, the confessions introduced the public to two extraordinary and unlikely killers who appeared to revel in each particular of the elaborate crime they had planned since November of the previous year. After the two confessed, columnist Edwin Balmer put the spotlight on them and on their parents: "The day before yesterday the horror of this crime was the horror of the fate of Robert Franks and the horror of the grief of his father and mother. Today it is the horror of being Nathan Leopold, Jr. and Richard Loeb and the ghastly tragedy of being their parents." Eleanor Glyn, a well-known popular writer, summed up the fascination somewhat differently. The case "has arrested the attention of the world through its jazzy juvenile delinquents whose backgrounds of wealth, overeducation, and indulgence has had this criminal climax."[14]

By the 1920s, Americans had become familiar with the idea of juvenile delinquency. Indeed, the introduction to the first major published collection of documents relating to the crime noted that "Parents and teachers as well as persons whose professions bring them into frequent contact with juvenile delinquency will find in this volume rich material throwing light upon hitherto unrevealed problems of adolescence and the causes of crime." The juvenile courts had been in operation since the turn of the century, and the concern with juvenile crime had been one of the staples of progressive law enforcement and penology. This was an early arena to which progressive social policy had been applied with its dual vision of moderation in punishment and wide discretion for expanded state authority. Most experts had linked juvenile delinquency with deficiencies, deprivations, and neglect in families, inheritance, education, and most recently, in mental endowment. While the literature in this expanding field was by no means uniform and new studies beginning in the 1920s would further erode the idea of a fixed or single exemplar, juvenile delinquency had not heretofore been publicly associated with the very gifted, and extremely privileged, educational elite. In this as in so many other ways, the case of Nathan Leopold and Richard Loeb upset earlier assumptions. The *Chicago Herald and Examiner* played on this assumption as it mocked its readers. "You perhaps thought that all lawbreakers were of a low type mentally and possessed little culture."[15]

The decade of the 1920s is replete with stunning kidnap-murder cases in which the confessed perpetrators are juveniles. "Boy slayers" the *New York Times* called them. Leopold and Loeb at nineteen and eighteen were only the first and the most socially prominent, and they captured the lion's share of the public's attention. They were followed by twenty-year-old Harrison Noel in 1925 and then in 1927 by William Edward Hickman, eighteen, in a case that roiled the West Coast.[16] In none of them did the young men fit the usual social expectations of delinquency. All were either college graduates or college bound. Of the four, only Hickman came from an economically deprived background and a broken home. But Hickman's previous behavior, his stellar academic record, and the high regard in which he was held by teachers, preachers, and community leaders removed even him from the ranks of the usually suspect. All of these cases would challenge the conventional views of juvenile delinquency. Leopold and Loeb, because it was from the outset a media sensation, was the most vivid and unsettling.

Immediately then, Leopold and Loeb's confessions upended conventional categories and definitions. Even though beliefs about crime in the 1920s no longer gave much credence to Cesare Lombroso's visions of criminals as primitive types, the use of intelligence tests before the war by psychologists like H. H. Goddard had created an association between crime and subnormal intelligence. This association was strongly challenged in the 1920s by some, like Carl Murchison, who used the same kinds of tests, much popularized since the war, to question the relationship between crime and what was called feeblemindedness. "The same characteristics that make for wordly success in business and professional life also make for success in crime," Murchison announced. But Murchison also concluded that the "evidence is very strong that college training is a strong preventive of violence. For all practical purposes, crimes of violence on the part of college men can be ignored."[17] The Murchison connection between intelligence and crime could not quite explain the case of Leopold and Loeb, boys who were not simply smart criminals or juvenile delinquents but highly educated murderers who challenged their society and its definitions to the core. How then could one categorize two such boys who had committed this kind of crime? Initially, at least, they seemed to dissolve ordinary categories just as they upturned traditional motives.

Sniffing the sensationalism inherent in the case of two rich young thrill killers (an idea with historical staying power) and intoxicated by the whiffs of sexual perversion provided by Bobby's nude body, the press initially presented the killers, especially Leopold, as a breed apart and invested them with larger-than-life proportions. Fascinated by Leopold's appropriation of himself and his partner to the image of Nietzschean supermen, the crime became an exotic flower of evil, supremely titillating but so extreme as to be without didactic possibilities. "The diabolical spirit evinced in the planned kidnapping and murder; the wealth and prominence of the families whose sons were involved; the high mental attainments of the youths, the suggestions of perversions; the strange quirks indicated in the confession that the child was slain for ransom, for experience, for the satisfaction of a desire for deep plotting"; the *Chicago Tribune* observed, "combined to set the case in a class by itself." Interviewed by the *Chicago Herald and Examiner*, one man on the street noted that "I can't conceive of normal persons committing such a revolting deed," thus capturing the sense of the criminals as entirely apart from the ordinary and picking up the theme of "normality" which would eventually dominate the case.[18]

Leopold lent himself well (and intentionally) to this early portrayal. With his assistance, the press hounded his every step and hung on his statements, concocting an image of an egomaniacal "scientist" who had destroyed his feelings in the interest of cold ratiocination. He was quoted as saying "anything is justifiable in the interest of science" and that he "did it as easily as he would stick a pin through the back of a beetle" and other similar things. Nathan's brilliance, his precocity and haughty self-assurance, plus his uncommon interests (including the classic pornography of Pietro Aretino) made him the "psychic adventurer *de luxe*," who some speculated had even left his glasses at the crime scene to flaunt his invulnerability. "The most brilliant boy of his age I've ever known," prosecutor Robert Crowe called him. Leopold was the Svengali who had lured the more naive and innocent Loeb into a devil's pact. "Is Loeb the Faun, Leopold the Svengali?" the *Herald and Examiner* asked on its front page. Leopold—with his dark, brooding, Semitic looks, large nose, hooded eyes, and sensual lips—thus was said to dominate, indeed to "mesmerize," the less intellectual, more socially popular, better-looking Loeb—an all-American type and fraternity man (whose mother was not born Jewish). Just as Jewish Fagin was the evil genius of Dickens's underworld of delapidated London, Leopold was his upper-class Chicago equivalent. The *Chicago Herald and Examiner* even compared him to Caligula.[19]

At first then, the popular portrayal of the boys' uniqueness became a kind of substitute for a motive, setting the case apart and in a sense defusing its potential to cause social havoc. Limning Leopold as a monster with no conscience, a cold-blooded fiend whose devotion to science, philosophy, and learning (with its Jewish overtones), made him so alien that the evil explained itself.

But the case and the problems it posed could not rest there. Unlike 1874 when Jesse Pomeroy could be dismissed as a fiend from whom one withdrew one's mind in horror, Leopold and Loeb were both more obviously sane and their intellectual crime more commanding. By the 1920s the culture that had once been dazed by disappearing children was reeling from a great war in which often very young men had been wantonly slaughtered in uncountable numbers. Violence was a much more challenging matter in 1924 than in 1874. From the first, the case of Leopold and Loeb began to provoke all kinds of resonances and some commentators quickly concluded that with this crime and these criminals "it is our civilization that is on trial." Judge Ben Lindsey, the progressive advocate and analyst of contemporary youth, invested the case with pivotal significance: "Let no parent flatter himself that the Leopold-Loeb case has no lesson for him. Let us all clearly understand that the crime was the fruit of the modern misdirection of youth. . . . It was more than the story of a murder. It was the story of modern youth, of modern parents, of modern economic and social conditions, and of modern education."[20]

Soon the case occasioned a tide of self-examination as various commentators tried their hands at capturing the source of the new evil that had been unleashed. The university, with its secular philosophy and its obeisance to science rather than morality, was commonly invoked as an explanation. At a time when college attendance was becoming for the first time something of a normal experience for an enlarged middle class, Leopold and Loeb's lavish education provoked concern. Glyn was not alone when she described Leopold and Loeb as *over*educated. To questions about the ill effects of higher education were frequently added specific attacks on modern philosophy and the secularism to which it often led. Indeed the boys readily admitted their lack of religious belief, and Leopold often boasted of his aggressive atheism. So, too, the great wealth of the boys' families and their indulgence in materialistic excess became a regular target for blame. The case reeked of cultural corruption and defilement, and it was not just ministers who lamented the amoral materialism of the culture and its educational institutions. A psychologist-neurologist noted: "The materialism which is spreading throughout the world tends to lessen the moral principles. . . . Boys of very wealthy parents tend to become abnormal because they possess all the powers with which to gain their desires." Billy Sunday, the well-known evangelist, brought some of this together when he described the problem as "precocious brains, salacious books, infidel minds." Sunday had

a way with words and he proceeded to condemn, "the moral miasma of un-
belief oozing from our higher institutions of learning."[21]

In the newspapers these social lamentations were joined to various
forms of pop psychology, notably the reading of physiognomy, especially
faces and hands, which was believed to be a via regia for understanding the
psychology of the two boys who had everything. The newspapers presented these explanations in an eclectic hodgepodge of possibilities, none of
them very satisfying, but all suggesting how the case of Leopold and Loeb
could be connected to broader cultural worries. Most of these, however, became secondary cultural news and information when the legal phase of the
case began and Clarence Darrow presented his innovative defense.[22] With
that defense, the issues highlighted by the kidnapping of Bobby Franks
changed profoundly and the problem of motives was dissolved into an
issue of psychology.

ᗡ|||ᘉ

As soon as the parents of the young Leopold and Loeb became aware of the
extraordinary danger the boys faced, they wasted no time hiring the very
best defense team, with Clarence Darrow as chief defense counsel. The
Loebs were especially well connected in Chicago and their ability to persuade the great defender of the common man to speak up for two millionaires' sons was facilitated by Walter and Benjamin Bachrach, who were
Loeb relations and served together with Darrow for the defense. Both
Bachrachs, Walter especially, had a deep interest in modern depth psychology, and the case, which from the outset raised questions about human motivation, would now take a sharply psychological turn. This fit well with
Darrow's own dark and deterministic inclinations, and the young ages of
the boys suited his generally well-known liberal sentiments.[23]

When Darrow accepted the offer (initially reported to include a $1 mil-
lion fee), the newspapers began to prepare the public for what was, by this
time, the expected defense in a case where the evidence was airtight and the
odds on acquittal very long—the insanity defense. As psychiatrist Thomas
W. Salmon observed, discussion "turned abruptly from the terrible details
of the crime and the amazing characteristics of its perpetrators to those
larger issues which the type of defense rather than the crime itself forced
upon the attention of the public." Despite some exaggeration, Salmon cap-

tured the swing in the case, as it now moved to a consideration of categories of personality and crime. From a crime which had from the start left old structures behind, the case of Leopold and Loeb would now construct a new vision of criminality and a new source of danger for American children. Indeed, once Darrow arrived on the scene, frontpage headlines began to prepare the public to expect a "battle of the alienists," as psychiatrists were still sometimes called.[24]

The *Chicago Herald and Examiner* began informing it readers about the nature and history of the "insanity defense" within a week of the confessions. On June 4 the paper ran an article on Illinois insanity laws. The next day, F. Dalton O'Sullivan began a long series on the history and meaning of the insanity defense, which took note of the fact that the public was highly suspicious of these long-established legal pleas. Prosecutor Crowe was reported to be attending an insanity trial in Geneva, Illinois, to better prepare himself for the forthcoming case. The legal dimension was soon augmented by interviews with psychiatrists, psychologists, and other mental experts. The battle of the experts, which the newspaper had led the public to expect, had begun.[25]

This battle was not, however, to be only between one group of medical experts, paid by the defense, and another group, paid by the prosecution, as the newspapers proposed, although much of the best front-page copy would eventually be devoted to this supposed battle between the hired medical guns. The war in the Leopold and Loeb case, and in subsequent cases in the 1920s, was between the developing expertise of psychiatry, and its growing visibility in court, and the prevailing legal definitions of insanity, whose language and methods were increasingly at odds with twentieth-century psychiatric concepts and visions. None of this was entirely new. For almost one hundred years, legal pioneers had sought to bring the conflicting perspectives into greater harmony and to leaven legal understanding with medical insight. At a time when the Leopold and Loeb case brought the conflict into open battle, S. Sheldon Glueck, whose book on *Mental Disorder and the Criminal Law* (1925) would soon become the standard text, noted that "The perennial conflict between members of the legal and medical profession on the question of the relation of mental abnormality to criminal responsibility is a matter of common knowledge."[26] The Leopold and Loeb hearing would bring the conflict, well known in professional circles, to sensational public attention.

Despite the antagonism, the role of psychiatry increased in law throughout the 1920s. In 1927 when William Alanson White, a dominant figure in American psychiatry and one of the defense experts in the Leopold and Loeb case, was asked to address a special session of the American Bar Association devoted to psychiatry, his appearance in that context helped to mark psychiatry's arrival in American law. White unflinchingly put his finger on the source of the conflict: "The psychiatrist in his contact with the legal machinery finds that the methods of procedure are such as to make it well-nigh impossible for him to mobilize his knowledge in any useful way for the assistance of the courts in dealing with the individual problems that come before him. . . . [T]he law with its emphasis upon the act rather than the actor . . . has failed to give to this factor [personality] adequate consideration. . . . Law and medicine because they have each been pursuing their own ends independently, have come to talk, as it were, different languages."[27]

The guiding concept in law was that of "personal responsibility," and this was the basis upon which a judgment of guilt or innocence could be made. Insanity pleas had a centuries-long history in English law, but the basic tenets of the modern legal idea were framed and standardized in the rules layed down in Great Britain in 1843 after Daniel M'Naughton tried to assassinate the prime minister, Sir Robert Peel, and shot and killed his private secretary instead. This action took place shortly after a similar attempt on Queen Victoria. When M'Naughton was judged not guilty on the grounds of insanity, the public outrage resulted in the promulgation of the "Rules in M'Naughton's Case" by ten high judges of the English court. In practice the three narrow guiding rules laid the basis for the knowledge of right and wrong criterion that long afterward served as the legal linchpin in English and American trials of insanity. As one student of legal insanity noted in 1927, "These rules are so drafted that in their strict interpretation it may be said that few are mad enough to come within them. . . . No doubt M'Naughton could never have come within the strict interpretation of these rules." The standards have been variously applied, but by strict definition, any individual who could be shown to know the difference between right and wrong was legally sane, even though the individual may not have been able to act according to that knowledge. When these rules were invoked in the Leopold and Loeb hearings and when William A. White was asked whether Richard Loeb "knew the difference on May 21, between right and wrong," the eminent psychiatrist shocked the court by calling the concept of "responsibility" that underwrote it "a legal fiction," something lawyers could argue about but on which doctors, from their medical perspective, could shed no light.[28]

The strain between legal and medical definitions of insanity broke into open conflict throughout the 1920s, both in the popular and the professional press. It was especially notable during and in the aftermath of the William Edward Hickman case. Hickman, an eighteen-year-old who claimed to be guided by a special providence, kidnapped twelve-year-old Marion Parker from the Mt. Vernon Junior High School in Los Angeles on December 15, 1927, by telling the school secretary that her father had been severely injured in an accident and had asked to see her. Later that same day, Marion's father, Perry M. Parker, received the first of several communications from Hickman informing him that his daughter (one of twins) was being held for $1,500 ransom but that she was safe and well. "Your daughter's life hangs by a thread. . . . This is business. Do you want the girl or 75 $20 gold certificates U.S. currency? You can't have both." Indeed, Marion herself twice wrote to her father pleading for her life. After at least one failed contact, the money was finally delivered on the evening of December 17. In return, the eviscerated partial body of young Marion, with her eyes wired open and her face rouged, was thrown at her father from a fast-moving car. Marion's limbs, lower torso, and internal organs were subsequently found in various packages all over Los Angeles.

Having successfully eluded elaborate police nets and detecting devices before the gruesome exchange, the man—who identified himself as the Fox, Fate, and Death in the notes—now led the police on what the *New York Times* called "the most spectacular manhunt the West has known in years." The *Times* proclaimed "Terror Grips City," as Los Angeles waited to find the perpetrator of this heinous deed. Very quickly the publicized reward money for Hickman's capture mounted, variously reported as $50,000, $60,000, or $100,000. Before he was caught, one man falsely identified as the kidnap-murderer hanged himself in his cell, and Hickman's positive identification (from fingerprint evidence) and capture in Pendleton, Oregon, almost resulted in a lynching. That lynching was prevented only by the clever strategem of a local chief of police who made the enormous crowd line up so each could get a personal look at the prisoner through the barred jail window.[29] Hickman confessed to the Los Angeles police officers after they arrived in Pendleton to take him back to Los Angeles.

Hickman's lawyers and progressive members of the Los Angeles criminal justice community were convinced that the young kidnap-murderer
was insane, utterly unable to control his behavior, and should not be held responsible for the crime. He confided to the junior defense counsel, Richard
Cantillon, then just beginning his career, that he had planned "the master
crime of the century" and that he heard voices ordering him to kill Marion
and directing him at each stage as he carefully disassembled her body. The
defense team attempted to demonstrate that Hickman suffered from inherited tendencies toward insanity, malign early childhood influences in his
fire-and-brimstone obsessed Ozarks family, and deep psychological disor-
ders and delusions. They used the latest psychiatric evidence for the etiol-
ogy of schizophrenia (*dementia praecox*), including the special vulnerability
of adolescents. They tried to draw strong analogies between physical and
mental disease: "You have seen a strong body rendered helplessly crippled
by poliomyelitis. Here you see a strong mind rendered hopelessly maniacal
by schizophrenia," Cantillon pled in his concluding remarks.[30] Since Hickman was not during the trial notably delusional or incoherent and had normal, even outstanding mental gifts, the insanity plea did not succeed in
either the initial trial or the subsequent appeal. The knowledge of good and
evil rule prevailed with the jury.

In Hickman's defense, Cantillon had argued that "The very conduct of
the defendant in the perpetration of the offense savors too strongly of tragic
madness. When Hickman hung that little dead body head down over the
bathtub drain and cut the throat with a kitchen knife, when he severed the
arms and legs, when he disemboweled the child, when he dressed what
remained of her in her school clothes, when he rouged her face, applied lip-
stick to that little dead mouth, and wired open the eyes, he was not malin-
gering—he was completely mad. These acts could only be the product of an
insanely deluded mind. There is a doctrine of civil law called *Res ipsa
loquitor*, interpreted, it means the thing speaks for itself. . . . If Hickman told
you personally he had just done these hideous things, but he claimed he
was sane, you would not believe him. The very acts speak for themselves."[31]
But this was just the problem: if certain acts in and of themselves proved
madness because they were so unusual or horrifying, then what remained
of the doctrine of responsibility? Could not some people deliberately choose
to commit atrocities, and should they not be held accountable for that
choice? Were normal humans capable of horrible behavior? Were there ob-

vious limits to what could be considered normal in human behavior?

These were the questions repeatedly raised in the 1920s as psychiatric experts defined certain kinds of behavior as abnormal, insane, or uncontrollable regardless of whether the individual could distinguish good from bad or seemed generally lucid. An editorial in the *Catholic World* expressed the fear that "a theory of ethics based upon the denial of a distinction between good and evil" will result in "the complete emancipation of the American criminal, . . . the final achievement of unrestricted personal liberty." James J. Walsh, a physician, voiced a similar concern: "because of all this discussion and minimization of responsibility . . . the criminal minded and cunning insane are taking advantage to do whatever they are tempted to do; in the confident hope that somehow or other they will, like so many others before them, escape the hand of justice." Indeed, in "Crime and the Expert," the *Outlook* concluded "At present there must be a strong temptation to anyone contemplating murder to perform the act in as cruel and coldblooded a manner as possible" since the more outrageous a crime, the more obviously insane the perpetrator could be judged to be from this viewpoint. Beyond this there was the gentle but unmistakable slide (of which Clarence Darrow was frequently accused) to explaining and thereby excusing *all* crime: "That the abnormal are not responsible for their conduct is a kindly teaching which by a certain logical *tour de force* can be extended to all offenders. This is the easy-chair 'proof' that the author of misconduct, because of the very fact of that misconduct, is to that extent abnormal and therefore to that extent to be excused."[32] In this view, law would soon be eclipsed by psychiatry. The verdict in the Hickman case, whatever its merits, was a barrier against this slide from legal to medical definitions and its perceived consequences.[33]

In a similar case two years earlier in New Jersey, the jury had also found the defendant, kidnap-killer Harrison Noel, guilty. Noel was luckier and escaped the gallows; not however until his case, like Hickman's, showed the problems involved in the volatile mixture of law, medicine, and public opinion so conspicuous in the 1920s. At twenty, Noel, who had "an exceptionally brilliant mind" and came from a cultured and wealthy home, had already spent a year at Harvard and six months in a private sanitarium when he kidnapped Mary Daly, aged six, from Montclair, New Jersey, on September 5, 1925. He then killed her and buried her in a ditch before demanding a $4,000 "reward" for her return. He had also killed a black man from whom he had commandeered a car. After twenty-two hours of questioning, he confessed when the child's mother urged him to speak.[34]

When he was institutionalized, Noel had been diagnosed as suffering from catatonic *dementia praecox*.[35] The press and public were outraged that Noel, who had escaped from a mental institution, was allowed to remain free on his father's recognizance. Newspapers held the director of the institution as well as Noel's father responsible for what had happened. But initially at least, perhaps because he had been in a mental institution, there was little dispute over his mental disease as the press reported general concord on the diagnosis of insanity; even the police captain called Noel "hopelessly insane." But when the alienists hired by the prosecution examined him, four found him sane and a fifth, "insane but responsible" because "he knew he had done wrong." On November 17, after deliberating for only a little over an hour, and despite Noel's mother's impassioned plea for mercy, the jury found Noel guilty and sentenced him to die in the electric chair. While the trial was still in progress, *The World* in New York declared "that all murders should be classed alike and that justice should not be consistently jeopardized by farcical pleas of insanity, dishonestly put forward, buttressed by dishonest evidence and leading to notorious results."[36]

The final disposition of the Noel case was not, however, made by a jury, a judge, or the press, but by the Court of Errors and Appeals in Trenton, which by a vote of 12 to 1 reversed the conviction and sent Harrison Noel to the state asylum in Morris County. New Jersey's unusual system of appeals gave the panel unique powers to overturn or amend verdicts. Even as Noel was thus snatched from death, courts were still not ready to act on the basis of the psychiatric expert but preferred, as the *New York Times* concluded, "to base [their] verdict on standards that are those of popular opinion rather than that of science." The Noel case had taken its place among the criminal trials that William A. White called "a blot upon our land . . . a battle of wits for the delectation of a sensation-loving public. Some sense of popular opinion can be gleaned from the response of Mrs. Estelle Lawton Lindsay to the Hickman case: "insanity's bunk. . . . People are weary to death of insanity as a defense in murder cases."[37]

Both the Noel case and the Hickman case, despite their different final outcomes, echoed the case of the two boy slayers from Chicago. Noel himself told examiners that he had read about and was influenced by the Leopold and Loeb case, while Hickman's planning of the perfect crime was clearly also an imitation. And the press readily drew comparisons among the boys. Prosecutors in the Noel case carefully studied the moves of their predecessors in Chicago. Newspapers, judges, juries, as well as the young kidnap murderers had read about, imitated, and learned from the "crime of the century," which *The World* in a large feature on young maniacs called "the classic parallel to the crime of demented young Noel Harrison."[38] While the young killers were influenced by the famous pair, their juries and the public had also been informed by the results of the case carefully managed by Darrow.

In the spring of 1924, Darrow had anticipated the intense and widespread hostility that an insanity plea would arouse, and he was fully aware of the acute limitations created by the criterion of knowledge of good and evil if applied to his urbane and knowledgeable defendants. When Darrow was called in to handle the case in early June, he had apparently planned to proceed along this conventional route, and the two boys were subjected to long and intimate interviews and an extensive series of tests of their physical and mental functions. The newspapers carefully recorded the elaborate preparations and the boys' responses, including Leopold's increasing irritation with the tests and growing hostility to being pled insane.

Then Darrow and the Bachrachs changed their strategy. Foreseeing the likely outcome should a jury, inflamed by public opinion and a populist prosecutor ambitious for higher office, be asked to bring in a judgment that Leopold and Loeb were not guilty by reason of insanity, the defense tried an innovative court procedure. They pled the boys guilty and laid all their hopes on using the evidence of the psychiatric reports to mitigate the sentencing by the judge. They were hoping in this way to take the boys out of the shadow of the gallows and into prison with a life sentence. A judge, rather than a jury, could more readily be persuaded of the ways in which psychological problems had distorted the pair's emotions, rendering them not entirely responsible for their behavior, while leaving them technically sane and legally responsible. "We raise no issue as to the legal insanity of these defendants and make no contentions that by reason of the fact that they are suffering from a diseased mental condition, there should be any division or lessening of the responsibility to answer for the crime, the commission of which they have confessed. We do assert that they are suffering and were suffering at the time of the commission of the crime charged from a diseased mental condition, but we do not concern ourselves with the question of whether such mental disease would constitute in the present case a defense to the charge of murder."[39]

Darrow's proved to be a historically consequential maneuver. But initially, it was not certain that any of the evidence gathered by the medical and psychiatric experts engaged by the defense could be presented. Prosecutor Crowe and his team, basing themselves on a strict interpretation of the M'Naughton rules, argued that since no one was suggesting that Leopold and Loeb were insane this kind of evidence should play no part in the hearing. In his all-or-nothing strategy, Crowe was trying to throw the case into the hands of a jury. He noted that if psychiatric evidence was used at all, then the boys should be pled insane and a jury impaneled. Only a jury could make a judgment about guilt or innocence and a plea of insanity always involved the question of guilt or innocence since an insane man could not be responsible and was therefore necessarily innocent. By pleading guilty, Crowe argued, the defense had made psychiatric evidence unusable since its only function was to cast light on the responsibility of a defendant for a crime, something only a jury could decide. Throughout the proceedings, in fact, Crowe spent much time trying to trip the defense into an insanity plea. But Judge John Caverly allowed the defense to walk the very fine line they had laid out for themselves. He accepted the defense argument that although Leopold and Loeb knew what they were doing (and that it was wrong), their emotions were so disordered that, although this did not release them from responsibility, it should be weighed against the extreme sentence of death. Because of that balancing act, the American public was given a significant lesson in the new psychology and exposed to a long discussion of what was and was not normal youthful behavior. The maneuver probably also cost Robert Crowe his public hanging.

IV

With their confessions, Loeb and Leopold had shocked the nation, but their story was still largely of their own making. The first press presentations of the pair as evil geniuses had in most ways fulfilled their glamorous self-representations, although the press early began to seek ways to connect their story with larger cultural matters and anxieties. Now, however, as the lawyers hired by their parents tried to save their lives, the young kidnap-slayers lost control of their story. Instead, with the fascinated assistance of the media, the psychiatrists hired by the defense constructed a new public portrait. That portrait used psychiatric concepts to provide Americans with alternative ways to grapple with the evil that had befallen their children. Instead of the corruptions of the city with its sordid haunts that had been used to explain Charley's abduction, the source of the new threat lay buried in the distorted emotions of even the most reputable and upstanding. If the threat to children had once been lurid and titillating but subject to policing, the new threat was much more elusive, requiring new technologies and explanations. As a first approximation to understanding the source of crimes against children in terms of the new psychiatry, it was a modest effort and not entirely persuasive, but as the entering wedge of a new psychological era, it was sensational.

"Fifty Alienists to Fight for Slayers" the *Chicago Herald and Examiner* announced in its headlines for June 14 in a typical burst of exaggeration. In fact, Darrow's experts were a much smaller team. The three star witnesses (mockingly called "the Three Wise Men from the East" by the prosecutor) included: William Alanson White, chief of staff at St. Elizabeth's Hospital in Washington, D. C., and Professor of Nervous and Mental Diseases at Georgetown University, who as the head of St. Elizabeth's, was one of the most important figures in American psychiatry. He was also an early and very influential American interpreter of Freud's ideas and would have a large role in bringing European psychoanalytic theory into an American framework. The second star was William Healy, a renowned authority on juvenile psychopathology and a pioneer in expert court testimony. Healy had been director of the psychopathic clinic in Chicago and was at the time of the trial the director of the Judge Baker Foundation in Boston, an organization devoted to issues of juvenile crime and justice. Healy had written extensively about the causes of juvenile delinquency. Dr. Bernard Glueck, the third witness, was former director of Sing Sing prison in New York, a translator of several European authorities on psychoses, and an expert on the relationship between law and psychiatry, who had published in 1916, *Studies in Forensic Psychiatry*. Less well known nationally, was Ralph C. Hamill, a local and well-regarded neuropsychiatrist who did not testify in court but helped, together with the others, to prepare the written psychiatric evaluation on which the defense case was based. This evaluation was described by the *Journal of the American Institute of Criminal Law and Criminology* as "the first instance of the offer of elaborate psychiatric analyses as the basis for remitting the law's penalty."[40]

The defense team had also enlisted the aid of two other doctors, H. S. Hulbert and Karl M. Bowman, to write a complete profile of Leopold and Loeb. They examined Nathan and Richard extensively for fourteen days, probing and measuring their body functions, mentality, intelligence, family histories, and fantasies, as well as the then popular matter of the function of their endocrine glands to appraise the physical and mental basis for their behavior. The result of their investigation was the notorious 80,000-word Hulbert-Bowman report, which would serve as a basic text of the defense case. Before these studies got to court, however, their entire contents were somehow stolen or leaked to the press and served up, together with eggs and toast, as breakfast food for American newspaper consumers.[41]

The Hulbert-Bowman report thus became famous even before it became evidence. Through it the public learned the most intimate facts about Loeb's and Leopold's lives. Paraded before the public, their fixations and their "master-slave" relationship became staples of the Chicago newspaper diet. The report anchored "perversions" in childhood fantasies and intellectual precocity in endocrine malfunction and in compensation for fears of physical inferiority. The report also forced an entire revision of the assumed relationship between Leopold and Loeb: Loeb was now the "master" criminal and Leopold his willing "slave." This seemed initially to be the "shocker" ("Loeb is the king. It is he who has been the mastermind throughout. He is almost without emotions. . . . He has always been fond of crime stories"). But any reader who went beyond the attention-grabbing summations would be presented with two very troubled boys. Much of this material, except for "the unprintable matter" (very small segments in the report and testimony that described their sex play), appeared in the major Chicago newspapers, as well as in the volume published very shortly after the trial by Maureen McKernan, a reporter for the *Chicago Herald and Examiner*.[42]

The Hulbert-Bowman report and the subsequent psychiatric testimony transformed the horror into pathos as the pair went from being monsters to being boys. And it completely altered their story and its meaning. The defense psychiatrists insisted on calling each of the boys by their nicknames, "Dickie" (Loeb) and "Babe" (Leopold), while their reports and testimony were directed at showing the childlike quality of the killers' behavior ("There is not an act in all this horrible tragedy," Darrow insisted, "that was not the act of a child."). Even without the endearing names, however, no one could read the medical reports and not be affected by the fragile loneliness of Leopold's childhood, scarred by feelings of physical inferiority, the sexual abuse of a governess, and the death of his mother when he was fourteen. "He [Leopold] states that his mother was beautiful, loving and kind. . . . The patient states that there have been two experiences in his life which have completely altered his philosophy of life. His mother's death is one of these . . . if his mother, who was such a good and exceptional person had to suffer so much in the world and that if God took her away from this world, then that God is a cruel and senseless God."[43] It was just as difficult not to condemn the evil committed against a vulnerable Dickie Loeb by a well-meaning but pretentious and outrageously strict governness who literally took him over, denied him playtime, and pushed him into extreme academic overachievement.

The defense team (doctors, psychiatrists, and lawyers) were very careful to avoid blaming the families (and specifically denied any genetic taint). But whether parents or parent substitutes were at issue, it was the boys' childhoods that had been distorted. As the case unfolded daily in voluminous detail in the press, the psychiatric testimony embedded the warped childhoods of the two killers in the public's awareness of the case. Even the prosecution's attempt to undermine the defense position backfired. While the prosecution would hold up to derision White's image of Dickie nightly speaking his dreams and fantasies to his teddy bear, the mental picture of the lonely child with his teddy lingered in the newspapers.[44]

Leopold and Loeb were not entirely tamed by the Hulbert-Bowman report or the psychiatric testimony, especially as the boys' sexual compact as master and slave became more firmly limned. And this testimony did not diffuse the ugly mob spirit that hung in the Chicago air and that included cross burnings by the KKK. But for readers who were willing to be informed and not just inflamed, the bold self-sufficiency of the two criminal masterminds had been deeply shaken. The exposure of their privacy in the press was profoundly humiliating, a humiliation that had begun even before the hearing when, in preparation for their defense, their every bodily and mental function became the subject of news and publicity. Day after day, the newspapers showed the pair hooked up to machines and discussed their every test result. "Questions are hurled at them—staccato, urgent questions. They answer. More questions. More answers. Then come the examinations—the hopping, the skipping, the jumping. First the one under examination stands on one foot, then on the other. Searching, prying fingers go over him. He winces and grins." At one point, Leopold railed that "Loeb and I are being trained like fleas to jump through hoops just to entertain the curious."[45]

In exposing Leopold and Loeb to prying fingers as well as the prying public, the testing and the psychiatric evidence subverted their glamorous self-sufficiency. The new psychology transformed them from arrogant Nietzschean criminals (the early representation of Leopold) into vulnerable boys (Loeb and his teddy bear) and linked them more directly to the ordinary boys of America. Leopold and Loeb's experiences in childhood were extreme, but not after all so very different than those of other young boys. How could anyone know if one's own child (or a neighbor's) might not become the next child slaughterer? Dr. Carleton Simon, a criminologist and police deputy, took the occasion to instruct parents about the dangers of adolescence. "It is during the adolescent transition that so many youth turn toward a career of crime." And the newspaper that carried Simon's essay editorialized, "This is an article which every parent should read, an article which may result in saving many a youth from the wages of sin." By its use of an old-fashioned metaphor, the paper neatly transcended the difference between older religious views and the scientific expertise offered by the criminologist. Given such lessons, it is hardly surprising that a minister confessed that the crime "caused more heart searching on the part of parents than any crime within my memory of forty years in the ministry."[46]

At a meeting of psychiatrists, Dr. Llewellys Barker, professor of clinical medicine at Johns Hopkins University, explained the broad significance of the case: "If the public could be accurately informed of the prevalence of *abnormal* thought, feeling, and behavior in the United States, such indifference as now exists regarding prevention would become inconceivable." Such knowledge would, of course, elevate the professional status and social role of the experts who controlled it. It would also make Americans acutely aware of the extreme danger under the surface of everyday behavior. During the hearings, the public was thoroughly inducted into the new concept. The defense psychiatrists' joint report repeated the terms "abnormal" and "normal" more often than any others and added to them the special term of "supernormal" when referring to Leopold's intelligence. The defense argued that Leopold and Loeb suffered from emotional disease and from an imbalance between their mental and emotional levels. "These boys—I do not care what their mentality—that simply makes it worse—are emotionally defective," Darrow asserted. Walter Bachrach described their ills in more technical terms: "The evidence demonstrates the existence in Nathan Leopold, Jr., of a paranoid personality, and in Richard Loeb of a schizophrenic condition of mind, which in each boy resulted in diseased mental reactions and made possible the perpetration, in combination, of the crimes committed."[47]

But the term "abnormal" was much more loosely applied by the defense throughout the hearing, and this vaguer concept was widely applicable. Among the "abnormal" childhood behaviors were too much private fantasizing, excessive reading of "exciting detective fiction," drinking alcohol at too early an age, and associating with those much older than oneself. Leopold "was not only precocious in his mental interests, but these interests assumed a degree of intensity and showed themselves in special directions which were in themselves indications of abnormality." Leopold's special brilliance and extraordinary interests became signs of "abnormality" much aggravated by the fact that "Early recognition of his superior attainments by his teachers and by his mother made him feel unlike and apart from others and superior to them." In Loeb's case, the "unscrupulousness, untruthfulness, unfairness, ingratitude and disloyalty assume a particularly abnormal nature when one views them in the light of the kind of home and social setting that he came from." In other words, these traits, usually condemned as dishonorable or possibly immoral, were abnormal because Loeb could not possibly have learned them in the kind of home he came from, one "noted for its high standards of virtue and culture."[48] These were generous definitions of abnormality indeed, and so broad and flexible as to be extremely frightening. If applied generally, any special trait or eccentricity became a source of concern, every character flaw a mark of emotional disease.

Above all, Leopold and Loeb seemed to have indulged extreme fantasies. "In contrast to the imaginative life of normal childhood which is always in touch more or less with the realities surrounding child life, Leopold's phantasies were from the beginning out of accord with the usual demands of social life, and never seem to have undergone the natural fate of phantasy life in being increasingly matched or assimilated into the facts of reality. Thus the normal child identifies himself with the persons in his immediate environment, he day-dreams himself being a motorman, an engineer, a policeman, showing thereby in his desires a normal response to the influences which surround him." Probably neither Leopold nor Loeb daydreamed about being motormen or policemen (although Loeb's perfectly ordinary cowboy fantasies were damned as evidence of excessive aggression), but the psychiatrists' banal views of reality and realistic fantasies (while even then criticized as substituting doctrine for insight) helped to provide easy didactic lessons and fit well into the newspapers' needs to link the case to the bedrooms and nurseries of their readers.[49]

The newspapers had moved early toward using Leopold and Loeb for contemporary lessons. This required that they be made accessible, even familiar. Some papers began to ask readers to take the same IQ tests and puzzlers as Leopold, the genius. The most extreme of these strategies was to involve readers in a subtle process of identification as when Winifred Black, a woman's columnist, asked her readers to imagine "If Your Son were [the] Slayer": "You who sit there at your breakfast table, so comfortable, so much at peace with the world. . . . Would you stand for justice and for right, no matter if by taking such a stand you had to walk to the very foot of the gallows with your son?" In this ploy to sell papers, the press moved in the same direction as the defense strategy of sympathetic identification with the killers and their families: "I know that any mother might be the mother of little Bobby Franks. . . . I know that any mother might be the mother of Richard Loeb and Nathan Leopold, just the same . . . any mother might be the mother of any of them," Darrow declared, effectively erasing the difference between victim and killers through his rhetorical strategy. Indeed, he concluded, "these two are the victims."[50]

As the defense attempted to understand and explain Leopold and Loeb's behavior as a function of distorted (but not so very alien) development and the newspapers tried to maintain their readers' fixed attention through identification, concepts of normality and abnormality were effectively reprocessed. Abnormality now became not so much the opposite of normality, in the way that innocence was of guilt, as it became the unfortunate extension of normality. Thus Leopold and Loeb were like other "boys," only bent and malformed emotionally. As such they could be (and possibly were) like any of the sons of readers of American newspapers, so close to home as to be chillingly familiar.

Prosecutor Crowe tried mightily to oppose both the defense claims and its legal consequences by insisting that the pair had a clear motive—ransom—and that they were criminals, not abnormal. Crowe had called the crime "the most atrocious, cruel, brutal, cowardly, dastardly murder in the history of American jurisprudence." He dressed his traditional prosecution up in populist rhetoric and antics. Crowe usually presented himself as the democratic David against the Goliath of highly paid and obscurantist expertise and subjected the "Three Wise Men from the East" to withering cross-examination. A dramatic figure, who frequently changed his sweat-soaked shirts in the stifling August courtroom, his circus antics and populist treacle only increased the carnival atmosphere and the case's media visibility. By attacking the psychiatrists (and using his own group of psychiatric witnesses), Crowe inflamed the contemporary debate over the role of psychiatry in the court, but he could not alter the transformation in popular imagery that had taken place.[51]

The defense had insisted that "There is justification for stressing the uniqueness of this case if for no other reason than that it has created widespread panic among parents of young people,"[52] but the defense strategy was, in fact, to link the once strange kidnappers to ordinary experience. Not just the "criminal classes" as the nineteenth century had called them, but the families of Hyde Park could nurse and nestle a predator. By removing an obvious social purpose from their crime (ransom) and by attaching to it (possible) sexual goals, the defense psychiatrists had refashioned the nature of crimes against children and given them a psychological home.

🜨√🜨

Who was to blame? In the traditional legal view, blame was responsibility and responsibility was guilt. But the Leopold and Loeb defense had effectively obscured these once firm connections. The boys were guilty, but not responsible; sane, but not completely blameworthy. The crime resulted from the boys' childish pact and, further back, from each of their "abnormal" personalities, developed in a distorted childhood. But the defense had been careful not to blame the parents either. This defense strategem appears to have succeeded: in letters and interviews ordinary citizens were not strongly inclined to blame the parents or hold them responsible, and Judge Caverly received numerous letters that sought to bring the "horrible suffering" of the boys' "guiltless parents" to his attention.[53]

Indeed, one of the more remarkable features of the case was this largely sympathetic posture adopted toward the unfortunate parents of the two kidnap-murderers. In the context of the overwhelming need to make sense of the crime, few sought to blame the parents. Given their wealth, Jewish religion, and social prominence, this is strange. It is even more strange in light of the enormous attention directed to the killers' childhoods. Part of the explanation lies in the fact that the families quickly assumed a posture of conciliation with the public and acknowledged its right to participate in the case that shocked everyone's sensibilities. Thus, in response to the growing rumors about Darrow's astronomical fee, the two fathers, Nathan Leopold, Sr., and Albert H. Loeb, issued a joint statement. Prominently displayed, together with pictures of each, on the front page of Chicago newspapers, the statement declared the families' willingness to abide by a fee structure set by the city bar association. To this the fathers added a significant statement accepting the norms of community justice for their sons: "If the accused boys are found by the jury to be mentally responsible, their families, in accordance with their conscious duty toward the community, agree that the public must be fully protected from any future menace by these boys. In no event will the families of the accused boys use money in any attempt to defeat justice." This simple statement prevented neither the prosecution from railing against the power of money to buy justice throughout the hearing nor the public from expecting the families to use their power, money, and influence in whatever way possible.[54] But the statement expressed a basic regard for outraged opinion and spoke well for the families.

The Loeb and Leopold skill at public relations was surely not all that was involved. Even before Clarence Darrow, in his extraordinary summation, pled for justice and mercy for the families, a plea that the newpapers believed helped to sway public opinion, the press had largely sheltered the families from public wrath and from blame. Indeed, the extension of sympathy had begun as soon as the boys confessed, as the papers carried stories such as "Agony of Mothers of Slayer and Slain" and told how Jacob Franks "Voices Deep Sympathy for Families." On June 3, the lead article in the *Herald and Examiner* portrayed both Mrs. Franks and Mrs. Loeb (Nathan's mother had died) in "a state of collapse" as the paper proceeded to discuss how "the deepest pity was felt for those who were there [at the hearing] because they were the same blood as these two boys who took the right to plunge three families into the depths of despair."[55] This remarkable compression of the families of both victim and criminals into a single poignant category underlined how the case had become a parable of family pain.

Gradually, the reluctance to blame and the ready sympathy for the parents of the boys was transmuted into a sense of tragedy. Darrow's brilliant concluding remarks helped to attach it permanently to the case, but it was also congruent with the larger drama of which the case and the hearing were part. Loeb's mother and father early withdrew from the scene and retreated to their countryplace in Charlevoix (Loeb had a heart condition and died within the year), leaving Richard's older brother, Allan Loeb, to represent the family. But Nathan Leopold, Sr., was visibly and painfully there. And it was the elder Leopold who was cast in the role of tragic hero. Dignified and silent, Nathan, Sr., faithfully attended the hearings, where, like a brooding Job, he became the focus of press attention and national sympathy. "In all the earth," nationally known columnist Arthur Brisbane observed, "you would not find agony more intense than in the face of that unfortunate man." Another reporter noted that "Nathan F. Leopold, Sr. . . . bore an expression of pain far more poignant than that of the murdered boy's father. Leopold, Sr. is ever silent. He never speaks a word to any, even the relatives at his side. There is no outlet to his grief, and his face shows it." When Darrow delivered his summation (a major public event), Judge Caverly's wife, who reportedly wept, sat next to the elder Leopold and told the newspapers: "The look of hope upon his face, the desperate intensity with which he drank in the lawyer's plea for his son's life was the most tragic thing I have ever seen."[56]

In another instance contemporary playwright William Anthony McQuire began by distancing himself from the brouhaha that swirled about the case and the trial: "Morbid curiosity has never been an attribute of mine. . . . Of course, I have found, during the last few weeks, that if one is to participate in conversation at all he must at least have a casual acquaintance with the biographies of Loeb and Leopold. . . . It annoyed me greatly to discover that unless I could quote correctly Loeb's words at the age of 5 to his teddy bear I was socially extinct and of no verbal importance in any discussion whatsover." McQuire continued in this barbed vein with various quips about the assorted courtroom participants. But before the image of Leopold, Sr., he turned serious and reverent: "I see Leopold's father. He is a tragedy. My heart aches for him. . . . I shall never forget Leopold's father," and he returns to the refrain, "My heart goes out to him."[57]

Of course, not everyone was sympathetic to the slayers' parents, and the papers also carried features in which ministers or psychologists used the occasion to blame modern parents for the neglect and misbehavior of their children, but they tended to berate parents generally, rather than blame these specific parents. And even the critics were inclined to describe the situation as "tragic." "The tragedy recently enacted in our city . . . is the fruitage of homes where religious and moral training has had no serious place in family life," one clergyman proclaimed. According to another critic, "I was a tutor once in a home of a millionaire, and I saw how a retinue of governesses and servants destroy the intimate touch of parenthood." It was, of course, nannies who were condemned in the psychiatric evaluations as well. This emphasis on the evils of parent substitutes not only left the parents guiltless, since they themselves had sought only the best for their children, but provided a lesson concerning the need to cement real family life. Instead of suggesting, as later psychiatrically influenced views would, that parents were to blame for what went wrong in their children's early years, the Leopold and Loeb case made the case for greater (not necessarily better) parental involvement so that one could avoid the fate of a Nathan Leopold, whose faithfulness had to be expressed when it was too late, when it was indeed tragic. Thus the message that emerged in the context of the early influence of psychiatry was not unlike the lesson of the lost children of fifty years before: Parents needed to find their children and put them first. "The lesson to the public is a lesson to all fathers and mothers," the *Herald and Examiner* told its readers the day after Caverly delivered his decision, "live *with* your children and *for* them, no matter what the sacrifice! There is no other road to happiness."[58]

The tone for this had been set by Darrow's extraordinary summation, which brought the parents of the defendants under the umbrella of his defense of the sons and then connected them with the eternal sorrows of parenthood:

No one knows what will be the fate of the child he gets or the child she bears. . . . I am sorry for the fathers as well as the mothers, for the fa-

thers, who give their strength and their lives for educating and protecting and creating a fortune for the boys that they love; for the mothers who go down into the shadow of death for their children, who
nourish them and care for them, and risk their lives, that they may
live, who watch them with tenderness and fondness and longing, and
who go down into dishonour and disgrace for the children that they
love.

All of these are helpless. We are all helpless. . . . [W]hen you are pity-
ing the father and the mother of poor Bobby Franks, what about the
fathers and mothers of these two unfortunate boys . . . and what about
all the fathers and all the mothers and all the boys and all the girls who
tread a dangerous maze in darkness from birth to death?[59]

With his Biblical phrases and Lincolnesque cadences, Darrow firmly connected the mothers and fathers with the sorrows of their children. But it
was a tale of helplessness, not responsibility, that Darrow constructed from
his murder case, a helplessness that defined the parents as well as the psychology of the two boys.

Not the least remarkable feature of this story of guiltless parents is the
fact that the parents of Leopold and Loeb were used not in a cautionary tale
to warn future parents to avoid those behaviors that would so psychologically mar their children that they would grow up to commit kidnap and
murder. Instead, they became part of a drama of endurance: How in the
midst of the twentieth century, parents and families could withstand the
worst of fates—to have their children murder other children—and survive.
"Nothing that could ever be done to these two criminal boys, not all the in-
genious agonies of the ancient torturers, could inflict upon them such pain
as they have inflicted upon their fathers and mothers." If Americans in the
1920s were ashamed of their young people, whose most extreme exem-
plars—Leopold and Loeb, Hickman, Noel—had committed atrocious acts,
it was not the families who were finally to blame. While milder forms of
youthful misbehavior, like petting and drinking, caused much consterna-
tion in the 1920s and were often blamed on parents, these much more serious crimes, these crimes of brutality and insanity, were too disturbing to
attach to parental negligence. For them, at least, early psychiatry provided
tragedy in lieu of blame. These cases suggested that the parents' role was to
stand by their children as Noel's mother did when she pled for her son's life

and as Nathan Leopold did in silence. Kidnapping had once again exposed modern parents' vulnerability. But while this vulnerability was now extended in two directions, their obligations remained very much at home, with their own children. Americans had been led to sympathize with the parents of Leopold and Loeb as well as Bobby Franks as psychiatry became a means for cementing the most enduring bond.[60]

◰ V ◳

On September 10, 1924, Judge John Caverly passed sentence in the kidnap-murder of Robert Franks. "Impelled to dwell briefly on the mass of data produced as to the physical, mental and moral condition of the two defendants," he concluded that the slayers "have been shown in essential respects to be *abnormal*; had they been normal they should not have committed the crime." Walter Bachrach had argued just this point in the hearing—that the crime itself demonstrated the mental condition of the accused. Cantillon would propose it again three years later in the case of William Edward Hickman. But just as he stepped toward this radical view, Caverly withdrew. His final decision had *not* been affected by this material, which had "been of extreme interest and is a valuable contribution to criminology." Instead, he was influenced "chiefly by the consideration of the age of the defendants, boys of 18 and 19 years." He was "satisfied that neither in the act itself, nor in its motive or lack of motive, nor in the antecedents of the offenders, [could] he find any *mitigating circumstances*." With that confused picture, he sentenced them both "for the crime of murder and kidnapping for ransom" to life plus ninety-nine years in prison. The most notorious boy criminals of the early twentieth century had been spared the death penalty. Loeb would die in Joliet prison twelve years later, the victim of a horrible slashing attack by a fellow prisoner who used Richard's notoriety to accuse him of making unwanted sexual advances. Leopold would serve thirty-five years of his sentence. After several unsuccessful attempts at parole and a few years after writing his prison memoirs, he was finally released in 1959.[61]

In sentencing them to prison, to "life," Caverly believed his decision followed the precedents of the state of Illinois in which only two juveniles had been sentenced to death and "to be in accordance with the progress of criminal law all over the world and with the dictates of enlightened humanity."[62] Caverly appeared to discount the evidence of the defense psychiatrists, but in taking note of it and allowing it to be placed in the record and before the public, he had provided it with an unusual legitimacy and visibility.

That visibility gave psychiatry the occasion to demonstrate its most useful new concept. In a new age, what Ben Lindsey called "the stream of modern life," what was normal? At a time when young people were experimenting with new fashions, behaviors, mores, and ideas, what was normal? Usually unspoken but significant nevertheless throughout the case were questions about what was normal for young men who had lived through abnormal times, and how a new "normalcy" (a term just coined by President Harding) could be established. The young had been socialized at a period when war propaganda (confusingly mixed with news) inflamed passions of sex and violence. "When the rules of civilized society are suspended, when killing becomes a business and a sign of valor and heroism;" the Reverend Charles Parsons noted in 1917, "when the wanton destruction of peaceable women and children becomes an act of virtue, and is praised as a service to God and country, then it seems almost useless to talk about crime in the ordinary sense." While the relationship between crimes among young people and war is far from clear, there is evidence for an increased rate of delinquency during war, including World War I.[63]

More to the point, perhaps, than the actual effect of war on youth crime is the social concern and anxieties released during and after periods of war. In the 1920s, the Leopold and Loeb case became the focus for many of the fears about aggression and how it could be contained that emerged from the war. It also became the vehicle for the new psychological insights that the war offered. Darrow brilliantly evoked this theme in his summation:

We read of killing one hundred thousand men in a day. We read about it and we rejoiced in it. . . . We were fed on flesh and drank blood. Even down to the brattling babe. I need not tell your Honor this, because you know; I need not tell you how many upright, honorable young boys have come into this court charged with murder, boys who fought in this war and learned to place a cheap value on human life. . . . These boys were brought up in it. The tales of death were in their homes, their playgrounds, their schools; they were in the newpapers that they read; it was a part of the common frenzy—what was a life? It was nothing. . . . I know that out of the hatred and bitterness of the Civil

War crime increased as America had never known it before. . . . I
know it has followed every war; and I know it has influenced these
boys so that life was not the same to them as it would have been if the
world had not been made red with blood.[64]

Like so many other things to which the young have been exposed in the
twentieth century and to which violent behavior has been linked, Darrow
was seeking to explain how modern life had created new and horrible behaviors among honorable boys from good homes, boys whose parents had,
in effect, lost control over their upbringing.

Darrow was suggesting that Richard and Nathan had participated in the
abnormality of their time and should not be blamed and made the source of
more bloodletting. But the frenzied concern with the case suggests that the
case was being used to make just those distinctions between peacetime and
war. And Darrow's defense assisted this process by defining Leopold and
Loeb as abnormal. If Leopold and Loeb were abnormal, at least a new line
could be established. In adopting this concept, the publicity around the case
may have helped to halt the sense of violent contagion as the new concepts
of normality and abnormality (though loose, maybe especially because they
were loose) provided a substitute for good and evil in a culture that craved
such redefinitions. It was revealing in this regard that the newspapers gave
as much space to psychiatrists and psychologists to reflect upon the meaning
of the case as they gave to ministers. And even ministers who were outspoken in their condemnation of the pair and the evil they had committed were
usually eager to adopt an idea like abnormality in defining Leopold and
Loeb.[65]

The intial portrait of Leopold and Loeb had been frightening because it
broke from categories. What the defense psychiatrists provided was a new
kind of category to quell the sense of disorder. In this light, the tendency for
psychiatrists to conflate the abnormal and the unconventional is not so surprising since Americans now learned to define in terms of disease those behaviors that had previously been immoral or unnatural. The looseness of
the boundary between normal and abnormal, whatever its psychoanalytic
roots, was also congruent with this war experience in which, as Darrow
suggested, ordinary boys became killers and peaceable citizens lusted for
blood. With the Leopold and Loeb case, psychiatrists acquired a new visi-

bility as arbiters of normality, and with their new position, the sense of a society giving way to chaos ceased.

As significant as violence was the issue of sex. Sexual issues clung to the Leopold and Loeb case from the beginning, and they were still palpable when Caverly issued his ruling: "And here the Court will say, not for the purpose of extenuating guilt, but merely with the object of dispelling a misapprehension that appears to have found lodgement in the public mind, that he is convinced by conclusive evidence that there was no abuse offered to the body of the victim." The image of Bobby's body (discolored by acid in a number of places), as sexually mutilated, the site of perverse practices, had indeed "found lodgement in the public mind," despite the coroner's report to the contrary. That image was multipled in the course of the newspaper publicity as, first, sexual "perverts" were rounded up for questioning and, then, psychiatrists discussed the boyish pacts, with their clear sexual underpinnings, of the two defendants' *folie à deux*. Judge Caverly had not helped matters when he cleared the courtroom of all women (including women reporters) at those points in the psychiatric testimony when the most explosive sexual matters were discussed or when, in the midst of Dr. William Healy's testimony, Caverly insisted, "This is not for the papers at all," and asked for the rest to be told *in camera*. Years later Leopold remembered that "the newspapers reported the proceedings . . . in terms that misled a large part of the public. 'At this point the testimony became of such a nature as will not be reported in this paper,' and this would be followed by a whole row of asterisks. What a lot of sordid imaginings laid behind those asterisks." Prosecutor Crowe was champing at the bit for the exposure of "perversions" against Bobby, and tried repeatedly to introduce these into the record to further inflame public opinion. He also pointed his finger at the killer's sexual abnormality: "These two defendants were perverts . . . they entered into a childish compact so that these unnatural crimes might continue. . . . My God! I was a grown man before I knew of such depravity." Crowe's remarks were ruled out of line by Caverly, but the popular concerns that Crowe exposed (and to which he was speaking) were not out of line.[66]

Whatever happened to Bobby, there was a clear and explicit erotic relationship between Leopold and Loeb that went beyond what was usually described as ordinary. This relationship was intimately linked by the psychiatrists to the boys' abnormality and to their crime. As the Hulbert-

Bowman report noted, "the crime as finally devised and acted out would have been impossible except for this extraordinary association." Even though explicit sexual discussions and graphic descriptions were not made available to the public in 1924 (indeed the decade was, despite its reputation, still quite prudish in public discussions of sexuality), the period was full of a vaguer sense of the new potency of sex, often linked to youth. Sex and youth were publicly connected in the 1920s, and Leopold and Loeb, by expressing a more extreme form of sexual "license" than the commonly acknowledged loosening in sexual mores among youth generally, highlighted the popular concern. As Ben Lindsey knew, the Leopold and Loeb case was related to "joy rides, jazz parties, petting parties, freedom in sex relations and the mania for speed on every turn." Just as the case created new categories of mental abnormality for violent behavior, Leopold and Loeb may well have helped to squelch the sense of sexual danger of the period by confirming a boundary against sexual license. In being more "terrible" as Lindsey put it, they may have helped to normalize the less terrible heterosexual experimentation of twenties youth, making this behavior more acceptable, even wholesome. In this regard, it is revealing that the defense team was intent on portraying the two as having girlfriends with whom they experimented sexually. In so doing, the case helped publicly to put homosexuality into the same category as abnormality and crime.[67]

The Leopold and Loeb case raised into active public discussion, a variety of questions about the limits of normality in psychologically related areas like sexuality and violence. To these questions older definitions like those that informed the law—issues of responsibility and insanity with their governing visions of good and evil, knowledge and will—seemed no longer satisfactory. As V. C. Branham observed in the *Journal of Criminal Law and Criminology*, "the hiatus between the legal and psychiatric viewpoints toward delinquency is widening daily," and daily the public was learning about some of the newer ways of understanding guilt, crime, and other behavior. This does not mean that the case of the "boy slayers" legitimated the role of expert medical testimony in the courts, because it did not. As we have seen, neither the Noel nor Hickman cases benefited from any redefinition of insanity in the courts. In many ways the case of Leopold and Loeb undermined that testimony because of the circus atmosphere and its sensationalism. In 1926, Branham described psychiatrists as still smarting from this experience. But in a culture eager for new answers, the Leopold and Loeb case forced the American public to consider new sexual and psychological motives for crimes committed against and by their children.[68]

We will probably never know why Leopold and Loeb decided to kidnap a child on May 21 and then kill him and put acid on his genitals. Certainly, Leopold's prison memoir never elucidated the issue. But in wrapping their new crime in an older form, the two young men had neatly connected the older kind of kidnap to new twentieth-century concerns about violence and sexuality. They had set a precedent in the 1920s for others like Noel and Hickman. And they had provided the occasion for a first public display of the interpretive power of the new psychiatry and as importantly of the public's craving for new ways to understand and to explain heinous crimes against children. They had also opened the door wide to a new set of parental fears for their children. In this case, it was a toss-up which was more to be feared—to be parent to a victim or a victimizer. While ransom kidnappings would remain very much a part of parental anxiety in the early twentieth century and even grow in fearsomeness, the case of Leopold and Loeb had exposed newer vulnerabilities all around.

CHAPTER THREE

"The Nation's Child . . . is Dead"

The Lindbergh Case

The child was born at an inauspicious time, at the beginning of the most serious economic depression in American history, on June 22, 1930, to parents who were young, handsome, rich, and very famous. Blond and blue-eyed like his father, he was the picture of privilege. The first grandchild on one side of a rich and powerful international banker and ambassador, he was on the other side a grandchild of a quirky, maverick populist and isolationist congressman from Minnesota. After his birth, his parents began to build a mansion, an aerie, far from the madding crowds, to protect themselves and him from the curiosity that had become his birthright and from the cult of celebrity that was beginning to define mass society in the twentieth century.

On Tuesday night, March 1, 1932, he was stolen from his crib in the just finished house while his parents and several servants were at home. He probably died on that same night, either from an injury received during the abduction or because he was intentionally killed. On April 2 his parents paid a ransom of $50,000, but he did not return. When his body was found, not far from his home, on May 13, he was hardly recognizable except for his hair and a set of overlapping toes. After the remains were cremated, no one but his parents knew where the ashes were scattered. On April 3, 1936, Bruno Richard Hauptmann, an unemployed carpenter, German immigrant, and himself the father of a young son, was executed in Trenton, New Jersey, after an extraordinary trial for what everyone called the crime of the century.

The life of Charles Augustus Lindbergh, Jr., was short, but it was engulfed by an enormous story that has fascinated Americans for more than sixty years, and it has left in its wake a mystery to which Americans still cling: Did Hauptmann really kidnap and kill the Lindbergh baby? As books continue to proliferate trying to answer that question, the real mystery has remained unexamined. How could the abduction and killing of a small child have become the defining crime of a decade?

🝁┃🝃

On March 3, 1932, two days after Charles A. Lindbergh, Jr., was kidnapped, the *St. Louis Post-Dispatch* published a gripping cartoon: an enormous rapacious hand and arm marked "kidnaping" poised over a nation of tiny huddled homes. Captioned "A National Peril," the cartoon was meant to be a vivid representation of a nation haunted by the specter of kidnapping. Indeed, by the time the most famous baby in America was abducted, the American press had already described kidnapping as a national disease that was destroying the peace and security of its citizens and a sign of the ravaged condition of law and order in the nation.[1]

But the cartoon was also an uncanny anticipation of the hold that the abduction of the Lindbergh baby would have over the American people in the days, weeks, and even years to come. In the early days of the case, the disappearance of the Lindbergh child was still shadowed by that of an earlier Charles, a poignant story of loss that until then had defined the terrain of ransom kidnap horror. The memory of that case was soon buried in the Lindbergh avalanche. The *New Republic* foresaw this within weeks of the new trauma: "The men and women who were children in the days of the Charlie [*sic*] Ross kidnapping can remember how their mothers warned them to stay in the house, never talk to strangers, and regard every old-clothes man as a potential ogre who would carry them off and strangle them and cut them into little pieces. The Lindbergh case is likely to produce an even wider reaction. One can hardly estimate its effect on popular psychology." In its prescient vision, the journal predicted that "the effect on public consciousness is likely to be as extensive as an earthquake, a flood or even a minor war." By the seventeenth of March, when the *New York Evening Journal* reprinted, side-by-side, the reward posters for the two boys in order to draw upon emotions still available in popular memory, it was hardly necessary any longer to evoke Charley Ross.[2] By then the press had enshrined many of the themes of that earlier kidnap trauma—sentimentalization of childhood, parental anguish and anxiety, fears about social order, and police ineptitude—in the new story. Within two weeks of the Lindbergh abduction, these had been played out for the American public in a quantity sufficient to render the pathos of the earlier memory obsolete in face of the new commercialized emotionalism.

While there was much that resonated between the two cases, there were also many differences. Charley Ross was the youngest of seven children, in a well-positioned but obscure middle-class family. Charles Lindbergh (sometimes called Charlie by his mother, but never in the press, which preferred "the lone eaglet" or "little Lindy") was the first and (at the time) the only child of the most famous man in the world. Five years earlier Lindbergh had mesmerized hundreds of millions of people by his youth, courage, modesty, and singleness of purpose when he overcame extraordinary hazards to became the first man to cross the Atlantic in a solo flight. That event had represented a frantic moment in the history of mass psychology when people everywhere seemed collectively to hold their breath in anticipation of either tragedy or exhaltation. In that context, Lindbergh had become, in the words of one of his biographers, "the last hero."[3] That moment of suspense was to be repeated endlessly in the time between the first news of the Lindbergh baby's abduction on March 2, 1932, and when the baby's body was found on May 12, 1932, even though the drama itself did not end for almost four years until the child's convicted killer was electrocuted. One of the fundamental differences between the stories was, of course, the closure offered by the discovery of the dead child. Although some people were not entirely satisfied about the identity of the child—for years people continued to claim that they were Charles Lindbergh, Jr.—the fact that the parents accepted that the child had been slain brought the abduction, at least, emotionally to a conclusion.

In 1932 the sensationalism that had been dramatically aroused by the press's portrayal of the mutilated body of young Bobby Franks eight years earlier would be raised to lascivious heights when photographers bribed their way into the funeral home (where only moments earlier the child had been identified by his father) to get a glimpse of the corpse, now decayed beyond recognition. Here was perhaps the most significant historical difference between the Ross and Lindbergh cases. The press, already hungry for news during the 1920s, literally devoured the Lindbergh story and followed little Charles Lindbergh into the crematorium. The publicity about Charley Ross took months to penetrate the American landscape via posters, traveling circuses, Western Union, and word of mouth. News about Charles Lindbergh, Jr., was instantaneous and for months dominated front pages and whole front sections of newspapers throughout the country, while millions of news extras were published to stimulate and satisfy the public's rapacious curiosity. The Lindbergh story also created major innovations in the way news was carried to Americans. On the radio, news about the Lindbergh case was broadcast twenty-four hours a day in half-hourly bulletins, creating radio history. "For the first time . . . the country's great national chains of broadcasting stations remained on the air all night last night to broadcast latest developments of the hunt for the Lindbergh baby." Radio coverage of the Lindbergh story significantly expanded the limits of radio broadcasting beyond entertainment and took it into the night. According to the *New York Times*, most of the radio waves were given over to reporting on the case during its early phase while regularly scheduled broadcasting was displaced. Ticker tape was also used to issue the first notice of the child's disappearance and Lindbergh family home movies were broadcast in newsreels. Even television in its infancy was recruited to beam a continuous picture of baby Lindy to its still very limited audience.[4]

But the press and the new communications media were far more than innovative conduits of information. Christian Ross's memoirs had defined the public narrative of Charley's life and abduction as the tale of a child who never returned and a father's endless sorrow. Charles Lindbergh never wrote about his son and was said never to have mentioned him or referred to the events of that time for the rest of his life. Although Anne Morrow Lindbergh did write about Charlie, it was the national press that created the Lindbergh story.[5] The story it created was about the ravishment of the home and the vulnerability of even the most famous and beloved. Like the stories about Charley Ross and Leopold and Loeb, the public story of the

Lindbergh kidnapping was about family life. Far more than these others, it was also about social disorder and crime. Crime had been critical to these earlier stories, and the Leopold and Loeb case had pointedly equated it with abnormality. With the abduction of the Lindbergh baby, crime became a national preoccupation, an element so powerful that it altered the image of Charles Lindbergh forever in the national imagination. In the Lindbergh story, criminality endangered the republic. Finally, in telling these other stories, the press created new levels of sensationalism through the exploitation of public emotions. By completely overshadowing the gentler emotions experienced by those most immediately involved, Charles and Anne Morrow Lindbergh, the media became a significant part of the case of Charles A. Lindbergh, Jr., and set a new milestone in the commercial exploitation of childhood.

𝔭 ‖ 𝔤

On the evening of March 1, 1932, sometime between 8 P.M., when he was put into his crib by his young mother and his nursemaid, Betty Gow, and 10 P.M., when Betty Gow found the crib empty, twenty-month-old Charles Augustus Lindbergh, Jr., was kidnapped. There was one set of muddy footprints in his room, but everything else, including the covers in the crib, was undisturbed. By the nursery window (whose shutters would not close properly and through which his son was presumably snatched), Charles Lindbergh found a ransom note with an unusual logo, three intersecting circles as an identifying signature. The note demanded $50,000. Outside this same southeast-facing window, Lindbergh found a series of footprints and, a short distance from the house, a homemade three-part ladder with a broken rung. Charles and Anne Lindbergh, who were both home that evening, had only recently moved into the newly finished, white French-chateau-style house, still sparsely furnished and unlandscaped, that they called Highfield. While they usually stayed there only on weekends, spending the rest of the week at Anne's family estate in Englewood, New Jersey, this week they had remained through Tuesday because their son had a chest cold. And it was on this Tuesday night, marked by an unusually gusty wind, that the child was taken from the room right above where his father was working in his study.[6]

The many details of this simple scene have been examined thousands of times by professionals and amateurs alike. Since Bruno Richard Haupt-mann was executed on April 3, 1936, without making a confession, the the-ories about who, why, and how, as might be expected in the circumstances, have grown in number and fancy. The nature of the prosecution's case, Hauptmann's defense and attempted appeal, had never entirely satisfied the millions who became engaged in the story and who subsequently kept it very much alive and in the news.[7] Unlike these many others, I am interested not in a solution to the Lindbergh mystery, but in its portrayal and its con-tribution to the unfolding history of kidnapping.

One of the most significant aspects of the portrayal of the crime was the obsession with the house itself, a large, white structure perched high and lonely in the remote Sourland Hills of central New Jersey, a few miles from the small town of Hopewell and about twenty miles from Princeton. In the weeks following the abduction, that house and its invasion became the most important site for the evolving narrative and a metaphor for the tragedy that had befallen the nation. It was repeatedly pictured in the press as the kidnap tale was retold, and the papers bulged with descriptions of its ground plan, details of its construction, and obsessive renderings of its dese-cration. Besieged by the curious (who were offered airplane rides over it for $2.50[8]), invaded by state and local police (who set up their headquarters there), and surrounded by the press (150 reporters and photographers gath-ered almost immediately on the front lawn), the house was not only the site of the tragic abduction, but became the locus of the unfolding story. When-ever any new development took place, some insight achieved, or some sus-picion expressed, it took place in the house. Since Charles Lindbergh very early insisted on maintaining control of the hunt for his son, all strategy planned by the state troopers, who were officially responsible, and Lind-berghs' circle of chosen advisers took place in the house. Clues were discov-ered in the house, around the house, or near the house. John F. Condon, the man Lindbergh came to trust as his emissary to deliver the $50,000 ransom (which later created the money trail that led to Hauptmann's arrest), was received into the house. He was even allowed to sleep on the floor of the nursery. When the Lindberghs were finally fed up with what they saw as press interference with their pursuit of the case or police interference with their strategy, these groups were evicted from the house.

Nelson Harding presented an unusually potent image of the house and what it had come to represent in a *New York Evening Journal* cartoon. A large, French-chateau-style house, clearly discernible as that of the Lindberghs and labeled "Security of the Home," tilts precariously while floating on a sea of grasping fists. Floating just below it is an unhinged door marked "Safety of the Nursery." The entire cartoon is marked "Kidnap Crest of the Crime Wave."[9] The Lindbergh house, which was to have been their refuge from the public curiosity and clamor brought on by Lindbergh's fame, became instead the arena for lost innocence and the violation of domesticity. The *New York Times* described the national impact well: "It is impossible to escape the awful symbolism of the crime at the Lindbergh home. . . . For that home has come to represent . . . the beauty and the sanctity of romance and youth. Somehow it seemed unspoiled and untouched by mundane evil and ugliness, and remained apart as a sort of common ideal. The ravishment of that home by crime becomes a challenge, a personal affront to every decent man and woman, and a disgrace to the nation in which such a thing should occur."[10] It is hardly necessary to comment on the significance of the house as an image of threatened family life. Coming as it does in the depth of the Depression, the assault and devastation of the house and the threat this seemed to pose to the American family was an ominous national image.

That assault was not against this house alone. It was against the homes of all Americans. "This kidnapping," the *North American Review* concluded "was a challenge to the home itself. Every mother knew by instinct what it meant and shuddered." The journal drew the obvious conclusion: "The nation is now *putting its house in order*. The Lindbergh case contributed largely to its determination that house breaking shall cease." After the baby was found dead, the *Literary Digest* published an appropriate companion to the cartoon of the looming hand. Captioned "Can't We Make the World Safe for Infancy?" it showed a man's threatening shadow on the partially opened door to a nursery where a curly-haired child slept peacefully. The cartoon perfectly reflected the sense of invasion of the nation's own security. The larger issues engrossed by the kidnapping were unmistakable. As an editorial in the *Christian Century* observed: "Behind the Lindbergh baby (God preserve him!) and the Lindbergh parents (God sustain them!) lies an issue which every American citizen must be made to face. That issue is whether American democracy . . . can preserve itself against downfall at the hands of the organized lawlessness which it has allowed to grow up within its own body."[11] The *North American Review* called it "a cancer, which . . . infected the entire body politic." Whether within its own house or within its own body, the desecration of the Lindbergh family had exposed the nation's insecurity and vulnerability in the most shocking manner.

Since the story had become one of assault against and penetration of the emblematic home of the nation, it became altogether appropriate for Anne Morrow Lindbergh to take a prominent place in its portrayal. Unlike Charley Ross's mother, who hardly existed, Anne Lindbergh assumed a critical role in the unfolding story. Never before (or after) would the mother of the kidnap victim play such a prominent part.

It was both appropriate and ironic for Anne Morrow Lindbergh to assume this role. Although her books would subsequently make her famous in her own right, Anne was shy, sensitive, and hardly one to seek out attention or acclaim. Yet her protected and privileged life as the well-educated and well-bred daughter of Dwight R. Morrow, a former J. P. Morgan partner and ambassador to Mexico, had culminated in a much-envied marriage to the world's most eligible bachelor. During the first several years of her marriage, she accompanied Lindbergh on his world tours and his pioneering explorations of routes for the fledgling airline industry. In the various dangers to which this exposed her and the attendant publicity, Anne had learned grace under pressure and an uncommon courage. These qualities she now displayed in the agonizing days and weeks when she suffered from both the uncertainties surrounding the fate of her child and the rapt attention of the world. Anne's quiet strength and bearing in the very worst circumstances made her an ideal focus for sympathy and an easily exploitable model for a press eager to dredge the emotional depths of the case.[12]

But Anne's qualities were not immediately visible since she was initially portrayed in the usual stereotypes of motherly sorrow. Gradually, that representation evolved. In its first report on the kidnapping on March 2, the *New York Evening Journal* described Anne as "Broken by Grief"; melodramatically, fulfilling long-standing expectations of womanhood. She is "a broken-hearted mother" in a feature story by Laura Vitray, the reporter assigned to get the woman angle: "The almost proverbial coolness is gone. In its place is a pleading terror-stricken look. Her eyes . . . are tear-filled and her low, even, well-bred voice is high-pitched with fear. . . . No longer is she the woman who was the guest of kings of the earth, no longer the girl who made 'the best match in the world.' She was just a mother—desperate over the baby." This was accompanied by a news report that Anne feared that her cold-stricken child would not be adequately cared for. Directly below a full eight-column photo of the Lindbergh house, it was noted (accurately) that Anne was pregnant with her second child. To complete its first day of coverage, the *New York Evening Journal* had another eight-column spread of photos of Anne headlined: "Changed From the Most Envied to the Most Pitied of Mothers—By Kidnapers." That headline not only democratized an aristocratic lady, but introduced just the right note of democratic resentment that would shadow the case. This would eventually be much less evident in the coverage of Anne than of Lindbergh himself. The facing page was composed entirely of family photos. The following page had three more photos of the house.[13]

By the second day of reporting, Anne had largely dropped from sight as an individual, to be replaced by a cartoon of a young, lithe woman made to resemble Anne, with dark hair and eyes and oval face, standing bereft in a thorny lane and blown by the wind. Entitled, "The Worst of All Crimes: Kidnapping More Terrible Than Murder," the cartoon is followed by an article describing the agony of kidnapping as a mother's pain: "There can be no pain for a mother beyond this." Although Anne had appeared nowhere by name in the article, the author, Nell Brinkley, does not allow the obvious connection to pass without emphasis: "This is a hard story to write. We have written of little 'Anne' and her husband adding to the world's happiness in their happiness. And now we must join with every father and mother in the hope that they will get their happiness back again."[14]

But "little Anne" was neither the stick figure of the cartoon nor the stock figure of earlier kidnap portraits. By March 4, Anne was back in the news, now as a staff for her husband's ebbing strength. "She is calm. She does not give way. Perhaps she does not dare give way. The Lone Eagle [Lindbergh's sobriquet] is depending on her now.... Visibly, he draws new strength, new courage, new fortitude from this gentle girl he married." Having penetrated Anne's home, the press had to contend with the reality of her presence. And since Anne was, in fact, bearing up and even helping to provide innumerable meals for the state troopers who had settled into her house, the older portrait of female hysteria was giving way to one of courage. As if in compensation, however, the paper provided Anne with a wailing chorus, "Thousands of Mothers Pray for Return of Lindy's Baby."[15]

Not only was Anne in her home, but her mother joined her to oversee its burgeoning operations. The *Journal* appropriately paired this holy family portrait with a picture of Anne and the kidnapped child, entitled "Flying

Madonna and Baby." It took a few more days for feature writer Elsie Robinson to bring this new portrait of inner strength despite outer sorrow, of the *mater dolorosa*, to it full flower: "Quietly, steadily, Anne Lindbergh goes on with life . . . her mind, at times, must falter and fall, behind those wide, fine eyes, but it still has charge. . . . All through the day, Anne Lindbergh goes on, making carefully, deliberately the small, fine controlled gestures of civilization. Today, in the face of the most desperate and terrible agony which a human soul can suffer, Anne Lindbergh is controlling herself—and maintaining civilization against 'the powers of darkness.' . . . This is the greatest thing I have ever seen. I, too, have had a son and lost him. I thought I lost him bravely—but I stand shamed before this girl." The newspapers had, for the first time, created a true antidote to the portrait of the faceless hysterical mother. While not exactly human, that portrait was heroic and noble. This new portrayal of womanhood proved, according to Laura Vitray, "what a mistake it is to imagine that overwhelming grief must find its expression in wild hysteria."[16]

By March 8, one week after the abduction, Anne had come into her own as a fighter who assisted in the search for her child. She helped to open the mountains of mail brought to the house in the hope of finding another ransom note. It was she who demanded control of the house. "The entreaties of Anne Morrow Lindbergh were behind the sudden and surprising exodus of state troopers from the Lindbergh's estate. " Soon, the *Journal* described her as "intrepid Anne," her stamina sapped by a cold, but "not in a state of collapse." Anne had emerged as such a strong person that even when the baby was found dead, when "women were torn by pity," Anne remained strong, "Spartan-like." "No tears came from the eyes of Anne Morrow Lindbergh. Hers was a courage too fine for that." By the time Anne testified at the Hauptmann trial, her dignity was her defining characteristic. In the *New York Times*, Alexander Woolcott described her as a "gentle and gallant woman" with "grace of spirit" who gave the courtroom "a final dignity," which not even the hullabaloo surrounding the event could destroy.[17]

What was it that had so transformed the standard portrait? It was not just a historical change, for contemporary portrayals of the mothers of other kidnap victims continued to define them as "prostrated" and "hysterical," as was the mother of Jimmy de Jute's (kidnapped just hours after the Lindbergh baby). Obviously, the reality of Anne Lindbergh's presence had something to do with it. More important no doubt was the power of the image of the invaded house. That house, the nation's house, required a hardier female presence than a fragile, hysterical woman. Beyond these, however, Anne was necessary to the didactic lessons the papers began to offer as the case progressed. The case had touched such an overwhelming chord of social helplessness and opened to view so many criminal possibilities, that some figure was required to oppose the enveloping darkness. J. Edgar Hoover argued in an article in the *Delineator* that attempted to advise parents about what to do "When the Kidnapper Comes": "The mother's strong moral influence . . . must be our first line of defense against this shocking crime situation."[18]

Anne seemed to provide just such a line of defense. Despite her wealth and privilege, she was seemingly without pretense and her outer calm was a barrier against despair. That this was clearly a part to which Anne was enlisted is suggested by the unusual inclusion by the press of Anne's mother into the story. In one article, Elizabeth Morrow, a woman of impeccable social credentials, is portrayed "Wearing a white apron over her widow's gown [Dwight Morrow had died six months earlier] . . . waiting on the table and making the beds," thereby astonishing the state troopers who were "amazed to see a woman of her position and financial importance pitching in and doing her share of the work like any housewife." It was the housewives of the nation, it seemed, who were providing its strength in trying times. In giving Mrs. Morrow the common touch, the papers also gave her the common sense necessary to raise a model daughter and mother like Anne. Mrs. Morrow was the "type of mother whose head rules her heart— and no other type . . . is so much needed!" Too many children became dangerous menaces to society because they were "dependent children with mother fixations [shades of Leopold and Loeb?]." But Anne was "a mother of intelligence" because her own mother was such a mother. By including some of Elizabeth Morrow's little didactic poems as aids to understanding ("Fear no celestial gibe 'I told you so'—Good mothers never say that even in heaven"), the article concludes confidently, "Could the daughter of any mother who sums up so perfectly the meaning of motherhood, be less than a perfect mother?" Whether by nurture or nature, the family circle so brutally ruptured in the loss of the child was completed in the wisdom of the ideal grandmother. Lest we imagine that only a Hearst paper would adopt this line, it is worth noting that the very first picture published by the *New*

York Times on its front page coverage of the kidnapping was an almost Renaissance portrait of Anne, the baby, Mrs. Morrow, and Mrs. Morrow's own mother, assembled as a holy family.[19]

Anne became an important figure in the case because she served the purpose of creating an effective barrier to the social disintegration that the kidnapping of the world's most famous baby seemed to threaten. In this, Anne's position is genuinely ironic. The wife of a man of extraordinary bravery and character, an international hero, it was she and not he who opposed the tide of lawlessness. To understand why this was so, we need to understand how Lindbergh had been compromised by his actions in pursuing just the lesson—negotiate at any price—that Christian Ross had learned so painfully and that had been inscribed in public memory as the only way to retrieve one's child.

⊡ ||| ⊟

By the early 1930s, the nation was portrayed as in the grip of a kidnap epidemic. Kidnapping had become a business pursued by members of organized gangs and gangsters among their own as a form of blackmail and extortion, as well as part of power wars between rival groups.[20] Almost all of the victims were adults. In many cases, the gangs were part of the organized liquor rackets, familiar to the public in an era of Prohibition and Al Capone. Most of the reported kidnap activity took place in the Midwest, but no place was immune, and the problem seemed to be a coast-to-coast phenomenon. The most infamous of these gangs, like the Detroit Purple Gang, had brought kidnap-extortion to a high level of public terror and personal profit.[21]

On the eve of the Lindbergh abduction, the kidnappings had also spread to the general public, as wealthy businessmen and professionals became targets for raising large sums of money. The figure usually thrown around in the press was 2,000 kidnappings in the years between 1930 and 1932, although this number was never substantiated. The much more modest figure of 285 proposed by the *Literary Digest* and based on a partial survey by the St. Louis police of other police departments was probably closer to the mark. More important than numbers was the alarming sense that kidnapping was, in the words of one headline, "A Growing Racket" for criminals ready to use organizations left over from a declining bootleg liquor business. With the kidnapping of the Lindbergh baby, officials across the nation were poised to demand new action and intervention against a crime perceived to be out of control. And the Lindbergh kidnapping gave them a powerful new symbol and lever. One day after the Lindbergh abduction was reported, Congressman Hatton W. Summers, chair of the House Judiciary Committee asked for immediate consideration of a new federal kidnap statute (long held up in committee) that would make kidnapping a federal offense punishable by death in order to deal with "the terrorism of crime in this country."[22]

Kidnapping was an important symbol for the general lawlessness that seemed to pervade the period of the early 1930s as a population devastated by Depression seemed also beset by a collapse of the instruments of law or the will to lawfulness. Americans had become helpless victims of gangland crime with a "governmental philosophy which has surrendered to gangdom almost every public function except the raising of taxes and regulation of traffic." This sense of a society immobilized by crime was captured in Albert E. Ullman's novel, *The Kidnappers*, written in the midst of the Lindbergh hysteria. The plot revolved around an omnipresent and surreal group called the Purple Band, which terrorized citizens and public officials with impunity. The head of the gang, Purple One, was a suave, brilliant foreigner whose evil genius was matched only by his apparently unlimited power.[23]

In Ullman's novel, the terrifying prediction that the evil gang would demonstrate its omnipotence by eventually "snatching helpless babies" comes true when the governor's son vanishes from his home, seemingly by magic, finally to be rescued only through the efforts of a secret agent and his girlfriend, recruited from among newspeople. Ullman's surreal tale with its comic strip tone, written in the midst the unfolding Lindbergh events, was meant to capitalize on the latter's breathless suspense ("Every mother's heart in the land was beating for baby George"). In fact, the story reveals the context within which the Lindbergh kidnap took place and how it was immediately interpreted by the press and the public. In Ullman's story, an invisible gang moves from preying on criminals to preying on adult citizens to the unthinkable—snatching the son of the most powerful man (in Ullman's words) in America. It is a logic of unopposed power. The Lindbergh kidnap was seen immediately and almost unanimously as such a crime, the result of criminality run amok in America, "a national disgrace."[24] Who else but an organized gang would undertake such a daring crime, such an unthinkable act? Who else would challenge the power of a national hero?

Because he was the nation's baby, the crime against the Lindbergh child and the Lindbergh house was a crime against the nation. Its successful execution evidence of the pusillanimity of the forces of law and order. The logic of the crime also revealed the logic of its solution.

> Is a child safe in his home?
> Is he safe in his nursery?
> Is he safe in his crib?
> Can we catch criminals?
> Can we convict criminals?
> Can we punish criminals?

In the glare of the Lindbergh kidnap, the press was literally filled with articles on organized gangs, many titled like a Sunday series in the *New York Evening Journal*, "First Full Facts About the Astounding Plague of Organized Kidnapers, America's Latest and Vilest Racket," or like that in the *New York Times*, "Kidnapping Wave Sweeps the Nation." In this context, the case resulted in a hysterical upswelling of shame about the civic state. "The baby's blood is . . . on the hands of the average American citizen" because of "his long complacency to crime," the *Minneapolis Journal* observed. Likewise, the *Christian Century* condemned "A complacent public, which has allowed a system of organized crime to grow until now it dares to challenge all the national forces of law and order." The *Brooklyn Eagle* proclaimed that the case "stands as a disgrace to this nation. It presents the shameful spectacle of *criminal supremacy*, under which the forces of law stand by powerless, blocked, and thwarted."[25]

This nearly universal view that the Lindbergh crime was lodged in the disgraceful state of American justice and the helplessness of the people against organized forces of lawlessness led to several conclusions. One of these was that the crime against the child would lead to a rededication to national honor. According to the *Arkansas Gazette*, "out of our national sorrow and a national humiliation should come a new consecration in citizenship." For many this meant strengthening the instruments of law and punishment. In a long article written from the point of view of American mothers, Margerite Mooers Marshall called for legal vengeance: "Every instinct, every thought of woman calls down the vengeance of man and of

heaven. Here is the unpardonable sin. . . . So long as capital punishment remains on our statute books, why should it not menace our most callous and
cold-blooded criminal, the baby stealer?" Another columnist in the *New
York Evening Journal* concluded that "It seems to me the plainest thing that
the proven tormentor—a KIDNAPER—of a child deserves to die." Another
writer was more graphic: "The penalty for kidnapping should be flogging
to death in the public square or slow torture with red-hot knives. These
might make even a 1932 gangster hesitate."[26]

The call for strengthening the law and for the death penalty was not the
only conclusion possible since, above all, the kidnapping was an indictment
of the efficacy of law, "a symbol of the widespread sense of helplessness."
Historian Harry Elmer Barnes concluded that the entire conventional approach to crime, the jury system itself, should be discarded, replaced by a
more scientific form of justice administered by experts. Only such a radical
solution could counter the "uniquely disgraceful condition in respect to
crime which exists in the United States." Various paralegal and usually secret crime commissions like those in Chicago and St. Louis were also held
up as models for a more effective law enforcement. Not long after the
crime, one article addressed to mothers fearful of kidnappers urged them to
bypass the ineffectual and indiscreet local police and go directly to the
newly invigorated Bureau of Investigation (forerunner to the FBI), which
would act quickly and with complete secrecy.[27]

The Lindbergh kidnapping also encouraged more radical solutions. The
Literary Digest reported that "There has been talk of America needing a
dictator to curb crime." And the specter of vigilante justice could be dimly
heard everywhere, as the *New York Evening Journal* warned the baby's kid-
napper(s) that "Justice would not be pleasant at best, and extremely uncom-
fortable if they were identified and left at the mercy of any American
crowd." In the *New York Times*, after the Lindbergh baby was found dead,
one correspondent called for a committee of women vigilantes, a secret
group to function "with entire self-effacement and . . . with no thought of
credit or reward." The committee was to be entirely nonsectarian and "no
sane, discreet, unselfish, well-balanced, non-notoriety seeking person
should be excluded." This call for respectable, responsible, and interfaith
women vigilantes was more restrained than the public lynching publicly
advised by Charles Lindbergh's friend, Will Rogers. No doubt many others
concurred in this conclusion. This supercharged atmosphere, where law

was perceived to be impotent in the face of crime, would lead to a public lynching in California just one year later when the suspected kidnap-killers of Brooke Hart, son of one of San Jose's leading citizens, were stripped and hung by a mob of several hundred respectable college students and businessmen.[28]

It was in this atmosphere of shame, repentance, and vengeance, in which the meaning of law in a crime-ridden society seemed at stake, that Colonel Charles A. Lindbergh, a genuine American hero, sought to retrieve his son.

◨ IV ◧

On the evening of March 1, after being unable to locate his son in a search of the house and the grounds, Charles Lindbergh asked his butler to notify the local police. Despite the presence of the police, Lindbergh was clearly in charge, and he remained in charge even after state troopers replaced the local officials as more suitable to the investigation. Lindbergh, like most fathers ever since Christian Ross's infamous hesitation, expected to bargain directly with his son's kidnappers. Indeed, when only a few hours after the Lindbergh kidnapping eleven-year old Jimmy de Jute was abducted on his way to school in Niles, Ohio, his father was quoted as eager "to pay the $10,000 ransom for the return of the boy." While the police were never happy with this kind of decision, they had come to expect to compromise their own goals with those of parents of kidnap victims. Even the former chief of the United States secret service, William J. Byrnes, publicly advised that "There is nothing for the Lindberghs to do but pay the ransom and get the baby back." No less an official than the governor of New Jersey asserted that "the main thing is to get the baby back."[29]

Lindbergh, like his far less famous Ohio counterpart, was willing to pay and ask no questions. This was well understood by the police and clear in the press reports. By March 4, when he still had not been given a means to effect an exchange for his son, Lindbergh made a radio appeal asking the kidnapper(s) to communicate with him and offering every assurance that they would suffer no legal consequences. And the newspapers acted in concert with Lindbergh's wishes. The *New York World Telegram* expressed its support in the form of a question: "If it were your child, would you hesitate for one moment? Of course you wouldn't. You'd give everything you possess, compound the felony and shut your eyes if you could get him back in his little crib." The *New York Evening Journal*, even assured the kidnappers in its editorial that Lindbergh could be trusted: "He has no thought of revenge or punishment. He will gladly pay the money that is demanded, and will gladly see to it that the kidnapers depart with the money in safety, if only they will return his child." They added their own plea, imploring "the kidnapers to communicate with the father and mother . . . return the child, accept their money and GO IN PEACE."[30]

But it was hardly so simple. Not only did it seem that everyone in America was searching for the child and his abductor(s) (5 million according to the *New York Evening Journal*), not only were 100,000 officials reported to be involved, but Lindbergh, as the most famous man in America and a national hero, could not simply act as other fathers did. While other fathers could agree to ransom demands and even make legally problematic public statements, when Lindbergh did so it carried the force of his importance and prestige, and it implicated the nation's honor in his action. To offer amnesty was literally to flout the laws and to do so in a manner that threatened to invite future lawbreaking. If the kidnapper of the Lindbergh child could get away unpunished, then what chance would a lesser snatcher have to be caught? To allow the kidnappers to go unpunished and to do so publicly was to acquiesce in "the breakdown of American life."[31] Gretta Palmer of the *New York World Telegram* gave voice to the complex problem when she both condoned Lindbergh's willingness to negotiate and asked in the same breath "But what of law and order?" The *Nation* magazine understood some of the inevitable problems posed by Lindbergh's dilemma. "The parents of this and any kidnapping have only one thought—the safe return of their child; punishment for the kidnappers as a means of revenge is almost unthought of; punishment for the protection of society is thought of even less." But while parents surely needed some cover to negotiate, the *Nation* was immediately struck by the problem of a hero sheltering criminals: "Society, of course, out of its very sympathy as well as to protect itself from similar crimes in the future, could not consent that the penalty for kidnapping be abolished."[32] Even though Lindbergh had obtained the acquiescence of the head of the New Jersey State Police, Colonel Norman Schwarzkopf (father of the future general), to his bargaining with the kidnappers, Schwarzkopf had never agreed to the kind of amnesty that Lindbergh seemed to be offering in so public a fashion, and various state officials quickly issued disclaimers.

The obvious conflicts of interest in the case were profound. Surely in his moments of anguish, Lindbergh must have dreamed of being an entirely private citizen like Neil C. McMath of Harwichport, Massachusetts, who bargained successfully for his daugher's return in 1933 by calling for a forty-eight-hour kidnap truce in which he "would not inform police" of his contacts with kidnappers. McMath even had the extraordinary foresight to deny the press pictures of himself and his wife until after the child was returned, thus obliterating the publicity that would make the kidnappers fearful of discovery and providing an incentive against an intrusive press. But Lindbergh did not have the privilege of anonymity. Unlike McMath, Lindbergh's house had become the public's house, and while he might fancy himself in charge, his decisions were never merely personal. Moreover, whatever sympathies the public might have felt for the Lindberghs, these were squashed by the weight of sheer curiosity. When, for example, rumor about a ransom drop spread on the night of March 7, several hundred people gathered to observe, a situation that would surely have buried any possibility of exchange had one actually been arranged. This made Lindbergh even more obsessive about maintaining secrecy in his activities and led the press to far-fetched speculations.[33]

The police, too, were trapped. If they interfered and the child was not returned, they would be held responsible for the loss of the nation's best-known child, the "First Baby in the Land," a kind of democratic prince. If Lindbergh managed to shield his child's abductors and regain his child, the impotence of the police and the laws they were supposed to defend would have been reinforced in full public view and at a time when public officials were denounced as ineffective against criminals. Caught between their duty and the public's omnipotent gaze, the police allowed Lindbergh to take charge and gave him the wide berth he needed to issue even public statements that implied police amnesty (to which he did not, in fact, have overt agreement).[34]

In the not so long run, this experience would provoke a serious reaction. Just as Ross took the blame for his hesitation to act vigorously on his son's behalf, Lindbergh was blamed for the public chaos that his eagerness to come to any terms threatened to incur. The public disillusionment soon took an unexpected turn. In 1933, Governor Herbert H. Lehman of New York proposed penalties against those who privately negotiated with criminals: "We cannot afford to consider the feelings or interest of an individual when it conflicts with the safety and welfare of the people as a whole," Lehman announced. Dr. Carleton Simon, a former deputy police commissioner in New York agreed: "To my mind, the man who pays a ransom is a selfish individual endangering the lives of untold number." Indeed, Canada had such a law and suffered from few kidnap crimes. Although initially scoffed at as impossible to enforce (what jury would convict a father for negotiating for his child's life?), the law soon had a larger national following. By 1938, in the wake of a continuing "epidemic" of kidnapping following the Lindbergh case, the public was reported to be prepared for just such an outcome. By a two-to-one margin, Americans polled in the wake of yet another kidnap-murder (of a five-year-old Princeton, New Jersey, child), agreed that "it should be against the law for a family to pay ransom to a kidnapper." Most of those polled believed that the law would be futile against kidnappings committed for sadistic or vengeful reasons, but would be effective as a deterrent to organized crime.[35]

In fact, Lindbergh's violation of the public trust went well beyond a willingness to negotiate with any and all parties with no questions asked and no penalties threatened. He had been prepared to cooperate actively with the very tools of lawlessness that seemed to hold the society hostage. Very early in his strategy, Lindbergh had engaged the services of an underworld character, Morris Rosner, whose gangland connections and criminal history were supposed to provide the access to the world of gangs that Lindbergh assumed (together with almost everyone else) was responsible for his son's abduction. And Rosner had employed two assistants as negotiators, Salvatore ("Salvy") Spitale and Irving Bitz, with equally unsavory associations. Indeed, Spitale was described as someone who "knew men engaged in the kidnapping as well as other rackets." All of these characters had been *taken into the Lindbergh home*. Although some had argued all along that organized crime was hardly so stupid as to have attempted the brazen abduction of America's best-known child and that all signs pointed to an amateur or an inside job (involving the Lindbergh or Morrow servants), Lindbergh obviously hoped for a quick connection with the world of gangsters that he believed could be provided by his seedy associates. This maneuver brought no positive results, although Bitz and Spitale's public posturing several times misled the press and the public that an exchange was imminent and that the Lindbergh baby would be home shortly.[36]

If this dabbling with thieves and hoodlums was not enough, Lindbergh's fame and the obvious public relations value of the case brought out the big gun of the rackets, Al Capone, who was serving time in federal prison on income tax evasion charges. After initially offering a personal $10,000 reward for information leading to the child, Capone proposed to serve personally as an emissary. As king of the underworld, his limitless contacts and power would surely bring the right rats out of their holes. The possibility that the two most powerful figures of the American imagination, public enemy number one and public hero number one, might cooperate to rescue a child was a truly stunning possibility. The opportunity for Capone was irresistible, and his offer was that of a gentleman with a deep respect for family values: "I don't want any favors," he told Hearst columnist Arthur Brisbane, "if I am able to do anything for that baby. . . . I will send my young brother to stay here in the jail until I come back. You don't suppose anybody would suggest that I would double-cross my own brother. . . . It would be hard for anybody, any man that found that baby not to take a crack at him. But I would give my word through my different angles, as I give it now, and nobody would be afraid to trust me." Capone added that, in his opinion, "That child is not taken by an organized mob. It isn't the work of any organization. . . . To kidnap that child was as foolish as it would have been to try to kidnap President Hoover."[37]

By the end of the second week of the child's disappearance, Capone was not alone in doubting the mob's involvement. It seemed too stupid and public an action and the ransom too puny. As one columnist, exploring various theories about the kidnapping, explained: Mrs. Morrow (Anne's mother) had inherited $20 million from her husband, and gangsters had asked for and received in other abductions twice what was being asked for the Lindbergh child.[38]

Lindbergh, his advisers, and the police, too, were beginning to discount the gangland hypothesis. Lindbergh turned Capone down, but the publicity surrounding Lindbergh's dealings with the underworld were beginning to sully the purity of the case, just as the presence of its underworld affiliates were tainting the famous house. The press and the public had initially been willing to give Lindbergh a wide berth. "If promises of immunity and enlistment of notorious New York gangsters as intermediaries would result in hastening the return of the baby to its parents, the end would be generally held to justify the means." But the baby was not returned. After the futile payment of the ransom, the Reverend Robert Russell Wicks of Princeton

University drew the damning conclusion: "From now on each man who pays his tribute to the underworld for the purchase of his drink may see what sort of viper he helps to nourish in our midst."[39] Lindbergh, because he was firmly "in charge," took the brunt of the disillusionment, both for its lack of success (which might have "justified the means") and for the means employed. In this context, Anne's calm grief and simple nobility was an inspiration. Where Lindbergh's hero credentials were beginning to tarnish, Anne became a proper princess.

This gendered reversal of fortune has lasted to this day. Part of the story of the Lindbergh case is the development of conspiracy theories that have haunted the case for over sixty years. In most of these, Lindbergh plays a prominent part. This was, at least in part, because he played such an active part in the unfolding story. But it was also, I think, because Lindbergh was tainted by the choices he made and by his single-mindedness. Unwilling or unable to see the public's large stake in a heroic opposition to lawlessness, he pursued his objectives with the same obliviousness that had helped him to conquer the Atlantic, the same disregard for anything but his own goal.

By the time the baby disappeared, Lindbergh already had a rocky relationship with the press, mostly because he was niggardly in giving them access to himself. That relationship also reflected his attitude toward the public that had enshrined him willy nilly as their living symbol of youth, adventure, and courage. Because of his desire for privacy, Lindbergh had also kept "the first baby in the land" shielded from the press. "Perhaps nowhere in the world at any time in history," the *New York Times* observed, "had a child been the object of such wide public interest as was the Lindbergh child." The child was "the son of the most famous young man in modern history" and was listed in the 1931 edition of Britain's *Who's Who* together with the future queen of England. But Lindbergh had only very rarely released pictures of the child to the public in the twenty months since his birth.[40] Indeed, this reluctance to share the baby with the public had led to the first whispered suspicions about a conspiracy—the belief that the child had been disposed of because he was mentally backward or otherwise abnormal. The lack of public access had early on led to an undercurrent of mistrust.

Laura Vitray, a Hearst reporter, disposed of this theory publicly in a book published shortly after the child was stolen and replaced it with an even more bizarre suspicion. Vitray was troubled by what she portrayed as police reluctance to pursue serious leads, and proposed that the baby was, in fact, alive and well. The Lindbergh baby had never been kidnapped at all. Rather the entire event was staged, part of a conspiracy to deceive the American people, carried out with the full consent of Lindbergh, President Hoover, and the upper echelons of the press in order to deflect the public's attention from the nation's serious foreign and domestic ills. As a reporter who had been at the house, Vitray knew all about and participated in what she called the *Great Lindbergh Hullabaloo*, the enormous upswell of national media attention created by the abduction and orchestrated by the press. Her book is an important measure of how a reporter who was on the inside looked at a case that seemed tailor-made for publicity purposes. Vitray took this insight only a step further, to suggest that it *was*, in fact, tailored for just that purpose. Vitray also drew some damning conclusions about Lindbergh's connection with the underworld. Rosner, she noted, "made the Lindbergh dwelling his headquarters, flitting in and out of it on errands whose purpose we never were able to ascertain. . . . Lindbergh and his underworld advisors were not taking the detectives and State Police into their confidence. . . . The gangsters felt themselves the real force in solving the kidnapping."[41]

Vitray put Lindbergh, the underworld, the newspapers, and the American government in bed together in a conspiracy aimed at creating a national diversion of mammoth proportions. In a final convulsive conclusion entitled "I ACCUSE!" she drew upon the style of Emile Zola's great anticonspiracy tract: "I accuse the powers of the Underworld, who have become the powers which guide and move the financiers and the administration of our government, of having deliberately arranged the Lindbergh kidnaping, not for ransom, but *as a story*, to divert public attention from the grave disaster that threatens this nation at their own hands today."[42] The accusation suggests the emotional impact of Lindbergh's dabbling with the underworld. The great hero had succumbed to the very forces that his son's abduction had enshrined as the evil empire. Vitray did not accuse Anne.

The intense outrage of Vitray's tract shadowed the case throughout its history, although usually in more subtle form. In 1935, it first peaked in the Hauptmann trial itself when Lindbergh was accused (and has been so repeatedly since) of knowingly bearing false witness against an innocent man, a foreigner and a scapegoat. Lindbergh was in the vicinity of the cemetery on the evening of April 2 when Dr. John Condon passed the $50,000 ransom to a man who identified himself as "John." Lindbergh claimed to have heard this man's voice when he called to Condon: "Hey, Doctor." Although the trial was nearly three years after this event, and Lindbergh had often claimed that it would be difficult to remember the voice with complete accuracy, he never hesitated to offer this testimony to the prosecution case. At the time, in 1935, Lindbergh was still too much the hero (though sullied), too much the grieving father to be publicly disgraced. After Hauptmann's execution, however, when Lindbergh, Anne, and their young son, Jon, fled the country to take up exile in Britain, Lindbergh became increasingly the fallen hero, no longer immune to public rebuke, vulnerable for his behavior, and perhaps even guilty on various counts. Some began to suggest that he had fled from his own guilty knowledge.[43]

Not until the 1980s and 1990s did these suspicions and accusations result in a direct thrust at Lindbergh. In several recent books, Lindbergh is either guilty of consciously giving false witness in a trial that had been faked by the police and prosecution in order to bring the very public case to a successful conclusion or, more treacherously yet, himself guilty of his son's murder or complicit in his death. Just as Lindbergh's light faded while his wife's rose during the press coverage of the abduction and its immediate consequences, Lindbergh's reputation has recently been blackened to make way for the emergence of Richard Bruno Hauptmann as a heroic victim, a reflection probably of our own need to raise victimhood to new heights of glamour. In 1985, Ludovic Kennedy, a British journalist, wrote an impassioned book in which Lindbergh acquiesced in Hauptmann's victimization by the prosecution. In it, Hauptmann is a man plainly innocent of the kidnapping and probably innocent of the extortion as well. By 1993, Lindbergh's alleged complicity had been transformed into active guilt in the first book openly to accuse him of murdering his son, published privately by Gregory Ahlgren and Stephen Monier. Then in 1994, Noel Behn published *Lindbergh: The Crime*, a book that topped other conspiracy books to become the focus of renewed national publicity. In most of the Lindbergh conspiracy books, the police and a politically ambitious prosecutor, David Wilentz, set up and convicted an innocent man. In Behn's book, Lindbergh committed the crime himself, having either killed his son or covered up the murder committed by his deranged and insanely jealous sister-in-law, Elisabeth Morrow. The police knew and knowingly scapegoated an innocent foreigner, thus making Hauptmann a symbolic victim of the American justice system and Lindbergh complicit in the death of two innocent victims. The mighty had indeed fallen. Anne, it should be noted, has been kept out of these various conspiracy theories, just as she had been by Vitray.[44]

Behn's story (and before him, Ahlgren and Monier's) is notable because it provides not a new plot, but a new conclusion to a story whose plot had always been about the larger society and its instruments of justice. From the start, the stories about the Lindbergh abduction have been about power and powerlessness. While the initial story was about how even a hero of Lindbergh's stature had been rendered powerless by organized crime, this final story is about Lindbergh's immense power to control and subvert justice and to destroy another human being with impunity. Lindbergh takes the place of the underworld in the public's imagination, having become just as evil, just as devious, and just as potent. How else could one explain the kidnapping of the most famous child in America, whose abduction Capone had argued was as foolhardy as kidnapping the president of the United States? How else could one explain the death of the son of the man who controlled the American imagination?

Once during a scarce news time, the *New York Evening Journal* published a far-fetched story in three parts connecting the Lindbergh case to that of Leopold and Loeb. The paper was trying to draw on the sensationalism of this earlier explosive news story. The specifics are too contrived to warrant serious review,[45] but the comparison is nevertheless stimulating. In the case of Leopold and Loeb, the press had very early turned its fascinated attention to the perpetrators of the crime and focused on their plotting. That early interest with mad genius gave way to psychological discussions, which dissected the pair's inner lives and motives. Leopold and Loeb, as well as Hickman and Noel, were fascinating evil geniuses, whose madness or contrivance were basic ingredients in each kidnap's plot and whose individual psyches created the kidnap threat. In the 1920s, explanations for kidnappings had been lodged in intrapsychic forces, either genius or madness or some lethal combination of both. While some were eager to blame the schools or the lack of morality, these issues were secondary, significant only as forces that might mold or unhinge the development of personality.

Initially, the abduction of the Lindbergh baby told a completely opposite story. It was lodged in malevolent social forces—political corruption, legal helplessness, and civic decay. It was a story of human weakness and social vulnerability. "If a Lindbergh baby is not safe in society, what safety is there for any baby anywhere?"[46] Kidnapping reflected the general helplessness of the society. Lindbergh's helplessness had been used as conclusive evidence for this condition. In the world of the 1930s, even a hero could be a victim.

But Lindbergh had always been a reluctant hero, and during the ordeal of his son's kidnapping, he was also a reluctant victim. In acting boldly and adopting all means to find his son, even those that were illegal and complicit with the very forces seeming to unhinge social order, he had tainted himself. He was no longer a hero, but his monumental status meant that he could also not simply be an ordinary man. In the long run, when his heroism no longer sent shivers down the spine of the American people, when they no longer understood the sense of helpless despair Americans had experienced in 1932 in the depth of the pre-Rooseveltian Depression—when gangsters did prey on people's fears as well as on their imaginations—Lindbergh would be transformed into a villain. In the period between his son's abduction and the American participation in World War II, especially after he returned from European exile, Lindbergh accelerated his swift descent by his right-wing politics (a stupid embrace of America Firsters, fascists, and Nazi-lovers), and by an isolationism spiced with political ambition. But his downfall had begun when he could not save his own son, or the nation's house.

◲ √ ◳

Lindbergh had always been a bonanza for the American press. On May 22, 1927, the news of the successful completion of his transatlantic flight at Le Bourget airport outside of Paris filled the front pages of newspapers everywhere. Even the staid *New York Times* gave him full banner headlines, a large front-page photo, and most of its first page of newsprint. But the excitement inscribed by that extraordinary adventure paled in comparison with the press fever that surrounded the abduction of his son. The *New York World Telegram* devoted not just the first page and seven following pages of its March 2 edition to the story but the first page for an entire week. The *New York Times* provided four full columns of its front page for four days after the abduction and several full inside pages to the story. The case was such a significant news story that it received continuous coverage in *Editor and Publisher*, the newspaper industry's own newspaper, thus making the coverage of the case itself news. Indeed, according to *Publisher's Weekly*, the journal of the book publishing industry, the final episode—coverage of the Hauptmann trial—so drained the reading energies of the public that "the reading of detective fiction has taken a drop during these weeks when the Hauptmann trial has been so fully reported in the newspapers from coast to coast." While that final convulsion of press sensationalism would define the worst aspects of its exploitation, the case was a press event from the beginning. Two weeks after news of the child's disappearance, the *New Republic* was describing the kidnapping as "an opportunity for displaying at their worst the vulgar arts of ballyhoo," noting in particular "the patent insincerity of the [radio] announcer's accents of woe" and the written media's "egregious display of sentimentality and bad taste."[47]

From the start, the press recognized the story's potential as "the greatest human interest story of the decade." Starting with the first day of coverage, newspapers reported "soaring sales" on the basis of extra copies printed, and New York and Philadelphia papers (the largest local markets) saw an increase of 15 to 20 percent in their circulation. Photos, as well as news stories, were very much in demand. While the Associated Press bought the use of a Lindbergh neighbor's phone for its transmissions of about 10,000 words a day, the Hearst International News Service sent 50,000. As soon as Lindbergh released the initial photos of his son in order to assist in his recovery, the AP chartered an airplane to bring them in. International News Photo Service (Hearst) chartered two ambulances and fitted them with developing equipment so photos could be developed while bells and sirens smoothed the way for a high-speed delivery to New York. The general manager of the International News Photo Service was quoted as saying that "Our service at present is given over almost entirely to the Lindbergh story. It's the greatest picture story I've ever known from the point of view of rapid distribution." By March 16, one and one-half million words had been reported from Hopewell and Trenton, the towns to which the press had retreated when the Lindberghs had asked them to leave their grounds.[48]

While newspaper editors fell over each other with delight at the "universal appeal of the kidnapping" and its "splendid human interest," all was not entirely well from the point of view of competition. The written word was being threatened by the radio's new potential as a more rapid source of information and its ability to encourage listener engagement. The radio carried popular (and politically reactionary) Father Charles Coughlin's urgent appeal for the return of the baby, as well as the appeal of the baby's father. And it also carried frequent, and often misleading, spot bulletins about progress in the case. One news editor thought "the radio people were . . . over bold," another that radio "put out reckless reports." The flash bulletins on the radio probably did not hurt newspaper sales but cut into the news extras that would have been greatly profitable in this instance.[49]

More seriously, the radio broadcasts could stir urgent emotions by capitalizing on the immediacy of the spoken word. *Editor and Publisher* observed that "they aimed for pathos, and, except for the nature of the news, were nearly funny. . . . As a news and advertising medium, it appears to be developing along purely emotional lines." Although the newsprint medium was criticizing its new competitor, the papers were both imitating the radio's exploitative emotionalism and themselves increasingly becoming targets of serious contemporary criticism. As Silas Bent observed in *The Outlook*, "they outdid themselves and one another in verbosity and vulgarity." And Walter Lippmann, a journalism luminary, denounced the press for forcing Lindbergh to "devote so much energy to evading publicity when he needs his whole strength to search for his child." In fact, contemporary criticism was often so severe that *Editor and Publisher* was regularly put on the defensive. The extraordinary publicity attached to the case even brought an early scholarly evaluation in the *American Journal of Sociology*, which placed the issue in a comparative cultural and historical perspective.[50]

The media attention came to a first climax on May 13 with reports of the child's death, then topped even this with Hauptmann's trial. It is hard to imagine any story that had more potential to capture the public's attention or to inflate newspaper sales. Through a fortuitously timed phone call to Governor Moore, Francis A. Jamieson, the Associated Press correspondent at Trenton, New Jersey, learned of the discovery of the body and was able to flash news to the public well in advance of Schwartzkopf's announcement. *Editor and Publisher* concluded that "From the circulation standpoint the finding of the baby's body was the biggest story since the Armistice and in some cases *the biggest story of all times*." In New York, the *Daily News* sold 600,000 extras, and the *World Telegram* and *Evening Post* saw increases in their circulation of between 20 and 25 percent, while the *Daily Mirror's* circulation grew 40 percent. Across the continent in San Francisco, the six city newspapers had a combined additional sale of 260,000.[51]

The profits were large and the emotions high. Even the normally re-strained *New York Times* expressed outrage when the baby was found within a few miles of the family home on May 12: "The story which has had its tragic and heart breaking ending during the last week in the finding of the dead child has revealed the worst in human nature, if indeed those who committed the most merciless, perfidious and despicable of deeds deserve to be called human. . . . There could be no welcome for [them] even by the fallen angels in hell." Calling it "An Unspeakable Crime," the respectable *St. Louis Post-Dispatch* labeled the kidnappers fiends and concluded that "Justice, swift and sure, must hound their footsteps, ferret them out of their holes and bring them to justice. It is unthinkable that one of the vilest crimes in history shall remain unsolved and unavenged." The tabloid *New York Daily News*, featured a picture of the baby on the entire back cover and only two words, "Baby Dead," on the front. The words needed to be hand lettered because there was no typeface of adequate size. The *New York Evening Journal* provided the most bloodcurdling verdict and did so on be-half of mothers: "Women are the givers of life, not the takers. Yet some-thing red and murderous swims before the gaze of every woman who dares to let herself think of the callous brutality coloring every circumstance in this horrible case." Calling the perpetrators "DEVILS," Marguerite Mooers Marshall counterposed a sentimental description of the golden-haired, blue-eyed youngster in his little crib half-sick with a cold against the "butchered baby" whose "blood cries aloud against human cruelty." Mus-tering the "fury of pity" from women "lost in sick rage," Marshall identified the kidnappers with "raiding red Indians" and proposed that "Hanging is too good for them!"[52]

A few days later, another *Evening Journal* woman columnist, Nell Brink-ley, featured a drawing of a young mother hugging her lovely (and quite disturbingly sensual) child in her lap and evoked the same ricocheting im-ages of delicate motherhood and maternal vengeance. In trying to create reader immediacy and identification, this drawing and its accompanying saccharine thoughts both roiled emotions and debased them. This was not because genuine sympathy for the woman another columnist called "Poor Anne" or anger on her behalf was not possible, but because what papers like the *Evening Journal* created was an indulgence in emotionalism rather than an expression of true feeling. And it was exploitative of Anne and her dead child rather than supportive. In so deranging the reader's real need to know and to sympathize, newspapers like the *New York Evening Journal* and others commercialized the experience of the kidnapping. This was clearly understood at the time, enough so that *Editor and Publisher*, at one point, defended the constant parade of emotionalism by announcing that the newswriters, too, had "honest sentiments" and, like the nation, were "torn by love and fear for the child of the heroic Lindberghs."[53]

This commercialization did more than sell newspapers. It attached certain emotional titillations to the tragic experience of losing a child to kidnappers. I have already suggested that the horror introduced by Charley Ross's abduction was associated with the titillations common to gothic tales of the period. In the Lindbergh case, the rabid commercialization of grief, which was attached to an already insatiable curiosity about the famous, turned horror into another kind of sensation—a kind of salacious pity. This was an invertion of identification and allowed readers actually to distance themselves from the participants, though not from the anxieties about kidnapping, which increased furiously at the time.

The attention given to the details of the kidnapping and murder and the striving to bring to readers every particle of potential "human interest" also loaded the *crime* of kidnapping with a certain kind of thrill. Someone with criminal inclinations, like Richard Loeb, was already fully aware of this possibility in 1924. After the Lindbergh case, with its reams of publicity and its association with fame, the crime of kidnapping would be infused with the glamour of association.

⧉ VI ⧉

The *Orlando Morning Sentinal* (Florida) headline announcing the death read "Baby Lindy Sacrificed on Altar of Crime." In fact, from the point of view of the evolving story, the criminal altar was erected only after the baby's death. Until the discovery of the child's badly decomposed corpse (presumably dead for two months) in a shallow grave by two black draymen, the case had focused on the Lindberghs, their home, and the problem of social order that the kidnapping represented. While the social issues associated with criminality were palpable, the heart of the case was a human one: Could the father get his child back? When he failed, the mystery shifted to the police's attempts to find and to convict the perpetrator(s). As the *St. Louis Post-Dispatch* announced in a large headline, "State and Federal Forces Combine to Run Down Kidnappers Who Killed Baby Lindy."[54] Crime control had always been an issue. Now with the passage of new federal legislation and the shift to capturing the kidnapper(s), it dominated the story.

The child's death removed the extreme restrictions and self-imposed rules governing press access to information about the strategies pursued by the Lindberghs and the police. Until then, it was feared that releasing significant details might impede negotiations. Most of what the press knew came from the police in highly structured briefings; the Lindberghs themselves had been largely off limits. While it had seethed at this treatment, the press had deferred to the importance of the family and to the case.[55] Journalists were able to gather details of several of the wilder attempts being made to retrieve the child, but they had not been informed about the most serious of the ransom negotiations, initated and completed by "Jafsie," the name assumed by John F. Condon.

Condon was a seventy-two-year-old former schoolteacher and principal who lectured at Fordham University. A man of principle and unabashed patriotic ferver, who was proud of his accomplishments and eager to uphold American honor in a situation where it seemed at serious risk, Condon had offered a small personal reward and volunteered to serve as an intermediary. The Lindberghs had heard nothing from the kidnapper(s) before Condon placed his initial notice in the *Bronx Home News*, where he occasionally published essays and poetry. After a few days he received a note, which because of its logo "signiture" convinced the Lindberghs that it might well be from the kidnapper of their son. After an initial meeting with a man who identified himself as "John" in a Bronx cemetery and who subsequently sent Condon the sleeping suit that the Lindbergh baby had worn on the night of his abduction, Condon gave $50,000 to this same man at St. Raymond's Cemetery in the Bronx on April 2, 1932. Everyone had been extremely hopeful that the child would then be returned and Lindbergh, together with Condon and Lindbergh's lawyer and closest adviser, Henry Breckinridge, flew all night and the next day over Cape Cod, where John had indicated the child would be located on a boat named "Nelly."[56]

Some press leaks had taken place before this event since the initial contact came through personals in a local newspaper. Still, it remained largely a secret operation and remained so for a week after it took place. Publicity came only after the exchange had failed to produce the child. Ten days after the money was handed over by Jafsie to John, the *New York Times* published all the serial numbers of the bills, which, while unmarked in accordance with the ransom demands, had their serial numbers duly recorded by agents of the Treasury Department. This filled one and one-quarter full pages. The secrecy surrounding this exchange and other early attempts at negotiation sowed the seeds of wild rumors and conspiracy theories; they would bring a rich harvest in the long term.[57]

With the discovery of the child's body, the gloves were off, and when the police finally reeled in their prime suspect, Bruno Richard Hauptmann, in September 1934 on the basis of a trail of U.S. currency notes (made more easily traceable because of FDR's withdrawal of gold certificates from circulation), the scene was set for the greatest exploitation of a criminal case that the press and the public had ever known. This was foreshadowed by the immediate coverage in the *New York Times*: one-half of the front page and all of pages two, three, and four were devoted to the story of the capture, as was a similar amount of space the next day. It all recalled, but far exceeded, the attention the *Times* had given to the strange capture and death of the men presumed to have abducted Charley Ross, and for the same reason—it provided a vindication of law and order in the society and the potential end for an extremely unsettling story.[58]

The Hauptmann story has been often told and told in many different ways. The final exploitation in what many called the story of the century provided the sharp continuation of the impulses that had governed the press coverage from the beginning of the case. By the time, Hauptmann went to trial on January 2, 1935, the 150 reporters and photographers who had gathered on the front lawn of Lindbergh's house had grown to 700 crowding the stately courthouse in the small town of Flemington, New Jersey, where the trial took place. Most newspapers had given precedence to the trial over President Roosevelt's message to Congress. Wire services transmitted the entire trial transcript of about 55,000 words a day. Indeed, James S. Kilgallen, head of the International News Service noted that he had never been at a trial where there were so many women reporters, a mark of the trial's potential for generating varied kinds of "human interest" stories; some of these reporters specialized in "Flemington Fashions." It also attracted the attention of very famous reporters, like Walter Winchell, Arthur Brisbane, and Adela Rogers St. John. Hearst's *New York Evening Journal* had over thirty people in attendance. And because the trial had become the center of national media attention and publicity, it became the place to be seen and to be admired. The trial became a society venue where, according to Edna Ferber, fashionable mink-clad New York ladies gathered for the most "divine" experience. The courtroom was also packed with names familiar from the world of entertainment: Jack Benny, Ginger Rogers, Moss Hart, Lynn Fontanne, Jack Dempsey. In fact, the trial had become a form of entertainment, an early instance of the modern fascination with real life experiences as better than fiction. Novelist Kathleen Norris drew attention to how easy it was to connect the Hauptmann trial to motion picture fantasies: "Hollywood. We have been regaled by so many prison pictures, so many crime and detective and district attorney pictures, that as the day dawdles . . . it begins to seem like a picture. Presently the reel will end, and Minnie Mouse and her white shoes will take the screen." It is worth noting that Bobby Franks's brother, Jack, had a similarly mediated response to news of his brothers' abduction. He explained that he didn't believe that kidnappings ever really "happened outside the moving pictures. . . . I wanted to laugh." By the 1920s and 1930s, Hollywood had already recreated the public's experience of crime, just as the radio was in the process of recreating the nature of news.[59]

The trial had become such an orchestrated media event that many questioned whether it could also become the site of real justice. Eleanor Roosevelt asked publicly, "what might happen to any innocent person in a similar situation," and Clarence Darrow thought the atmosphere made a fair trial unlikely. In the wake of the trial, a committee of the American Bar Association hoped to control publicity of this kind in the future and presented a proposal to its convention in July 1935: "The committee believes . . . that to treat a simple trial as a public show, as was done in the sensational criminal trial of Bruno Hauptmann, is to cheapen life itself by causing people generally to undervalue the life of the criminal and to increase the morbid desires of sensation seekers." And the solicitor general of the United States told a meeting of the American Bar Association that the "town of Flemington, New Jersey, became the center of the most shocking example of the evil practices which have surrounded the trial of sensational cases in this country for years." Members of the press, too, were outraged. The *New Republic*, which had been critical of press excess from the beginning, called what happened at Flemington "less a process of justice than a mass orgy of hatred and revenge." Much revered journalist William Allen White became indignant (and also caught the Hollywood connection): "The disgrace and scandal of movietone trials like the Hauptmann case reflect upon American intelligence and undoubtedly lower the tone of American justice." And he denounced the shaming of the courts as "the price of . . . vacuous morbidity."[60]

While hawkers sold miniature ladders as souvenirs and the press sent cartoonists to draw "the funny side of the trial," one young man came with a different purpose. Twenty-four-year-old Harmon Whaley was learning how to avoid Hauptmann's mistakes. In May, he would kidnap nine-year-old George Weyerhaeuser, heir to a Washington state lumber fortune, while the boy walked to school. Signing himself "Egoist," Whaley asked for a $200,000 ransom, which the parents gladly paid.[61] The publicity about the Lindbergh kidnapping had brought a certain kind of glamour and reaped another kind of harvest.

The press had turned its spotlight on kidnapping and murder—and turned "Child Murder Into Entertainment," in the words of the *Catholic World*. As a result, the nation took "orgiastic delight" in the battle over Hauptmann's fate. The trial, even more than the kidnap coverage, led American journalism into spasms of self-accusation, as many began to recognize the implications of what had occurred.[62] The nation had witnessed an unparalleled manipulation of emotion, in the most intimate and searing terms—childhood loss, parental anguish, murderous guilt, and retribution. Because honest sympathy and desire for justice could hardly be sustained at a high pitch, the press had turned the emotional screws until all honesty and genuine wishes for justice had disappeared. In the attempt to convey intensity, the representations of emotions had created titillation. In the attempt to create disgust for lawbreaking, the news had often created sympathy for the daring of lawbreakers. This was certainly part of the appeal of the Hauptmann trial. Just as Lindbergh's heroism had worn thin, so criminals conversely became fascinating. Whaley had captured this in his signature "Egoist." Richard Loeb in his precocious brilliance had anticipated much of this thrill of outlawry, just as he had managed to collapse the real and the fictional in his mind in anticipation of later events. Earlier still, in 1900, after Patrick Crowe had kidnapped and then freed Eddie Cudahy for $25,000, he had become to the public a glamourous adventurer, whom a jury refused to convict even after he turned himself over to the authorities and despite abundant evidence of his guilt.[63] Now, with the help of various news media, many Americans who were less gifted or daring than these began to experience the thrill as well as the horror of crime. Hauptmann too, became the focus for an inversion of values, made so much easier by Lindbergh's own fall from primal grace.

Certainly some of this was the result simply of a pervasive resentment against the rich and privileged, a resentment that was just below the surface, even in the portrayals of "poor Anne." That sentiment was surely acute during a period of deep economic pain such as the 1930s. In this context, some began to portray the Hauptmann trial as a new version of Sacco and Vanzetti, a miscarriage of American justice against the foreign and helpless. It was, therefore, not altogether surprising that Sam Leibowitz, famous for his defense in the Scottsboro case, was called in to assist in the Hauptmann appeals process. (He did not take the case.)[64] But some of the inversion of values resulted from the press's attention to crime and criminals and the "orgiastic delight" being attached to crime watching as the media propelled the public into both vengeful and lustful thoughts.

In the wake of the Hauptmann trial, even the usually complacent *Editor and Publisher* began to take notice of the press's potential for creating crime. The journal admitted that the chorus of condemnation about crime news had grown significantly since 1930 and had been recently joined by some newspaper editors. "It is undeniable that today, criminals, outcasts-of-society, are as famous as the most distinguished scientist and scholar. Perhaps more so." In fact, a survey conducted by the Medill School of Journalism of Northwestern University, eliciting the views of several kinds of professionals with interests in crime, found some stunning results. Seventy-six percent of all those questioned believed that crime stories incited further crimes. While only 3 percent of editors "would exclude crime news from the front page," 71 percent of penitentiary wardens, 67 percent of sociologists, and 52 percent of psychologists favored such an exclusion. Most of the professional groups were of the opinion that "present methods of handling crime news make heroes out of criminals," and even 41 percent of the editors believed this to be true. While experts debated the results of such publicity, not very far from the Lindbergh home, in Highland Park, New Jersey, a man put a ladder up against the nursery window of pharmaceutical manufacturer, I. Howard Johnson, in an attempt to kidnap his daughter.[65]

Whatever its effects on the glamorization of kidnapping or crime generally, the continuous attention to the Lindbergh kidnapping had made Americans extremely anxious for their own children. "Thousands of mothers are sick with apprehension and thousands of fathers dread to hear the telephone ring because of this terror." The *New York World Telegram* captured the mood with an especially effective cartoon: Two parents sit silently huddled together with a child in the mother's lap. Their chairs are pressed together in an image that evokes nothing so much as the circling of wagons against Indian raids. The cartoon is entitled "A Matter of Concern in Every Home." That fear, churned up by the news media, "that it might have been their little boy or girl," lasted for years during the ordeal of the long drawn-out public case, and remained as a residue of the experience. It had become, in the words of the *New York Times*, "a lively and real fact in the lives" of parents everywhere. Although psychologists testified about the ill effects of a too close surveillance of children, many parents began to take special care about their children's safety. Those who were prominent or rich often hired private guards for their children or had their homes barricaded. They could now also buy kidnap insurance, which was issued by Lloyd's of London after the Lindbergh kidnapping. Others could simply watch their children more carefully and with heightened anxiety.[66]

The role of the press in the exploitation of child kidnapping was made clear when the *Delineator* advised parents about what to do in the event of a child's abduction. The journal cautioned parents to avoid "news leaks" by contacting the Bureau of Investigation rather than the local police station, where "the host of reporters . . . will broadcast it." A similar moral ran throughout a short story called "Front Page Stuff," published in the *Saturday Evening Post* in 1934: an ordinary advertising man, Lee Spencer, comes home to find his home ablaze with lights and the place occupied by police and press when a prowler is found loitering on the grounds of his house (their "remodeled carriage shed . . . rented for a nominal sum" ends up described as an "estate" in the papers). He and his family are prominently featured in the newspapers, where they become famous as the most recent victims of an attempted child kidnapping. Initially, Spencer thinks "of Charley Ross, who never came back home," but then discovers that his son is safe. Soon, however, they receive ransom demands, and their anxieties become acute with his wife fearing that "if her vigilance relaxed for an instant," their son "might be spirited away." As they become a focus of press attention, their friends, fearful for their own children, regard them as "carriers of the plague" and abandon them. By the end of the story, only the press is benefiting from their plight, and the father begins to suspect that the whole story had been concocted to sell papers. When he balks at continuing to provide information to the newspaperman covering the story, he is told, "Man you're news now. You're on the front page." "No wonder gangsters keep scrapbooks of their clippings," Spencer responds and walks out. In his disillusionment with the police and the press, he grasps more than the facts of his own victimization. He gets some perspective on the nature of news stories and the particular spiciness of stories about child kidnappings.[67]

The story is unlikely to have reversed the fear that the Lindbergh case had instilled in parents. It was also unlikely that the experts' reassurance that the crime was rare and that the chances that any child would be kid-napped was four and one half million to one made much of an impact. Then as now, the fact that other more common childhood risks posed far greater threats to child safety (in the 1930s, a host of childhood diseases and the "murderous automobile") hardly put a dent in kidnap anxieties. Like the parents in the cartoon, Americans were once again circling the wagons, clutching their own children tightly to their chests.[68]

As the first popular medium, the press had always played some part in the historical evolution of kidnapping. Even in Charley Ross's day, it had been the first avenue for parents seeking their children, as well as the con-veyance for wild rumors. By the 1920s, the press had taken an active part in hunting down the evidence that led to Leopold and Loeb's confession, and its rapt attention to the pair had made them famous. In making the Lind-bergh case the most famous kidnapping in history, the newspapers and their newer descendents left all their past work in the dust. In riding a trail of fear and sensationalism, they provoked a national hysteria. In the end, that public experience also left behind a new federal law making kidnap-ping a capital offense, as well as new and revised state statutes; a restruc-tured, more vigorous, and renamed Federal Bureau of Investigation under J. Edgar Hoover; and an international reputation for the United States as the kidnapping capital of the world.[69]

When Bruno Hauptmann finally died on the electric chair on January 13, 1936, as the convicted kidnapper of Charles A. Lindbergh, Jr. (after a series of dramatic delays, amply charted by the press), the entire deathwatch delegation appointed to observe the event—the six designated reporters and the twelve additional witnesses—was appropriately composed all of newsmen.[70]

The Lindbergh kidnapping brought to an end the innocent view of children fashioned in the nineteenth century out of religious sentiment, enlightenment philosophy, and a commitment to moral progress. While the Lindbergh baby's cherubic image—its curly blond hair, dimpled chin, and blue eyes—were omnipresent, the press's exploitation of that image and its cynical manipulation of the grief of the child's parents turned the emotions it was meant to evoke into other channels. The commercial exploitation of childhood implied in a demand for monetary ransom that had so horrified observers in Charley Ross's day had become the defining characteristic of the Lindbergh kidnapping. This commerce in childhood was hardly restricted to the $50,000 that was futilely exchanged for the child's life. It was contained as well in the little bits of enterprise, such as the family that exhibited their "little Lindy" lookalike in a profitable sideshow (fifteen cents a peek), or the $2.50 airplane rides over the Lindbergh estate, or the sale of souvenir ladders and locks of baby's hair at the Hauptmann trial. These entrepreneurs were doing on a small scale what the press and radio, together with the vast public turning compulsively to their news, and the bleak theater of the Hauptmann trial were doing on a much grander scale—commercializing the emotional commitment to childhood and consuming the parents' grief at the loss of their child. Since according to one columnist for the *New York Evening Journal*, "Every Woman's Heart Goes Out to Mother of Slain Eaglet," it is not entirely surprising that one California mother offered to give her baby to Anne as compensation for her loss. The gesture not only showed the results of the consumption of other people's griefs, but gave the generous mother a part in the story. Her offer put her "in the news."[71]

In the 1920s, the coverage of kidnapping cases had begun to exploit children's bodies—the mutilated bodies of Bobby Franks and Marion Parker as well as the troubled minds and emotions of young criminals like Edward Hickman, Richard Loeb, and Nathan Leopold. Whatever social innocence was left after that could hardly survive the onslaught of the case against the most famous baby in America.[72]

CHAPTER FOUR

Baby Hunger and Sexual Pathology

The Abductions of Robert Marcus
and Stephanie Bryan

By the time the United States entered World War II, Americans had witnessed a full range of kidnap horrors. The loss of a child, his or her possible death and mutilation defined the terror of kidnapping. The issue of extortion, which had initially alarmed Christian Ross and his nineteenth-century contemporaries, had receded in the context of the even greater threat to a child's life and well-being contained in the newer twentieth-century stories. Indeed, while ransom abductions had been the initial focus of publicity and had formalized the threat, kidnappings for ransom became, after the surge in the 1930s, increasingly less common as the source of concern. Because of the new federal laws and beefed-up local statutes, it had also become a very dangerous way to raise money.

While most of the publicized abductions in the late nineteenth and early twentieth century had been for ransom, in the second half of the twentieth century the press and the public sensed that the danger for children moved to new arenas. The exposure to ransom abductions had, however, familiarized Americans with the many social issues to which the abduction of a child was publicly attached. Indeed, child kidnapping called forth the culture's most sacred affirmations. Most conspicuously, kidnapping threatened the physical and emotional integrity of the family and the sanctity of child life, which was the modern family's central responsibility. It also raised very serious questions about community safety and the problems of crime and punishment.

Early twentieth-century ransom abductions had also brought to the cultural foreground two features of twentieth-century life that became increasingly central to the public's later experience of child kidnapping—the means by which kidnappings were understood and the methods by which they were advertised. Psychological explanations had been entirely absent in the moralistically charged drama of the Ross abduction. But the Leopold and Loeb case had shown how issues relating to sexuality and abnormal psychology could envelop kidnapping in a new sense of menace. And even Hauptmann—who was in the end executed for a theft—was accused during his trial of attempting the crime of the century to gratify an inflated ego and had been examined by psychiatrists eager to define a particular emotional profile.

The press and the newer media, like radio and motion pictures, also became essential to the experience of kidnapping in the twentieth century. Increasingly the press's role, understandable in the Lindbergh case, became a harassing presence even for the humble and unheralded. In at least one instance, they brutally altered the outcome of a case. On July 4, 1956, five-week-old Peter Weinberger was kidnapped from the patio of his parents' home in Westbury, Long Island. The Weinbergers were ordinary people, chosen at random by John deMarco for a $2,000 ransom demand. "I'm scared stiff," the ransom note said, "do not notify the police until noon tomorrow or I'll be forced to kill the baby." The resolution would have been simple enough if the newspapers had not entered the picture. Despite a demand for a one-day news blackout by the police, the *New York Daily News* broke the story in its evening edition, including the facts concerning the ransom payment. Other papers followed suit the next morning, considering themselves released from their bond of silence. By the time deMarco went to the agreed-upon rendezvous one day after the kidnapping, he saw a crowd and, turning on the radio news, learned the details of the police trap into which he was about to fall. Fleeing, he left the child by the roadside where it was found dead three months later when deMarco was apprehended. After the ransom exchange fell through, the enraged mother, who was described as "near collapse," told the gathered press that "I could cut all your throats." Even before the child was found, the experience had left "many thoughtful New Yorkers...wondering whether their enterprising newspapers had succeeded in murdering a month-old child." *Time* magazine concluded that the New York press had "failed their severest test." The case led many in the press to a consideration of its ethical obligation in cases of this kind but hardly changed its hunger for baby kidnapping news.[1]

In fact, news about kidnapping had never been strictly informational. From the beginning (when it spread unfounded rumors about the Rosses), the newspapers combined news with entertainment. In the twentieth century, news media, later amplified through the outlet of television, would take this combination and create a new emotional mix in kidnap stories—a mix where the thrill of mysterious disappearances was replaced by an ever more exciting fascination with the fate of the child. Death had all along offered exciting possibilities. Sex could provide other angles. By the middle of the twentieth century, child abduction became a natural human interest story with cascading media possibilities. By then, stories of child theft and of missing children were a means to create an intense emotional buzz while offering endless little lessons on family feeling and parental roles, and recharging broad social commitments to law and justice.

From the spring of 1955 to the winter of 1957, the San Francisco Bay Area became the site of two very different abductions. Both attracted intense news coverage. But the happy outcome of one and the tragic result of the other could not have been more different. Both cases remained largely local affairs. Saturating the San Francisco Bay Area and northern California, they reached out briefly to audiences in Los Angeles and then the world through the *New York Times, Newsweek*, and *Time*. Indeed most kidnappings, despite the extraordinary publicity attached to very famous cases like Ross, Leopold and Loeb, or Lindbergh, usually were decidedly local events, seizing momentarily the humdrum lives of local people as their neighbors' lives were transformed forever. As these two stories make clear, by the middle of the twentieth century child abduction could reach out and devastate the lives of ordinary Americans. These stories also raise serious questions about the seemingly placid surface of family and community life in the 1950s—a period far more tranquil and wholesome in memory than in experience.

🔳 | 🔳

In September 1955, Dr. Sanford Marcus was an attending physician at Mt. Zion Hospital at Post and Divisidero Streets in San Francisco. At thirty-four, Marcus was married and the father of two children, Richard, three, and Susan, two. After graduating from the University of California at Berkeley, Marcus obtained his medical degree at the University of Pennsylvania in 1944. While doing postgraduate work in surgery in Pennsylvania, Marcus met his future wife, Hanna Eichenwald, a refugee from Nazi Germany, who at thirteen had initially fled to Holland and subsequently to England and the United States. Hanna was working at a settlement house when she and Marcus met on a blind date in 1950. They were married the next year. By 1955 the Marcuses, with their two children, had just moved into a home of their own in Daly City, a modest San Francisco suburb of small pastel-colored houses that was growing like topsy in the postwar period.

On September 17, Hanna gave birth to the couple's third child, Robert, at the same hospital where her husband worked. Two days later, on September 19, Robert Marcus was taken from the maternity ward on the fourth floor of Mt. Zion Hospital. Several witnesses saw a woman, described as an overweight blond, carrying an infant late that afternoon in the vicinity of the hospital. Almost immediately, reports about the abduction proposed that the woman had taken the child not for ransom, but as a result of "a twisted desire for a child of her own."[2]

Despite strict hospital security, the abduction was both simple and unobstructed. At about 3:45 P.M., a woman carrying a pink blanket had come to the nursery and was seen observing the five babies on the ward at the time from behind the glass partition. When asked for her pass, she claimed to have left it with the child's mother. The duty nurse left briefly. By the time she returned, Robert Marcus had disappeared. The woman must have singled out the Marcus child since he was farthest away and most inaccessible. The Marcuses were in shock, but Sanford Marcus kept enough of his composure to beg journalists to relay the message that he would not prosecute the kidnapper if the child were returned "quickly and unharmed."[3] He also tape-recorded a radio message appealing to the kidnapper to return the child. The message was sent over the radio at intervals throughout the night. Mortimer Fleishhacker, Jr., president of the Mt. Zion board of directors acted quickly to offer a $1,000 reward for information leading to the child's recovery. The story would remain front-page news in the San Francisco area for over a week as numerous people reported seeing suspicious-looking women with infants all over the Bay Area, from Novato in Marin County to San Jose on the peninsula, and the press reported obsessively about the parents' emotional distress.

On the day of the abduction, the San Francisco police department was put on immediate alert to locate the child and began what would become the largest house-to-house search in the city's history. From the outset, the police devoted a very large number of people to the task. According to the *San Francisco Examiner*, "The police search" on the first day, "included forty-one inspectors, . . . seventeen motorcycle officers, nine crime prevention detail officers, four men from the juvenile bureau, ten officers from Park and Richmond stations, and twenty other miscellaneous men." Stationed at airports and bus depots, these police officers also called at every drugstore and other stores in the area where baby bottles and formula were sold. In fact, the police did an extraordinary job and, had the child still been in San Francisco, it is possible that they would have located him then or on the next day when more than 600 policemen, one-third of the entire police force in the city, were enlisted in the search for the Marcus baby. By the evening of September 20, the search for the infant boy had grown into "the biggest police effort in San Francisco history," as police officers conducted a house to house search of three of the nine police districts, and the acting police chief, John Engler, "promised that by tonight, the same crews would have worked door-to-door" through three more. Indeed, Engler vowed that "no home in San Francisco would remain unchecked until the baby was found." In the end, the police examined 260,000 dwellings, the most massive house-to-house search in the city's history. As 400 officers knocked on doors, Lt. Don Scott was supervising the operation from a command center on the fourth floor of the San Francisco Hall of Justice, where the hundreds of calls that came in were evaluated and coordinated with the enormous force conducting the search in the field.[4]

The task set for all these men was simple—to return "the breast-fed baby to the arms of his mother." The image of the helpless child wrested from his mother so quickly after birth was irresistible, a perfect icon for a culture newly absorbed in the 1950s by issues of marriage, home, and child rearing. The child's vulnerability was accented by more than his very tender age and that he had literally been deprived of his mother's breast. Robert Marcus also still had open wounds from his umbilical cord and recent circumcision. Dr. Louis Goldstein instructed the kidnapper through the press on the care of both wounds and warned that "the baby should be only sponge-bathed until the umbilical cord and circumcision wound heal." These facts, together with the pitiful picture of the tiny footprints and the exact specifications for the baby's formula prominently printed in the papers, made the case of the missing Jewish child a heartrending drama.[5]

In this case and at this time, the fact that the child was Jewish and born to a woman who had narrowly escaped from Germany, where her parents and brother had been consumed in Hitler's ovens, made the drama even more wrenching. Where an earlier period might have found the ethnic details a source of emotional distance, in the 1950s the Marcus case stirred a profound pity and sympathy laced by a general knowledge of the very recent past where enormous numbers of Jewish children had been violently torn from their mothers' breasts and arms. In the mid 1950s, the American press had hardly explored the gargantuan family tragedy that had taken place in Europe, and few aspects of popular culture had made available the emotional details of the destruction of European Jewry. The Marcus case provided the local audience of the San Francisco Bay Area with a personal tragedy with much larger historical reverberations. It also gave Americans a chance to demonstrate their humane and charitable sentiments, a fitting culmination of the war effort.

The Marcus story allowed San Franciscans to remember past suffering through a vivid present experience. This was strongly reinforced by Hanna Marcus's trauma as she was confronted by the loss of her child. Like most mothers of kidnap victims in the past, Hanna Marcus was described as having collapsed when she learned that her child had been stolen. But Hanna, already hospitalized and vulnerable from the birth experience, lived out the literary trope that had become attached to the mothers of kidnapped children. Her collapse was so complete and profound that there was a serious question about whether she would ever survive her hospital confinement. Rather than becoming the publicly absent mother of most kidnap history, Hanna's collapse brought her enormous publicity and attention. By the second day of the kidnapping, while Dr. Marcus "could only wait and pray," confounded by his utter helplessness, the grief-stricken Hanna, whose still-fresh memories of family loss and separation must have returned uncontrollably to her mind, had retreated into a state of semiconsciousness. She had given up eating entirely and was heavily sedated. She was remote, out of reach, and shut off in some inner chamber of anguish and remembrance. When Sanford Marcus appeared on television to appeal for his son's return, he recounted his wife's earlier experiences and pleaded: "She has had so much to bear. . . . Help her now." By this time, an additional $5,000, raised by Marcus's family and friends, had been posted as a reward.[6]

The newspapers milked the family's anguish unmercifully to confirm traditional family values. The story was almost too perfect, juxtaposing the torment of family disruption with the possibilities of reconciliation, life and death, happiness and sorrow. Under a delightful picture of the pretty Hanna feeding her oldest son, Richard, when he was three days old (centered on the first page), the *San Francisco Chronicle* announced, "Doctor, Husband Fears Mrs. Marcus May Die." Dr. Marcus was quoted as believing that his wife was "going downhill so rapidly it's almost as if she's lost the will" to live. In their eagerness to keep their readers abreast of events, the newspapers even helped to provoke an attempt to use the tragedy for personal gain that would add a note of bathos to its real pain. Early in the unfolding case, the police had discounted the possibility that the child had been abducted for ransom and Marcus repeatedly announced that he was too poor to be the victim of extortion. On the third day of the baby's disappearance, however, the Marcuses received a ransom demand. The note had been intercepted by an alert Oakland postal clerk who notified the newspapers immediately. While the papers kept the note's existence secret for twenty-four hours to protect the child and possible private negotiations, the demand for $5,000 ransom and the threat to inflict bodily harm brought the FBI into a local police matter. But the extortion failed when the writer of the note recanted and apologized two days later. Possibly frightened or genuinely remorseful, the writer noted, "I realize I have done a horrible thing by sending you that letter threatening your child's life. . . . I needed the money. I now realized [*sic*] it was a cruel and fiendish trick. Tonight I will [ask] your's and the Lord's forgiveness." The pathetic ransom note and its retraction was not the only hoax inflicted on the family or the police, who were beset with "sadistic jokers, cranks, and publicity seekers." One such false lead, left with Dr. Marcus's answering service, instructed him to go to an address on Eddy Street. When Marcus rushed to the address, he found "a startled family at dinner—but no trace of the missing baby."[7]

In fact, the police were all along searching for a woman who stole the child for herself and not for ransom. The profile that the police had put together of the abductor included a police sketch of an unkempt, heavyset blond woman in her late twenties who was, according to the lieutenant in charge, "a thwarted mother." When the police consulted Mt. Zion psychiatrists for "a scientific picture of the type of woman who might be involved in such a crime," they were given the same answer with some window dressing: "The psychiatrists decided she must be mentally disturbed and with some sort of psychic baby fixation."[8]

This evaluation had not changed much since the 1920s when, in the wake of similar abductions in New York City, the police and psychiatrists added a new profile to their portfolio of criminals: women who stole babies. At that time, Inspector John Coughlin, head of New York's detective division, indicated that these "distraught" women had "gained a recognized place in the gallery of criminology." Having suffered the loss of a child, unable to bear children themselves, or pregnant at the time, these women were psychologically unhinged and could not control their "mother mania." "Grief has unsettled them, and they . . . lose all control in some temporary wildness to relieve their empty arms." The kidnappers tended to care for the children with devotion. By the middle of the century, this portrait had become a commonplace. One year after the disappearance of the Marcus child, when a six-week-old infant disappeared from its carriage, authorities also "theorized that a deranged woman, starved for a baby" had taken the child—that is until the infant was found dead and suspicion began to shift to the mother herself, who had mysteriously lost two other children in the last four years. Indeed, the picture of the infant kidnapper as a deranged mother aching for a child in her arms has remained the prevailing criminal diagnosis in such cases, especially where infants are taken from hospitals. In the 1980s, "psychotic" women suffering from baby hunger became a standard category of child kidnapping for the FBI. This picture has become generally absorbed in the popular culture as well. A contemporary mystery novel, *Grievous Sin* (1993), used it as the basis for a plot.[9]

As Hanna's condition became progressively more serious (she had been put on intravenous hydration), her husband tried one last strategy to reach her: he brought her children to the hospital. This "dramatic therapy" lifted Hanna from her semicomatose state, jolted her from her utter despair, and provided readers with evidence of the wonders that children could perform. While the cure was miraculous for Hanna, it was heaven-sent for the newspapers. In an extraordinary photograph published on September 25, 1955, Hanna was shown smiling blissfully while hugging her children, clearly on her way to recovery. This photo competed for attention in the *San Francisco Chronicle* with a glum picture of Dwight David Eisenhower, who had suffered a serious heart attack on the same day. While the suspense surrounding Ike's condition knocked the Marcus baby out of the headlines temporarily, it could not dislodge the family drama from equal front-page billing nor from gobbling up the majority of articles on the inside.[10]

The hunt for the baby had also become increasingly desperate. The papers now printed a new baby formula, which was supposed to be enriched as the baby aged by the addition of two ounces of "placebo." The new formula, with its bogus ingredient based on a term presumably not yet in common currency, was supposed to flush out the abductor, who would be eager to follow an appropriate regimen. (No one raised the possibility that many mothers, ignorant of the term and without personal doctors, might also have been eager to add placebo to their week-old babies' formulas.) As the papers tried to assist in the search, they also encouraged at least one possible copycat abduction. In Ventura, California, on September 25, the bassinet of two-day-old Charles Montano was found empty at Foster Memorial Hospital. The abductor was never found, but the child had fortunately been left unharmed at the exit door to the hospital.[11]

The Marcus search had spread to the East Coast; as the days stretched past a week, the hopes for a quick recovery faded. But just as the best leads were exhausted and Hanna finally left the hospital (by ambulance) to resume her life with her other children, all the appeals and the publicity in the case paid off. On September 29, nine days after the initial story broke, the Marcuses were photographed beaming with their baby, securely in Hanna's arms, being fed from a bottle. This photo appeared above the newspaper name in the *San Francisco Examiner* and occupied one-quarter of the front page. Next to it was the photo of a weeping woman, Mrs. Betty Jean Benedicto, "blond, blowsy, and blubbering," who had both taken and returned the child. The *San Francisco Chronicle* headline, "Baby Safe," was in two-inch high and one-half inch bold typeface. In southern California, the *Los Angeles Times*, which had covered the initial story, carried a large front-page picture and story about the return, and a full page of photographs. Even the *New York Times*, although far back in the paper, carried a very tender picture of Hanna with her son in her arms while a gleeful father stood in the background. And Dr. Marcus could not resist the fairy tale quality of the moment: "The baby's fine and my wife is fine—so now we're going home and live happily ever after." For Hanna, "it was like a miracle. . . . She bounced out of bed full of pep—a new woman at the thought of seeing her baby." The newspapers had developed all the possible homey qualities of the story with its built-in drama of family courage and redemption. It was only surprising that the newspapers had dashed past their opportunity to draw a real Old Testament connection. While the *Chronicle* had a large picture of Hanna and her son in "a madonna-like embrace" on the day after the child's return, no newspaper drew the parallel with the biblical Hanna who, taunted by her female rival, had prayed fervently for a child and was, after years of desire, finally blessed with the prophet Samuel. The suspense of the local drama was over. Safely in his mother's arms, though not quite at her breast, Robert Marcus was home.[12]

◲ ‖ ◱

Betty Jean Benedicto's drama was just in midcourse. At twenty-seven, Benedicto was indeed blond and large, having grown to over two hundred pounds during the past year. She was recently married to a fifty-two-year-old Filipino man who owned a run-down hotel in Stockton in California's central valley, where he had once published a weekly Filipino newspaper. Even though she was unable to bear a child because of an earlier surgery, Betty Jean had convinced her husband that she was pregnant rather than just grown fat. In late August, she went to southern California to be near her mother when the baby was born. After telling her husband that the child was ill and needed to stay in the hospital, Betty Jean found it increasingly difficult to forestall his desire to see his son. Rather than admit her lie and desperate to show her husband a son, she decided to steal one. She had chosen the Marcus child because its name coincided with her husband's first name, Mark. The child, it seemed, was meant to be theirs. Betty Jean took good care of the baby. Her husband, "supposing himself the child's father, changed diapers, sterilized feeding equipment and was the one who usually arose for the baby's middle of the night feedings." After she returned the child, Betty Jean claimed that she had feared the loss of her husband's love and she linked the child's abduction with what she believed was her need to satisfy her husband. "How could he love me. . . . You don't have a man 'pass out cigars' and throw out his chest about being a father and then tell him he has been fooled."[13] Indeed, this desire to satisfy him, rather than her own maternal needs, probably motivated the abduction.

The newspapers played up Betty Jean's "baby hunger," often connecting her uncontrollable appetite for a child with her very size. "The need was so overwhelming that ten months ago her plump round body responded to her subconscious drive and she became 'pregnant,'" according to the *San Francisco Chronicle*. And the *Examiner* readily accepted Betty Jean's claim that she suffered from "an irresistible maternal longing" and "frustrated mother love." Betty Jean even asserted that she decided to return the child because of her sympathy for his real mother. After seeing "the picture of Hanna Marcus, little Robert's mother 'going home with her two other babies. After that . . . I couldn't keep this one.'" Claiming to have loved the child, she noted, "I was good to the baby."[14]

Whatever the nature of her feelings of mother love and guilt, the actual story of the baby's return was considerably more complicated, midwived by both the Stockton police department and a local Catholic church. On September 27, just a week after the abduction, Betty Jean Benedicto took the baby and joined her husband at a prizefight, where she was seen by Deputy Sheriff Osvaldo ("Kelly") Vanucci. His suspicions raised by what he knew about the Marcus case, including the description and sketch of the abductor, Vanucci asked Betty Jean and her husband about the child. "I looked closely at the child and decided that maybe that was not Benedicto's child." At the conclusion of the fight at 11:30 P.M., he followed the Benedictos to their apartment at the Mayford Hotel and asked for the baby's birth certificate. In fact, Betty Jean had anticipated just such a demand and had prepared a phony one from an unofficial certificate given to mothers as souvenirs by the St. Francis Hospital in Lynwood, California, near her mother's home. When Vanucci went to his office to call the hospital in order to confirm the details, Betty Jean, realizing that her story would be discredited, phoned the Marcuses and told them they could find their baby at St. Mary's Church in Stockton, where she took the child at 1:15 A.M. and turned him over to Father Alan McCoy. The priest had already been called by Dr. Marcus a few minutes before Betty Jean arrived at the door. At the church, Betty Jean "was holding the baby tightly to her breast. It was asleep and it slept all the while she was here." The Stockton police and local FBI agents then came and took Benedicto into custody. The priest took the child to St. Joseph's Hospital.[15]

After a high-speed police ride to Stockton, the Marcuses were directed by the Stockton police to St. Joseph's Hospital. It was from the nuns at St. Joseph's that Hanna Marcus finally got her now ten-day-old child back. Hanna noted, "I didn't need anyone to tell me this was my baby. . . . I recognized him immediately." He had gained eleven ounces. Betty Jean and her husband had clearly taken good care of the child; the Marcuses "bore her no rancor or animosity. . . . I am grateful that she took such good care of him and brought him back," Sanford Marcus declared. Later, during his grand jury testimony, Marcus made that clear. "Both Mrs. Marcus and I are happy that we played no part in causing her arrest. We bear her no ill will." Although the Marcuses would later receive "many letters accusing them of vindictiveness," in fact, the case was no longer theirs to resolve.[16] As a police matter, Betty Jean was subject to full legal punishment.

Almost at once, Betty Jean's drama was given additional spice when her mother, Ruth Berg of Mira Loma, California, turned against her daughter, challenging her story of mother love and exposing Betty Jean as an unruly child. Calling her a "psychopathic liar," Ruth Berg urged that her daughter "be punished for doing such a heartless, cruel thing." According to Berg, Betty Jean had been an incorrigible child, a repeat runaway who was taken to several psychiatrists. She had married at fifteen, but was without real maternal feeling, since she had deserted her own daughter (now twelve) when her husband, "'a fine man'—divorced her . . . for desertion more than 10 years ago." "My daughter did not even have a mother's affection for her own child. . . . She deserves no sympathy." While her mother questioned both her maternal feelings and her stated age, Mark Benedicto described her as "drink addicted." But the public, whose fears had dissolved when Betty Jean returned the child, were not ready to condemn her. Indeed, to some, Berg's behavior and attitude was unforgiveable, far worse than Betty Jean's. While Betty Jean appeared to be acting out of maternal need and had treated the child with care, "her mother deserts her in her hour of need." As one letter to the editor said, "Mrs. Betty Jean Benedicto deserves a break for two reasons. She took wonderful care of the little son of Doctor and Mrs. Marcus (and) her mother . . . turned against her."[17] The family drama enacted in the papers was complicated indeed, with the public willing to forgive a woman who stole a child because of maternal feelings, but unforgiving of a natural mother who turned on her own. Still, whatever Betty Jean's publicly proclaimed maternal longings, there was clearly something askew.

Betty Jean's peculiar mental state quickly became a matter for speculation and evaluation as she was arraigned on September 30, 1955, for the kidnapping of baby Robert Marcus. When a court-appointed psychiatrist pronounced her legally sane, the chief district attorney sought a grand jury indictment on kidnapping charges, which could carry a sentence of from one to twenty-five years in prison, and asked that bail be set at $100,000, a severe punishment but surely no more than (male) kidnappers could expect. However, Betty Jean, who admitted that she had taken the child, immediately proclaimed herself "sick." "I'm not a maniac but I'm sick. . . . Can't somebody please help me? I know I did wrong, but I must be sick."[18]

In the days and weeks that followed, Betty Jean Benedicto helped to fill in the contours of that description by her strange and histrionic behavior in jail. On the day of her arraignment, San Francisco observer and columnist Herb Caen had already noted that when Betty Jean lived in the city she "was widely known around the Hall of Justice as an '800' (the police radio code number for an alleged psycho)," but nothing could quite prepare the public for Betty Jean's prison antics. After plaintively screaming out her guilt at the arraignment and then collapsing, she cried hysterically in her cell and refused to be quieted. Then, just as Hanna Marcus had, Betty Jean refused to eat. "I know Mrs. [Hanna] Marcus didn't eat while the baby was gone—and if she went without eating, so can I." She also began the first of four suicide attempts and wound up in San Francisco General Hospital's psychopathic ward, where she was declared "entirely rational." She would eventually swallow several foreign objects, including mattress clips, hairpins, and glass, in her several suicide attempts. When, two weeks after her arraignment, Betty Jean's lawyers finally called for a jury to determine her sanity, she had been in hysterical collapse, having spasms, or recovering from a suicide attempt during the entire six weeks she spent in county prison awaiting her early November insanity hearing. In addition, she had eaten no solid food and was living entirely on coffee, tea, and water since her arrest. By then Herb Caen, noting that she was being represented for free by the former Dean of Santa Clara Law School, quipped that "His tales of her hallucinations are fantastic."[19] Betty Jean was acting as she believed a mother deprived of her child would behave. Caen's reaction was not to take the whole thing completely seriously. Unlike male kidnappers, even psychologically unhinged ones (especially psychologically unhinged ones), female kidnappers were not dangerous, merely nutty. They were like ordinary mothers, but with a few screws loose.

The initial court response was more serious. The court-appointed psychiatrist's conclusion, presented at her November 9 hearing, was that Betty Jean was "suffering from 'paranoid schizophrenia'—a split personality," marked by delusions. All four psychiatrists concurred in this view, which concerned only her present state and not her state of mind when she kidnapped Robert Marcus. On the stand, Benedicto claimed that she had not stolen "my baby." It had been given to her by the Virgin Mary. When asked if she might be faking, one psychiatrist, Dr. Abram E. Damsky, noted that to do so "she had to be a combination of a psychiatrist and Sarah Bernhardt." When her hearing concluded, presiding Judge John B. Molinari declared Betty Jean Benedicto insane and incapable of assisting in her own defense. He committed her to the Mendocino State Hospital in northern California, where she was to be held until she recovered sufficiently to stand trial for the kidnapping of Robert Marcus. Sanford Marcus issued a statement: "Mrs. Marcus and I are relieved that this unfortunate woman is to receive the psychiatric help she needs so desperately. We do not believe that a rational person could have committed an act of this enormity. We hope that she can be restored as a happy and useful member of society."[20] Both psychiatric and lay opinion thus concurred in the view that while mother love was laudable, too much mother hunger was a dangerous thing. Both Hanna and Betty Jean had tempted death in their travail. Each had looked to a child to save her. For Hanna, the miracle had happened. Betty Jean would have to depend on a psychiatric institution.

▣ ‖ ▣

As Betty Jean Benedicto was being transferred from her San Francisco jail to the Mendocino State Hospital, across the bay in Oakland, Burton Abbott was awaiting trial for the kidnapping and and murder of fourteen-year-old Stephanie Bryan. A jury of eleven members had already been selected, but Abbott's lawyers, trying to keep the process of jury selection going, had exhausted the first jury pool through their preemptory challenges. The long jury process anticipated what was to become "the longest and costliest trial in Alameda County history."[21]

Despite their proximity in time and place, the two abductions could not have been more different. And the newspapers, as if by some sixth sense, knew this from the beginning. While the possibilities implicit in an infant's abduction from the hospital seemed to promise a heartwrenching drama with possibly a heartwarming conclusion, thus propelling the Marcus abduction into the headlines from the start, the sleazier and more sinister possibilities lurking in Stephanie Bryan's disappearance made the initial newspaper story far more modest and retiring. In fact, the disappearance of a teenage girl presented vastly different possibilities than that of a helpless infant. The first notice of Stephanie's story received a single slim column on the first page of local papers, capped by a photograph of a sweet, reserved-looking, dark-haired young woman. The newspapers had waited the requisite day before releasing this information because the police and family, as in most such cases, were eager to stifle publicity that might discourage a private contact from the abductor. This protocol drew upon the typical ransom experience in which ransom demands, quickly made, could result in a quiet, private exchange. There was also always the strong presumption (in the absence of eyewitness accounts or ransom demands) that a teenager like Stephanie had simply run away. That was what had happened to another East Bay schoolgirl, Karen Boyington, a thirteen-year-old who had disappeared only a few weeks after Stephanie, on May 22, but was found safe and content living with a family of friendly strangers in the naval station town of Alameda.[22]

Stephanie Bryan had not been so rambunctious and would not be so lucky. At fourteen, Stephanie had been an outstanding student at the Willard Junior High School on Telegraph Avenue in Berkeley, then a quiet city that had grown up around the University of California. She was shy of strangers and well brought up. Her parents, Harvard-educated Dr. Charles S. Bryan and Radcliffe graduate Mary Bryan, insisted that she would never have accepted a ride from anyone she did not know well. She had no reason or inclination to run from the comfortable Mediterranean-style stucco home she shared with her parents, four younger siblings, two dogs, a cat, and her pet parakeet. When her mother did not come to meet her, Stephanie normally walked home from school alone or with her twelve-year-old sister, Cheryl, also a student at Willard, and she often took a short cut to her house through the grounds of the elegant old Claremont Hotel, nestled in the hillside just below her Berkeley home. In fact, that was where she was last seen at 4:00 P.M. on April 28, 1955, after she had said good-bye to an acquaintance, Mary Ann Steward, with whom she had walked from school that day. The girls had found their way to the Claremont in a leisurely walk, during which they had stopped first at the Berkeley Public Library, at a local doughnut shop, and then a pet store where Stephanie bought a book on the care of parakeets.

Stephanie's mother waited for her daughter patiently until 4:15. After Mary Bryan contacted three of her daughter's friends to find out if they knew what might have caused a delay, she kept the telephone line open in case Stephanie was trying to reach her. By the time Mary Bryan called the school the switchboard was closed. She went to the school herself but found nothing. It was a little after this that Mary Bryan contacted her husband, a radiologist at Peralta Hospital in Oakland, who called the police at 6:30 P.M. and began his own search of the immediate neighborhood and the grounds of the Claremont Hotel, a search that lasted into the night.[23] At 4:45 P.M. local police in neighboring Contra Costa County received a report of a young girl struggling with a man in an automobile on Tunnel Road, which led over the crest of the Berkeley hills to Contra Costa County, just minutes from the Claremont Hotel. Several such eyewitness reports would come in during the next day after the story was released to the public. But by May 1, three days after her disappearance, the police were still treating the case as that of "a missing person" because there was no "tangible evidence of ab-duction, such as a communication from kidnappers." Although the Bryans, like the Marcuses, had received an extortion demand for $5,000, police quickly exposed it as the work of "an opportunist," a former inmate of the Sonoma State Home for the insane. In fact, the Bryans would be the objects of two extortion attempts, neither of them taken seriously by the police.[24] The FBI had not entered the case because of the absence of evidence of in-terstate transportation or explicit threat of bodily harm. As in the Marcus case, increasing publicity brought leads from all over the Bay Area as people claimed to have seen Stephanie alive in various places.

Mrs. Bryan's brother, a colonel in the Air Force Reserve, made a private aerial search of the East Bay hills area. Then when Stephanie had been missing for a week, the police mounted an extensive search and "mailed out

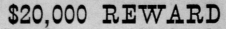
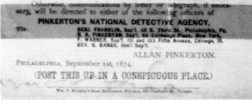

After his kidnapping in July 1874, reward posters helped to make Charley Ross famous as the "lost boy." This is a photograph of the poster I found at a small general store in Woodside, California, now a historic site. *Photograph by the author.*

Charley Ross is pictured at the age of two *(left)*, and as he would have appeared at the time of his abduction in 1874 *(right)*. Since his parents had no recent photograph, they commissioned this age-enhanced representation, which is the first of a kidnapped child. *The Historical Society of Pennsylvania (left). Courtesy Kathryn Turman (right).*

The title page to Christian Ross's story of his experience as the father of the first kidnapped child in America. Christian hoped that his memoirs, published in 1876, would help to locate his son. *The Historical Society of Pennsylvania.*

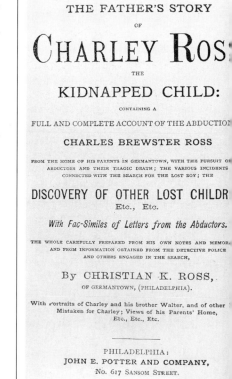

THE FATHER'S STORY

OF

CHARLEY ROS:

THE

KIDNAPPED CHILD:

CONTAINING A

FULL AND COMPLETE ACCOUNT OF THE ABDUCTION

CHARLES BREWSTER ROSS

FROM THE HOME OF HIS PARENTS IN GERMANTOWN, WITH THE PURSUIT OF
ABDUCTORS AND THEIR TRAGIC DEATH; THE VARIOUS INCIDENTS
CONNECTED WITH THE SEARCH FOR THE LOST BOY; THE

DISCOVERY OF OTHER LOST CHILDR
Etc., Etc.

With Fac-Similes of Letters from the Abductors.

THE WHOLE CAREFULLY PREPARED FROM HIS OWN NOTES AND MEMOR
AND FROM INFORMATION OBTAINED FROM THE DETECTIVE POLICE
AND OTHERS ENGAGED IN THE SEARCH,

By CHRISTIAN K. ROSS,

OF GERMANTOWN, (PHILADELPHIA).

With Portraits of Charley and his brother Walter, and of other
Mistaken for Charley; Views of his Parents' Home,
Etc., Etc., Etc.

PHILADELPHIA:
JOHN E. POTTER AND COMPANY,
No. 617 SANSOM STREET.

Part of the first recorded ransom note in American history, received by Christian Ross on July 4, 1874. It reads: "Mr. Ros—be not uneasy you son charley bruster be all writ we is got him and no powers on earth can deliver out of our hand—You wil hav two pay us befor you git him from us—an pay us a big cent to—if you put the cops hunting for him yu is only defeating yu own end—we is got him put so no living power can gits him from us a live—if any approach is maid to his hidin place that is the signil for his instant anihilation—if you regard his lif puts no. . . ." *The Historical Society of Pennsylvania.*

Flora and Jacob Franks at top attending the funeral of their son, Robert (Bobby), pictured in circle, with pallbearers and coffin at bottom. The attention paid to Bobby in the press largely evaporated after Leopold and Loeb confessed and stole the limelight. *Illustration from Maureen McKernan,* The Amazing Crime and Trial of Leopold and Loeb *(Chicago, 1924).*

Nathan Leopold, Jr. *(seated left)*, and Richard Loeb *(seated right)* with their famous lawyer, Clarence Darrow *(center)*, at the time of their hearing in July 1924. *Courtesy of Gertz Collection, Northwestern University Library, Evanston, Illinois.*

This newspaper mock-up of the heads of Loeb *(above)* and Leopold *(below)* was one of the many attempts to understand the motives of the pair. Note the emphasis on "glands" and the admixture of moral and psychological characterizations. *Copyright 1924, The Chicago Tribune Company. Reprinted with permission.*

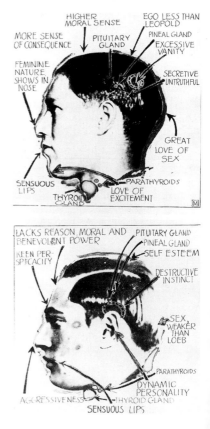

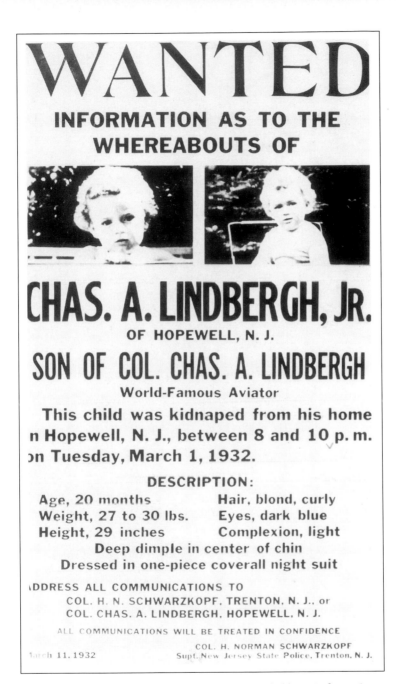

The reward poster for the Lindbergh baby provided basic information about the child and the names of the individuals to contact. Some newspapers, like the *New York Evening Journal,* placed this poster alongside that of Charley Ross (first illustration) as a reminder of that earlier shocking abduction. Although the context of the abductions and the historical periods differed, many of the themes concerning threats to the family were similar. *AP/World Wide Photos.*

Anne Morrow Lindbergh and her infant son, Charles A. Lindbergh, Jr., were pictured in many newspapers on the day after the child's kidnapping. *NYT Pictures.*

This famous photograph of Charles Lindbergh, Jr., was released by the Lindbergh family after the abduction on March 1, 1932, and appeared on the front pages of newspapers across the country as the most current photo available. *AP/World Wide Photos.*

Charles Lindbergh arriving at the courthouse in Flemington, New Jersey, to testify against Bruno Richard Hauptmann in January 1935. Many have questioned Lindbergh's ability to make an accurate voice identification after the long time lapse. *APA/Archive Photos.*

Bruno Richard Hauptmann *(seated right)* conferring with his attorney, Edward Reilly, during his trial for the kidnapping of the Lindbergh child. Hauptmann was convicted on February 13, 1935, and executed in April 1936. *The New York Times Company/Archive Photos.*

This artist's rendering was one of the many portrayals of the Lindberghs' newly built house, from which the Lindbergh child was abducted. This one appeared in the *New York Evening Journal* on March 3, 1932, and shows the location of the ladder and footprints as well as other possible clues to the kidnapping. *UPI/Corbis-Bettmann.*

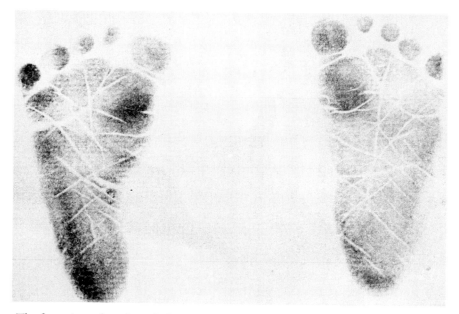

The footprints of newborn Robert Marcus appeared on the front pages of local newspapers on September 20, 1955, after the infant disappeared from a San Francisco hospital on the previous day. *UPI/Corbis-Bettmann.*

Betty Jean Benedicto, who kidnapped the Marcus baby, fit the prototype of a female abductor, an overweight woman with low self-esteem who sought to keep the child (usually an infant) as her own. *UPI/Corbis-Bettmann.*

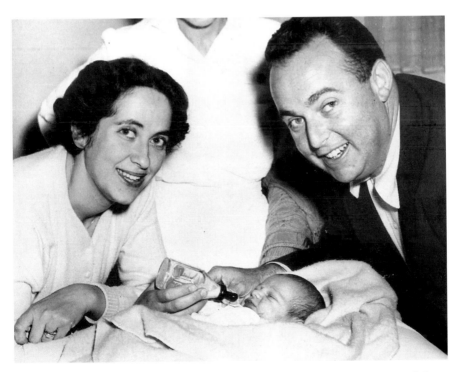

When Hanna and Sanford Marcus were reunited with their infant son it created the very picture of 1950s domestic happiness. In this photograph published on September 25, 1955, the Marcuses are the fortunate participants in a story that ends happily. *UPI/Corbis-Bettmann.*

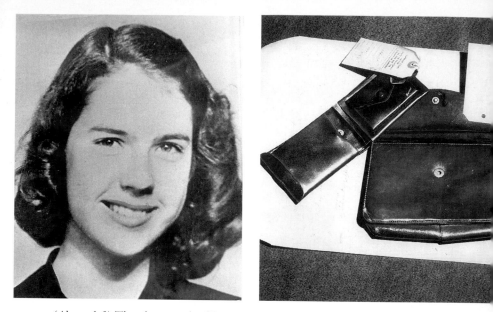

(*Above, left*) The photograph of fourteen-year-old Stephanie Bryan that appeared in San Francisco Bay area newspapers after she disappeared on her way home from school in Berkeley on April 28, 1955. *Reprinted from Keith Walker, A Trail of Corn (Santa Rosa, 1995), courtesy Oakland Tribune. (Above, right)* Stephanie Bryan's purse, wallet (here with police tags), and other personal items were found on July 15, 1955, in a box in the basement home of Burton Abbott in Alameda, California. Although Abbott disclaimed any knowledge of them, he thereafter became the prime suspect in Stephanie's abduction. *San Francisco Chronicle.*

Stephanie Bryan's gravesite near Burton Abbott's Wildwood cabin in Trinity County, California. This shoe and other clothing Stephanie wore on the day of her abduction helped to identify the body found by two local San Francisco reporters. *San Francisco Chronicle.*

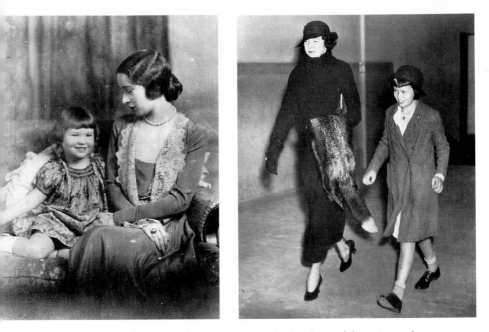

(*Above, left*) Gloria Vanderbilt at a happy moment with her beautiful young mother, Gloria Morgan Vanderbilt (Mrs. Reginald Vanderbilt). Mrs. Vanderbilt lost custody of her daughter after her sister-in-law, Gertrude Vanderbilt Whitney, seized the child and went to court to keep her in 1934. *UPI/Corbis Bettmann.* (*Above, right*) Gloria Vanderbilt at ten with her aunt, Gertrude Whitney, on their way to a New York City court during the custody hearing in November 1934. *UPI/Corbis-Bettmann.*

The custody hearing in the case of young Gloria Vanderbilt was a grueling event that created punishing publicity for Gloria Morgan Vanderbilt. She lost custody of her daughter on November 21, 1934. She is pictured here after leaving the courthouse. *Archive Photos.*

(*Above, left*) Milo Abercrombie and her two children in January 1927 after she lost custody of the children to their father, Captain Lyman K. Swenson. Milo refused to give them up and disappeared with the children. *UPI/Corbis-Bettman. (Above, right)* Jon Ramierez, pictured here with a portrait of his daughter, is one of thousands of parents who have lost their children to family abductions. The most difficult cases to resolve are those in which the child is taken out of the country. This is what happened to Ramierez's daughter. *Copyright 1994, Los Angeles Times. Reprinted by permission.*

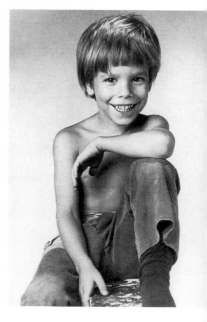

This is one of the many photos taken of Etan Patz by his father. A handsome, happy child, Etan was six when he disappeared from a Manhattan street in 1979 to become one of the first well-known victims of contemporary child abductions. The case remains open. *AP/Wide World Photos.*

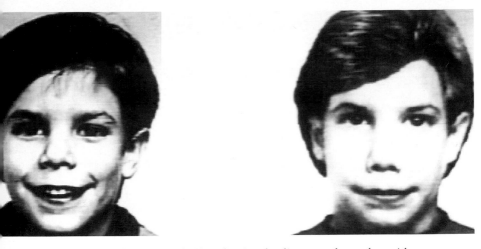

This is a photograph of Etan Patz *(left)* at the time he disappeared, together with one that has been age-progressed *(right)* so that Etan is pictured as he might have looked ten years later. The technique is used by the National Center for Missing and Exploited Children in their efforts to locate abducted children. *Courtesy National Center for Missing and Exploited Children.*

Kevin Collins disappeared in February 1984 from a San Francisco street and, like Etan Patz, was never found. Here he is depicted in an original photo *(left)* and age-progressed as he might have appeared in 1989. David Collins, Kevin's father, helped many others try to find their abducted children through the foundation he ran in Kevin's name. *Courtesy National Center for Missing and Exploited Children.*

JACOB ERWIN WETTERLING
Non-family abduction

JACOB ERWIN WETTERLING

Age progression to 13 Yr

Age Progression by NCMEC 8/91

(NATIONAL CENTER FOR)
**MISSING &
EXPLOITED
CHILDREN**
2101 Wilson Boulevard · Suite 550
Arlington, VA · 22201
(800) 843-5678 · (703) 235-3900

Missing: 10/22/89   **Age Now:** 18 Yr
Missing From: ST JOSEPHS, MN
Birth: 02/17/78   **Age Disap.:** 11 Yr
Sex: M   **Race:** WHITE
Height: 5'0"   **Weight:** 75 lbs
Hair: BROWN   **Eyes:** BLUE

Id Info: Child has a mole on his left cheek, a mole on his neck and a scar on his knee.

Circum: Child was last seen at approximately 9:00 p.m. He was with his brother and another friend when they were threatened at gunpoint by an unknown individual.

ANYONE HAVING INFORMATION SHOULD CONT
The National Center for Missing and Exploited Chil
1-800-843-5678
OR
STEARNS COUNTY SHERIFF'S OFFICE
(MINNESOTA) MISSING PERSONS UNIT
1-612-259-3700

Jacob Wetterling's abduction in October 1989 from a small Minnesota city became the occasion for an enormous community effort to find him. This poster circulated by the National Center for Missing and Exploited Children gives the basic information and an age-progressed photograph. Jacob is still missing. *Courtesy National Center for Missing and Exploited Children.*

REWARD
$200,000

KIDNAPPED

POLLY HANNAH KLAAS

Date of Birth: 1/3/81

Brown Hair & Brown Eyes

HT: 4' 10" WT: 80 Lbs

SUSPECT

White Male, 32-45 yrs, 5' 10" to 6' 3"
Thick, Wavy, Salt & Pepper Hair
Full Beard and Full Face
Slight Age Lines on
Forehead & Around Eyes

POLLY WAS LAST SEEN OCTOBER 1, 1993 IN PETALUMA, CALIFORNIA

IF YOU HAVE ANY INFORMATION, PLEASE CALL:

The Petaluma Police at 707-778-4481 or the F.B.I. at 415-553-7400

Or the Polly Klaas Search Center at 1-800-587-4357 • PO Box 800 • Petaluma, CA 94953

The City of Petaluma, California will reward any person or persons who supply information leading to the safe return of Polly Klaas in an amount not to exceed $200,000 in aggregate. The qualification of any person for the reward and the amount of reward for any person so qualifying will be determined by the City of Petaluma in its sole discretion. The total amount of all rewards given shall not exceed $200,000. This offer will expire on the safe return of Polly Klaas on its revocation by the City of Petaluma. This reward is offered in accordance with and pursuant to the laws of the State of California.

Polly Klaas's abduction from her home in Petaluma, California, in October 1993 created a national sensation. This reward poster includes an artist's rendering of the man who intruded into a sleep-over party to take the twelve-year-old girl. Richard Allen Davis was convicted of Polly's kidnapping and murder on June 18, 1996, and awaits execution. *Courtesy Polly Klaas Foundation.*

The media loves beautiful children. This photograph of Polly Klaas suggests the appeal. *Courtesy Polly Klaas Foundation.*

5000 circulars to law enforcment agencies throughout eleven Western States." By this point, eight witnesses had reported the struggle on Tunnel Road to police. One woman noted that as she passed, she heard a "loud, horrible scream." She had reported it immediately to police when she arrived home in Walnut Creek, but by the time the police went to the scene, they found nothing. Most of these reports concurred in identifying the car as a gray-green or light blue 1949 to 51 Pontiac or Chevrolet sedan. By the fifth of May, local television stations were broadcasting Bryan home movies in the hope that someone could identify Stephanie and assist in locating her. The story, which had largely been confined to the inside columns of the local papers, was gradually emerging as front-page news. Then, two weeks after her disappearance, Stephanie Bryan was finally in the headlines as a massive hunt by 800 searchers, including the National Guard, scoured the brush of the East Bay hills. It was to be the first of many such headlines for the shy Berkeley girl. With the massive searches, the FBI had finally joined the local police, who also conducted house-to-house searches in Contra Costa County in hopes of finding someone who had seen Stephanie. As searches continued, they included contingents of local boy scouts. Stephanie was still being spotted in various locations, in one case as far away as Fall River, Massachusetts, but gradually the searches were suspended since they had yielded no clues. In mid May, Stephanie's father told the police that he was not interested in prosecuting anyone and would "take Stephanie back any way I can get her." He offered a $2,500 reward, saying he was still hopeful that she might be alive, but that "it is impossible to believe that she may be a runaway. . . . She is not that type of girl." New circulars were printed in red and white to advertise the reward, and prayer vigils were held for pretty, shy Stephanie all over the area.[25]

Stephanie Bryan began to receive banner headlines in mid July, when serious clues turned up in the house of Burton W. ("Bud") Abbott in the naval base city of Alameda, fifteen minutes from Berkeley. A twenty-seven-year-old accounting student at the University of California on the G. I. bill, Abbott had become one of the last to qualify when he began his army service just before those benefits were due to expire. The father of a four-year-old son, Abbott was married to an attractive red-haired woman, six years older than he, who worked in a beauty shop in Alameda. Slight, frail, bespectacled, and with a pencil-thin mustache, Abbott had lost a lung and several ribs to tuberculosis in 1951.[26]

Georgia Abbott, Burton's wife, found Stephanie's belongings in the basement of their home on July 15 when she went searching for a costume to
wear to an amateur theatrical. In one box she found a lady's red leather
purse, which contained a wallet with an identification card for Stephanie
Bryan, as well as photographs, a junior Red Cross Card, an unfinished letter to a Massachusetts friend, and several other minor but clearly identifiable personal objects. Recognizing the name as that of the missing Berkeley
girl, Georgia was excited by her find and ran to tell her husband, who was
preparing dinner for a family friend, Otto William Dezman, and Abbott's
mother, Elsie. Abbott claimed not to recognize the name, but Dezman
urged him to notify the police. When the police searched the basement, they
found other articles belonging to Stephanie buried in the dirt floor of the
basement, including her library books, notebooks, eyeglasses, and brassiere.
The objects were quickly identified by Stephanie's parents. Berkeley's police inspector, Charles O'Meara, described the circumstances surrounding
this incident as "weird."[27]

Burton Abbott immediately disclaimed any knowledge of the articles
and noted that his basement had recently served as a polling place. Access to
the basement, Abbott noted, was available through an unlocked garage
door. Abbott and his wife were questioned by police, who also observed that
he owned a 1949 gray Chevrolet, a car "rather close" to the one reported in
the Tunnel Road incident. The Abbotts had also owned, but recently sold,
another car, a 1950 Pontiac. Berkeley police called in Professor Paul Kirk, a
criminologist from the University of California known for his scientific mi-
croscopic studies that often helped to uncover minute clues.[28]

Burton Abbott hired an attorney, Stanley D. Whitney, when he became
the subject of intense police questioning. Throughout his interrogation, he
stayed close to his story that he was not in Berkeley or the Bay Area on the
afternoon of April 28 when Stephanie disappeared or during the succeed-
ing weekend. Instead, he had left that day at 11:00 A.M. on his way to a fam-
ily-owned cabin at Wildwood in the Trinity Alps, a rough and remote
mountain area a considerable distance away, where he went for the opening
of the fishing season. At 2:30 P.M., he stopped in Sacramento to inquire at a
land office on his brother's behalf and reached his cabin at 8:30 P.M. Police
acknowledged that his story checked out for April 29 and 30, "But as to
April 28—the key date—we're still not satisfied." Because the police were

unconvinced, Abbott agreed to take the first of two lie detector tests administered by Paul Kelly, a professor of criminal psychology at Berkeley, and A. E. Riedel, a Berkeley police inspector and a well-regarded polygraph authority. Indeed, Abbott was soon pictured in the papers hooked up to the polygraph, the results of which were described as inconclusive.[29]

While Abbott was being questioned, a crowd of 500 gathered outside his home as police completed additional digging in the basement. The story had become a big news item. From the time her purse was found in Abbott's basement and for the next half year, Stephanie's story was rarely absent from the front pages of local newspapers and dominated their headlines. The papers were now filled with photos of Abbott's pretty, slender, red-haired wife, the "pitiful clews" about Stephanie, and pictures of Abbott, his cars, his home, his basement, his cabin, and maps of the region. The case of the missing girl had become a "mystery," peppered with physical clues and a weird, unsettling suspect, hardly threatening in any conventional sense but slightly creepy nevertheless. In 1955, the case of Caryl Chessman, who had been convicted of kidnapping and raping two girls (one of whom went insane), was still very fresh in the public's mind, especially in California where Chessman was on death row. Chessman appeared to have rehabilitated himself in prison and became an author, eliciting widespread sympathy from Americans opposed to the death penalty—a hot issue at the time in California and elsewhere. The disappearance of a young girl had all along resonated with the Chessman case. While Burton Abbott claimed, "I don't know anything about it [Stephanie's abduction] because I never read crime news in the papers. . . . Articles about crime just don't interest me at all," the possibilities presented by the conjuncture of the frail, weirdly composed suspect and the shy schoolgirl made the crime compelling reading throughout the Bay Area.[30]

The Berkeley police and the FBI had checked Abbott's cabin and found nothing incriminating, but the lure of the mystery and the possibilities of sensational news had provoked a *San Francisco Examiner* reporter, Ed Montgomery, and an *Examiner* photographer, Bob Bryant, to try again. On July 20, they hired two Trinity County ranchers and a pair of bloodhounds to check out the cabin. That evening they uncovered the grisly remains of Stephanie's corpse, still clothed in the aqua pleated skirt, white pullover, blue sweater, and saddle shoes in which she had disappeared. The sweaters were hiked up around her shoulders like a cape and her underpants were tied around her neck as a garrote. Stephanie's brassiere was missing. Although her body had been attacked by animals and been long in the ground, the Bryan family dentist made a definitive identification of the fourteen-year-old girl. She had been buried on a steep, thickly wooded area, 350 yards from Abbott's cabin. While Abbott proclaimed that "I don't know how the body got there. . . . I'm staying with my story. It just can't be," the police arrested him for Stephanie Bryan's kidnap and murder. Stephanie's father expressed the wish that Abbott be "turned over to me . . . I'd take care of him." While he apologized for his bitter outburst, he could not restrain further comment, with its implied reference to the Chessman case, on the nature of contemporary justice. "I'll wager you right now that he never goes to the gas chamber. The only question in my mind now is how soon they'll turn the sob sisters loose and get him off."[31]

Bryan was not alone in his concerns. Correspondents to local newspapers also bemoaned inadequate criminal punishments in the American justice system. Recalling the contemporary sympathy for Chessman and the calls for his release, one newspaper correspondent noted, "I suppose, and I am afraid, that he [Abbott] will be free in a short time and will appear on TV on the program 'This Is Your Life.'" Another asked, "Why aren't stiffer penalties imposed on all these crazed sex murderers? . . . Why can't something be done? We don't dare let our children outside the house. . . . Can't the government step in and pass a law making child molesting good for thirty years instead of thirty days and the death penalty mandatory on these sex criminals? Something must be done." "Has Stephanie Bryan died in vain, or will the tragedy of her young girl's life finally shock our society into a correction of its judiciary system? . . . Even animals do not attack their young—and if they become mad, we kill them." These questions would remain very much in the public mind throughout Stephanie's story and for the next forty years. The Bryan case had clearly become more than the sad story of an abducted schoolgirl. The case began to reverberate with issues of appropriate criminal penalties as well as with an unbounded sexual danger that seemed to haunt the seemingly placid 1950s.[32] As it happened, both Dr. Bryan and the correspondent who worried about Abbott's television debut were wrong. Abbott and Chessman would both be executed for their attacks on young girls.

ⓟ|Ⅴⓖ

Stephanie's body, badly decomposed and incomplete, could not be made to yield any evidence of sexual abuse. But the presumed motives for the abduction as well as some of the clothing evidence suggested that this kidnapping, like those committed by Chessman, were sexually driven. It was always unclear how the frail, tubercular Abbott could have gotten "well-reared Stephanie" into the car and how he could have brought her up the steep hillside, although Erle Stanley Gardner (of Perry Mason fame), who was hired by the *San Francisco Examiner* to write a long series of commentaries during the trial, speculated that she was dragged by the underpants Abbott had knotted around her neck. It was hardly ever doubted that Abbott had gotten some sexual pleasure from the encounter. The day Abbott was arrested, Stephanie's father told the newspapers that his studies had convinced him that "sexual psychopaths are beyond the reach of medical help." At one point, the University of California psychiatrist who initially examined Abbott told the newspapers that Abbott might have a "sadistic sex urge" in which "satisfaction came with killing." And District Attorney J. Frank Coakley suggested in his concluding remarks, among other things, that Burton Abbott had fetishized the objects in his basement. Coakley was emphatic that Abbott was a sexual pervert, and in his summation to the jury, he stressed that Stephanie's underpants had been slashed. "Those things happen only in murders committed by sex maniacs, by perverts and by psychopathic personalities." He also told the jury that the day Stephanie was killed, Abbott "had perhaps the greatest sexual satisfaction of his life." The precise nature of Abbott's sexual depredation was left murky, however. All the things alluded to, in addition to more conventional penetration of the body—dead or alive—were conceivable. It was, of course, the multiple possibilities that made the case so sinister and horrifying. "Are you going to set him free to sing again his siren song of sex?" Coakley asked the jury, painting sexual desire of all kinds as potentially socially dangerous. Not surprisingly, when Abbott was arrested, his wife immediately tried to put the sexual speculations to rest by stating, "Since his lung operation five years ago, he has not been highly sexed." In raising the specter of the range of human sexual appetites, Abbott's very frailty was an additional element since his passion had evidently allowed him to overcome his physical weakness, turning him into a veritable monster. The jury foreman called him "a mad dog" who had "to be put away." "I have no more compunction stepping on him than I would on stepping on the head of a rattlesnake."[33]

The aura of corrupt and unbounded sexuality that clung to the Abbott case is both curious and significant, not only because there was never any physical evidence of abuse, but because the prosecution never presented a motive for the abduction and the killing during the trial testimony and no evidence was ever presented concerning Abbott's state of mind or his psychosexual proclivities. Indeed, although the trial dominated the newspapers for weeks, most of the news was quite tame and much of it was boring. Even Gardner had a hard time milking the proceedings for much more than a thin thrill. If the newspapers had expected fireworks, they had to wait until the final days, when the innuendos that hovered over the case exploded in Coakley's summation for the jury.

In addition, although four psychiatrists were called during Betty Jean Benedicto's sanity hearing, none was ever called during the very long trial of Burton Abbott. The Abbott case was prosecuted on the basis of (very strong) circumstantial evidence, which included microfiber evidence presented by Dr. Kirk (a star witness) placing Stephanie in Abbott's car; Abbott's flawed alibi for April 28; and the fact that Stephanie's belongings were found at Abbott's house, while her body was buried near his cabin. During the forty-seven days of the trial, the prosecution called seventy-six witnesses, some of whom testified that they saw Abbott in Berkeley on the afternoon of Stephanie's disappearance (rebutted by defense witnesses who placed him in Trinity County or along the route to his cabin). But they never put Dr. Douglas M. Kelly on the stand, the University of California psychiatrist who had examined Abbott when he was first questioned.[34]

Like the beliefs concerning Abbott's sexual proclivities, most of the psychology surrounding the case was intense and vague. Kelly had told the newspapers after his first interview with Abbott on July 19 that Abbott was "legally sane, and he is not psychotic." After Stephanie's body was found near Abbott's cabin, family members claimed that he was "too meek and gentle by nature" to have committed such a crime, but Kelly concluded that "his is an infantile personality. This sort of act is compatible with this type of personality." Later, Kelly surmised that Abbott had remained in a juvenile state emotionally, always supported by sturdy females. "Such persons are characterized by immaturity and constant demands on other people. In effect his mother has never left him and his wife acted much as a second mother." District Attorney Coakley's summation called Abbott both "cunning" and "crafty" and described him as "a juvenile emotionally," suggesting a kind of psychological profile or syndrome where infantile emotions resulted in an inflated sense of self. It was clearly also part of Kelly's evaluation that Abbott had an inflated ego that made him "feel superior to all the persons with whom he came into contact." As part of its profile of Abbott, the prosecution also suggested that Abbott's unfailingly polite, cool, and unruffled demeanor on the stand during three days of heavy cross-examination and his ability to laugh off the evidence was a sign of his "disordered personality," but no clinical evidence was ever presented concerning either this supposed syndrome or of his condition as a sexual psychopath. The closest the prosecution ever came to psychological testimony was when Albert E. Riedel of the Berkeley police (who had administered the polygraph) described Abbott's response to Dr. Kelly when the latter provided Abbott with a detailed description of the corpse. "The purpose was to make the defendant realize the seriousness of the situation and stop him from laughing and making jokes about it."[35]

The most balanced and up-to-date study of sexual offenders published just after the Abbott trial would have supported the portrait of Abbott that the state had planted in the public mind since it concluded that most serious sex offenders were "sexually inhibited and constricted rather than over-impulsive and over-sexual individuals. . . . Ninety-one percent . . . proved to be distinctly emotionally immature." Why then did the prosecution fail to make Abbott's psychology an issue in the case or at least a specific part of the indictment of his motivation? Since Abbott always maintained his innocence, it was hardly a question of the prosecution presenting evidence that would open up the possibility of some kind of insanity defense. Rather the state must have felt that, given the absence of hard evidence of Stephanie's sexual violation, the vague psychologizing in which it was engaged was a more effective weapon than hard clinical evidence, which might have been open to defense refutation or to their own expert witnesses. Indeed, most of the psychological materials then available on the sexual psychopath were vague and often clinically unsubstantiated.[36] Thus, the prosecution used psychology to influence the public and the jury's vision of Abbott, but was reluctant to make the case hinge on this. It is tempting to speculate about the possibilities if Abbott had confessed or pled insanity, when these vague

bits might have cohered into a portrait of a man ravaged by emotional disease (as in the case of Leopold and Loeb). Instead, Abbott's firm stance left a
portrait of psychological menace and directed the case into other channels,
especially those concerned with criminal justice and the death penalty.
Nevertheless, and perhaps because of its vagueness, the public was encouraged to psychological speculations.

Stephanie's family had certainly concluded that Abbott was a psychopath, just as they were completely convinced "that Abbott [was] the
man who killed" their daughter. Charles Bryan noted, "From what I have
read . . . he doesn't seem to worry. He just sits in his cell and plays cards,
and jokes with his fellow prisoners and always has a smile on his face."
Bryan shrewdly concluded that this was also "why some people wonder if
he is guilty." But making psychological judgments like this was tricky. If a
controlled and cool demeanor in the face of severe adversity was evidence
of mental disturbance or illness, Bryan might have looked carefully at his
own Radcliffe-educated wife. Mary Bryan had remained publicly completely composed during the entire ordeal, so much so as to elicit comment
from the press. She even volunteered to testify before the grand jury in
order to spare her husband, who was more prone to emotional outbursts.
She had shown no emotion when discussing the case with journalists and,
more strikingly, when called as a witness to identify items from a box full
of Stephanie's clothing found in Abbott's basement and on her decomposed
body, clothing whose stench sent others fleeing from the courtroom—a
truly gruesome task. In fact, Mary Bryan's composure stood in marked
contrast to the frequent outbursts of emotional exclamation and sobbing
from Burton Abbott's mother, Elsie. Mary Bryan's emotions came to the
surface publicly only when the trial was over, and then only momentarily,
when Abbott had been convicted and she felt justice had been done. As the
San Francisco Examiner reporters who interviewed the Bryans on the day of
the verdict observed: "Her voice trembled with emotion, the first she has
shown openly since her daughter's disappearance. . . . But even as her anguish escaped in a sentence 'Now we can have Steffie back,' [because they
could now claim the body]—Mrs. Bryan was regaining her self control." In
this Mary was also like Burton Abbott, who at the moment when his verdict was announced (after six days of jury deliberations) "could not quite
mask his emotions. . . . He bowed his head and bit his lower lip, fighting to
maintain the almost impregnable shell of calm that he displayed during the

fifty-five days of trial."[37] Whether victim or victimizer, the emphasis on public composure was hardly an effective diagnostic tool.

Despite its loose contours, the psychopathology of the case, like the sexual danger it implied, was clear. The case's power as a public lesson, one that would continue to haunt the region and community for the next several decades, depended on an aura of psychological menace and sexual perversion. It hung around from the moment Abbott appeared on the scene and probably showed even earlier, as Stephanie's disappearance stretched from days into weeks in a California recently saturated by the debates over justice for Caryl Chessman. When Abbott was arrested, Dr. Bryan noted that, while there were 1,200 registered sex offenders in the local area, "There are perhaps tens of thousand in the Bay Area who could have been capable of this thing." It was impossible to protect children from such a menace. Of Stephanie, he observed, "No child could have been better taken care of or better *warned.*" Indeed, that generalized orientation to psychological explanations (whether they stood up in court or not) and the fears of a lurking dangerous sexuality were very much part of the 1950s environment that nurtured the story of Stephanie Bryan. Abbott gave them a reason to come boldly forth from imagination to reality. Not surprisingly, it was in 1956 that Meyer Levin dredged out the Leopold and Loeb case from his own memory and fictionalized it as *Compulsion.* In Levin's story, a Freudian framework encased a story of sexual desire. Abbott was tried and convicted on two counts: murder and kidnapping with bodily harm (a capital offense under California's "Little Lindbergh" law), neither of which involved sexual crime. Nevertheless, the community assumed that Stephanie's disappearance and death was "sex-inspired" and that Burton Abbott was a "mad dog."[38]

ｐ√ｇ

It is intriguing but largely coincidental that the San Francisco Bay Area in 1955 should have been witness to two such distinct and disparate experiences of child abduction as the cases of Robert Marcus and Stephanie Bryan. Apart from indicating the new forms of child abduction that pushed to the forefront of public attention beginning in the 1950s—as well as providing an eerie anticipation of more recent Bay Area kidnappings, the abduction and return of Baby Kerri (1992), and the kidnap-murder of Polly Klaas

(1993)—the significance of that coincidence is in how these local stories were implicated in larger historical and cultural patterns. While the cases confirm certain aspects of 1950s' culture with which we are quite familiar, they also provide unexpected twists to our historical expectations about the period.

In both cases, the families of the victims expressed complete confidence and satisfaction with the local police. Indeed, the extraordinary commitment demonstrated by the San Francisco police to finding the child of a reputable, but hardly renowned, citizen is notable. And Dr. Marcus was unstinting in his appreciation and praise. "Only in America could it happen that everyone is so concerned and, at the same time, so considerate," he observed in a typical expression of the kind of ethnic gratitude that was very much part of the period's self-identity. "I have nothing but praise for the police and the job they have done." Indeed, letters to the editor also expressed the general good faith in the police. "Maybe now some other mothers can rest a little bit easier, as their babies sleep in their cribs, or their brothers and sisters go off to school, knowing that a man like Deputy Sheriff Vanucci is looking out for them." The Marcuses, in their justified delight, also thanked the newspapers.[39]

Stephanie Bryan's parents had less reason for gladness, but they were satisfied with the outcome, Abbott's conviction, and Mrs. Bryan went out of her way to remark on the hard work of the police and law enforcement. "I am particularly relieved that the hard work of so many sincere people in the Berkeley Police Department, the District Attorney's office, and the FBI have been justified. They are the finest group of gentlemen ever assembled." The uniform satisfaction with police behavior clearly sets these 1950s experiences apart from the complaints of victims in the more recent past and the far less satisfactory behavior of the police in many of the earlier cases. And it is notable that while so many at the time questioned the nature of the laws and the justice system, either because they rejected capital punishment or believed it was too infrequently imposed, there was very little complaint about the role of the police or their behavior. The support for local police seemed generally widespread and certainly a mark of the kind of respect for community authority with which the period is often identified. This attitude was amplified by Erle Stanley Gardner, who used his series on the Abbott case to emphasize that "The big problem presented by the Stephanie Bryan case is the problem of policing our community ... of making our streets safe for the young girls who must walk along the sidewalks each day." Gardner did not challenge police authority or question police tactics; rather he asked for more cooperation "with our police so that we can have a better system of police protection." He urged a return to more cops on the beat, policemen known to and knowledgeable about their communities—the local kids' best friend.[40]

The 1950s quality of trust in established institutions like the police is also obvious in the gendered expectations and descriptions that clung to these cases like the scent of musk. Georgia Abbott was always slim, attractive, and red haired; Betty Jean Benedicto, a blowsy blond. In fact, Benedicto was at one point outraged that she should always be described by her physical characteristics. "I really don't want my picture taken. . . . I don't want to be called a blowsy, blubbery blond." But she was quite happy to have her picture taken after her stay in the Mendocino home when she was trim, well-kempt, and attractive. Beyond description was the extraordinary gendering of approved behaviors and of motives evident in both cases. Hanna Marcus's collapse, complicated by her traumatic personal history, was perhaps less notable than her miraculous recovery in the presence of her children. And Betty Jean's hunger strike and hysteria were stunning evidence of how much a child could mean to a woman's identity. Newspaper correspondents repeatedly pleaded for mercy for Betty Jean because she had been either kind and motherly to baby Robert or the victim of her own mother's emotional abandonment. And Judge Molinari ("normally a stern judge") in rendering judgment observed, "The instinct of wanting a child was natural and commendable. She treated the child well; there was no element of ransom."[41] Indeed, her motherly desires and her nurturant behavior toward the child could almost excuse her behavior, since the desire for children seemed to result in a kind of mania that clouded the mind. Certainly that was true for a real mother like Hanna.

Burton Abbott's implied mania was, of course, the opposite of this, since his predatory sexuality led to violence and death. It was this vague but sinister gendered sexuality, rather than clear psychological theory, that provided the basis for Abbott's conviction and the public revulsion against him. That this violent sexuality existed beneath a meek, frail, and hardly conventional masculine exterior probably made the portrait of perversity more convincing. Thus, when Abbott took the stand in his own defense and faced a grueling cross-examination, the *San Francisco Chronicle* observed that "The microphone underscored his pleasant even voice's lack of vitality and his prim, almost female quality of speech."[42] Just as Betty Jean's blowsy and sloppy blondness troubled her feminity, Burton Abbott's slight stature and the lack of overt aggression (as well as the absence of one lung) troubled his masculinity. Indeed, when he was arrested, Georgia had noted that he was undersexed since his lung operation. But where Betty Jean's underrefined but eager femaleness resulted in mother hunger, Abbott's reduced masculinity, his male inadequacy, led to sexual perversion. Both abductors were presented as examples of troubled gender categories, and these skewed representations were assumed to have negative social as well as psychological consequences.

As a gendered representation, fourteen-year-old, shy Stephanie Bryan was the ideal victim, a retiring, innocent female, just awakening to sexuality. Throughout the case, participants like the police, members of the jury, and witnesses noted that they had "daughters" who needed protection against the danger Abbott represented. And while the rapist presented a real threat (young teenage girls are still today the most vulnerable to abduction and sexual assault), there was more than a hint here that the sexual danger was as much from Stephanie's nascent sexuality as from external aggression. In the 1950s, sex was both pervasive and deeply threatening—an obvious explanation for a crime of this kind but more than what it seemed on the surface.

The period's concern with lawfulness, gender, and sexual order were nicely represented in the public portrayals of these cases. Far less congruent with our clichéd picture of the 1950s was the extremely interesting ethnic mix in the Marcus case. Here was a story that featured immigrants from across two oceans, and Jews and Catholics to boot, treated in sympathetic and humane ways. Hanna Marcus, a Jewish refugee with her circumcised son, elicited an ecumenical sympathy as well as interfaith prayers, and she received her child back from two Roman Catholic nuns. That Betty Jean Benedicto was married to a Filipino hardly provoked special comment let alone condemnation. Far more interesting to the press was Mark Benedicto's paternal devotion to "his son" and his obvious helplessness vis-à-vis his looney wife. In fact, the ethnic portrait in the case was further enriched by the obvious professionalism and civic-mindedness of Stockton's Lieutenant Vanucci and the concern and sympathy of Judge Molinari, not immigrants to be sure, but ethnic nevertheless. All this called up the rich cosmopolitanism not just of the city of San Francisco but of the entire northern California region. When Sanford Marcus was subsequently elected president of Congregation Judea in San Francisco, this was considered a newsworthy expression of civic responsibility.[43] Indeed, the Marcus case suggested the deepest kind of comfort with San Francisco's multiethnic and multiracial society, a comfort we hardly associate with the Ozzie and Harriet portraits of the period.

From the perspective of the history of kidnapping, it is also significant that while neither the Marcus nor the Abbott cases involved ransoms, the public in the 1950s still sufficiently associated child abduction with ransom demands to invite at least three extortion attempts in these two cases. The continuing connection in the 1950s between child theft and extortion even led Judge Molinari to commend Betty Jean on the absence of this motive in her behavior, thus lessening the blackness of her deed. In the Bryan case, the local police as well as the FBI were looking for a ransom demand in order to declare Stephanie an abduction victim. It took them some time to shift gears and to consider other motives. The 1950s thus provided a period of transition, as the ransoming of children gave way to far different and socially more potent (because less easily negotiable) fears. The Leopold and Loeb case had already anticipated a new criminal genre of kidnapping (where the motives were dank and obscure), but that crime had been enclosed in the form of a ransom kidnap. The Marcus and Bryan cases, while certainly not the first of their types or unique, opened up the closet of community fears about child abduction. Haunted not by potential extortion, such fears in the 1950s became more democratically inclusive in their potential victims while they revealed new nooks and crannies for the sociopathic personality.

Neither the public's appraisal of Betty Jean's psychological condition nor her imprisonment were harsh. Despite the havoc women who steal babies cause to the parents of the children they steal, they have hardly been portrayed as a threat to society. Since their motives are viewed as benign and an extension of maternity, the fate of the children they abduct rarely elicits either the society's deepest vengance or their worst fears.

Other kinds of kidnap fears did result in reinvigorated calls for stronger punishments. While the punishment in the family-healing Marcus case was merciful, Stephanie Bryan's abduction and murder brought loud cries for stiffer prison sentences and more frequent and clear application of the death penalty, especially for perpetrators of crimes the public found both titillating and horrifying. Indeed, the more that was left to the imagination in these crimes, the more anxious Americans became to impose harsher and harsher sentences, as if the punishment with its definitive severity could squash the ambiguous, nightmarish imaginings. Certainly the Bryans can be forgiven for seeking an end to their own nightmare in Abbott's death. But this response was more general. Anticipating more recent experience, Stephanie Bryan's case revealed the public's immense need for clear, punitive retribution. It was as if Abbott's deed was so infinite in its possibilities and so deep in the darkest corners of the human mind that only his complete extirpation could rid society of the truths about the human condition and psyche to which it testified. Capturing the special odiousness and lack of clear boundaries of the crime, Gardner noted that if, indeed, "Abbott is guilty, he is guilty of a diabolical crime."[44]

Despite the apparent desire on the part of many to impose maximum penalties on kidnappers, both the Marcus and Bryan cases produced public sympathy for the accused. There had always been a streak of gruesome malice in the public's response to the families of kidnap victims—crank letters, crank calls, and cruel hoaxes, as well as unfair accusations. Certainly this was true for the Ross family, and there was always an undercurrent of resentment in the coverage of the Lindbergh case that, as we have seen, finally affected Charles Lindbergh's reputation. In the Marcus and Bryan cases, these hoaxes continued even as the defense of the accused became more vocal. Indeed, both of these cases conspicuously brought public outcry against the unfair treatment of kidnappers. Dr. Marcus received letters accusing him of vindictiveness toward Betty Jean Benedicto, and Abbott was frequently portrayed as unjustly accused and convicted. "How in the name of justice could the jury accept the flimsy evidence presented? ... Law is one thing, justice another," one local correspondent noted about the Abbott trial. Whether the Chessman case had prepared Californians to come to the defense of the accused or the Hauptmann spectacle had raised questions about publicity-prone trials or the times were more conducive to open expressions of disagreement with authority than has usually been suggested is not clear. Public opinion was far less uniform about Benedicto and Abbott than the enormity of their crimes might lead one to expect, and each had her and his defenders.

In the Bryan case, some loudly protested the fact that Abbott was steamrollered by the press. The outcry was sufficient to stimulate an investigation by a Berkeley journalism student who completed her masters thesis shortly after the case. Grace Curtis articulated many of the common concerns about whether a jury could remain immune to the press innundation that accompanied a sensational trial such as Abbott's. "The atmosphere of the Abbott trial, created by publicity and the presence of thirty or more newsmen in the courtroom, was one of drama and excitement. It was not the calm, dispassionate atmosphere which ought to surround a court of law." "A bevy of photographers, rather than a quiet dignified front section of the courtroom, often confronted the defendant when he entered the room." At one point, the judge even warned the jury not to read the papers after a juror was seen glancing at the headlines. Curtis calculated that over thirty thousand column inches had been given over to the case in the three largest Bay Area newspapers, and from November to February, during the trial and sentencing period, the story had either headlines or banner headlines in each of these three papers in seventy-seven out of ninety-three days. And these papers were sold out as soon as they arrived in other northern California locations.[45] The Hauptmann trial twenty years earlier had made Americans aware of potential media abuses, and Curtis, among others, was alert to them in this context.

But the press overkill may have created dissension rather than consensus. By getting people involved in the case and with its protagonists in a seemingly intimate way and on such a daily basis, the overwrought press attention may have made it possible for some readers, at least, to reidentify the victim in these cases. Ever since at least the days of Leopold and Loeb, the media had been striving for popular engagement. During the Abbott trial, Erle Stanley Gardner's long series presented readers with various hypotheses, motives, and scenarios, many of which involved Abbott's innocence and the possibility that he was framed. Self-conscious about accusations that the press manipulated readers' sentiments, Gardner claimed in his very first installment that he was aiming to educate, not indoctrinate, his readers. "You folks will understand that while we don't want to 'try this case in the newspapers,' we DO want to give you the facts and the benefit of any conclusion we may reach just so everything is presented fairly." Similarly, the competing San Francisco newspaper, the *Chronicle*, announced that it hoped to provide a "balanced" summary of the evidence and asked in a prominent headline, "You Are Abbott Juror:

How Would You Decide?" The papers were making the trial of Burton Abbott into a riddle and posing it as a mystery as good as fiction. In mystery fiction the reader actively participates in the story,[46] and so the local newspaper readers were openly encouraged to become in the course of these extremely overexposed stories. Whether such "active" reading and reconstruction actually freed readers from their sources is an open question. But the Bryan case anticipated the complex and tangled fallout of media-hyped cases like that of O. J. Simpson, where readers, listeners, or viewers participate in the case and are not just receptors of media views and opinions. In this as in so many other matters, the kidnappings of Robert Marcus and Stephanie Bryan link the 1950s firmly to the present, providing us with a means to rescue not just the cases from the obscurity of an exclusively local interest, but the period from the far more brutal obscurity of nostalgia.

VI

It would be wrong to leave Betty Jean Benedicto and Burton Abbott in the special obscurity imposed by a broadened historical focus. In fact, their histories continued.

Betty Jean Benedicto was sent to the Mendocino State Hospital in Ukiah on November 11, 1955, where she was soon diagnosed as sane. One month later, on December 12, a much slimmer Betty Jean appeared in court, where she pleaded "not guilty by reason of insanity." The district attorney noted acidly that "Everything she did after she surrendered the baby was an act—her suicide attempts, her hysteria." Reconsidering her plea, Betty Jean waved her right to a jury trial and threw herself "on the mercy of the court" to ask for probation. Judge Molinari said, "My objective will be to satisfy the tensions that have been built up in the community and to fit the punishment to the offender." Betty Jean went back to San Francisco county jail to await her sentencing. On April 12, Judge Molinari sentenced Betty Jean to five years probation, with one year to be spent in county jail. Molinari concluded that she needed to spend time in jail because, though not "medically or legally insane," Betty Jean was "emotionally unstable." "During the period she has been confined thus far she has become a changed person. The benefits of her incarceration are obvious." Molinari concluded, "She must be reeducated. . . . She must be taught not to yield to her feelings."[47]

Two weeks later Betty Jean applied for the reward posted for the safe return of the Marcus child (which she did not get). And just two months after her sentencing, she tried to have her sentence commuted to time served. After serving a little more than eight months of her sentence, Betty Jean Benedicto was released from prison on the day before Christmas and "sent home to her husband in Stockton." Now "tawny-haired" and "forty pounds thinner," she was prepared to lead a "good full life, making her peace," according to the *San Francisco Chronicle*, "both with life and her own emotions." Judge Molinari told her, "I believe in you . . . I want you to forget this unhappy incident and rehabilitate yourself completely." Betty Jean responded in the spirit of the season, "I greatly need forgiveness and I shall ask for it at midnight Mass tonight." She looked to the future where she would try to be "a good wife to my good husband."[48]

Three months later, Mark Benedicto sued Betty Jean for divorce after she deserted him. In September 1957, nine months after her release, a bench warrant was issued for her arrest because Benedicto failed to report to her probation officer. Betty Jean Benedicto could not be located. But when a baby disappeared from a Brooklyn (New York) hospital in early 1959, the suspect was reportedly someone who looked like Betty Jean, which was not surprising since the profile of the infant abductor compiled by law enforcement was of an "overweight" woman who "suffers from low self esteem."[49]

In the fall of 1961, Francesca Uganza was accused of stabbing her common-law husband in Seattle. When she was booked and fingerprinted, Francesca Uganza turned out to be Betty Jean Benedicto. By then she had regained her weight and was described as weighing two hundred pounds. Agreeing to return to California for parole violation, she was quoted as saying "the only thing that bothers me . . . is facing those people there who were so good to me." In February 1962, Benedicto was back in San Francisco country jail. Described by her public defender as "a good girl," Benedicto got ninety days in county jail and one year on probation to complete her sentence for the kidnapping of Robert Marcus seven years earlier.[50]

While Betty Jean was awaiting her first sentencing in early 1956, Assistant District Attorney Folger Emerson was asking a jury in Oakland to convict Burton Abbott of what he called "one of the foulest and blackest offenses ever committed in the State of California." Contrasting the "humane way the state was asking that Abbott die" with what had happened to Stephanie Bryan, Emerson asked the jury (in numbing prose) to consider whether it would not have been "a blessing to Stephanie that if she had to die that she could have died that way than the way she did?" All along, the case against Abbot had hinged on sexual innuendo as well as the weakness of Abbott's alibi, and the jury as well as the public was left to ponder what Stephanie's death was like.[51]

The jury took seven days to reflect on this and the accumulated evidence, which they reviewed methodically in their unhurried and unanimous deliberations. On Wednesday, January 25, Burton Abbott learned that the jury had determined that he should die in the gas chamber. One juror told the *Oakland Tribune*, "We felt Burton Abbott should have shown more emotion on the witness stand. . . . We knew he had lied and he had admitted he had lied on the stand. We all wanted to believe him when he went up there, . . . and despite his crime, we all felt bad about having to make the decision." Abbott seemed completely surprised by the verdict, but immediately afterward, he rejoined a card game he had begun with three other prisoners. When interviewed by newsmen, he continued to maintain his innocence, claimed he had been framed, and proposed to have an alternative suspect. The trial had cost Alameda County an estimated $100,000.[52]

Dr. Charles Bryan, Stephanie's father, who had all along been unable to suppress his rage, expressed the belief that the gas chamber was not "much of a punishment, really, for this fellow. . . . I think he probably sleeps better than I do. . . . It's impossible for anyone with a normal mind to analyze the mental processes of someone like that." Mary Bryan was much more self-controlled, but ventured that "his only feeling must be that the verdict is unfair."[53]

Whatever the Bryans' thoughts on the matter and in spite of Judge Charles Wade Snook's opinion that, in his legal experience, he "never saw a more conscientious jury," a capital punishment verdict produced an automatic review in the California State Supreme Court. When Abbott appeared for sentencing on Friday, February 10, his attorneys anticipated arguments in that appeal when they asked for a new trial on the basis of the fact that one of the jurors, August C. Rettig, Jr., had been replaced during the trial. Rettig had lost his place on the jury when it was discovered that he worked just a few feet from Burton Abbott's brother, Mark, at the Alameda Naval Air Station. Abbott's lawyers also claimed errors by the judge and by District Attorney Coakley during the trial and that the news media had undermined Abbott's right to a fair trial through their presentation of prejudicial and sensational facts. On that same day, Judge Snook twice denied the defense a new trial and sentenced Abbott to die in the gas chamber for the kidnapping and murder of Stephanie Bryan. Because of bomb threats, the Alameda County Courthouse where Abbott was sentenced was under special surveillance by twenty deputy sheriffs. After his sentencing, Abbott was transferred to death row at San Quentin prison, located on one of the spits of land where Marin County cradles San Francisco Bay. Several weeks later, on April 1, 1956 (April Fool's Day), Abbott's Wildwood cabin, where Stephanie's body was found, was burned to the ground, apparently by "two lumbermen on a beer bust."[54]

On July 16, 1956, Abbott's new attorney, Leo Sullivan, filed a 162-page appeal to the Supreme Court of California, based largely on Coakley's "inflammatory" summation, which according to the brief, containing "unfair and completely destructive arguments in no way based on the testimony in the case." Citing Coakley's references to notorious cases like Leopold and Loeb, the brief accused Coakley of "pretending that the evidence in this case supported him in his arguments." The brief disputed Kirk's fiber evidence and argued that Rettig's removal had been illegal and prejudicial. Indeed, Abbott's attorney claimed that the two hairs that Kirk had taken from the car and identified as Stephanie's were put in Abbott's car by "two Berkeley police officers investigating the case." Sullivan's brief also questioned the jurisdiction of Alameda County since the body had been found in Trinity County and there was no evidence for the time or place of Stephanie Bryan's death. In response, the state attorney general's office filed a 195-page brief claiming that only Abbott could have committed the crime, an act of "perverted sadism." In defending the jury's kidnapping conviction, the brief also concluded that, in addition to "motives of sex, robbery and deliberate killing to conceal his crime," Abbott "also entertained an intention of obtaining a monetary profit out of the whole episode by using the books and glasses for purposes of reward or ransom," a contention never raised in the course of the trial.[55]

The California State Supreme Court reviewed the two briefs and rejected Abbott's plea by noting, "The evidence is clearly sufficient to support the judgment" of the lower court. The Supreme Court found no merit in the accusations against Judge Snook or District Attorney Coakley and concluded that Alameda Country had jurisdiction in the case since "the trial court of the county from which the victim was taken has jurisdiction." On December 10, Leo Sullivan filed a thirty-one-page petition asking for a rehearing by the State Supreme Court. That petition was denied without comment nine days later.[56]

Burton Abbott learned that his execution date was set for March 15, 1957, from a fellow inmate who had heard it on the radio ("Bud, it's March 15 for you, Snookie Boy"). As the days wound down, Abbott's mother, who all along proclaimed his innocence, offered a reward for any new information or leads.[57]

Shortly after Abbott's execution date was set, one of Abbott's cellmates, John Douglas Cober, in jail for passing bad checks, attracted star newspaper billing when he claimed that Abbott "Made It Plain He Killed Her." Accusing Abbott of having a "mind with a set of values so weird and distorted that there is no such thing as good or evil," Cober added that Abbott could make "any good schizophrenic" look like "a healthy man" in comparison. Cober, like other participants in the case, was using sophisticated psychological terms loosely. Cober claimed to know all about the case because Abbott and he would discuss the trial in progress and engage in banter about how Stephanie had been killed. Stephanie was nothing to Abbott except "an instrument in his creation of a famous criminal trial that would attract attention to himself." Abbott never called Stephanie anything other than "that girl." He had made it *look like a sex crime* (one that could never be proved), but in fact had no sexual motives in abducting and killing her. Although Abbott had "selected his victim as impersonally as if he were shopping for a bargain of some kind," he had "planned murder for years. He plotted the specific abduction and killing of Stephanie Bryan for months. . . . He deliberately created contradictions in the crime. He wanted to be a 'famous case.'" Cober's story recalled so many of the issues of the Leopold and Loeb case that one wonders whether it was he or Abbott who had read about it.[58]

According to Cober, Abbott lured Stephanie into his car by posing as a man delivering groceries to her house. Anticipating her attempts to escape, he had removed all door and window handles. Abbott had nothing to lose. He was already seriously ill. As Cober told Abbott: "You probably got the idea to commit murder when you were lying in the veterans hospital after the doctor told you that another operation on your lungs would mean only a 1000-to-1 chance for life . . . no matter what happens, you can't lose. If you are acquitted, you are forever after the famous Bud Abbott of the Abbott trial. And if you are sent to the gas chamber, what difference does it make because your life is dead anyway and you leave behind a world of doubt about your guilt. There will be thousands of people who will say you were innocent." Cober claimed that Abbott concurred in this explanation. In dissipating the sexual aura around Abbott's mind, Cober did nothing to bury its stench. But letters to the editor repeatedly questioned the veracity of Cober's account. "Your Bud Abbott story is the poorest type of journalism that can be practiced. . . . It's just trash." "This story by John Douglas Cober is for the birds." Abbott publicly denied Cober's story.[59]

One other person would also claim that Abbott had admitted his guilt, but that claim did not come for more than a decade. While testifying in another capital case, San Quentin psychiatrist Dr. David G. Schmidt disclosed that Abbott had indirectly confessed to him. During a "routine conversation between a psychiatrist and a condemned man," Schmidt suggested that Abbott admit his guilt and throw himself on the mercy of the governor to ask for executive clemency. Abbott declined to do so in order to spare his mother the grief and added, "I hope this will be confidential." Schmidt took this as a confession. He was roundly condemned for his conclusion and for the publication of his views.[60]

The case of Bud Abbott would become famous as part of the 1950s struggles over capital punishment, and Albert Camus even included it in his "Reflection on the Guillotine." But the case was certainly as much a reflection of the period's drive to understand human behavior in psychological terms and its fascination with "sexual perversion." Not only were the newspapers full of psychological terms and theories, Abbott's cellmate spoke in the newest lingo. That Abbott was seen by a psychiatrist as part of the deathwatch suggests the pervasive institutionalization of psychiatric practices as well as psychological perspectives.[61]

Bud Abbott never made a public confession. Between March 4 and March 8, Abbott's final lawyer, George T. Davis, made a series of last-minute attempts to stay his execution, including a plea to California Governor Goodwin Knight for clemency, an appeal for a stay to the State Supreme Court, and a last-minute appeal for a stay to United States

Supreme Court Justice William O. Douglas. All these were rejected. On the day before his scheduled execution, California Attorney General Edmund G. Brown (the state's highest-ranking Democratic politician, who was known to have anticapital punishment views) wired the United States Supreme Court urging a rejection of any last minute attempt for a *writ of certiorari* in the case.[62]

On the morning of March 15, Burton Abbott was led into the gas chamber. At 11:18 the gas chamber was sealed. Seven minutes later, Abbott was pronounced dead. He was twenty-nine years old. A large number of people had requested passes to witness his execution. One of them stated, "I've got a daughter myself, and I'd like to be the one who drops the pill." At 11:20, two minutes after the gas chamber was closed, Governor Knight, who had twice reviewed the case and rejected a request for delay and who had been unavailable through much of the morning, called San Quentin to issue a brief one-hour stay in order to give Abbott's lawyer a chance to prepare another appeal. By that point, it was too late to stop the process of execution. But the dramatic ending (two minutes too late) made national news and instantly gave the local crime international stature. Knight claimed that this had all been carefully stage-managed and timed by Abbott's lawyer. "I did everything possible to give Mr. Davis every opportunity to develop anything new in the case. This he could not do. In return he staged a dramatic stunt—with no legal ground to stand on—by waiting until the very last minute—then appealing for still another stay of execution."[63]

On March 26, a few days after Abbott's execution, his mother, Elsie Abbott, his brother, Mark, and his aunt, Mona Marsh, were present at a rally of 300 against the death penalty in San Francisco's St. John's Episcopal Church. Speakers included professors from the University of California and prominent clergy. The long process of unsuccessful appeals and especially the strange last-minute twist had turned the local kidnap and murder into a major issue in California politics and injected the case into the vociferous debates over the justice of capital punishment that took place in the mid 1950s. Eventually Abbott would make national news as his story appeared in magazines, and his cause became an occasion for public rallies, political gestures, and long contentious exchanges in local newspapers. Bud Abbott had made it into the limelight as his death became an object lesson for those who opposed the death penalty.[64]

On the day of Abbott's execution, Dr. Charles S. Bryan, Stephanie's father, went to work as usual at Peralta Hospital in Oakland. Eighteen months later, on October 28, 1958, he died of a heart attack, at the age of forty-seven. He had been working on a garden fence in the new house into which the family had moved after they abandoned the house above the Claremont Hotel to which Stephanie never returned.[65]

CHAPTER FIVE

"An Innocent Child Caught in the Web of Legal Jargon"

Parental Abduction in America

In the summer of 1873, "a gentleman of high social position" in Williamstown, New York, "the quietest of summer resorts," hired a "fast livery team" and carried off both his children. He presumably fled with them to Europe since as "a man of means," he would "spare no money to cover up the trail." Although the courts had given this man, Mr. Neil, custody of one his daughters in the "decree of separation on the ground of incompatibility of temperament," the other daughter, whom he also took with him, had been awarded to his wife, who now suffered "fearfully over the theft."[1] Thus, even before the Charley Ross case defined for Americans the horror of stranger kidnapping, other children were being snatched by their own parents in what was all through the late nineteenth century, and ever more frequently in the twentieth, the single most prevalent kind of abduction.

The neo-Solomonic divison of the girls between the parents that had given Neil custody of one of his children was probably unusual. But by 1873 it was not at all unusual for children to be legally assigned to their mothers in the event of divorce or separation. Despite their other considerable legal and civic handicaps, women were frequently awarded custody of their children, precisely because the nineteenth century ideology of separate spheres sharply differentiated women's roles from men's and kept women in places apart from men. By the late nineteenth century, the belief that staying with the mother was in the best interests of the child had become a legal guidepost "notwithstanding the father's natural right." While women were more frequently granted custody of their children than men in the late nineteenth century, this was not, however, uniformly the case. As a result, children were even then pawns in an uncertain legal struggle between the mother, the father, and the state. Indeed, the role of the state as the overseer of marriage and family life was never so visible as in their dissolution. Paradoxically, the state's role in family custody disputes, especially when parents kidnapped their own children, could be variously seen as tyrannical or impotent, and often both at the same time. In fact, it is peculiarly the double bind of custody disputes and parental kidnapping that the state is both too much a party to the issues and unequal to the task.[2] This has been the case since the nineteenth century, and it has been so for the rich and powerful as well as the poor and the displaced.

Since the nineteenth century, parental kidnapping has been not only the most common form of child abduction, but the most blind to social distinctions of all kinds. Parental kidnapping even altered customary gender distinctions. The perpetrators of most child kidnappings were men, with two exceptions: women stole children (usually infants) to raise as their own, as Betty Jean Benedicto tried to do; and they were active snatchers of their own children. In depictions of parental kidnappings, women were rarely portrayed as passive or hysterical. Instead, women actively intervened to obstruct the abduction of their children, and women, sometimes with the assistance of kin, abducted their own children.

In 1878, after a divorce, Mrs. J. De Trafford Blackstone of Norwich, Connecticut, stole her child from the well-staffed home of his father. Although she had been a member of a theater company and had an uncertain background, her former husband, "Traft" Blackstone, had impeccable social credentials; his family was "wealthy and honorable," and prominent enough to make the abduction front-page news in the *New York Times* for two days. Less elite, but also quite respectable, Henry Coolidge and his former wife, Belthiede, were found quarreling on West Sixteenth Street in Manhattan over possession of their daughter. "The woman had the child by one arm and the man by the other arm and they were pulling the little girl hither and thither." Pending the outcome of the divorce instituted by Henry, the judge had ordered one of their daughters to be placed in the custody of the maternal grandmother and the other with a friend of the family. Henry had taken the older girl from the grandmother's house, "ostensibly for a walk," but he had not returned her. The mother, with the assistance of her own father, had retaken the girl and had just met Coolidge on the street, where he attempted once again to take the child. This was the background for the little drama enacted on the street in New York. When brought before the local magistrate, Coolidge did not deny his wife's story but noted that he was rescuing his daughter from being subjected to "immoral influences," a charge strenuously denied by Mrs. Coolidge and her mother. The judge ordered the child returned in accordance with the original determination of temporary custody.[3]

For the Coolidges and for many divorcing couples in the nineteenth century, the court had rendered a judgment that at least one of the contending parties found painful, harmful, or unjust, and it led to personal attempts to correct the situation. As was the case with the Coolidges, it was often difficult to evaluate the validity of various accusations against the other party. Like them, too, many cases, then as now, would involve extended kin who became actively involved as contending parties in the dispute over the children, and then as now the cost was often best expressed in the striking visual image of "pulling the little girl hither and thither."

One of the most sharply etched abduction stories from the 1870s concerned parents who were not rich, or even respectable, but whose experience brought out the issues with a special poignancy and power. Brooks McQuiston had lived with "an octoroon" for seventeen months as her common-law husband but then "deserted her." Some weeks later, returning to claim his child, he broke down her door and "snatched the child from his cradle." Mrs. McQuiston (she is given no other name) discovered the abduction, leaped from a second floor window, and ran after McQuiston and her child in a spectacular chase that eventually landed all three in New York's Jefferson Market Police Court.[4]

Claiming that he wanted to rescue his child from the mother who "kept company with a negro waiter," McQuiston asked the judge to grant him the right to the child, whom he intended to send to his mother in Baltimore to raise. "The woman wept bitterly and pleaded piteously that the court would consider a mother's feelings"; besides, she announced, the child was not McQuiston's but had been born just two months after they met. Further, he had not deserted her but "had grown so brutal and drunken" that she threw him out. The judge decided that since "the father had possession," he should keep the child and that the mother could seek through a "civil process" to pursue her claim. Shrieking, "Oh Judge! for God's sake don't be cruel to a mother—don't drive me mad—don't give a stranger my baby!" the woman ran after McQuiston, who had already departed the courthouse with the child and hailed a cab. "Quick as a flash she darted across to the car, sprang onto the platform, struck McQuiston a powerful blow under the chin . . . pulled the child from his arms and sprang away with a scream of triumph." When captured, she gave the judge a brilliant lecture: "Judge, I could not help it—he was stealing my baby. I'll do it again. Forget where you are and remember only that you are a man, that I am a woman, and that I am a mother in your power. . . . What is law for one parent ought to be law for the other. I stand here just exactly as he stood a few moments ago. Now give him the law as you gave it to me. . . . I could not see the justice then—I can see it now and beg it now for myself." The judge responded, "Woman, you have the child; keep it until the law order otherwise."[5]

The story contains not only a stunning instance of the power of the courts to give and take children from parents but a portrait of an extraordinary woman who could see instantly that the courts' treachery was haphazard rather than intentional. And the story contains all the elements that would define parental kidnapping to this day: Two parents, each claiming to represent the welfare of the child, each often exercising heroic means to capture or retain possession of a child; a brutal parental relationship, often strained by alcohol or other substance abuses; overtones of sexual misconduct; a legal system hard-pressed to render a decision and often changing its mind; and a helpless child (not even identified here by name or gender) sometimes violently abducted and caught in a poisonous triangulation.[6]

In 1993, a federal appeals court in Richmond, Virginia, ruled that a natural mother was exempt from federal kidnap laws (the Lindbergh Act). In this case, a woman, with the aid of two friends, had tied, gagged, roughed up, and robbed her children's foster parents, and then abducted the children from their new home in Missouri. This attempt to retrieve adopted or fostered children was not unusual; it had happened often enough in the past, although the mother's behavior in this instance was certainly extreme. In excluding the mother alone (the others had already been sentenced to prison), the judges noted that the Lindbergh Act exempted parents from the crime of kidnapping. The ruling further asserted that the state court could "not alter the identity of a biological parent" even though it could end a parent's right to custody. The case represented an extreme instance of a more general social problem and the ruling provoked considerable controversy, but it suggests some of the legal complications implicit in the very concept of parental kidnapping.[7]

The Lindbergh Act was the first federal kidnapping legislation in the United States, but its predecessors both in England and the American states had also excluded parents either entirely or from the full force of kidnapping penalties. In England, the first legislation, "An Act for the More Effectual Prevention of Child Stealing," was enacted in 1814, purportedly because child stealing "has of late much prevailed and increased." It specifically *excluded* "any Person who shall have claimed to be the Father of an illegitimate Child, or to have any Right or Title in Law, to the Possession of such Child," effectively excluding all natural or legal fathers from kidnapping. Since the law presumed that the child was being stolen to "deprive its Parent or Parents . . . of the Possession of such Child," it axiomatically excluded fathers of legitimate children as possible violators. The updated Act of 1892 excluded all those "claiming in good faith a right to the possession of the child," thus bringing mothers under the protective umbrella, commensurate with their newly gained status as potential custodians. The law effectively remained the same until the 1980s, when the Child Abduction Act of 1984 made it an offense for a parent or guardian given custody to remove a child from Great Britain without appropriate consent, or for a person not having custody or guardianship to take such a child or "to keep him out of lawful control of any person entitled to his control." This updated vision of custody, as we shall see, corresponded to a growing recognition in the West of the explosive possibilities of child custody cum kidnapping offenses. The English Custody Act of 1985 brought English law into compliance with new protocols in international custody disputes.[8]

In the United States through most of the nineteenth century, case law had evolved erratically concerning parental kidnapping by drawing on the

English common-law definition of kidnapping—the forcible carrying of a child to another location (initially out of the country) without consent. In a Massachusetts case of 1862, the court ruled, "A child of the age of nine years is incapable of giving a valid assent to a forcible transfer of him by a stranger from the legal custody of his father to the custody of his mother, who had no right thereto; and evidence of such assent is incompetent in defense to an indictment of an assault and battery upon him in making such transfer." In another case, the theft of a four-year-old by his father was defined as "unlawfully and forcibly carrying the child out of the state," in accordance with the kidnapping definition. These cases were ambiguous because the parents used intermediaries in the transfer. But a Georgia court ruled in 1894, "A father cannot be charged with kidnapping his minor child, where he has not parted with his parental right to its custody"; and in Kansas in 1889, another court ruled even a third party "who assists a mother in leaving her husband and taking away the infant child of herself and husband is *not guilty* of kidnapping, since she is as much entitled to the custody of the child as its father." In these last cases, both parents were absolved of guilt in child stealing. But enforcement of the laws in the nineteenth century was erratic and the laws were hardly specific.[9]

Starting in the early twentieth century, after Charley Ross and subsequent kidnappings, as more and more state legislatures began to institute or beef up laws against kidnapping, they often found it necessary specifically to distinguish abductions perpetrated by strangers from those by parents. In so doing, they sometimes also instituted punishments for parental kidnappings. In Iowa, in 1900 the legislature turned its attention to creating harsh sentences for kidnapping for ransom. The prevalence of parental kidnappings even then is suggested in an observation by the *New York Times*. "Heretofore the cases of kidnapping in this state have been by divorced persons who wanted to get possession of their children, but with the inauguration of the kidnapping practice to extort money from the parents for the return of the child, it was found that the Iowa statutes do not provide punishment to fit the crime." As long as kidnapping had been a largely domestic affair, presumably, it required few severe penalties. In New York in 1911, state legislator Artemas Ward, Jr., specifically exempted parental kidnappers from the newly harsh penalties called for in pending kidnap legislation. Ward noted that it was "pretty generally recognized that there are extenuating circumstances where, through affection and love, a parent tries to get possession of his child." And for a long time both social attitudes and criminal justice proceedings reflected this belief. Just as nineteenth-century English law assumed that no father could steal what was already his, most American courts and police in the twentieth assumed that parental kidnapping bespoke an act of love, which could hardly be a serious crime.[10]

One wonders whether Ward, the son of a millionaire, might not have had specifically in view the interests of an affluent and increasingly divorce-prone constituency of glittering socialites and upper-class swells. For the explicit division of kidnapping in this way was a response not only to the belief that strangers and parents had different objectives when they kidnapped a child. It developed from the understanding that the temptation to kidnap one's own children grew proportionately with the divorce rate. And in the first decades of the twentieth century, that rate had already begun the rise that would accelerate rapidly with the unfolding century.[11]

The distinction between kidnapping by strangers and by parents begun in state laws at the beginning of the century and subsequently enshrined (by excluding parents) in the federal statutes of the 1930s remained in place until the 1970s and 1980s, when the astronomical increase in divorce and the resulting custody and jurisdictional disputes projected parental kidnapping into the center of a much larger public discourse over lost, missing, and stolen children. That discourse eroded the sharp boundaries between parental and stranger kidnapping earlier put in place. The strong move to criminalize parental kidnapping in the 1980s marked a major turning point in kidnap history and defined a wholly new public posture toward family life. Until then, while the courts would intrude in unprecedented ways and in extreme detail in the relations between parents and children as families exposed themselves to state regulation through breakup, parental kidnapping remained largely a social rather than a legal issue.

回 || 回

In the early twentieth century, perhaps the most notable social change to influence parental kidnapping besides the sharp rise in divorce was the introduction of the automobile. Just as the automobile put the lives of young children at risk generally, especially in the cities, it increased the risk of abduction for children of feuding, separated, or divorced parents. Where parents had earlier hired horse-drawn cabs or escaped on foot, most children in the twentieth century were whisked away, occasionally within sight of their other parent, in an automobile. "Boy Spirited Away By Five Men in Auto" read one headline that recounted a parental abduction; "Boy Kidnapped By Woman in Auto" read another. While the car changed the dynamics of abduction, the social patterns that had prevailed in the nineteenth century remained much the same as the tempo of divorce increased rapidly with the twentieth century.[12]

In sharp contrast to the horror expressed at stranger abductions and the solemnity with which they were discussed, newspapers adopted a tone of amusement when they described parental kidnappings. Thus when nine-year-old Dean McLaughlin was abducted in an automobile, the *New York Times* observed, "The boy has been kidnapped so many times by his father and his mother that he appears to be enjoying the experience." This attitude prevailed even though the abductions were deadly serious for the parents and sometimes involved physical force or the use of threatening weapons. In abducting Beverly Lorraine Whitgreave, eighteen months of age and great granddaughter of a local Chicago hero—Colonel James Mulligan of the famous Illinois Irish Brigade—the mother was reported by the *Chicago Tribune* to have announced, "I've come for my baby. . . . I've got a revolver and I'll kill you if you don't give her up." This was the fourth time that the baby had been kidnapped. "The first time she was taken by her father, the second time by her mother, and the last time by her father." Even this phrasing in the *New York Times* turned the experience into a game or a contest.[13] Portrayed as a joke, parental kidnapping was hardly considered a serious social problem.

The view of parental snatchings as somehow part of the rather droll battle between the sexes or a drawing-room comedy was exaggerated in the 1920s and 1930s by the fact that most of the news stories involved custody disputes among the socially prominent. This public emphasis on the glitterati was, I think, a specific choice, not just a reflection of the fact that the poor rarely bothered with divorce. In the late ninteenth century, and to some extent even in the early twentieth, the domestic disputes of poorer folk also made news, and children were reported as abducted even in the absence of divorce decrees. Thus abductions among working people were common enough to lead the police to assume in 1913 that when three-year-old Florence Sauter was abducted by a women who lured her from the vicinity of her tenement house on First Avenue with promises of an ice cream, the abductor was probably acting as an agent for the child's father. In this instance, the police were wrong because Florence had, in fact, been kidnapped by an "insane" woman who, like Betty Jean Benedicto forty years later, tried to keep her for her own child. The Sauters, like many of the poor, were not divorced, but since Florence had been Gustav Sauter's favorite, the police readily assumed that after Sauter deserted his family, he was implicated in her abduction.[14]

The newspaper's fixation on the abductions of the rich and famous between the world wars reflected a prurient fascination with those who were either spirited enough or rich enough to step beyond the bounds of convention. By the 1930s, the newspapers' depiction of all child abductions had some entertainment value, but the abduction of children by strangers carried a heavy emotional load with elements of horror and anxiety. This could be entirely discarded where the child was assumed not to be in danger, as in a parental abduction. Through the peephole of parental abduction, the public could enter into the unsavory domestic affairs of the socially prominent, who were thereby shown to be in no way morally superior. This selective coverage emphasized that parental kidnapping was exceptional rather than ordinary and largely confined to those whose lives were in all ways exceptional—and fascinating. The narrow range of reported abductions gave the impression that it was hardly a general social problem. As a result, when the media shifted its vision to the democratic masses and dramatically reported on the prevalence of parental abductions in the 1970s and 1980s, the phenomenon seemed to be unprecedented. In fact, parental abductions have been firmly a feature of twentieth-century domestic relations, with deep roots in the nineteenth century.

In 1915, Milo Abercrombie was a spectacular San Francisco debutante, one of two sisters born in New Orleans to a rich and prominent family. In addition to pedigree and wealth, Milo and her sister Margaret were extraordinary beauties, and Milo was often described as the most beautiful girl in California. She was the talk of artists and connoisseurs; Charles Dana Gibson called her "one of the most beautiful girls in America." That same year, she married Baron Wilhelm von Brincken, the handsome and very eligible military attaché at the German consulate. The dazzling wedding was followed by a dazzling divorce and a subsequent marriage in 1920 to Navy Lieutenant Lyman Knute Swenson. Although the blush was somewhat off the bride, she remained very much in the limelight, sufficiently beautiful and respectable to be asked to play the role of the Madonna in an Easter 1925 pantomime of the "Resurrection" under the auspices of the Salon of International Artists. But that part was promptly canceled when she signed a divorce complaint against her second husband. Within three years of the marriage to Swenson, there had been hints of trouble and rumors of infidelity on her part, but the divorce was not pursued until 1925. It was granted in September 1926. This marriage, like her first, had produced two children.[15]

Unlike Milo's first husband (who after spending some time in jail as a spy during World War I, retreated quietly to Hollywood, where he changed his name to Roger Beckwith and got involved in films), Swenson was not content to disappear from his children's lives. Despite his efforts to gain custody, Milo received custody of the Swenson children, Cecilia and Laurence, when she won an interlocutory decree. Problems really began when she refused to allow her husband the visitation rights granted by the court. It was only under a specific court injunction that Swenson was able to visit with his children in January 1926, just before he began an extended tour of duty, and even then officers of the court had to force entrance to the apartments at the luxurious Stanford Court Hotel where the children were staying with their maternal grandmother. An angry Judge E. P. Shorthall insisted that the father had a right to visit his children. "I'm going to give this father the right that God gives him; the right the laws of nature give him, and the right the laws of California give him. . . . The children's mother has compelled me against my will to send the sheriff to bring these children into court. I am moved only by their interests, but I don't think their mother has the right to ask much at my hands until she realizes the law reaches into the Stanford Court as well as the homes of the poor." Having asserted the majesty of the law and its equal treatment, Shorthall could do little more than threaten and refuse Milo the court's assistance when she sued for payment of back alimony. Milo's continued refusal to allow her former husband to visit the children led to several contempt of court citations against her. Finally, on January 6, 1927, the court transferred custody of the children to Swenson, concluding that "Mrs. Abercrombie was not a fit guardian." The transfer was confirmed by the Court of Appeals in October 1929. By then Milo and the children had disappeared.[16]

When Swenson last saw his children, under sheriff's escort, he had given Milo a letter proclaiming, "I love my children as much as you do, and their welfare is my first interest. Aside from my instinctive desire to want to be with them, I owe it to them to see them and talk to them as much as our tangled affairs will permit. You can't point out one dishonorable act I ever did in the time you have known me, so why should you do this foolish thing which has been such a strain on us all." The letter may already have hinted at hidden accusations, some mark against his honor, which if true might cancel his rights with the children, accusations he strenuously denied. In giving custody to the father, the judge took note of these accusations and rejected them: Milo "was instrumental in inspiring and promoting a scheme directly involving the children which had for its obvious purpose the ruination of the respondant's character, the bringing about of his complete disgrace as a naval officer and the destruction of the affection which his children had heretofore manifested for him." Although the newspapers never stated the accusation baldly, the nature of these accusations was undoubtedly widely known at the time. A recent book about Swenson's last, ill-fated assignment as captain of the SS *Juneau* during World War II when Swenson and his entire crew were killed makes it clear that Milo was accusing Swenson of sexually abusing his daughter, who was three years old at the time of the divorce. This accusation resulted in Cecilia's lifelong alienation from and rejection of her father.[17]

Either because she believed these things about Swenson or because she could not bear to give over the custody of the children, by the time the appeals were settled in Swenson's favor, Milo Abercrombie Van Brincken Swenson had fled to Oregon with her children. By March 1930 they could not be located, and because Swenson had to return to China, a Superior Court judge issued an order placing them in temporary custody of the court if and when they were found. Milo eventually turned up in Lima, Peru, after she married Pedro J. G. C. de Flores, "a former French marquis," in Reno. She divorced de Flores in 1935.[18]

This chequered path, from marriage to marriage (including titled ones), kept the beautiful Milo in the news, often indeed on page one in the San Francisco press, where a less stellar figure might have been ignored. But other women, too, were kidnapping their children, often in an effort to protect them from real or imagined injuries. When Josephine Sullivan Kieffer (who like Milo was charged with infidelity) snatched her two-year-old daughter, Elizabeth, in the midst of a divorce action, Mrs. Kieffer charged that her husband had not only been unfaithful, but that he "neglected and has at times slapped, beaten and otherwise abused the said child." In addition, he was "a person of erratic and exceedingly vicious habits . . . an unfit and improper person to have the custody of said child." Kieffer was a wealthy New York lawyer, a graduate of Harvard and a Rhodes scholar. Like the Swensons, the Kieffers had found the right lever to push in their contentious quarrels over custody.[19]

Impuning the reputation of the opposing party was only one of the means used in custody battles that could serve to legitimate kidnappings. The other tactic was to use the power that came from divergent jurisdictions. Milo Abercrombie took her children out of California, but she does not appear to have used another state court to try to regain custody. When Charles Bliss kidnapped his son from his wife's hotel room in Chicago in September 1924, he took him back to Tulsa, Oklahoma. Beryl Brown Bliss, the child's mother, was a "beautiful soprano" with the Chicago Civic Opera. Bliss, a millionaire Tulsa oil and real estate man, then sued Beryl for divorce in Tulsa, claiming that she was "too modern" and did not "recognize the long established custom of husband and wife living together." Whatever effect this tainting of his wife's character and his claim that Beryl "gave all her time to a career in opera" had on the judge, it was certain that Bliss's possession of the child in Tulsa helped him to obtain temporary custody. The judge allowed him to keep Charles, Jr., in "the jurisdiction of the Tulsa county court until after a settlement of the divorce case." Having the child within the jurisdiction of only one of the contending parties often resulted in at least temporary orders acknowledging that parent's right. In this context, it was not uncommon for the other parent to attempt to rekidnap a child and thereby achieve a legal victory in another jurisdiction. In the case of four-year-old Charles Bliss, Jr., it was reported that "servants are keeping a close watch on the boy for fear the mother will try the same coup that the father used successfully and get the child beyond the jurisdiction of the local courts." Because custody came within the exclusive jurisdiction of each state, the courts were quite impotent beyond their own borders, and conflicting order were often in place.[20]

While Abercrombies, Kieffers, and Blisses might capture readers' passing interest as their domestic quarrels and questionable morals satisfied a prurient curiosity, the single most compelling custody-snatch case in the period between the wars concerned a Vanderbilt. Like Milo Abercrombie, Gloria Morgan had been a great beauty. She and her twin sister, Thelma (who was the Prince of Wale's mistress before his attachment to Wallis Simpson), had captivated café society while they were still teenaged girls living on their own in New York. There they achieved fame because of the effusive praise of society columnist "Cholly Knickerbocker" (Maury Paul), who gave them titles like the "Magical Morgans" and "Glorious Gloria." Gloria's father had been attached to various American consuls and her Latin American mother had social pretensions, but Gloria's parents were hardly at the pinnacle of society, and they were certainly not rich. The social glare surrrounding Glorious Gloria became a conflagration when, in 1923 and barely eighteen, she married Reginald Vanderbilt, a middle-aged sportsman and alcoholic roué, the designated heir of Cornelius Vanderbilt. Cornelius and his wife, Alice Gwynne Vanderbilt (and after his death in 1899, she alone), were the self-styled arbiters of Newport and New York society. Preferring the café to the salon, Reggie (sometimes Regi), who already had a daughter Gloria's age, was hardly the type to uphold that position. Even Gloria admitted that Reggie was "too self-indulgent, too indolent to surrender any of his time" to caring for the approximately $70 million that had been left to the family by Reggie's father. Whatever Reggie's tastes and abilities, however, it was the Vanderbilt name, power, wealth, and position that was to bring Gloria great fame and also ignominy.[21]

Gloria's incorporation as a Vanderbilt was hardly enthusiastic. Despite the cool welcome she received from the family, Gloria's life was briefly enchanted and certainly made more important when a child, also named Gloria, was born on February 20, 1924. When Reggie died the next year (he literally exploded internally as a result of alcoholism), Gloria was not yet twenty-one, the legal age required to be a guardian of her child, who was a direct descendent of the Vanderbilt line, an heir to possibly the richest family in America. Gloria received a relatively small (though not insignificant) personal inheritance. But the child's portion of $5 million was, in the midst of the Depression, a fortune. It permitted her mother (under the guidance of a legal administrator) to receive a $4,000 monthly allowance, ostensibly for the child's maintenance and care. It was finally that money, how Gloria spent it, and how she cared for her daughter with it that became the central matter in the great legal controversy *Vanderbilt v. Vanderbilt* that exploded on the front pages of newspapers in the 1930s.[22]

Gloria was nothing like a doting mother. After Reggie's death, she took all the money she could gather together from the sale of various assets and moved herself and her daughter to Europe, temporarily to the Ritz Hotel and then to a sumptuous apartment in Paris. There she rejoined her mother and other relatives and became a fixture among the young and fast international set, a set fueled by American money and decorated by faded European titles. In time, Gloria's escapades with the rich and titled in Europe would eventuate in an engagement to a needy, but noble German prince (that dissolved in the midst of her legal troubles). With an obsessive nursemaid utterly devoted to her and the attention of her grandmother, the young Gloria was more or less taken care of. But the mother's carefree life and the child's careless upbringing came to the attention of Gertrude Vanderbilt Whitney. Gertrude Whitney was little Gloria's imposing and astoundingly rich aunt who, according to young Gloria, "lived on an extraordinary scale . . . unusual even in that more affluent day." After the death of Alice Gwynne Vanderbilt, Gertrude was the doyenne of the Vanderbilt family, as well as a sculptor and art patroness *extraordinaire*.[23]

Concerned that the child was not being properly raised or adequately cared for, Gertrude Whitney decided to take the matter into her own hands. With the connivance of little Gloria's nursemaid and grandmother, the child was taken from the mother's home in New York during one of her mother's temporary returns to the city and kept first in Gertrude Whitney's Fifth Avenue apartment and then at her Long Island estate. She effectively "snatched" the ten-year-old from her mother and made it impossible for Gloria to see her daughter in unchaperoned circumstances.[24] Gertrude asked to become the child's legal guardian. When the mother refused, Gertrude instituted the suit to gain custody and Gloria replied with the countersuit to retain custody that became the front page event "*In re Vanderbilt.*"

Gloria Morgan Vanderbilt's life became the stuff of daily public discussion as Gertrude Whitney's attorneys presented evidence that little Gloria had been subjected to the immoral influences (drink, pornography, sexual liaisons) of her mother's lifestyle. Even Mrs. Morgan and the child testified against her. In this case, as in most others where an attempt was made to remove a child from the custody of its mother, the burden of proof was on Gertrude to demonstrate that Gloria Morgan Vanderbilt was an "unfit mother." This explains why almost all these kidnappings—Kieffer, Abercrombie, and, more indirectly, Bliss—trailed sexual innuendoes in their wake. In the case of Gloria Morgan Vanderbilt, the trail was thick and rich, with the most damaging evidence involving accusations of lesbianism. As Gloria said in one of her memoirs: "If Gertrude Whitney had sought throughout the earth for an instrument to blast her dead brother's wife and shatter her life, and stamp that brother's child with an undying mark of infamy and degradation . . . she could find nowhere so deadly and searing a weapon." When she lost custody of little Gloria, the judgment was front-page news across the country. According to the final decree, the life that Gloria Morgan Vanderbilt had provided for her child was "in every way unfit, destructive of health, neglectful of her moral, spiritual and mental education." Gloria Laura Vanderbilt, an orphaned heiress, became, in the words of the final order, "the ward of the Supreme Court of the State of New York," and her aunt, Gertrude Vanderbilt Whitney, was granted custody as a representative of the state.[25]

Describing herself as "robbed by Mrs. Whitney," Gloria Morgan Vanderbilt lost "her natural privilege as a mother to have the custody of her own child" and vowed to do everything to get her child back. Scorned in court, Gloria became the object of popular pity and support. Before the judgment was rendered, three hundred women who often gathered outside the court-house signed a mother's petition asking that Gloria be given custody of her child and attempted to present it to the judge. One wife of a tavern keeper in the vicinity of the sensational trial was quoted as "praying night and day for Mrs. Vanderbilt's success." She had even "sent a string of rosary beads" to Gloria, who had been raised a Catholic. After the decision was handed down, *New York World Telegram* columnist Evelyn Seelye concluded, "Most mothers doubt that it means Gloria's [the child] ultimate happiness... most mothers have a sort of mystic belief ... that, no matter what occurs, a child belongs to her mother." From then on little Gloria (the "poor little rich girl") became the object of frantic public attention, surrounded by crowds everywhere she went. She also became the object of kidnap threats and extortion notes. Gloria stayed with her aunt or under her supervision until, in her mid teens, she decided to move in with her mother, who had by then taken up residence in Los Angeles and joined the Hollywood crowd.[26]

The Vanderbilt custody case departed from the scenario of other parental abductions because there had been no divorce or separation and no open breach between the child's parents. Instead, one of the extended paternal kin had acted on behalf of the child's perceived welfare. The active intervention by extended kin was, and is, very common in snatch cases. In the Vanderbilt case, the paternal kin took an even more prominent part than usual, standing in for rather than just standing with and in support of the parent. Perhaps more uncommon was the role of Gloria Morgan Vanderbilt's mother, Laura, who supported Gertrude Whitney and whose defection dealt a lethal blow to Gloria's case. Most of Gloria's other relations stood staunchly by her side.

After she lost custody of her daughter, Gloria was able to visit with her during a regular court visitation schedule. In this sense, the snatch had effectively achieved its limited ends—the shift in custody. Gloria Morgan Vanderbilt, like any lesser figure, but much more visibly and publicly, became hostage to the court's determination of how, when, and where she could see her child. The final decree seriously impaired Gloria's hyperactive and travel dependent social life. Not only could she visit with the child only in the month of July, on Christmas Day, and each weekend (the most hectic times in a social calendar), but because of the court order, little Gloria could not be taken out of the state of New York. This provision was intended to prevent another abduction and attempts at new proceedings in another jurisdiction.[27]

The Vanderbilt snatch was notable in its punishing publicity and because it strongly overlapped in time with another famous kidnapping, the abduction of the Lindbergh child. Indeed, the same front page often featured both events side by side. Barbara Goldsmith, who has written the most comprehensive account of the Vanderbilt case, argues that because of the Lindbergh publicity little Gloria was terrified of being kidnapped and that this explains the child's bizarre behavior during the custody proceedings. Certainly there is plenty of evidence for the family's concern about a possible ransom attempt. In fact, however, little Gloria *was* kidnapped, though not by a stranger. And she probably feared being kidnapped again, this time by her mother (who she apparently feared might kill her). Indeed, Gertrude Whitney established elaborate protections against just such an eventuality. Gloria senior entitled the chapter in which she lost possession of her daughter "Kidnapped!" This coming together of the two kinds of kidnappings—by family and by strangers—anticipated a later period of kidnap anxiety, when both kinds of kidnappings would be brought together by media coverage of stolen children. In 1934, the coincidence between the abduction of Charles Lindbergh, Jr., and the custody battle over

Gloria Laura Vanderbilt suggested not that the two kinds of kidnapping were the same, but that family life, even then, was precarious. In each case, someone rich, prominent, or powerful lost a child. In the midst of the Depression, the unpredictability of social life had no more vivid representation. So, too, no more telling a case could be made about how the period's mixture of curiosity and resentment against the privileged was expressed than the public's fascination with how a Lindbergh or a Vanderbilt had lost a child.[28]

▣ ||| ▣

Fifty years later, the basic issues in parental kidnapping had changed very little, but the public representation of the problem had been utterly transformed. The source of society sensations had become the democratic "Agony of the 80s," in the words of *USA Today*. By then, parental kidnapping was usually described as an epidemic—a rapidly spreading and terrifying illness of the society. Newspapers, women's magazines, and news journals, as well as novels and personal memoirs, focused on the problem and gave it extensive popular exposure. Parents who lost their children testified in the press and at congressional hearings and told their stories on television talk shows. Americans still occasionally learned about the snatches of the rich and famous, like the Mellons, but these had receded like sand under the giant waves of the perceived problem. Starting in the 1970s, the media portrayed the painful experiences of middle Americans and purveyed statistics that showed parental kidnapping to be a problem for thousands, even hundreds of thousands, of families. Those numbers and the fact that it happened to people like themselves made parental kidnapping a common experience of family life rather than an aberration. The new profile of the kidnapping family was composed not of society swells and their beautiful but unconventional wives, but of ordinary people whose lives were seared when their spouses or former spouses kidnapped their children. Precisely because it was so ordinary, parental kidnapping suggested that even families that seemed normal might hide some deep pathology. Parental kidnapping had become a massive disorder of family life in the late twentieth century.[29]

Certainly the dimensions of the phenomenon had changed. Although we have no figures for parental abductions in the nineteenth century (or for most of the twentieth century either), the enormous increase in divorce, especially of divorce where children were involved that started in the 1960s, created a greater potential for abductions. And just as the automobile had changed abductions in the early twentieth century, the democratization of plane travel after the 1960s made escape to other states and even to foreign countries accessible to more than the rich.

Initially, indeed, it was this new mobility and its potential for jurisdictional disputes in custody that rang the alarm bells and called for action. Snatching seemed to be a by-product of jurisdictional shopping, as a disaffected parent, unhappy with the custody ruling in one state, took the child to another where he was granted custody in the absence of the other parent. With an appropriate court order, the parent could feel himself or herself comfortably in compliance with the law. Although the child had been snatched, the custody decree in a new jurisdiction seemed to legitimize the action. And if shopping for custody was the problem, the remedy seemed simple—a stricter enforcement of the initial decree and compliance by sister states. In fact, rationalizing custody procedures was not simple because the Supreme Court imposed the full faith and credit clause of the United States Constitution only to a limited degree to custody cases and because state courts, according to an expert observer, "believed strongly that flexibility was necessary to best protect children's interests."[30]

Throughout the 1970s, much attention and energy, both in the popular media and among experts, was directed to enforcing custody decrees across state lines and much of the discussion took as its objective the enactment by the fifty states of the model laws proposed in the Uniform Child Custody Jurisdiction Act (UCCJA). This was not a law but a voluntary agreement to which states could subscribe. Initially approved in 1968 by the National Conference of Commissions on Uniform State Laws, by the mid 1980s the models had been adopted by almost all the states.[31]

As compliance took shape, however, the UCCJA turned out to be less than the solution many had foreseen. In part because parents often abducted their children before any custody order was in place, in part because communications and enforcement between states was slipshod, in part because police were not eager to be bothered by what they saw as "domestic disputes," the act seemed to have only marginal impact on the incidence of the problem or the sense of social malfunction it represented.

In 1980, in response to growing media attention, the federal government finally took note of the problem, and with much fanfare and publicity, Congress passed, and President Jimmy Carter signed, the Parental Kidnapping Prevention Act (PKPA). The PKPA did not reverse the protection offered to parents by the Lindbergh Act and did not make parental kidnapping a federal offense; custody was still a state concern. The new law was intended to enhance the UCCJA, required states to give full faith and credit to custody decrees of other states, and made the Federal Parent Locator Service available to parents trying to find their children. It also facilitated the work of state and local agencies in enforcing their own parental kidnapping laws. Throughout the period of the 1970s and 1980s, states were enacting legislation that made parental kidnapping an offense. Although these laws differed among themselves, with some states defining parental abductions as felonies and others merely as misdemeanors, by 1991, every state and the District of Columbia had a criminal statute prohibiting parental kidnapping.[32]

In 1982 and 1984, the federal government increased its role in parental kidnapping cases (and other forms of child disappearance) by passing the Missing Children's Act and the Missing Children's Assistance Act. Both provided informational and material assistance to parents and state and local governments in their attempts to locate children. These acts also, for the first time, made the FBI available as a resource of information. By 1984, the federal government had authorized the establishment of a national clearing house for information about missing children and established a toll-free hot line for reporting abductions and to gather information about missing children. The United States had also been instrumental in negotiating the Hague Convention on the Civil Aspects of International Child Abduction and became in 1988 one of only a handful of signatories who voluntarily agreed to surrender children brought into their jurisdiction in international custody disputes.[33]

Federal action had developed a new network of information and means to expedite compliance across jurisdictions, but these activities had not entirely quelled either the alarm over the abductions or their visibility. In good part, federal action was a response to an already flourishing grassroots movement of private self-help agencies, like Child Find and Children's Rights, Inc., which offered information and tools to help parents locate children lost to all kinds of abductions and mischance. Hardly an article, pamphlet, or book published on the subject in the last twenty-five years does not give parents advice on how to respond in the event that they had a child snatched or how to prevent such a snatching. Parents were often advised to seek assistance from these private organizations. The federal government had merely added another layer to a burgeoning industry based in a deeply rooted network of information and alarm. In addition to the work of these organizations and their spokespeople and in part as a result of it, throughout the 1970s and 1980s popular news journals as well as women's and parents magazines were full of haunting pictures of children stolen from their parents and presumably lost forever, together with stories of their parents' anguish.[34] With new laws, widespread publicity, and federal assistance, parental kidnapping was now perceived as a major social problem.

To sway legislation, victimized parents, child find organizations, and their congressional supporters marshaled statistics and personal tales of horror. Some of these statistics were simply made up and then cited by others, as they ricocheted from a low of 25,000 to the most common figure of 100,000 to over 1 million each year. These numbers were intended to include all lost, stolen, and missing childen and became part of a general effort to bring together the previously separated problems of stranger abduction and parental abduction in a fuller dedication to finding *all* missing children. As it had more than one hundred years before, the different problems of America's lost, stolen, and missing children once again came together; with all of their stories emblematic of serious social change. In the 1980s, as in the 1870s, the intentionally abducted became the emotional focus of a much broader threat, absorbing a general concern for beleaguered family life and community breakdown, although it was generally acknowledged that the largest group of *stolen* children were victims of parental snatchings. In focusing on the stolen, the public was often led to overlook the lost and the abused. As in the past, the legitimate concern with society's obligation toward its children was narrowed and criminalized.[35]

As the issue became widely publicized, it became part of other contemporary agendas, especially the feminist critique of the family and its patriarchal social supports. The question of child custody had always been a woman's issue. Since the nineteenth century, unless they were judged unfit or they were incapable of caring for them, women were considered the proper custodians of their children. And as we have seen in the popular sentiments concerning the Vanderbilt case, that sense of the matter had sources well beyond the courthouse. By the late 1980s, however, the presumption that mothers should get custody of their children except when unfit had faded with older stereotypes of women. By then, thirty-seven states had adopted joint custody in child dispositions. Even though the original feminist agenda helped to underwrite changes in custodial determinations that stressed greater paternal involvement, women increasingly saw the difficulties for themselves and the conflicts for their children that resulted from the need to continue negotiating with former spouses in matters concerning their children. Less immediately apparent but just as significant for parental kidnapping was the fact that joint custody often rendered laws concerning parental abduction inoperative. As a 1989 Justice Department pamphlet to parents observed: "Ironically the increased use of joint or shared custody—often pursuant to newer State statutes establishing a legislative preference for joint custody arrangements—has had the unintended side effect of hindering successful prosecution of some parental kidnapping cases . . . in several cases . . . defendants have successfully argued that an accused parent cannot, by virtue of his or her joint custodial rights, be guilty of criminal custodial interference."[36]

Kidnapping has always focused attention on family rather than social obligations, and parental kidnapping was no exception. In fact, parental kidnapping rapidly became interlaced into almost every conceivable issue related to the contemporary family from child custody to wife battering and sexual abuse. And it became a gauge of contemporary anxiety about the family. Stories of parental kidnapping always had a very different potential for telling about family life than tales of stranger kidnapping because the source for disruption and loss came from within the family group itself. By the 1980s, what had been in the 1920s and 1930s a window on other people's misbehavior and figured in a psychology of *schadenfreude* became the basis for fears about more broad-based family pathology.

Indeed the issue, which even in the 1970s seemed a simple matter of getting states to comply with the custody decrees of other states, became ever less simple and clear. The once straightforward objective in most kidnap stories, returning the child to its custodial parent, became in the 1990s strongly contested. By then public sympathy often turned to parents who kidnapped their children in order to rescue them from situations where they were exposed to sexual abuse or physical neglect, situations in which the state had placed them when it granted custody or visitation rights to the other parent. The state's role, once sought after, became much murkier and deeply problematic. Even a government pamphlet noted that "Parental kidnapping is not the right answer; but it is an anwer to which many parents resort in desperation. To the degree that judges and law enforcement officials can pay closer attention to parents with serious and apparently well-grounded fears for the physical, mental, and emotional well being of their children, one important part of the overall parental kidnapping problem may be eliminated at its source." The issue had come full circle as the officials became not the saviors but suspects in the problem.[37]

In the 1990s, as the government at all levels came in for increasingly harsh scrutiny, the state's role as an arbiter of family feelings and relationships became ever more suspect. Indeed, the state, the laws, and the police seemed incapable of dealing with the community's legitimate concerns about the welfare of its children. Just at the time when the family was viewed as unstable and pathological, the state itself was viewed as incompetent to perform the tasks of oversight. Paradoxically, a now deeply wounded family was once again called upon for social healing. As in the past, kidnapping forced the problem of child welfare inward, on the family.

⧉ IV ⧉

Parental kidnapping in the last twenty-five years has been defined as a common pathology through a huge, variegated literature and through media presentations. These include news reports, expert social science analyses and conference reports, novels and television programs based on true and fictional stories, and personal snatch narratives. The most interesting and revealing of these forms are the snatch narratives, which offer a personal *cri de coeur* in what is often a morass of statistical anonymity. They are also witness to the unique combination of the common and the extraordinary that has come to define the public representation of parental kidnapping. The narratives testify to the stunning, even heroic, experiences of ordinary people. More even than novels and television programs, the personal narratives give the sense of a life transformed by the loss of a child and propelled into articulation. The experience of child loss creates the need to share with other victims and potential victims the understanding, techniques, and personal wisdom gained from this experience. Indeed, this is the defining quality of most of these narratives—an urgency to testify and to relate circumstances that have made the participants at once victims and heroes but above all communicators, sharing their plight with others in the modern world.

In some ways, of course, these narratives are like Christian Ross's story of his search for Charley. But there are also important differences. Most parental kidnap narratives end with the child successfully recaptured and the healing provided by a new family created out of the painful death of the old. Thus, unlike Christian's, the typical parental kidnapping narrative is the memoir not only of wrenching loss and victimization, but of family disenchantment and the creation of alternative family forms, often involving extended kin or a new mate. Parental kidnapping narratives thus dethrone the conventional family and legitimize the family changes of the 1970s and 1980s, proposing that these changes are healthful and therapeutic. Also unlike Christian's, these narratives assume the commonness of the experience. They exist within an already alarmed environment, in which every article or book on the subject has cited huge numbers of parental abductions and each has given advice to readers on action and prevention. Where Christian told readers about a singular case, with which he assumed everyone was somewhat familiar, parental abduction narratives give an instance, hitherto unknown to the reader, of a supposedly familiar phenomenon. The narratives are thus both unique and democratic, related more to television talk shows like *Donahue* and *Oprah* than to Christian's lonely quest. In fact, these shows have often included parents of lost and missing children.[38]

The personal narrative is a variation and extension of the human interest stories developed in many magazine articles in the 1970s and 1980s to publicize the phenomenon of parental kidnapping. These articles usually told several painful tales together, conflating the experience into a type. The articles were accompanied by a series of smiling pictures of children before they were lost. Like Charley's poster, the pictures were haunting reminders of loss; except where Charley was singular, this was a group portrait. Each story was thus part of a larger package, a social profile rather than an individual tragedy.

"It was a cool evening in March 1977 when Robin Reiss, her parents and two-and-a-half-year-old son, Kevin, walked away from a friendly diner in Brooklyn, N.Y.," one such article in the *Ladies' Home Journal* begins. "The boy was giggling when Robin felt her grip on his hand suddenly tighten. It was at that moment that a horrible, ongoing nightmare began. From across the street, six burly thugs were sprinting toward her family. . . . Kevin screamed 'Mama,' and Robin saw the toddler reaching his arms toward her before she was blinded and silenced by a faceful of burning mace." Here the violent abduction plays on (and the article specifically alludes to) fears about stranger abductions as it attempts to create an emotional equivalence between the two. Like the conflation of statistics, this helped to criminalize parental kidnapping by blurring boundaries among types of abductions. The authors, Sally Abrahms and Joseph Bell, go on to tell several similar stories (later expanding their efforts in a book), including one of the most distressing, that of Cody Cain. In 1976, Steven Cain kidnapped his son, Cody, from his wife's Oklahoma home. When Steven Cain drove off with him, he was pursued by his wife and her brother. In the resulting high-speed chase down an Oklahoma highway, Cain's car crashed and both father and son were killed. This article, like many others, escalates the level of terribleness with each successive segment, selectively choosing the most harrowing details and combining them into a tale of horror.[39]

While the group portrait was a common magazine form, some journals began to tell individual stories. These narratives tended to be more realistic and less dependent on horror because they developed a different kind of drama. What most distinguishes the group horror tale from the single account was the latter's successful outcome. While group stories are always tales of victimization, in the individual tale the victim becomes a hero. The story of Eileen Crowley told in *Good Housekeeping* was much more true to the patterns of most snatches than the dramatic opening of the Abrahms and Bell article. Crowley's problems began two years after her divorce, when her daughter, Robyn, did not return after an ordinary visit with her father. Crowley recounts her problems with the authorities, who did not want to get involved in "a domestic matter." She hires lawyers and detectives, the usual devices of stunned parents. None of these legal means work. Neither do *habeus corpus* writs and court orders. Friends and family provide support, assistance, and comfort. Even after her husband is traced to a location on Long Island, he disappears when he suspects he has been discovered. Like other stories in the genre, Crowley tells of the tormented trail of search and disappointment, the impotence of legal instruments and authorities, and the frustrating and agonizing acceptance of loss.

As in most such narratives, the child is eventually found through a happy coincidence, almost never through the work of law enforcement agencies.

In Crowley's case, "on Friday, June 4, 1982 [seven years after the abduction], I received a letter from an old friend on Long Island. 'Yesterday I heard a girl yell out "Robyn," . . . I turned around and saw a miniature you as I remember you from our childhood together.'" Crowley and her new husband immediately make plans to retrieve the girl, now almost twelve years old. But even after locating her daughter, and with her custody papers in hand, Crowley has a hard time getting to see her. When she does see her daughter, the child is both strange and familiar. Mother and daughter are terrified. Crowley, her second husband, and their son, together with Robyn, now form a new kind of family. There are some problems of adjustment, but the story ends happily: "Mommy, I love you."[40]

Though brief, Crowley's story reflects the general pattern of such accounts: loss, a desperate search, the help of kin and friends, the impotence and incompetence of authorities, a new family, and then an almost miraculous reunion. But while Crowley obviously blames her former husband for the loss of her child, she does not characterize him as anything more than a snatcher. The evil and vindictive possibilities of the snatching husband is developed in great detail in other narratives. Thus in Bonnie Black's *Somewhere Child*, Anna Demeter's *Legal Kidnapping*, Thomas Froncek's *Take Away One,* and the novel *Kiss Mommy Goodbye* by Joy Fielding (which closely parallels the personal narrative form), all written in the late 1970s and early 1980s, the child is kidnapped by a dominating, tyrannical husband whose need to control his wife and his rage at the divorce serve as the motive for the children's abduction.[41]

As the alarm over parental kidnapping increased, this theme of parental selfishness came to the fore. Traditionally, the distinction between stranger abductions and parental kidnapping hinged on the belief that parents stole their children out of love. As part of the effort to paint parental kidnapping as a real crime, many of the arguments used by participants and activists in the evolving public discourse and in the personal narratives began to paint a very different picture—not of a loving father, but of a vindictive husband. The father might well also love his children, but he kidnapped them in order to punish his former wife. Since this was the period in which the woman's movement peaked, this portrayal dovetailed with feminist pictures of family dynamics. In a *Ms.* magazine article, abducting mothers were almost completely ignored, with Lindsy Van Gelder concluding, "Many of the abducting fathers are newly spurned husbands, reacting to the news that their wives want a divorce." Van Gelder used parental kidnapping to attack "the myth that the cornerstone of American life and law is 'the sanctity of the family,'" arguing instead that the family was balanced on women's pain and that the law was not available to women. "In the course of researching this article I found one case in which the law *voluntarily* went after a child-snatcher: here the offender was a *woman*." Similarly, Adrienne Rich's introduction to Anna Demeter's *Legal Kidnapping* turns the story into a feminist exposé. "The mother-child relationship can be seen as the first relationship violated by patriarchy. Mother and child, as objects of possession by the fathers, are reduced to pieces of property and to relationships in which men can feel in control, powerful, wherever else they feel impotent." Rich argues that "Legally, economically, and through unwritten sanctions, including the unlegislated male-bonding network documented in this book, the mother and child live under male control although males assume a minimal direct responsibility for children."[42] Parental kidnapping could be made to serve a variety of contemporary purposes.

Perhaps the most poignant of the narratives because it is the least polished and commercial is by Margaret Strickland. Strickland's story of the abduction of her grandson, Danny Strickland, is nothing like a feminist tract, but it has all the elements that define the parental kidnapping narrative. And the issues raised by Strickland, especially issues of child endangerment and questions about personal pathology, connect it firmly with the evolving social science theories about family dynamics in abducting families. The Strickland narrative serves as a transition from stories focusing on parental kidnapping as the problem to newer ones in which parental kidnapping may be a solution.

David Strickland and Joan O'Brien were a couple of kids when they were married in 1971 in Cocoa Beach, Florida. She was a high school dropout; he, a student in a local community college. Joan was already pregnant. As she is portrayed by her mother-in-law, Joan "could charm the wings off a butterfly." She had been a habitual school truant and had run away from home twice. She was also a liar. Initially, however, the marriage seemed to work. Margaret Strickland took care of Danny, born in November 1971, while Joan finished up her high school diploma and David worked part time and finished school, then worked full time in a local ambulance service. In short order, however, the marriage began to fall apart. Margaret claims to have initially discounted "well-meaning telephone calls" telling her that Joan had a boyfriend until Joan left David for one of his coworkers. Joan took Danny with her.[43]

David Strickland and his parents soon became concerned over Danny's welfare. Joan put her own interests above the needs of the child, leaving him in parked cars until late at night while she cavorted with men or visited bars. She left him in the care of irresponsible sitters who were often drunk. She didn't want the Stricklands around any more. "David began to concentrate on one thing and one thing only: freeing Danny from the irresponsible environment in which it was evident Danny lived." The child was temporarily put into Margaret Strickland's custody. And "Joan went her irresponsible, irrational and merry way." She was caught shoplifting, and the police found narcotics in her purse; she forged checks; she was a hit-and-run driver.[44]

Having defined her daughter-in-law's character in this way, Margaret Strickland then moves to the heart of her story. After a series of accusations and counter accusations (mostly hinted at in the narrative), the court gave permanent custody to David Strickland. Joan had visitation rights—one week every month. The visits with the mother were not successful, but they were tolerated and a rhythm was established. But Danny began to bring home tales of his other "daddy," a small Asian man whose many sexual antics he had observed. Danny began to draw indecent pictures of sex acts and took his clothes off whimsically. "During his short, one week stay with Joan, Danny had undergone a complete change in personality. He was no longer the normal, spirited boy one knew so well." Worse was to follow. His body had a series of scabs ("Mama Joan did it with a knife."). He had a large head wound. Finally, he pleaded not to have to "go with Mama Joan again," and he warned them "they're going to keep me."[45]

Joan had become the daugher-in-law from hell—irresponsible, abusive, foulmouthed, erratic, untrustworthy, sexually permissive—even before the day that two cars with several burly men and their barely concealed weapons accompanied Joan when she collected her son for his usual visit. Suspicious, but initally not yet ready to give up hope and trust, the Stricklands finally had to admit that the child had been snatched.[46]

The Stricklands were upstanding members of the Baptist church and they went by the book. They followed all the rules. They got contempt motions, writs of attachments, and orders terminating visitation. They delivered these to the state attorney general's office. They had not yet learned that the state and law enforcement agencies were both incompetent and un-caring. They learned soon enough. They couldn't even get the sheriff to file a missing person's report. "If this child is with a relative, now mind you, I did not say *mother*, I can't help you." They appealed to the governor of Florida, who replied, "Depend on your local law enforcement agency." Margaret's response was, "What a joke!" They ran up massive legal ex-penses, requiring the sale of valued property. They hired a friend as a detec-tive. To pay him, Margaret kept his children for the summer at no cost while his wife attended nursing school. The Stricklands had a down-home attitude and values. They learned to do what they did best—draw upon their own resources and their friends for aid and comfort. The courts, the state, the local police, were a "joke." Even the local papers wouldn't print their story.[47]

Joan had not only been efficient in the abduction, she had been shrewd. She laid a series of false trails that consumed the Stricklands' time, money, and emotional energy. They followed up every and any lead. They met good people and bad. "But we persisted. If Danny were dead, we had to know. If Danny were alive, he must be found and allowed to lead a normal life." (This might have come almost word-for-word from Christian's mem-oir.) To this end, they were extraordinarily pertinacious; they developed se-rious leads. "We wrote letters to all the state superintendents of schools in the United States, giving vital statistics on Danny and including a picture of Danny and Joan."[48]

In the end, they were lucky. Following through on an FBI lead on the most recent man with whom Joan was living and the fact that Joan was pregnant, a wild set of coincidences put Margaret Strickland's good friend, Kathryn Case, in the same Colorado Springs maternity waiting room with little Danny Strickland. Kathryn Case had never seen Danny, but Margaret had asked her to search for him when she went off to attend the birth of a grandchild in Colorado (where Joan and her new man were believed to have gone), and she had armed her with pictures of the child and copies of the custody decree. To make the story even more real, Kathryn Case tells her own part of Margaret Strickland's extraordinary tale. When Kathryn met Danny in the maternity waiting room, she did not know who he was, but apart from the name Danny, he did not know who he was either. "The FBI reported to the Stricklands that Joan had lived with about a dozen dif-ferent men and changed last names no less than twelve times. It would have been a difficult proposition for a boy Danny's age to keep track of a constantly shifting homelife, not to mention a name." Kathryn says she identified Danny through her "sixth sense." Kathryn let the Stricklands know, and Danny's grandfather flew immediately to Colorado to collect the child and bring him home under FBI auspices. "Only God could have produced and arranged such a logical sequence of events, such happiness," Kathryn concludes.[49]

The Stricklands' happiness was not complete and was to be severely tried by the challenge mounted by the O'Briens (Joan's family) in the courts and the press in both Florida and Colorado. "We had never lived in the public eye. We did not like it. We did not know how to counteract the lies." The newspapers had supported "motherhood . . . a sacred word in the English language" and spread lies about the Stricklands. Now the court tangles began. "After Danny's return, we were on a legal merry-go-round that never stopped. Seldom did Danny go two consecutive days without court ordered activities. Keeping track of the whole mess was close to impossible." Their lives and the life of the child were not normal. The courts continued to allow Joan to see the child, and the judicial system instituted conflicting orders about what the Stricklands could say to Danny and to the public to defend themselves. In the end, this narrative and the final decree, which kept Danny in his father's custody, was their vindication.[50]

In Margaret Strickland's narrative, the divorce, the abduction, the pursuit, the reunion, and the acrimonious public battle were not the only costs of the experience. Little Danny Strickland, only six years old when he was finally returned to the Stricklands, had been the object of it all, and he became its real victim. He was, according to David Strickland, "an innocent child caught in the web of legal jargon." He suffered emotional wounds. Even the final custody order provided no real closure. The child is quoted as saying "he did not like himself—would like to kill himself." Confused and unable to keep up at school, Danny was assigned a court counselor (for whom the Stricklands paid), but he "had precious little peace of mind." Despite their continuing problems and worries, the Stricklands did have peace of mind. "It was much better having Danny home, though the circumstances were not perfect, than having him lost, not knowing if he were alive." It was a sentiment Christian Ross would have understood.[51]

Despite its down-to-earth tone, Strickland's narrative is shot through with a contemporary vision of personal pathology and child endangerment,

court interference in tandem with official incompetence, the costs of publicity, and the fragility of modern marriage. It all culminates in the need for
psychological intervention and anticipates the most recent perspectives on
parental kidnapping. Like other kinds of kidnapping, by the second half of
the twentieth-century parental kidnapping partook of the strong tendency
to explain, understand, and heal in psychological terms. And like other
kinds of kidnapping, the family and its resources were called upon, albeit a
new family composed of kin and a stepparent rather than both parents of
the child. In the Strickland case, as in others, the courts actions, though required, are neither helpful nor fully just. Danny's story did in fact, help to
change the laws as the publicity about the case finally forced Florida to subscribe to the UCCJA. But the story suggests how passage of the new laws
also shifted the focus of the problem. With its emphasis on emotional disorder and family self-help, and its innuendos of sexual abuse, the Strickland
story helps to highlight personal resources and family pathology rather
than legislation as the central issue in parental kidnapping cases. These
would be the issues of the 1990s.

◧\/◨

In 1990, in fulfillment of the requirements of the 1984 Missing Children's
Act, the Justice Department published the first comprehensive statistical
analysis of the missing children problem in American history. The study
was a response to the furor over missing children that had been created in
the 1970s and 1980s. In the attempt to criminalize parental kidnapping, advocates and the media had associated it with wrenching stories about
stranger abduction, whose history had been available for over one hundred.
In conflating the statistics of the two, missing children's spokespersons at
once made stranger abductions seem more common and parental abductions more frightening. As a result, wild figures for the prevalence of child
kidnapping were floated in newspapers and congressional hearings. These
statistics eventually brought on a number of jaundiced-eye examinations,
which attempted to deflate the balloon. Many of these cast serious doubt on
the scope of the abduction problem and raised important methodological
questions about the manner in which different kinds of phenomena had
been juxtaposed in order to inflame popular feelings. One of these exami-

nations, a series in the *Denver Post,* garnered headlines and approval when it won the Pulitzer Prize.[52]

In the tangle of publicity and advocacy of the 1970s and 1980s, statistics were inflated and categories blurred. The Justice Department study first of all refined definitions, treating different categories of missing children as distinct and separate issues and then giving two kinds of numbers within each category. This was because, in the words of the study, "Serious definitional controversies surround each of the problems studied." In responding to the tendency to aggregate the missing children problem, the Justice Department also distinguished the most serious kinds of cases from those that were minor since most advocates had counted every possible incident or attempted occurrence as part of the phenomenon. In first distinguishing among five different kinds of child loss and then differentiating what it called "broad scope" problems, which included all incidents (even very minor ones), from more serious occurrences, the study provided a more realistic profile of the problem. The second set of numbers was usually from one-half to one-fifteenth the size of the broad scope numbers. Thus in the case of nonfamily abductions, the study concluded that in 1988 (the sample year), 3,200 to 4,600 cases could be broadly defined as stranger abductions but only 200 to 300 fulfilled the narrower definitions of a serious "stereotypical kidnapping."[53]

Using only the stricter definitions, family abductions accounted for the most numerous group of missing children in 1988. The 163,200 narrowly defined cases exposed a very significant problem. By the more flexible definition, which included every instance when a child was taken "in violation of a custody agreement or decree, or a child was not returned on time from an agreed upon overnight visit," there were 354,100 cases, a number even greater than most of those involved in discussions of parental kidnapping had proposed. But this kind of violation of agreement hardly met the image of a parental kidnapping created in the media—an abrupt rupture in parent-child relations and long-term disappearance where one parent did not know the child's whereabouts. Indeed, the broad focus abductions were usually only defined as abductions at all because they conformed to a strictly "legal conception." The number of cases that met the more stringent definition were large enough, however. These cases met the criteria of "intentional concealment" and included cases where attempts were made to prevent contact with the child, or the child was transported out of the state, or "there was evidence that the abductor had the intent to keep the child indefinitely or to permanently alter custodial privileges."[54]

The Justice Department study created a careful, focused picture of the parental kidnapping phenomenon. The criteria by which over 150,000 cases were defined as narrow focus were congruent with the recognizable stereotype of parental abductions. The most common time for abductions was January and August during extended visitations. Parental kidnappings were rarely long term. "Most of the episodes lasted two days to a week, with very few, 10 percent, a month or more. In only a tiny fraction, 1 percent or less was the child still being held by the abductor."[55] In other words, most parental kidnappings were resolved in fairly short order.While the numbers seemed to substantiate the furor over parental kidnapping that began in the early 1970s, many of the facts did not. Most articles in the 1970s and 1980s had claimed that only about 10 percent of all children abducted by parents would ever be returned. In all the personal narratives, when children usually were recovered, the period of loss ranged from many months to many years. Danny Strickland had been gone for three years; Eileen Crowley's daughter for seven. The Justice Department study of national incidence quietly made it clear that only 10 percent of all children were gone even a month or more and that very few were never returned. In only one-half of all the cases did the caretaking parent not know *at all times* the child's whereabouts. The common media representations of parental kidnapping were hardly representative.

It is always important not to confuse numbers with significance. Each of the abductions was a serious loss and a painful experience no matter its duration. Certainly parents were victimized when their children did not come home, even for a few days or a few hours. Some of these parents were justified in their concern since children may well have been at risk for some physical harm, though in many others they had merely overstayed an otherwise normal visit with one parent. The figures do not absolve either the parents or the society of responsibility.

But it is also important not to read the statistics without the specific qualifications to which they were attached or to confuse them with the picture of children lost all over America with parents responsible for their lasting disappearance, which Americans were asked to believe since the 1970s. Predictably, however, these "official" statistics became a kind of Holy Grail to those connected to the missing children phenomenon. Indeed, the agency most directly affected, the National Center for Missing and Exploited Children, which had been assigned the information clearinghouse functions required by the federal law in 1984, soon began to redefine its own agenda, as it shifted from an emphasis on stranger abductions to pay greater attention to parental abductions in light of these statistics. Its director, Ernie Allen, while noting that the nature of child abduction was now understood to be "more complex" than previously assumed, identified parental kidnapping as monumental and still growing at "an alarming rate." Not surprisingly, Allen and the National Center for Missing and Exploited Children used the much larger, broad focus figures in their public statements and analyses. The NCMEC called the situation a "crisis" in its aptly titled pamphlet, "The Kid Is with a Parent. How Bad Can It Be?" and boldly pronounced that it was very bad indeed when 4 percent of all these children experienced serious physical harm, 4 percent physical abuse, 1 percent sexual abuse, and 16 percent mental abuse. The pamphlet noted that in absolute numbers the children affected in this way was greater than those who suffered from more familiar and feared diseases like measles or Lyme disease. In calculating the number of children presumably at risk for harm, the pamphlet assumed that the number of children who suffered from each type of abuse could be added rather than that many of these abuses were experienced by the same children.[56] Thus, the Justice Department statistics were now available for those who had all along been committed to using parental kidnapping as a window on family abuse and disfunction or for those who had a stake in portraying the problem of abduction (of any variety) as rampant.

All through the discussions of the 1970s and 1980s, statistics had been accompanied in the public portrait of parental kidnapping by personal stories of emotional distress and family disorder. As the statistics were stabilized and made "official," the center of discussion increasingly shifted to an examination of the psychological dimensions of the kidnap experience. While the newspapers in the early twentieth century had made the problem of parental kidnapping into a kind of high society game in which the children participated, by the late twentieth century, social science and psychology transformed the experience into childhood trauma. Initially, most of these studies were based on very small samples of individuals who haphazardly came to the attention of social workers, psychiatrists, and psychologists in clinical practice. The conclusions of most of these studies supported the image of children on the run as suffering and abused—by their circumstances, their parents' lies, and their own fears. In 1990, the Justice Department's national incidence study gave a number to this phenomenon when it found that 14 percent of abducted children experienced serious mental harm.[57]

The most comprehensive study profiling abducted children and "abducting families" was published in 1993 by two social workers. Based on interviews of people discovered through an innovative sampling technique, it captures a far larger and more diverse sample than usual. The authors worked hard to diffuse the sensationalism that had come to mark most of the publicity surrounding parental kidnapping. In fact, Geoffrey L. Greif and Rebecca L. Hegar provide "a complex picture" that refrains from laying blame and accepts few of the common stereotypes. Greif and Hegar's conclusions are temperate and evenhanded. Not all children who are abducted are abused or traumatized or unhappy. Unlike in earlier feminist accounts, Greif and Hegar show that mothers as well as fathers kidnap their children. They show that parents who kidnap are often loving and caring as well as vindictive and abusive. The authors shrewdly understand that many of the charges and countercharges about abuse come from escalated conflicts in custody disputes. They even see justification for some kidnappings.[58]

Nevertheless, as clinicians oriented to issues of pathology, Greif and Hegar's stories are similar in the commonness of the overall family pathology that they detail. There is an enormous number of drug- or drink-addicted parents, a startling amount of violence between parents (and in the parents' own childhood homes), and many of the homes from which abducted children come can only be described as chaotic. In so doing, in identifying the complex and varied pathologies of contemporary families, they implicitly raise questions about how children can be rescued from abuse, the issue that has come to define and legitimate parental kidnapping in the 1990s.

One of Greif and Hegar's most compelling findings is that a significant proportion of kidnapping families are international or intercultural. This conclusion correlates with mounting evidence that the UCCJA could hardly help many parents whose children had been abducted because the child had been taken overseas and beyond the jurisdiction of American courts. While any abducted child might be transported abroad (as even Mr. Neil's daughters were presumably transported in 1873), in fact, many of these children were abducted by parents who were nationals of other countries and who now shed American citizenship and returned to earlier cultural identities. This is the plot at the center of Thomas Francek's parental kidnapping narrative, *Take Away One*. So serious is the problem of international abductions that the State Department published a self-help pamphlet advising parents of their rights and options. Indeed, in 1996 the federal government agreed to pay the expenses of needy parents who had to travel abroad to try to recover their children. In the absence of cooperation from the country to which a child has been abducted, retrieving such a child is the most intransigent problem associated with parental abductions. Some countries, like Portugal and nations in the Balkans and Middle East, simply do not recognize a mother's right to her child, and since these countries are not affiliated with the Hague Convention, fathers who abduct their children to these locations are usually home free.[59] Many of the most difficult (and long-term) cases of parental kidnapping are of this type. These cases, reported to number 1,200 in 1994, have in the last several years drawn widespread media attention.

The media has also focused on the vigilante groups that have developed in response. Trained as a Delta Force Commando, Don Feeney and others in the North Carolina group he organized, "Corporate Training Unlimited," have had several spectacular successes "rescuing" children from Iraq, Bangladesh, Jordan, Tunisia, and elsewhere. Their successful adventure in reabducting a girl from Jordan even became the subject of a television movie. Sometimes caught and jailed, but always pursuing their cause with determination, the members of the group are portrayed as both American freedom fighters and dedicated to parental justice. Don Feeney and his wife, Judy, who works with him, have become modern-day frontier gunslingers, fighting along the boundary between law and justice. Operating along this erratic line, they kidnap children and break the laws of other countries.[60]

Thus the public image of parental kidnapping has taken a new turn, emphasizing individual righteousness operating outside the law and against it. This turn is at once unexpected and explainable. It is unexpected because a public campaign begun initially as an attempt to bring the laws into line with changing social conditions has taken on a new public face centered on desperate acts in opposition to law. It is explainable because these are presented as a courageous response to injustice and the threat posed to children by family pathologies. The 1990s attitude toward the state and the family can hardly be more effectively portrayed: rotting and unreliable, families breed emotional distress and psychological disorder, while the laws and the courts are unavailable, ineffectual, and unjust. Caught without traditional social supports, the individual is portrayed as forced to private means and self-help approaches.

Just as the Feeney commandos operate outside of American law to kidnap children from foreign countries and break the laws of those countries, recent stories about parental kidnapping often focus on parents who become heroes by kidnapping their own children in the United States. Thus, Dr. Elizabeth Morgan, with the assistance of her parents, kidnapped her daughter to prevent her dentist husband from exercising his visitation rights, accusing him of child molestation. She went to jail for her defiance of the court, only to emerge a media star and the subject of a very sympathetic television movie in 1992. In Marin County, California, Paula Oldham repeated the Morgan saga and became a local heroine in 1994. When popular columnist Anna Quindlen featured her in one of Quindlen's last *New York Times* pieces, Oldham became a national figure and a new feminist champion. Quindlen not only justified the abduction but condemned the courts and the law that put Oldham in jail and then sent "the child . . . to live with the man Paula believed was a pedophile: her daughter's father, who denies the allegation." Oldham's husband has not only denied the charge but refused to be identified, knowing the fate of those who are even vaguely associated with such behavior. He has strong allies among law enforcement authorities; according to Marin County Deputy District Attorney Al Dair, "Oldham simply made up the allegation to punish and deny custody rights to her former husband, whom [Dair] has labeled the victim in the case."[61]

In the past, it was usually a mother's access to her children that was threatened by aspersions about immoral sexual behavior, and this was the basis upon which she could be judged "unfit." Today, a father's visitation rights or custody can most effectively be threatened by accusations of sexual abuse of the child. The charges are not new; Milo Abercrombie had used them against Lyman Swenson. But the contemporary reverberations are more extensive. Now linked with spreading allegations about the prevalence of incest and questions about how common child sexual abuse is even in the most "respectable" families and how often memories of this abuse are recalled later in life under therapeutic conditions, parental kidnapping has become increasingly linked to a discourse of family pathology.

And just as the Feeney commandos have become famous for rescuing children from the clutches of foreign countries to which they were abducted by a parent, an underground woman's movement, best known as a result of the media's focus on Faye Yager, has emerged to save women and their children from male violence and the American legal system. Yager and the Children's Underground Network that she founded is part of a spreading self-help movement aimed at rescuing women and their children from abusive and sexually depraved husbands and fathers. Yager, whose own daugher was raped by Yager's first husband, has become a female Rambo, meeting out justice where the law has misfired. In *Life* magazine's hostile portrait of Yager, she is described as relentless. She has, "nothing but contempt for the judiciary; and she is comfortable in the role of avenger . . . she is obsessive in pressing her case that America has given up its children not merely to individual deviates but to a conspiracy of satanists—preachers and politicians and mafiosi and Masons—bent on stealing souls." According to *Life*, "If she believes that you have sexually molested your own brood, she will accuse you loudly and fearlessly, on TV and in print, oblivious to lawsuits for libel and slander, pointing a finger until she has divested you not only of your children but also of what remains of your reputation." Yager is a sharp thorn in the side of officials. But she has a devoted following who help her to relocate women and their children by providing them with safe houses and new identities.[62] Yager reports that she has helped "about half of the 2,000 families she has counseled to go into hiding." According to the *New York Times*, "She says hers is one of several networks that hide children or assist families running from the courts. Word is spread in shelters, by lawyers and social service agencies and by Mrs. Yager's appearances on television talk shows." Accused by police of hiding and browbeating children into making accusations against their fathers, Yager was herself tried and acquitted on kidnapping charges in Atlanta in 1990, an event that served loosely as the basis of a television *Law and Order* episode. At her trial, the defense, "was able to discuss child abuse in general and . . . turned the trial into an emotional, at times horrifying, evocation of children betrayed by abuse and perversion." According to the *Atlanta Constitution*, "Many jurors expressed anger over testimony they'd heard about children not being believed or removed from abusers." One told Mrs. Yager afterward that she'd made her want to start a "safe house for such children." As the *New York Times* concluded, Yager's trial "and those attending it provide a glimpse into the *darkest edges of domestic disorder*, in which truth can be exceedingly difficult to ascertain."[63]

Today, child abuse and its justification for lawbreaking is often at the heart of parental kidnapping as a public issue. The deep concern for children's welfare expressed by the juror at Yager's trial is testimony to the widespread concern Americans feel for their children. In the 1990s, as in the past, that concern has been most forcefully evoked when the children are endangered (by strangers or today by parents), most vividly represented in stories of stolen children, and most furiously expressed when issues of sexuality are attached to these. By the late twentieth century, children's rights to care of all kinds has hardly been addressed systematically. Instead, only in stories of the most extreme mistreatment do jurors and other citizens of the community seem prepared to act on their behalf.

The problem of how children can be protected has been further complicated by the fact that the legal system has increasingly come to be seen as part of the problem. Since the community's instruments are themselves tainted, as the parental kidnapping narratives make clear and Yager makes explicit, how can that same community protect a child's welfare? The family may provide no better protection since today parental kidnapping is increasingly portrayed as a recourse *against the family pathology* that is assumed by many to be endemic in contemporary family life. At the end of the twentieth century, parental kidnapping is like a bomb ticking away in the midst of Americans' legitimate concerns for their children. Since the family has always been their recourse in stories about child kidnapping (including, as we have seen, parental kidnapping), what happens when the family is itself the source of the threat?[64]

The location of this bomb within the family is hardly surprising, given the family's central role in emotional development, and the late twentieth century's obsession with psychotherapeutics. Similarly, as the courts became ever more frequently arbitrators in the most intimate family concerns, especially issues relating to child custody and welfare, the suspicion they aroused and their failures in this task led to disenchantment. The culture has, of course, legitimated this attitude, with its elevation of Dirty Harrys as heroes and with stories throughout the 1970s and 1980s in which the law was either a joke or a villain. Earlier, the judge's ruling in the Vanderbilt case was greeted with vocal hostility. Before that, in the nineteenth century, the humble Mrs. McQuiston got the judge to change his ruling by wresting the child from the man to whom the judge had just moments before given the child, helping to expose how much justice was a sham when it came to matters of the human heart. The law and the courts had never been up to the particular challenges posed by parental kidnappings. With an extraordinary increase in custody cases, even revised laws governing parental kidnapping were simply unequal to the many problems besetting families and children by the late twentieth century, let alone all the other social and psychological issues to which it had become attached. Parental kidnapping as a crime further burdened a court system ill-equipped to settle the custody disputes from which it arose. The courts had become a weak vessel of mediation in an arena of strong beliefs, hostile feelings, and free-floating fantasies.

Parental kidnapping, seen as impossible in the nineteenth century and entertaining in the 1920s and 1930s, has at century's end exploded the myth of family security with stories that engage the American fascination with child loss and endangerment. Previously, the institution of the family had benefited with each episode of kidnapping, since the family's violation led to a renewal of its strength and a recharged commitment to children. Now as the century drew to a close, the family hardly existed in the form the Rosses with their seven children or the Bryans with their five would have easily recognized. Reconfigured through divorce, remarriage, and blended forms, it was deeply challenged from within as it became implicated in the theft and violation of its own children. No more vivid representation of the dilemmas of modernity could be imagined. Presented as a new crime, the much older problem of parental kidnapping vividly documented the changes the family had experienced in the last several decades.

CHAPTER SIX

"Missing"

Child Kidnapping in Contemporary America

At one time or another most parents experience those terrifying few minutes when their child wanders away or is several hours late in coming home and cannot be immediately located. . . . During those initial moments, parents imagine their child in the most fearful situations either trapped in some unseen place; lying injured or unconscious out of everyone's sight; or, the most dreaded, abducted by some stranger for unspeakable purposes.[1]

This was absolutely the worst experience anybody can ever have.[2]

⊡|⊡

Just before 8 A.M. on Friday, May 25, 1979, six year old Etan Patz emerged confidently from his parents' co-op apartment in the SoHo district of New York to begin the two-block walk to the school bus stop. Etan had been eager for some time to do this on his own as a sign of a new maturity, and his mother had finally assented. She watched him briefly from her loft's third-floor fire escape as he proceeded from their home on 113 Prince Street to the intersection of Wooster. She then turned back into the apartment, and Etan vanished into the New York crowds.[3]

Julie Patz did not yet know that when her son vanished from her sight, he had disappeared forever from her life. Indeed, Julie assumed that Etan had boarded the bus and was in his first-grade class at the Independence Plaza School (an annex of P.S. 3) on Greenwich Street throughout the day. It was only when he did not return as usual at 3:30 that afternoon that Julie Patz suspected that something might be wrong. She soon learned from a friend who usually collected him from the bus and whose daughter was in his class that Etan had not been at school and that he never made it to the bus that morning. It was clear to Julie at once and it would eventually become clear to the police, the media, and through them, the city, and the nation that Etan Patz had been taken in broad daylight amidst the commercial bustle of normal life from the streets of New York.[4]

What happened to him has, however, never been made clear. Indeed, the case of Etan Patz—who would now be a young man of twenty-five—remains an open police case of a missing child.

When the police arrived at the Patzes' home at 5:30 that evening, they were confronted by a time lapse of nearly ten hours since the child was last seen. They were also confounded by the fact that it was not only a Friday, but the beginning of the long Memorial Day weekend. As a result, it would be very difficult to recreate the early morning scene the next day, a Saturday, when many possible observers would be absent. And it would be very difficult to piece together evidence or witnesses to that morning's events. Because the weather had been drizzly and because of the delay, the police dogs brought in the next morning to follow the child's scent and to reconstruct the route of his disappearance would be less than completely effective.[5]

In the Patz case, however, unlike many others, the police were not long delayed either by the assumption that Etan had simply run away or just wandered off. Runaways were usually older, and Etan was a happy, well-adjusted child who knew where he was going. Neither was he the victim of a potential custody dispute. Julie and Stanley Patz were, to all appearances, a stable couple with two other children, a two-year-old toddler, Ari, and an eight-year-old daughter, Shira. These were always among the first speculations in any case of a missing child. Whatever had happened to Etan, it was unlikely that he had either run off or been taken by one of the parents. Nor did it seem probable that he was the victim of foul play by one of the parents, as sometimes also happened when children were reported missing to the police. The parents seemed devoted and loving, and they were genuinely distraught. While the police would not discount this last possibility until both Julie and Stanley had taken the first of several polygraph tests, they proceeded on the assumption that Etan had been kidnapped. Etan's disappearance, according to Lieutenant Earl J. Campazzi, who commanded the missing persons squad, was simply "unique."[6]

For a long time, Julie Patz believed that, as an extremely handsome child with blond hair, an upturned nose, and glowing blue eyes (often fetchingly rendered by his photographer father), Etan had been taken by someone who desperately wanted a child of her or his own. "Whoever took him might be desperate for a child, but that person can't make Etan happy," Julie pleaded. "We won't press charges—all we ask is please bring Etan back to us." Almost one half year later, on Etan's birthday, October 9, Julie insisted, "We still think some misguided person who wanted to have a beautiful little boy took Etan." And Etan—friendly, bright, and outgoing, as well as smiling and pretty—would have been a desirable child. By 1979, it was becoming increasingly difficult to find attractive, healthy, white children for adoption. And while most children stolen for such purposes were infants taken directly from the hospital like Robert Marcus, it was not altogether impossible for a child Etan's age to be taken with these ends in view.[7]

It was similarly unlikely that Etan would serve as the basis for a ransom. The Patzes were far from wealthy—their loft was thinly furnished (Julie ran a child-care center there)—and ransom kidnapping had largely faded in the 1970s. A brief rash of cases followed in the wake of the spectacular abduction of Patty Hearst in 1974, but through that very connection to a political cause, ransom kidnappings became less likely as a simple form of criminal extortion. Moreover, ransoming had become a crime against adults (often the older progeny of the conspicuously wealthy like the Hearsts, the Gettys, and the Bronfmans) and increasingly the activity of non-American groups in Italy and Germany. The Patzes would eventually become the subject of an extortion demand of $2,500, but this was two years into the case and a clear instance of a secondary and opportunistic crime piggybacked on the original kidnapping. Stephanie Bryan's parents had similarly been subjected to this kind of kiting of parental anguish. In 1979, there were still other (more far-fetched) theories to explain Etan's disappearance. Among the thousands of letters the Patzes received, one urged them to "look for gypsies (*gitanos*),"[8] a reminder that, more than one hundred years after the first widely publicized abduction, some myths still persisted.

None of these explanations seemed to dispel the mystery of Etan's disappearance. "All the questions, it seems, lead nowhere," Etan's father Stanley noted. "Everyone is supposed to love a mystery. Well, we don't." Neither did the police, as Etan's case became the "No. 1 priority of the Police Department" in New York City by the end of May and the beginning of June 1979. One week after Etan's disappearance, the police were fielding 500 calls daily, and a force of forty men had completed repeated searches of all buildings in the four-block square area where Etan was last seen. As many as 500 officers were at one point involved in the police investigation, but the police appeared baffled. Lieutenant Ken Bauman speculated: "Is the child in a building where he is trapped? Is he with a male who is attracted to young boys or is he with a mentally disturbed woman who wishes that the child would be her child?"[9]

Absent meaningful leads, the police were reduced to chasing after "sightings" by concerned citizens. These started coming in large numbers after the city was blanketed by flyers (eventually more than 300,000 were broadcast) with a picture and description of the boy, distributed by the forty neighbors and friends of the Patzes who assembled in their home to aid in the search effort. Etan or someone very like him was soon spotted in many local places, from Sheepshead Bay, to the south in Brooklyn, to Yonkers, north of the city. As the media began to retell the story, the police got calls from as far as Michigan and California. Sightings, posters, and the media became the lifeline of the search effort. Very soon, too, in desperation the Patzes turned to leads by hundreds of psychics who offered their services, the likes of which have been offered in the search for missing children from Charley Ross's day to the present. Julie Patz tried to use every media occasion to draw attention to her still-missing child, and Etan had become, a month after he vanished from the city's streets, the subject of the "widest and longest search for a missing child undertaken by the city's Police Department in decades." Unlike a similar all-out effort that eventually led to Robert Marcus's recovery on the West Coast twenty-three years earlier, this one led nowhere. Detective James Williams had been in the missing person's squad for twenty years and observed that "there's never been anything like this before.... A child so small, so defenseless has never disappeared for so long."[10]

In fact, the search for Etan Patz would go on much, much longer. After the city had tired of the posters and handbills "plastered on every boutique and loft building" and they had become the site for graffiti and obscenities, the search for Etan would remain an obsession for the child's parents and for at least two law officers: Detective William Butler, who was initially in charge of the police investigation and worked on the case for over a year until his retirement, and much later, federal prosecutor Stuart GraBois. These diehards were haunted by the pretty little boy who disappeared inexplicably off the face of the earth. They remained with the case while other support faded. Two weeks after the disappearance, the police had disassembled the telephone command post they had set up in the Patz home, and after the first few months of rapt interest, the press coverage thinned down significantly to be reawakened only by the occasion of a birthday or an anniversary. But Etan Patz, a "Lost Child," was, in the words of his omnipresent posters, "Still Missing."[11]

The police and the parents had pursued many false leads and the parents' hopes had been both buoyed and shattered repeatedly. They were in many ways, of course, repeating Christian Ross's experience one hundred years earlier. In 1979 as in 1874, the disappearance seemed to signal something new to the society. In each, the loss of the child was inexplicably horrible. In a hundred years, many things had changed, especially the rapidity of the information about the kidnapped child and the new prominence given to Julie Patz's role in the search for her son. Indeed, it was Julie more often than Stanley who appeared on television and gave interviews, as a mother's public grief and Julie's own poise became culturally acceptable and a salable commodity. But many more things had not changed. Among them were the many crank and mean-spirited calls to which the Patzes were subjected and the endless advice offered by an array of specialists in psychic phenomona. One of these claimed that "Etan at age 6, had intentionally left home to construct a geodesic dome." Like Christian Ross, too, the parents, Julie especially, were blamed for Etan's disappearance. As Julie said at one point to the reporter from *People* magazine, "I am the woman who lost her child—not the mother whose son was kidnapped." And she had experiences of overt accusation. "One day I took Shira and Ari to Little Italy and a group of Italian mothers came up to me and said how sorry they were that Etan was missing and how terrible I must feel, especially since it was all my fault." At other times, too, she was accosted and blamed for allowing a young child on the streets by himself.[12]

Like Christian, too, the Patzes were recipients of both the help and the callousness of friends, neighbors, and fellow citizens. Just as Christian had to squelch rumors and libels about his involvement in his son's abduction, the Patzes had to dispute rumors and newspaper articles that claimed Etan was with his grandparents because of a family dispute over religion. (Stanley, but not Julie, came from a Jewish background.) In this instance, a group of "Anonymous Puerto Ricans of the SoHo section of Lower Manhattan," angered by rumors that Etan had been kidnapped by two Puerto Ricans in a car, countered with a rumor in *El Diario-La Prenza* (a Spanish language newspaper) that he was in Massachusetts with his paternal grandparents. The story was picked up in the *New York Post* and proved to be a serious setback for the investigation as New Yorkers assumed that they had been falsely alarmed and began to take Etan's poster from the walls, windows, and lampposts of the city. Even more seriously, a New York taxi driver waited three and one-half years to come forward with significant information about a young boy fitting Etan's description. He had been spirited into the cab by a nervous and jittery blond man on the day and in the place of Etan's disappearance.[13]

Like Christian also, the Patzes would suffer intensely the agony of not knowing what had happened to their son. "How," Stanley Patz asked, "do you learn to survive as the family of an abducted child?" "This is a psychological wound that will never heal, never close up, without a resolution of one kind or another." At the outset, the Patzes had refused to allow rewards to be posted for Etan, fearful that this would lead others to steal children in hopes of benefiting from the reward. They thus repeated Christian's reluctance to set bad precedents. When they finally relented three years later, it was in order to provide themselves with some ending to their story. An anonymous donor offered $25,000 "'for credible information' leading to Etan's return or proof that he is dead." Like Christian, who wrote a memoir to bring forth information about his child's fate, the Patzes finally used reward money to bring some closure, some end to Etan's unfinished story. "People get raped or murdered, and those crimes, as horrible as they are, at least are contained in time," Stanley Patz observed. "In this crime there was a beginning, but there is no end." Finally, Stanley and especially Julie Patz had to construct a meaning for their loss, to provide themselves a substitute for its emotional irresolution. And like Christian, they did so by devoting themselves to the effort to help find other children. Their meaning now came in subsuming Etan's identity to a larger campaign on behalf of missing children. In 1983, when President Ronald Reagan proclaimed a new National Missing Children Day, he chose May 25, the date of Etan's disappearance. Since then, the event, with a shifting date in May, has become an institution. It was fitting that when the New York City Police Foundation began a "new public campaign to find missing children in 1985," on a date almost exactly six years after Etan's disappearance, it was Etan's picture that was flashed two times an hour from a large electronic screen above Broadway. Here it competed with the other lights and icons of twentieth-century culture. The picture was accompanied by the words "Last seen 5-25-79. Still Missing."[14]

While his parents learned to cope with their loss and Etan became a symbol for other missing children, the explanation for his disappearance was beginning to emerge from another set of cultural concerns that allowed his disappearance to become meaningful. Only after the initial explosion of interest had subsided and after they had pieced together every possible shred of testimony (there was no physical evidence) from passersby who had either seen or been present in the neighborhood that morning—five full months after the event—did the police release a sketch of a man who was possibly implicated in Etan's disappearance. This man was "reportedly seen talking with Etan Patz shortly before the boy disappeared." By then Stanley and Julie, who had initially sought comfort in the belief that their son had attracted the attention of some desperate, but maternal, woman, were hanging onto their shredding hopes. Soon they would even draw "strength . . . in the story of Steven Stayner, the California boy who was returned to his family seven years after he was kidnapped." Whatever strength the Patzes were able to draw from Stayner's return could not possibly have come, contrary to the phrasing of the *New York Times* report, from his having been returned. On the contrary, Kenneth Parnell, who kidnapped Stayner in 1972, had just stolen another boy, five-year-old Timmy Lee White, who he also expected to keep permanently as "his son." It was Stayner's empathy for the new recruit, and what he anticipated to be the certain fate of the younger child, that crystalized Stayner's determination to escape from Parnell and take the new child with him. By this time, Steven was a strapping young man who, when he did escape, could not remember much more about his early life than his first name. Stayner had not "been returned," and his escape eventually led to an extremely tricky and far from successful reintegration into his family. Steven had been deeply wounded by the regular sexual and physical abuse to which he had been subjected by Parnell.[15]

It was, however, Stayner's story that helped to turn a particular corner in the Patz case as it precipitated a more settled picture of what had likely happened to Etan. Stayner's return from captivity together with other aspects of the Patz case began to jell into a new theory that eclipsed most previous speculations. That theory centered on the sexual abuse of young children and their entrapment by adults driven by uncontrollable urges, even to the extent of abducting their victims.

Both the police and his parents had always been aware of this possible fate for pretty little Etan. It was one of the speculations by Lieutenant Bauman as early as May 31, but the press had hardly followed in depth this line of investigation and had not advertised any police dragnet of suspected sex criminals. The search for Etan had been mostly an open-ended search for a missing child. Even a year after his disappearance, a long piece in the *Sunday New York Times Magazine* by Mary Cantwell had not alluded to the sexual possibilities in the kidnapping but dwelled instead on the existential torments of being a mother who must at some point allow a child to take wing, even with the possibility of such a loss literally lurking around the corner.[16]

By the time Beth Gutcheon's best-selling novel, *Still Missing*, was published in 1981, that new theory had become an all but settled fact. The book was universally believed to be based on the Patz case and full of deep emotional and physical parallels, but Gutcheon had attached an ending to the search. Gutcheon, who had been a neighbor of the Patzes, located "Alex Selky" in the clutches of a pedophile. Alex had been obviously (though never explicitly) abused, and the novel is full of the sexual themes of child exploitation.

One year later, in December 1982, a picture of a child very much resembling a somewhat older Etan was discovered in a police raid on a warehouse in Massachusetts used by NAMBLA (the North American Man Boy Love Association), which had also netted two teenaged boys. By then, what had been previously unspoken, but hardly unimagined—that Etan had been stolen in order to be sexually exploited—had become the governing assumption, even after it was firmly established that the boy pictured in the NAMBLA material was not Etan. It was this picture and its surrounding sexual sensation that eventually drew forth the so-called eyewitness report by the New York cabby. It also renewed the investigation of Etan's disappearance, to which eight New York police officers were once again assigned.[17]

Within a week of the finding in Massachusetts, the Patz case was back in the news. The *New York Times* put the issue bluntly on the front page of its "Living" section with the headline, "Etan Patz Case Puts New Focus on a Sexual Disorder, Pedophilia." Although, according to Dr. A. Nicholas Groh, a clinical psychologist, "abduction of a child by a pedophile was very rare," the *Times* nevertheless stated that "There is an epidemic of sexual abuse of children." Eventually Stuart GraBois would take this motive for granted in his pursuit of a local pedophile, Jose Antonio Ramos, whom he sought to link to the Etan Patz abduction.[18]

While Etan Patz would never return, and eventually even his parents no longer wished for the media attention that a continued campaign would require, his disappearance could now be "explained."[19] Its explanation lay in the deepest, dirtiest secret of contemporary American culture.

📑∥🔓

The secret was not exactly new to Americans, but its centrality as an explanation for stranger kidnappings was. It had been an innuendo in earlier cases. The possibility of perverse sexuality was a grey cloud hovering over the Leopold and Loeb trial in 1924 and permeated the prosecution's closing arguments against Burton Abbott in 1956. In both cases, an absence of physical evidence had relegated the issue to the fringes of the prosecution cases and to public speculation. In a larger sense, however, the sexualization of childhood was increasingly part (though a troubling and unassimilated part) of the culture. Despite the decade's ambiguities, this was certainly the case by the 1950s.

Since at least the late nineteenth century, the sexuality of children had been a potent cultural possibility, available not so much as an alternative to childhood innocence, but as a confluent current. The confluence had defined Freud's project, which boldly drew attention to infant sexuality and integrated childhood sexual fantasies into the family romance of bourgeois attachments. Since the 1920s, various institutions of American culture had made the connection among youth, vitality, and sexuality commercially profitable; throughout the twentieth century, strategic new media like the movies and advertising had exploited the connection with relish. In the 1950s, nubile young women like Tammy and Gigi, whose innocence had a romantic sensuality, were staples of movies, and the association between youth and eroticism eventually spilled into the much more richly sexual

Splendor in the Grass in 1961. By the time Americans read the teasing tale of Nabokov's preadolescent Lolita in 1958 and watched it on the screen, the sexual possibilities of young girls found fertile soil amidst the many baby dolls of the American imagination.[20]

The sexual abuse of children, as distinct from the cultural representation and exploitation of the sexual potential of childhood (if such a distinction is completely possible), had its own literature, also rooted in Freud and other early twentieth-century sexologists, like Richard von Krafft-Ebing. It was nurtured in the United States by the studies of human sexuality of Alfred Kinsey and his associates in the late 1940s and 1950s. Although a few earlier American studies like those of J. Paul de River had focused on the pathological in attachment to children, Kinsey's studies not only placed the issue in the context of the amplitude of human sexuality and its normal diversity, but denied any necessarily ill effects of early experimentation or childhood exposure. Kinsey, moreover, "normalized" such experience through the simple device of numbers. He had found that about 24 percent of all women (almost one-quarter) had some preadolescent sexual experience, ranging from being the subject of exhibitionism to active participation in coitus.[21]

While Kinsey's tolerant views and emphasis on catholic tastes contributed to the heightened sexualization of 1950s culture and influenced specialized investigations of the sexual experience of children, during the same period (the late 1940s through the 1950s), the American public was stirred up by a campaign based on the fear of sexual crimes, especially against young girls. And the period not coincidently saw a marked acceleration in the implementation of sexual psychopath laws. A few states—Michigan, Illinois, and California—had passed such laws in the late 1930s, but many others did so only after a 1940 Supreme Court ruling held valid a Minnesota statute that allowed sexual criminals, dangerous to others because of irresponsible behavior, to be committed "as if insane." Since those accused could be sentenced to an unspecified time in a mental institution, these states had turned into social policy Sheldon Glueck's conclusion in 1937 that "the aggressive sex offender is more a problem for psychopathology than for criminal justice." In California, in 1951 sex crimes comprised nearly one-tenth of all superior court dispositions. These laws were criticized by liberal observers, who saw in them the potential for a serious abrogation of civil rights. The distinguished criminologist Edwin H. Sutherland said in 1950 that "The sex murders of children are most effective in producing hysteria," upon which the laws depended. By midcentury, the sexual criminal who attacked children was not only a social pariah, as had already been brilliantly demonstrated in the 1931 film *M*, but was being put into a special penal category to be governed by psychological rather than legal guidelines. Thus by the time Stephanie Bryan's body was found near Bud Abbott's cabin, the sexual abuse of children was familiar enough to be terrifying but still sufficiently bizarre to create hysteria. As Sutherland noted, "The hysteria produced by child murders is due in part to the fact that the ordinary citizen cannot understand a sex attack on a child. . . . Fear is greater because the behavior is so incomprehensible."[22]

In the early 1950s, the image of a "shocking increase in sex crimes" was fanned by J. Edgar Hoover's pointed question, "How Safe Is Your Youngster?" *Parents Magazine* tried to allay concern by publishing a heart-to-heart article addressed to alarmed parents. According to the author, Edith Stern, "What I found out was quite different from lurid accounts of the imminent peril of 'sex maniacs' and 'sex fiends'—and infinitely more reassuring. . . . The number of these most frightful of all crimes, attacks on children, is really quite small." Although Stern concluded that "there is absolutely no way of telling who is suddenly going to commit a violent sex crime," she was hopeful that research could help solve the problem. And the article concluded that "much more study of abnormal sexual behavior is needed before it can really be controlled."[23]

Those studies were, in fact, growing in response to the laws and the public outcry. Like the *Parents Magazine* article, most of these studies refused to fan the flames of an agitated public fear. The 1950s saw a substantial number of investigations centered on the child victims of sexual crimes as well as their perpetrators as states with sexual psychopath laws began to make both the victims and criminals available for study. California was notable in this regard, and the California Sexual Deviation Studies, funded by the state and conducted at the Langley Porter Clinic in San Francisco, are important examples of the tendencies of this research. Grounded in the psychodynamic perspective (with its psychoanalytic roots) that had become professionally dominant in the 1950s, these studies also echoed the Kinsey commitment to an ecological and sociological investigation of the range of normal sexual behaviors. While the professionals engaged in these studies owed their status and their funding to the furor over sex crimes, most sought to distinguish their dispassionate scientific perspective from the highly politicized furor over sexual criminality and sexual deviancy of the time. Thus, for example, although sexual psychopath laws usually included homosexuality in their domain, Karl Bowman, the superintendent of the Langley Porter Clinic and a supervisor of the California studies (and a coauthor of the famous reports on Leopold and Loeb) concluded, "It is generally agreed that homosexual relations are common among men," and proceeded to quote Kinsey. In that light, the study advised that "Legislation should distinguish clearly between crimes dangerous to society and those disgusting or offensive to public decency and morals."[24]

It was from this same (for its day) liberal perspective, and with a similar inclination not simply to succumb to offended decency, that the California studies addressed questions relating to sex with children. While they concluded, "Concise laws, with appropriately severe penalties, must protect children and young minors against all sexual advances, whether heterosexual or homosexual," the studies asked that the laws be revised "in case of a defendant convicted of sexual relations with a girl who, though young is married, promiscuous or a prostitute." In this instance, the study was trying to distinguish the clearly culpable criminal from those offenders who were technically culpable but who probably shared responsibility with the young victim.[25]

In attempting to apportion blame carefully, these studies strongly suggested that many young victims were complicit in their sexual molestation or abuse. The California State Deviation studies, for example, often depicted young victims as highly flirtatious and sexually, or at least erotically, fixated: "One ten year old girl (L. W.) became very flirtatious with the psychiatrist (a male) and said, 'You know what a fanny is? You know what a butt is?' . . . A 13 year old girl (A. M.) told the male psychiatrist, 'I know I've seen you before because I never forget a face. Did I meet you on Market Street in one of the bars? I'm sure I did.' One four and a half year old (A. F.) sat with her dress up and her legs apart, telling with great relish of the way in which the neighbor had fondled her." There were many similar observations.[26]

With their psychotherapeutic outlook and scientific aims, the studies were not out to condemn the victims, but to ask broader questions, especially about the consequences of sexual experience for future personality development and how sexual experience was related to family relationships. According to the researchers, these family relationships (particularly relations with mothers) were emotionally inadequate and the families of many victims were characterized by severe instability; some were so disturbed as to be pathological. Since child molestation was thus usually linked to family pathology, it was not surprisingly supposed to become the occasion for treatment of the victim and her family. The victim, as much as the abuser, became the object of psychotherapeutic intervention. But the depiction of children as young as four as flirtatious, teasing, erotically wise, and sexually ripe was certainly not a firm basis for a broad-based campaign to ignite public sentiment against child sexual molestation, most of which, the study concluded and—"contrary to what might be expected"—was committed by acquaintances or even family members.

Thus in the 1950s, scientific experts like those who conducted the California Sexual Deviations Studies (whose investigations had grown from the furor over sexual crimes) refused to add fuel to the fire in a campaign against sex criminals. Indeed their research conclusions put a general damper on any broad-based campaign. In the context of the period's commitment to home and family, the disturbing conclusions that families were often the source of the sexual exploitation was largely ignored, to be resurrected in a different context and time. By making the victims complicitous and by establishing a base close to home for child sexual abuse, these studies helped to keep the social science expert on sex crimes against children out of the public arena. When he did contribute, he was likely to conclude, as Paul W. Tappan did in *Newsweek*, "The average sex offender is a mild-mannered, much maligned and nondangerous person who seldom repeats his offense and even more seldom becomes a murderer."[27] Hardly the image of the rampaging sex criminal.

Although there were some significant variations, most of the studies of sexual abuse of children between 1950 and the mid 1970s came to similar conclusions. Most child molestation was committed by neighbors, friends, or family members; the vast majority of the victims were girls, usually between eleven and seventeen; most of the serious offenses stopped short of physical penetration; and usually the victims could be easily seduced (if they had not themselves been the seducers) because they had inadequate attention at home or were not well taken care of, especially by cold, rejecting mothers and absent fathers. Many of the families were marked by separation or divorce. Craving love, the victims of molestation frequently exchanged sex for attention. Even studies that drew upon broad student populations and were not based on the victims of legally charged offenders (as was the case in the California Sexual Deviation Studies) came to similar, though more cautious, conclusions. Thus on the basis of a sample of 500 University of California students, Judson Landis observed that the girls who had been complicitous in molestation came "from the unhappiest homes."[28]

Some of the studies from this period were distressed by the extent to which children were sexually abused in America. But even these could not escape the familiar faultfinding. By emphasizing the pathology of victims' families, the studies tended to put the victims into a distinct and identifiable group. The victims were hardly random. By 1976, when Patricia Miller wrote a doctoral dissertation in sociology on the subject, she defined two theoretical possibilities: "The Random Victim Model" and "The Culpable Victim Model." She found no empirical support for the former. Miller attached a structural rather than a psychological explanation to her evidence—girls were complicit in their victimization because of gender socialization—but she put herself firmly in the research tradition in which "the child is believed to precipitate the offense in some way." The random victim model, in which a child was strictly the victim of a sex offense, was mere "folk wisdom." As late as 1976, therefore, most scientific studies had found that sexually abused children were drawn from a distinct social group; they were rarely random victims.[29] Whatever else was true of the sexual criminal, he did not come unbidden.

In view of the status of most psychological and sociological conclusions about the culpability of the victim and her family in child sexual abuse, it was hardly surprising that when Etan Patz was kidnapped, when he simply vanished from the streets of New York, neither his parents nor the police would have drawn automatically upon this literature and its portrait of child molestation to explain why he was "missing." While there had always been some small place in the literature for the entirely innocent victim of vicious sex crimes, the literature was sharply focused on the complicit child, with the "mild-mannered, much-maligned" molester hidden in the background. This portrait hardly served as a ready-made explanation for Etan's disappearance. Etan was an innocent child, not a runaway; he came from a stable, loving home. Etan, like Charley Ross, was unambiguously a victim. And just as the crime of ransom kidnapping was "new" in 1874, so the crime of sexual kidnapping was in some sense "new" as an explanation for

Etan's disappearance. During the long period of Etan's absence, the central tendency in the literature on child molestation was sufficiently transformed to give new meaning to Etan's disappearance.[30] That transformation was so thoroughgoing that ever since then almost every innocent child—in the absence of very strong evidence to the contrary—is assumed to have been abducted for sexual purposes. By the time Jacob Wetterling disappeared ten years after Etan, it was an unalterable conviction.

回|||回

There had been a troubling literature on pedophiles at least since the 1940s, when the psychoanalyst J. Paul de River published a graphic, illustrated, and stomach-churning chapter on the sadistic pedophile in his book on sexual perversion. And in the 1970s, some of the literature gathered on the sexual molesters of children increasingly put a vicious face on at least some of the victimizers of children. In 1978, A. Nicholas Groth noted that the "exploitative child offender" "exhibits a lack of concern for the consequences or costs to others of his sexual activity; he experiences his motivation to be strong sexual needs that he is incapable of delaying or redirecting."[31] But, it was not until the early 1980s, when the literature on child victims of sexual molestation had taken a new turn, that the rampant molester of children once more came out from behind the bushes. At that point, the literature on the child victim turned toward a massive documentation of the broad extent and serious consequences of the problem of child sexual victimization. This literature drew upon new statistics collected because of stringent state reporting requirements on child abuse instituted in the mid 1970s.[32] But the literature also drew upon previous studies (accumulating since the 1950s) that counted large numbers of children who had been sexually exposed. Those numbers were now given a new twist. Unlike the Kinsey studies, the new literature did not use the numbers to normalize childhood sexual experience. Instead, these were turned into an enormous tabulation of large-scale victimization of children in the society.

This transformation also involved a significant change in the objectives of the literature from detached scientific study that emphasized clinical observation and treatment to the tabulation of a rampant social problem that required social advocacy. The shift occurred most emphatically after the emergence of a strong victim's rights movement, symbolized politically by

President Ronald Reagan's appointment of the Task Force on Victims of Crime on April 23, 1982. In 1982 too, Congress enacted the Federal Victim and Witness Protection Act and passed the landmark Missing Children's Act which ushered in a new stage in public acknowledgment that child kidnapping was a serious and widespread social problem. This agenda coincided with a vigorous feminist outcry against blaming the rape victim and came a year after the exposure of the heinous serial murders of as many as twenty-nine African American children in Atlanta. These events brought to a new pitch the revulsion against what was increasingly portrayed as the special sexual pathology of those who preyed on children.[33] Since that time, the specialized literature on child sexual molestation, by emphasizing the many faces of the pedophile and the widespread nature of the child sex abuse problem, has made the danger to children seem both ubiquitous and endemic. That literature has brought the sexual molester out from behind the bushes into practically every house and neighborhood in America.

The transformation in the style and nature of the literature on child molestation can best be seen in two books written by the man who, in the last fifteen years, has become the most visible authority in the area of child sexual abuse, child abduction, and missing children, David Finkelhor. And it can be seen in a fairly brief period of time, between 1979 and 1984. In 1979, Finkelhor published his first book, *Sexually Victimized Children*. Firmly anchored in the by then growing view that child sexual abuse was widespread, affecting 19.2 percent of girls and 8.6 percent of boys aged 13 to 16, Finkelhor's 1979 book cautions his readers that these statistics almost certainly undercount the phenomenon. Well aware that these figures are very large and appear to reflect the sudden emergence of a social phenomenon, he notes, "Whereas ten years ago there was hardly a case anywhere, today the reporting rate is increasing exponentially and shows little sign of abating. The situation has been called an epidemic." But, he is extremely careful to downplay any tendency to base an argument about an increase in sexual victimization of children on this change in the number of reported cases. Instead, he is intrigued by the issue, and, as befits both a dissertation and the times, Finkelhor carefully weighs all possible factors and includes various explanations; he makes important comparisons with other studies. Finkelhor concludes, much as did earlier investigators, that there was a strong relationship between troubled families and sexually victimized girls. "We hope we have firmly established the idea that the family plays a crucial part in creating vulnerability to sexual victimization." Finkelhor thus adopts what Miller had called "the culpable victim model."[34]

Finkelhor draws no explicit conclusions about the sexually complicit child, though in accordance with the general evenhandness displayed in his book, he discusses the prevelance of this view. But his book still glows in the embers of the liberal sexual attitudes of the 1970s (whose firm base was in Kinsey's 1950s). Finkelhor raises questions about whether sex is as bad for children as is usually assumed, placing himself firmly within the earlier consensus summarized by Miller in 1976: "virtually every study published in the last forty years reporting data on more than a few cases has failed to find negative consequences of the childhood [sexual] experience reflected in subsequent years." Where researchers do find negative consequences, Finkelhor notes, they attribute these to the anxiety that attaches to the secretiveness about sex rather than to the experience itself. Sex is thus not necessarily dangerous or even emotionally unsettling to children. Finkelhor goes even further, giving potential standing to those who believe that "mild forms of sex play between parents and children" might well be good for children, as well as those committed altogether to reexamining the incest taboo.[35]

All this was not only in the spirit of post 1960s sexual liberation, but consonant with the assumptions behind the investigations of child sexual molestation conducted in the 1950s. Like these earlier studies, Finkelhor assumed that normal sexuality might include childhood sexual experience, that sexuality was not by itself the bogeyman of childhood, and that childhood sexuality was an arena for scientific study, to be defined by tempered discourse and neutral investigation.

By 1984, when Finkelhor's second book, *Child Sexual Abuse*, appears, the flames of liberal sexuality are entirely extinguished, and Finkelhor has now much more certainly entered the fray as a child advocate, a spokesman for the molested and abused child whose enormous numbers now smother all other issues. Finkelhor's new book is defined by the same strategy that guided the symposium sponsored by the United States Department of Justice that same year: to "produce better strategies for addressing child abuse" and "to convey to professionals and the public as a whole that child molestation is a serious criminal offense." Under the tutelage of Diana Russell, a feminist who had proposed that huge number of girls (35 percent) were victims of sexual abuse, Finkelhor's book is now firmly anchored in the child abuse movement and the women's movement. These had created mountains of testimonials by 1984, very like those presented by victims of parental kidnappings. Finkelhor sheds his earlier evenhandedness for an ungloved fist. The sexual revolution of the 1960s, once seen as offering multidimentional potentials that could liberate children, is now viewed as contributing to their exploitation: "Certainly one major effect of the sexual revolution has been the erosion of traditional externalized controls over sexual behavior. . . . One group for whom this state of confusion is particularly serious are those whose sexual behavior in the past was regulated primarily by serious external control. . . . This group might conclude, logically [as if logic would have much to do with it], that there are no longer rules . . . are the prohibitions against sex with children still in force?" Another potential erosion of inhibition, pornography, is now also suspect because it is an indicator of "the erosion of taboos."[36] Finkelhor's primary goal is now to serve as advocate. Since in this light children are in constant peril for sexual exploitation, his main goal is to remove anything that could possibly contribute to this situation, not to question his own assumptions.

Finkelhor no longer had the distance to ask whether the very success of the sexual liberation movement in eroding taboos against a whole range of sexual behaviors may have made *the taboo against sex with children at once more socially necessary and more* **apparently** *vulnerable*. The very need for some sexual boundaries somewhere in a society rapidly shedding earlier taboos made sex with children more repugnant and more socially explosive, increasing both the pressure to create more protective legislation and the tendency to report breaches. Indeed, the enormous growth in the ranks of child advocates and protectors like Finkelhor was an expression of the significance of the taboo, not a sign of its loosening hold. The veritable avalanche of attention to the problem of sex with children was the sign of a society enforcing explicit, vocal boundaries against sex with children. All this would explain why the number of cases of child sexual abuse may not have changed at all over time in the midst of what appeared to be an epidemic, thus elucidating the very problem that had intrigued Finkelhor in 1979. Ironically, an understanding of the newly reinforced taboo against sex with children could even explain some tendency to increasing prevalence of the activity or at least its cultural representation. As sex with children becomes more dangerous, it became more titillating and, as such, far more enticing to advertisers and the producers of movies and television programs.[37]

Observing the changes in Finkelhor's work as well as some comprehension of the newly shrill taboos against sex with children help us understand how Etan Patz's disappearance could be so much more easily "explained" in 1983 than in 1979. Whatever the actual prevalence of child molestation or pedophilia at the time, the perception of this as a serious threat to American children had grown immensely in a very brief time. The perception of that threat had increased significantly as a result of the new, vocal advocacy literature. That literature was itself the result of a new cultural awareness of the taboo against sex with children, a taboo that became both more necessary and seemingly more vulnerable as other taboos (against premarital sex, homosexuality, adultery, serial sex, and promiscuous sex) were eroded. Thus at the same time that sex with children was perceived as more dangerous than ever before (and more harmful to children), the large numbers used by child advocates made it seem very widespread.

By the early 1980s, sex with children had become both dangerous and apparently prevalent. De Groth had already identified one kind of pedophile as an exploitative child offender, a predator who could not control his impulses and had no regard for his victims. It only took a little more study to further categorize pedophiles, as the FBI was in the process of doing, and add new variants to those of the infantile and regressed pedophiles (more timid than actually dangerous), among them the "morally indiscriminate" and the "sexually indiscriminate" pedophile. To these observations was added also the reflection that "almost any child molester is capable of violence or even murder to avoid identification." The once mild-mannered and unthreatening child molester became a potential child killer. When this happened, it was simple (even logical) to conclude that a massive increase in child kidnapping was one consequence of the sexual molester's threat to society. By the early 1990s, the newly reinvigorated threat posed by the molester of children once again brought demands for laws against sexual predators. Some of these laws took over where the old sexual psychopath laws left off, while new public disclosure laws aimed to inform communities about recently released and still dangerous criminals in their communities.[38]

If we reflect on the period from 1950 to 1980, much seemed to have changed, although nothing strikingly new may have happened. The period probably did not produce a sudden new population of criminals who preyed on children. In the 1950s, these had already been quite visible in the media, in legislation against sexual predators, and in cases like that of Stephanie Bryan. What had changed was the social science evaluations of that behavior and the role that social scientists had assumed as child advocates. In the 1950s, psychiatrists like Karl Bowman had resisted participating in the social fears that surrounded sexual deviancy, hoping instead to understand scientifically and treat through family therapy the context of child victimization. By the 1980s, social scientists assumed a very different posture toward the problems they investigated and toward its victims. As child advocates, their concern was no longer evenhanded or therapeutic. It was to expose the problem and to protect the presumptive innocence of the child.

The times had also changed. While the much looser moral strictures of the 1980s made all kinds of sex all right, it made the possibility of sex with children much more ominous. Sex with children seemed both more likely in a society without clear boundaries of sexually right and wrong behavior and made barriers against sex with children seem all the more necessary. The sexual exposure of children, which Kinsey had found widespread and largely unthreatening, had become the newest kind of horror. Americans had once feared extortion and then death in their tales of child kidnapping. By the 1980s, parents feared that their children were being sexually exploited—by child-care personnel, former husbands, and rampant sexual predators. These last had become the most fearsome of all the enemies children faced.

IV

By the time Kevin Collins's picture appeared on the cover of *Newsweek* magazine on March 19, 1984, he had been missing for more than a month from his home and family in San Francisco. Even though the local police had initially hesitated to grasp the kidnapping implications in his disappearance and preferred to view him as a probable runaway, the nation, or at least the estimated twenty million readers of *Newsweek*, seemed far less reluctant to believe that when a ten-year-old disappeared, his fate was probably linked to whatever happened to Etan Patz.[39]

Saturday, February 11, was to be the big basketball game, and Kevin Collins, a fourth grader, was looking forward to it eagerly after his Friday evening practice at the St. Agnes School at 755 Ashbury Street. Because his brother was not there to protect him from the punches of sixth-grade kids who usually carpooled with Kevin after practice in their coach's car, Kevin decided to walk to the bus stop that evening and go home by himself. He had a city (Muni) bus pass. When he was last seen waiting for the number 43 bus at 7 P.M. on February 10, he was wearing his school uniform—brown corduroy pants, a blue shirt, and a green sweater. When Kevin had not returned by 7:30, his father, David Collins, and his coach, Paul Fontana, began to search the neighborhood. It was to be the beginning of a long process that would lead David, an unemployed truckdriver, into a new way of life, a life devoted to the search for his son and for the many other children missing in contemporary America.[40]

The Collinses and their nine children were well-regarded members of their local parish (David and Anne had met at the St. Agnes School when they were students there), and it was the parish and its school that became the initial site for assembling the volunteers and the posters that became the first line of defense against the enemy that was devouring America's children. By February 15, 2,000 posters had been distributed through the two-hundred-block area around the school. That number would grow into the hundreds of thousands in a short time. On the same day, San Francisco Mayor Dianne Feinstein issued a $5,000 reward for information and gave permission for Kevin's poster to appear on the city's public transportation vehicles. Kevin's picture showed a handsome, wide-eyed boy glancing slightly backward over his shoulder at us. That picture, with its questioning, somewhat startled look (which would eventually appear on the *Newsweek* cover), became a familiar sight throughout the San Francisco Bay Area and way beyond as the parents waited anxiously for someone to come forward with information to help them or the police find their ten-year-old son. By the fifth day after his disappearance, the local newspapers were not only beginning to register the fading of hope for a simple explanation, but also the national statistics on missing children. "About 150,000 children are reported missing annually and . . . roughly 50,000 of those cases are never solved." Kevin had become one of a multitude—his disappearance, like his iconic picture on a *Newsweek* cover headlined "Stolen Children," a symbol of a national tragedy.[41]

After a week, the Collins case was fed into the FBI computer, a service recently made available because of new legislation on missing children passed in 1982. This move indicated that the police were now persuaded that he was probably not a runaway, but scarcely meant that the new service would enable Kevin's return. The inclusion of missing children in the FBI network represented the new national recognition of the problem as something beyond the scope of local law enforcement, but it did not bring with it new national means for locating him. The vast majority of missing children's cases—whether suspicious or not—remained in the hands of local police who retained control over the investigation. The FBI computer contained simple information, but it could not generate leads or follow them up. For this the Collinses, like all families of kidnapped children, depended on public knowledge and the kind of publicity that posters and the media alone could provide. Their initial bulwark against despair were the hundreds of volunteers who gathered to distribute flyers and who eventually scoured the city in search of the child. Within three days of the disappearance, Kevin's picture was on local television.[42]

The volunteers soon enlisted the aid of the Reverend Cecil Williams, a local San Francisco hero, trusted by the down-and-out as well as the famous and powerful for the comfort he brought to the poor and the unfortunate. Williams became an intermediary who offered to meet with anyone at anytime in complete anonymity for information about the child or to receive the child. Williams could be a trusted alternative to the police. He made a simple appeal: "To whoever has Kevin or knows his whereabouts. We appeal to you to release Kevin or let us know where he can be found. We are not interested in seeking 'justice' or punishment. We are only interested in his safe return. We want to offer you a safe way to return him." Williams knew a lot of people and his pulpit at the Glide Memorial United Methodist Church was an important place for disseminating and gathering information. He was also very well known to the local media.[43]

In a short time, David Collins and his wife's brother, Michael Deasy, were becoming experts in a new enterprise—the search for missing children. David Collins learned to approach the problem in an almost clinical way, dividing San Francisco into thirty-three neighborhoods that were carefully bounded on a map and saturated by search parties. Within one week, hundreds of volunteers had conducted an extensive house-to-house search. Within ten days, Collins's energies and the pain of a community whose children seemed to be under threat had generated 100,000 flyers and 850 volunteers. The police were impressed. According to Police Inspector Richard Hesselroth, "This is the biggest citizen effort we've ever seen" in the search for a missing child. The newspapers were also impressed. And in the absence of any serious progress, the city was advised to take pride in its efforts. "Kevin's disappearance has pulled The City together," the *San Francisco Examiner* heralded in a headline. The search involved people well beyond the local neighborhood. At the city's military base, the Presidio, "military volunteers working on their own time searched the post for Kevin's clothes or signs of recent digging." Both those actively involved in the search and those on the sidelines were affected. As one parent noted, "It hits home. . . . You hope it doesn't happen to you. You just watch your own kids a little better."[44]

A largely gay organization, "Community United Against Violence," sponsored its own search for Kevin. And with good reason. Although the newspapers initially did not speculate about the reason for his disappearance, Kevin's parents as well as many in the community simply assumed that Kevin had been abducted to be sexually exploited. Their greatest concern was with what followed that exploitation—whether the child was released, kept as an object for long-term abuse, or killed. Two week after his disappearance, police were quoted as fearing "the worst." By then, the police had asked the California State Department of Justice to check out "registered sex offenders," of whom there were approximately 2,500 in the Bay Area alone. Shortly after that, local newspaper readers were informed that, according to Denny Abbott of the Adam Walsh Child Resource Center, "Child stealers fall into no stereotype and may seem as ordinary as the guy next door." But, "for the most part they're pedophiles, people who sexually use children." These same readers were also warned by the Office of Juvenile Justice and Delinquency Prevention of the United States Justice Department, "No one knows the extent of the problem. . . . Child victims are being enticed, blackmailed and kidnapped to satisfy the market for" kiddie pornography, pedophilia, and serial homicides. Child abduction was thus just a logical expression of a much wider phenomenon, the problem of sex with children. The Justice Department also usefully, if repellingly, outlined the possibilities. "If it's a killing, the body is usually found within 24 to 48 hours. . . . Most psychotic killers kill but don't hide the body. They enjoy the pain caused by having the body found." But a sadistic pedophile or even a serial killer was only part of the danger. "Children who are stolen and kept alive take about two weeks to become adjusted to their new situation. . . . One 6-year-old victim . . . had become so accustomed to his new life after less than three weeks that he was reluctant to leave the remote cabin where he was being kept."[45] It was no wonder then that local gays, concerned not to be tarred with the pedophile brush and its sometimes perceived link to sociopathic consequences, were actively helping the efforts to locate Kevin.

There were obviously many good reasons for different segments of the San Francisco Bay community to pull together to find a small boy who had been torn out of its midst in this brutal way. In the process, they helped to register their alarm about social predators and to confirm the presence of strong community norms that proscribed sex with children. To this effort, the gay community added its own voice.

But how could a community fully protect itself against such dangers and allurements? In an article in the *San Francisco Examiner*, Kevin was described as "strictly trained never to get into a strange car," and certainly the effort to protect children had by the time of Kevin's disappearance in 1984 created sufficient concern that parents did increasingly warn children in this way. After Kevin's abduction, many also had them photographed and fingerprinted so that there could be some link established to missing bodies that might turn up unidentified. But the larger problem was much more intractable. It was lodged in the contradictions of a culture that at once adulated children and treasured their innocence while their very vulnerability made them prey to those inclined to befoul that innocence. The extraordinary danger to children in modern America could not have been better illustrated than in the juxtapositioning on the same page of a newspaper of an advertisement for a "Children's Photograph Contest," including a total of $3,000 in prizes, with the picture of the search for Kevin's body by the Presidio volunteers. In the ad, a lovely, smiling, full-cheeked, little blond girl of about five smiles alluringly out at us, her audience. The appeal is devastating; an appropriate companion to the indelible, somewhat accusatory glance that stares out at us from Kevin's posters.[46] In a society that had learned to exploit the innocence of childhood, how could one prevent other forms of exploitation by those drawn to the attractive child? On a single page, this local paper had depicted both the appeal and the danger of childhood innocence.

Another part of the painful contradiction of child sexual exploitation in contemporary America could be found in the Collins family's desperate need for publicity. After Kevin's picture appeared on the cover of *News-*

week, David Collins noted, "You can't calculate the value of that kind of exposure." By then volunteers had distributed 400,000 posters of Kevin, and seventeen billboards around the Bay Area had been donated "carrying a plea for the public to be on the watch for him." But the magazine cover was the final coup; it had an international reach and acted as a stepping stone to other media coverage. If Kevin were still alive, he had probably become adapted to his new situation, but the man who abused him could hardly hide him altogether. The Collinses' only chance for recovery would lie in someone seeing Kevin (even if he were disguised), recognizing him from his picture, and making the connection.[47] Retrieving a missing child in 1984, as in 1874, still depended on sightings.

And just as Charley's identity could not be protected from being transformed by his repeated sightings, so Kevin's identity was necessarily altered as he became the poster boy for America's missing children. Eventually, his face was everywhere: on billboards, on bulletin boards, on milk cartons, and on any other object that could serve as a means to broadcast information. Like the goods that were usually featured this way, Kevin was used to sell the problem of missing children. Eventually other pictures took Kevin's place as the countless missing children in the society followed each other in rapid and pitiful succession. Initially, the newness led to intense concern and anxiety, each picture another sign of social failure. But eventually, as one picture succeeded another and each became a blip on an individual's consciousness, they became a part of the landscape, a scar rather than a wound in social awareness. The final, omnipresent expression of the campaign became the little Advo advertisements put into millions of mailboxes across the nation, with a lost child on one side and goods to be sold on the other. Americans began to adapt to the sight of these pictures, scarcely noticing their distinct characteristics, quickly glancing at the vital information—date of birth, size, and other evanescent physical characteristics—but registering very little of the individual contained within. What was left behind was an oppressive anxiety and a sense of child endangerment, but no real means to defeat the enemy who seemed everywhere.

After the mid 1980s, the poster children, the billboard children, and the Advo card children of all colors, both genders, and a variety of ages became everpresent, a psychic scar in American culture. They were everywhere "Missing."

◨√◧

A variety of organizations now kept the faces actively circulating in the public domain. Indeed, Kevin's abduction occurred at a moment of already elevated consciousness about the kidnap dangers lurking for America's children. Not only had Etan Patz become nationally known, but Adam Walsh, the six-year-old kidnapped from the toy department of a Hollywood, Florida, department store, had been memorialized through an extensive political and media campaign to alert the nation and its leaders to those dangers. Testifying before Congress and in the afterward to a famous television re-creation of his son's story, John Walsh became a charismatic and indefatigable spokesman on behalf of the missing children's problem. In the television re-creation, *Adam* (first broadcast in October 1983), Walsh was portrayed by Daniel J. Travante, the then hot star of *Hill Street Blues*, a popular television show. Starting in 1988, Walsh would become a media star himself as the host of the television program *America's Most Wanted*, which often features missing children among its segments. Like *Adam* before it, *America's Most Wanted* drew upon the experiences of voluntary organizations by enlisting the public in efforts to apprehend criminals and solve crimes. In *America's Most Wanted*, as in *Adam*, pictures of children are flashed on the ultimate billboard, the television screen, in an effort (sometimes successful) to encourage identification and discovery.[48]

Earlier, Walsh had started a private, nonprofit organization devoted to the search for missing children. That organization and its many imitators not only memorialized the lost child, but sought to aid many other families who, it was now presumed, would soon have similar experiences. Only experience with this kind of shocking loss could prepare one to help others cope with the emotional and practical problems that came with the abduction of a child. Thus, the organizations were at once search networks and support groups, performing the two basic functions needed by parents left bereft of a child and subjected to the often skeptical attitudes and inadequate knowledge and resources of the local police.[49]

Most of the private organizations grew naturally out of the spontaneous volunteer efforts that came together when a child disappeared. Beginning with the donation of time and services, the volunteers who gathered to search for a child often found themselves also soliciting other kinds of assistance to keep the search going—money for copying, printing, telephoning, postage. The organizations thus found it necessary to handle the sudden flow of monetary aid that usually came in the wake of a well-publicized kidnapping as the local community acted to show its support for the family and to express its outrage at the assault. Some of the volunteers found themselves actively working on behalf of the wider cause, not just the single case. The *San Franciso Examiner* caught this intertwined experience of grief and activism well in an editorial in the wake of Kevin's disappearance: "The idea of the child as victim is painful to contemplate; the reality is unbearable to behold. We look on in shock and try to imagine the unimaginable suffering of the families. . . . We stand in awe of the courage . . . that . . . has been demonstrated by Kevin's parents, and it has struck a heartening response in the community. . . . All over the country, parents of missing children have banded together to press for laws to help safeguard youngsters and to offer educational programs that may prevent other parents and children from suffering." Thus, the spontaneous efforts to search for a single missing child paradoxically helped to create organizations whose existence depended on the expectation of grief and bewilderment by the parents of future missing children. While grounded in the reality of grief, these organizations existed to predict dreadful loss and generated a sense of social anxiety. Many proceeded from offering assistance to individual families to serving as educational resources in communities and schools to lobbying in the state on issues relating to child kidnapping and other sex crimes against children.[50]

The Kevin Collins Foundation for Missing Children, one of the oldest and most active, was established in 1984 in the wake of Kevin's disappearance. Run out of a storefront in San Francisco's Tenderloin district, the organization was a no-frills operation that spent all the money it raised on behalf of its efforts. It offered, first of all, advice and assistance to parents suddenly confronted by the loss or the feared loss of a child through its twenty-four-hour hot line and live-answer service. It further helped to organize the initial community effort to find a child. In its own words, "Experienced on-site assistance pulls together a terrified community and gives them constructive direction." When this community effort was absent, the foundation distributed flyers and assisted parents in the basics of a search. It has also devoted itself to lobbying for state crime legislation "to keep predators off the streets and to keep track of those still on the street." Along these lines, its most recent efforts (which was strongly reinforced and finally rewarded in the context of the kidnapping of Polly Klaas in

October 1993 from her Petaluma home) has been the passage in 1996 of California Senate Bill 12X, the Violent Crime Information Center. The information provided through the passage of this bill will provide local police who stop a suspicious vehicle with complete background information on the past crimes of the vehicle operator. David Collins and others involved in lobbying on its behalf are strongly of the opinion that had such information been available at the time of Polly Klaas's kidnapping, her self-confessed abductor, Richard Allen Davis, would have been apprehended when his car was caught in a ditch not long after the kidnapping. Davis had a previous record of kidnap and sexual assault. Had he been arrested at that time, Polly Klaas might still be alive. David Collins and the foundation were also active in organizing the search for Polly Klaas.[51]

Organizations like the Kevin Collins Foundation have been involved in a wide range of lobbying activities that have made the problem of child abduction and laws relating to general questions about child sexual abuse an important part of many state legislative calendars. Their efforts have strongly distinguished the 1980s' campaign against child sexual abuse from that of the 1950s. These organizations have also helped to define the educational agenda of local schools and child-care centers, as well as local media and community-outreach programs, in a broad-based effort to instruct children in ways to protect themselves against abduction. And these organizations have taken root throughout the country. According to the *Los Angles Times*, over one hundred such organizations were created in the last ten years. Usually founded on the energies of a grief-stricken family, its friends, and its neighbors and set up to memorialize a single child, they have kept the issue of missing children an urgent part of contemporary culture.[52]

The national publicity generated in the early to mid 1980s by these organizations, fathers like Walsh, and other child advocates also resulted in the creation of a much more centralized response to the problem in the founding of the National Center for Missing and Exploited Children (NCMEC). NCMEC occupies an unusual middle ground between a public and private organization. While it has no governmental authority, its rationale as well as its funding is lodged in congressional legislation, and it has strong links both in information sources and joint publications with the Office of Juvenile Justice and Delinquency Prevention of the Justice Department. It also maintains a close relationship with the Adam Walsh Foundation and with John Walsh. Since 1984, the NCMEC provides the clearinghouse functions for national information on missing children required by the Missing Children's Assistance Act. By its own account, after ten years of operation, the center has received "more than 760,000 calls on its toll-free Hotline" from people requesting assistance, reporting sightings of missing children, or asking for educational information. It has also "printed more than 8 million publications," which provide training assistance to police and others on how to deal with and prevent missing-children-related crimes. The center also actively circulates pictures of missing children, often in large layout posters, but most famously by making selections from among its currently active cases for the Advo advertising cards. The center is a perfect example of the linkage between private and public action that defines contemporary efforts on behalf of missing children.[53]

In its efforts to locate missing children, the center is especially proud of its age-enhancement photographic service, which uses extant photos (that rapidly become out of date) and age progresses them to approximate the appearance of a child some years after an abduction. This computer-created photograph uses technology to the same ends as Charley Ross's parents achieved when they had an artist use an old photograph to approximate what Charley might have looked like when he was stolen since they had no very recent depiction. The center claims to have assisted in the recovery of one in seven children whose photographs it has distributed and one in six of those whose photos have been age enhanced. Since the center is organized to provide assistance with all missing children, that definition and its agenda includes not only children abducted by strangers, but also those abducted by family members and runaway children. The number of returns includes those recovered alive or dead. Recently, the center has also opened its computers to information about and assistance with Alzheimer patients.[54]

The center's agenda is best described by the particular conjoining in its title of the words "Missing and Exploited" since much of the center's literature is aimed at advertising the connection. Among its prominent publications are titles like "Children Traumatized in Sex Rings," "Child Molesters: A Behavioral Analysis" (published in cooperation with the FBI), as well as "A Lesson for Life: An Examination of the Accuracy and Adequacy of Traditional Child Protection Messages." As one of these publications notes, "The link between missing and sexually exploited children is a strong one." The center has fully adopted and is an active proponent of the governing paradigm that child molesters are not only a widespread danger to children, but the source of most stranger abductions. Although the center's publications are usually careful to divide molesters into a variety of different categories and observe that "sadistic child molesters do not appear to be large in numbers," one of its pamphlets concluded nevertheless that "If an offender has a sexual preference for children and at the same time has no conscience, there is no limit on how he might sexually victimize children. Such an offender is likely to abduct or murder children . . . his behavior is determined by a stunning lack of conscience." This publication also includes collectors and distributors of child pornography among child molesters, and this inclusion illustrates the connection the literature draws between the exploited and the missing. "Any individual . . . who collects or distributes child pornography actually perpetuates the sexual abuse or exploitation of the child portrayed."[55]

Although the center is not a governmental organization, it is a professional one, and unlike the many private nonprofit organizations (forty of these are approved by the NCMEC), its bureaucratically organized staff is trained to respond to other professional organizations, specifically the local police, rather than aggrieved parents. Its published training manual addressed to local law enforcement advises them that while local voluntary organizations can be useful in the search effort, "law enforcement control of the overall investigation must be firmly established and understood." The NCMEC provides technical rather than emotional support and is an organization honed to respond with information, statistics, and publications to media inquiries. Indeed, the media have increasingly used the center as their basic information resource. By the late 1980s, many articles about individual missing children referred to information or material furnished by the center. The NCMEC provides an efficient, organized response. Unsurprisingly, its relations with local volunteer organizations and with griefstricken parents is not always a happy one.[56]

Despite its status, polish, and the millions it receives as a line of the national budget[57] the NCMEC is, in fact, restricted in what it can do by the same problems that beset other kinds of efforts. Like all other organizations, its aim is to attract attention for its children and to its cause, for the two are interlinked. Above all, it depends on information fed into its national computer base: the child's name and birthdate and the child's picture. Thus, despite its national scope, the success of the NCMEC in locating a child is really limited by the fallible and evanescent nature of that information. For many missing children, their names, like their lives, can change overnight. And while the center might distribute the pictures of children much more widely than any local effort, those pictures, even age-enhanced ones, are only as good as the citizens who see the children and report it. In the end, that information on sightings, like information collected by voluntary centers, is turned back to local law enforcement officials. The success of the endeavor is limited by the latter's resources, commitment, and time.

The center's initial existence depended heavily on the inflamed atmosphere created by wild statistics that was part of public discourse in the early to mid 1980s, when Senate and House committees were told that as many as "two million children" disappeared each year and as many as "five thousand were murdered through kidnapping and abduction." Since 1990, however, the NCMEC has been eager to set the record straight and to serve as a reliable source of accurate information. To this end, it has been a significant conveyor of the study sponsored by the Justice Department known as National Incidence Study on Missing, Abducted, Runaway and Thrownaway Children (often called NISMART) conducted by David Finkelhor, Gerald Hoteling, and Andrea Sedlak.[58]

The NISMART study put to rest the gyrating numbers of the mid 1980s, which had unleashed a serious professional backlash, and carefully redefined the problem of missing children into five parts: Runaways, Lost/Injured/Otherwise Missing, Family Abduction, Thrownaway, and Non Family Abduction (also known as stranger abduction, although some parts of this category includes acquaintances). In each of these categories, NISMART additionally divides the problem into what it calls "broad scope" incidents (mostly less serious or very short term), and "policy focus" incidents (more severe, of long duration, and obviously dangerous to the child). Among nonfamily abductions, NISMART has identified 3,200 to 4,600 child abductions/kidnappings per year. These figures represent all those who fit the legal definition of a "coerced or unauthorized taking of a child, into a building, a vehicle, or a distance of more than 20 feet; the detention of a child for a period of more than an hour; or the luring of a child for the purposes of committing another crime. . . . *Many short-term abductions that took place in the course of other crimes like sexual assault were counted under this definition.*" Thus, sexual molestations that included detention or abduction for at least an hour, and which were reported to the police, would be included in the broad-scope figures, although these may have been brief sexual incidents rather than intentional abductions. NISMART was especially eager to separate the category of abduction from the media picture to which it had become attached and that defined the problem in the popular mind: "We need to emphasize this point: Legal Definition Abduction is far broader than the stereotype many people have when they think of stranger kidnapping."[59]

In the NISMART study, the more restricted category, "stereotypical kidnapping," included only the most serious cases of longer detention or intentional aduction, and those in which the child was gone overnight, killed, or transported fifty miles or more or there was evidence of intent to keep the child permanently. These cases, like the cases of Etan Patz and Kevin Collins, were comparatively rare, and in 1988 probably numbered between 200 and 300. The report also concluded that there were 114,600 attempted (broadly defined) abductions involving strangers per year. Finally, of the stereotypical stranger abductions, the report estimated that between 43 and 147 children had been murdered as a result.[60]

Despite the authority of this government-sponsored study, and the uses to which it has sometimes been put by the media to staunch fears about rampaging stranger abductions, the figures have been challenged by others in the missing children's movement. David Collins is unhappy both with the numbers, which he believes seriously underestimate the phenomenon, and with the popular assumption that the broad-focus abductions are not real kidnappings and not really serious. Collins draws on recent California experience to propose that the problem is significantly larger and that even short-term abduction-molestations are a serious and widespread phenomenon that is vastly underreported. At San Francisco General Hospital alone, 80 children a year are treated for sexual molestation occurring in what Collins calls the course of an abduction. In California, 89 cases of kidnapping were witnessed in 1994. Collins believes that the number of national abductions is closer to 12,000, rather than the 4,000 used in the broad-focus figures. Based on his own experience, he also claims that many of the children listed as runaways have actually been abducted but are not reported that way by unsympathetic or inexperienced police.[61]

Even the NCMEC has reacted ambiguously to its own officially adopted numbers. In 1994, in the wake of a series of frightening and widely advertised cases, including that of adolescents Polly Klaas and Sara Wood, Ernie

Allen, the director of NCMEC, urged parents to deemphasize "stranger danger," the stereotypical abductions on which the media had become fixated. At the same time, he urged an increase in vigilance over the much more widespead problem of parental abductions and the equally frightening problem of child molestation, which Allen proposed had been probably sharply underestimated in the broad-focus figures. Indeed Allen, along with NCMEC, had a stake in maintaining social vigilance over a broadly defined problem of missing children. Though he hoped to avoid the backlash that had grown in the wake of the *Denver Post's* widely respected (and Pulitzer Prize–winning) series that exposed the degree to which kidnap statistics had exaggerated the problem, he also sought to keep the light fixed on the children missing all over America. And for this problem, the Etan Patzes and the Kevin Collinses, by embodying the nightmare, had become the most effective public representatives. Because this was so, because the nightmare, the chill up the public spine, was the best way to raise concern about the wider phenomenon in which the center had such a vested interest, it was unlikely that the issue could ever completely be redefined even by NCMEC.[62]

It was not long until the cumulative cultural fixation led beyond private organizations based in community grief and beyond public agencies based in federal law to entrepreneurship. In many small stores and restaurants in California, enterprising individuals had set out jars for public contributions, mostly spare coins or single bills, collected by who knows who and donated to who knows what ends, labeled "For Missing Children." In April 1995, a far more large-scale effort was started as business entered the search for missing children. And it came in the likeliest, most practical of all forms—insurance. The idea of kidnap insurance was not new. The first policy had been written in 1920; immediately after the Lindbergh child was kidnapped, Lloyd's of London advertised it publicly. But the scale of the proposed contemporary undertaking bespoke the widespread popular anxiety about child abduction on which it rested. In the San Francisco Bay Area, New York, Boston and elsewhere throughout the nation, an organization called the Family Protection Network appealed to the basic fear now lodged deep inside American culture. In full-page advertisements in major newspapers, it announced, "We won't give up. As long as your child is missing, we will keep on looking." SafeCard Services, which claims to have started the venture with $25 million in start-up costs and engaged the services of 1,000 licensed investigators, is run by Paul G. Kahn, a man the *San Francisco Chronicle* calls "a credit-card wizard." Kahn attributed his "sensitivity" about the issue to the Polly Klaas case, and the fact that he had a "13 year old daughter." The company expects to offer parents two options: a simple registration for $50 a year and a search option for $250. Lower fees would be instituted for families who insured three or more children. The idea is basically to create a children's data base with vital information (picture, blood type, height, weight, fingerprints) that would immediately be mobilized in the event of an abduction.[63]

Whatever the actuarial calculations on which SafeCard hopes to conduct its (one presumes profitable) business, the question of what a private insurance company can actually do is left entirely to the imagination of the public, a public whose heads are well stocked with the roll call of still missing children. SafeCard claims, "We will have an investigator at home within two hours of a call." But, as one San Francisco private investigator asked, "What does the detective do after he comes up to the door and takes his hat off? He opens the drawer, takes out the picture and then contacts the media."[64] Like all other efforts—by friends and neighbors, by nonprofit organizations, or by NCMEC—the effort to find abducted children has a limited repertoire. What SafeCard has done is to prepackage a community response. In so doing, it may have answered to the fears of parents but taken away the only positive experience (if that is at all possible) that the abduction of a child offers—a lost child in exchange for a new community bond.

◧ VI ◨

When Jacob Wetterling was taken at gunpoint at 9:15 P.M. on Sunday, October 22, 1989, he had something rarely available to kidnapped children: witnesses. Also a variety of organizations and laws were already in place for precisely this kind of case. The National Center for Missing and Exploited Children had been in operation for five years, and after Jacob's name was put into its files, it drew upon the growing data collected for NISMART to assure the local media like the *Minneapolis Star Tribune* that cases like Jacob's were rare about 100 each year. David Collins, inducted through his own experience and now head of the Kevin Collins Foundation for Missing Children, was on hand to give emotional support and technical assistance. He helped to organize the original volunteer effort and the flyer campaign.

The police never questioned that an abduction had occurred since Jacob's ten-year-old brother, Trevor, and his eleven-year-old friend, Aaron Larson, had been with him when a man with a ski mask took Jacob away. And, after eliminating the possibility that one of Jerry Wetterling's disgruntled chiropractic patients or someone unhappy that Jerry was the president of the local chapter of the NAACP might have acted from revenge, the police quickly moved on the assumption that Jacob's abduction had been sexually motivated. Jacob's mother, Patty Wetterling, recalled, "As I sat there, numb, all kinds of horrible scenarios ran through my mind. Jacob could be raped or sexually abused—or worse." By 1989, the sexual was already presumed. By midnight, the FBI had been called into the case in accordance with new laws that allowed them to become much more quickly involved where foul play was suspected. By five o'clock the next morning, a friend of the Wetterlings had contacted local and national media and asked them to air the story. "Within hours," Patty recalled, "our house was filled with reporters."[65]

After two days, the police were tracking down 100 potential suspects as a result of tips. "At least three of them had records for sex offenses and were released within the past six months from correctional facilities or treatment programs." The police were confident that "the child was abducted for a specific purpose." And while County Sheriff Charlie Grafft noted that he was no expert in these matters, he thought that "this person is a pedophile." Within a very short time in the Wetterling case, there was a known crime, an explanation, and a variety of sources of support for what David Collins describes as the largest search effort in his experience.[66]

Jacob was the second of Jerry and Patty Wetterling's four children, and the oldest boy. The evening of October 22, he, Aaron, and Trevor rode their bikes to a convenience store a mile down the road to rent a video. St. Joseph, Minnesota, in Stearns County, was a very small city, an overgrown town, really, with a population of just over 3,000 people and a small college, St. Benedict, in its midst. Initially at least, Jacob's parents could not believe that anyone from St. Joseph or the vicinity could be responsible. "I just don't understand this," Patty Wetterling bitterly observed immediately after the abduction. "My worst fear is that some professional child abductor came in here looking for an eleven-year-old good-looking kid. My biggest fear is they drove all night and now he's gone." Patty was responding to the information that the masked gunmen had carefully selected Jacob for his age and looks. After asking all three boys to lie flat on their stomachs, the abductor had asked each for his age. Both Aaron and Jacob were eleven. After he had looked at Aaron's face, he told Aaron and Trevor to run into the woods. He then grabbed Jacob. By the time the other two turned around, Jacob and his kidnapper had vanished. In its information about pedophiles, the NCMEC publication (based on FBI information), notes that "Most pedophiles prefer children of a certain age, in a certain age range. . . . How old a child looks and acts is more important than actual chronological age."[67]

Patty Wetterling's belief that the abductor must have been a stranger, not only to the boys, but to the area, resulted from her views of the kind of place that St. Joseph was—an idyllic, semirural, peaceful place, ideal for raising children. "We don't live in a big city where crime is commonplace," Patty Wetterling later recalled. "It was a place where I thought my kids were always secure." It was not until later, after the police had searched through state records, that Patty discovered, "In Minnesota alone, there are several hundred known pedophiles." But whatever its hidden dangers, it seems fitting that St. Joseph and nearby St. Cloud, indeed, all of Minnesota, became the site of an extraordinary community effort to find Jacob.[68]

Almost immediately, the residents of the two communities raised a $25,000 reward, to which businessmen from the Twin Cities added $100,000. Although the large reward had a seventy-two-hour deadline to encourage a quick return, the response of the Wetterlings' neighbors had no such limit. Instead, the kind of concern initially expressed in raising a large reward blossomed into a multitude of activities to express the community's outrage over the abduction and Minnesotans fellowship with Jacob's family. Very quickly in response to Patty Wetterling's announcement that the song "Listen" by Red Grammer was Jacob's favorite, radio stations throughout the area began to play it at regular intervals as a kind of signal to Jacob that his parents were seeking him and wanted him back. It was "a way . . . to reach out to Jacob." During the first week, the 3M Company of Minnesota donated thousands of white ribbons, which every family in the area displayed on their mailboxes to "symbolize the theme of our search 'Jacob's hope.'" One week after the abduction, the search had moved out of the area as the Oakland A's star catcher, Jerry Steinbach, who was from the small Minnesota town of New Ulm, wore a letter 'J' on the "back of his batting helmet in the boy's honor."[69]

The massive search for Jacob had just begun. In addition to the usual searches by National Guardsmen and other public officials, the effort soon known as "Jacob's hope" got under way as a community tried to bring back one of its children. That campaign included everything from prayer to publicity. Among these efforts was the release of 1,000 helium-filled balloons by members of St. Joseph Catholic Church. With the words "Jacob's Hope" emblazoned on each, the balloons, like the song "Listen," were a message to Jacob. As a variety of tips continued to come into the police headquarters about strange men hanging around gas stations or convenience stores, or tussling with agitated children along the highways, sheriffs' deputies conducted a "barn-to-barn" search of four south-central Minnesota counties. They searched vacant farm lots as well as occupied structures. A thirty-six-square-mile area of cornfields, woods, and commercial sites was searched five times.[70]

Jacob's disappearance had created fears throughout Minnesota. One cartoon in the *Star Tribune* showed two women walking down a street among newly fallen leaves. One hugs a baby. The other has a toddler on one side and an infant in a stroller. "Watching, praying. . . . Hugging our own children a little tighter," one says. The other replies, "Yeah, we've been thinking a lot about Jacob Wetterling these days, too." Another columnist noted that everyone was eager to do something, "anything, to help find Jacob, for he has come to represent so many of our fears for our children. If this can happen to Jacob in a place like St. Joseph, Minn., where can our kids, any kids, be safe?" The wolf could come to any door in America. The disappearance of a child in such brutal circumstances had led since the 1870s to a renewed commitment to caring for one's own children. Fear, as it had in 1874, or 1924 or 1955, did not need numbers or the statistics; it was aroused by the specific case.[71]

On November 4, a Saturday, about three thousand people stepped somberly out of their cars along Highway 75 in Stearns County. It was two weeks since Jacob had disappeared. At 2 P.M., school buses began to shuttle people to a two-mile stretch between St. Cloud and St. Joseph. Everyone held hands, and for an hour the human chain swayed to Red Grammer's "Listen"—Jacob's theme. An hour later people were shuttled back to their cars and they returned home. It was a show of community solidarity. Indeed, Jacob's disappearance was the occasion for the re-creation of community bonds through the clear assertion that any child threatened (and threatened by a breach of the sexual taboo) was an assault on the community as a whole. "When Jacob was kidnapped," one letter writer to the *Star Tribune* observed, "the momentum and seeming security of daily life was shaken. We suffer for Jacob and his family because they are so much like us. . . . We respond to such tragedy with no holds barred. The health and survival of our spirits depend on the resolution of grief, fear, anger and confusion, through learning to cope with such events and, Lord, willing, through Jacob's return."[72] In its many activities on Jacob's behalf, the community fulfilled its own needs for survival. Even though the community effort obviously now had the support and assistance of national organizations, it was the community above all that exerted itself on Jacob's behalf.

The gesture of Oakland A's catcher Jerry Steinbach on behalf of his neighbors back in Minnesota had stimulated friends and acquaintances as well as strangers all over Minnesota to find other ways to show support and to generate publicity for "Jacob's hope." Because the National Football League's rules prohibited defacement of players' helmets, the Minnesota Vikings went for a much bigger show. As the Minnesota *Star Tribune*'s sportswriter Jim Klobuchar observed, an entire sporting event would be turned over to highlighting the search for Jacob: "On Sunday, 100,000 will think of Jacob." Among the planned events at the Metrodome, huge streamers would display Jacob's name and his picture. "On the sidelines, Viking players will wear billed caps . . . inscribed with "Jacob's Hope." In addition, television stations "across the country would be able to offer to their viewers an appeal by satellite from the Vikings' Hershel Walker" asking people to join the search for Jacob, with a phone number they could call if they had information or wanted to help. "This," Klobuchar noted, "is a community of four million people in Minnesota declaring its solidarity and doing it on a Sunday afternoon in a football arena, where it can physically extend its kinship to a missing boy and his family." In describing his efforts to assist the Wetterlings, Mike Lyon, the Vikings' general manager, noted that he had an eleven-year-old daugher, and he no longer allowed her to wait for the school bus by herself. Suspicion of strangers and kinship with neighbors had both become part of "Jacob's hope."[73]

The campaign to find Jacob became probably the largest and most extensive campaign of its kind in American history, spreading through every kind of personal and community effort to millions of people in Minnesota, throughout the Midwest, and beyond.[74] Miles from St. Joseph, people organized volunteer groups throughout the region. And offers of money rewards as well as donations toward the search poured in. A week after Jacob's disappearance, as many as 1,000 volunteers flooded into a school gymnasium. Within one-half year, the newly organized Jacob's Hope Foundation had received $350,000. When David Collins, who directed the initial organization of volunteers, asked for a quote for 340,000 leaflets (an enormous number) from a local printer, Maxwell Graphics offered to do the work for free. Jacob's campaign was so successful that Collins even used it to piggyback the search for another child, Jenna Ray Robbins, recently kidnapped in Texas, who had not received very much attention. By attaching Jenna's picture to flyers for Jacob, Collins hoped to bring her story to public attention. The Kevin Collins Foundation alone distributed 7 million of these flyers. Within six months, 52 million flyers of Jacob, an astounding and unprecedented number, had been distributed throughout the country. With the enormous publicity, the police received over 14,000 leads. And the family was receiving support from all over the country. At Thanksgiving, one third-grade class in Cumberland, Wisconsin, sent them 1,000 origami paper cranes because they had learned about a legend that 1,000 paper cranes brought good luck. As one volunteer from a nearby town said, "I don't know the family, haven't met any of them. . . . I have a nine-year-old boy. I'm just glad to have him." One wonders how much magical thinking was involved in the community effort (in addition to the obvious extension of sympathy and fellowship), thinking in which to search for another person's child was a way of protecting one's own, an effort on behalf of others to forestall a similar curse. As David Collins observed, the volunteering was "therapeutic for the community."[75]

Empathy, pity, fellowship, fear, magic, and hope all combined to make the search for Jacob Wetterling an expression of solidarity and a furious effort to protect the community from the predators who were stealing America's children. It was an effort ultimately at social healing. But the same need for healing also encouraged fantasies of success. Just before Christmas, two months after Jacob disappeared, a rumor spread rapidly through Minnesota and adjoining states that Jacob had been found in a Texas hospital. The rumor and the attendant glee spread so quickly that people greeted each other on the streets, in stores, and on telephones with the glad tidings. Over 1,000 calls with the happy report were taken by just one local radio station, WCCO. It was all a painful mistake; as one University of Minnesota sociologist noted, "a classic case" of people wanting to hear the end of a story. For a few hours, he observed, it was "a lovely Christmas story." By the end of the year, the Jacob Wetterling story, with or without an ending, had "topped" all other Minnesota news stories for 1989. When almost one year had elapsed since Jacob disappeared the police had received 40,000 tips.[76]

Unlike the fantasy of Jacob's return, Jacob's story has not come to an end—despite an extraordinary show of community support, despite the parents' continuing faith and the work of the foundation that Patty Wetterling set up and directs in Jacob's name, despite the efforts of the local police, the media, the NCMEC, and the Minnesota Vikings. It is perhaps peevish—in view of the enormous effort on Jacob's behalf, especially the ineluctable publicity, which was meant to bring Jacob home as well as to let him know how much he was still wanted—to ask if this immense effort had not instead sealed his fate. What abductor would dare to have Jacob in his possession when Jacob was so widely known? Not the least part of the tragedy of Jacob's abduction is contained in the paradox of publicity. Publicity is both the lifeblood of the search and the albatross for the abductor. Getting rid of the child may be the inevitable result. ("Almost any child molester is capable of violence or even murder to avoid identification," an NCMEC publication notes.) Some children who are abducted by strangers are found. Almost one-half of these are found dead. The children most likely returned are not like Jacob, but infants stolen by women from hospitals. The longer a child is not found, the less likely he will ever find his way back home.[77]

The children who are found, dead or alive, are part of the story of modern child abduction. But the story of Jacob and the search for Jacob, as well as the stories of Kevin and Etan and the others who have simply "vanished off the face of the earth,"[78] are the most painful of all. Without an end, without a resolution, these are the stories of the children who are simply missing from our lives.

⊒VII⊑

It is worth considering the significance of the repeated refrain that has come to signal the problem of contemporary kidnappings. "Missing" obviously suggests physical displacement—a child gone from the places to which she or he belongs and where that child is known. It suggests as well an unknown identity, as in the term "missing person." Indeed, one of the services provided at the NCMEC is a cross-listing of the missing with the FBI file of unidentified dead bodies.[79] Thus missing children are both displaced from their families and their identities are unknown to the many who may meet with them after their abduction. Any stranger's child may be a missing child, his identity altered, his origins unknown. Unlike Charley Ross, "*the* lost boy," known to everyone as a singular case, missing children are plural. Thus, the term "missing" calls up the magnitude of the problem as well as the anonymity of the society within which that phenomenon has developed. It was totally appropriate, therefore, for a community like St. Joseph, and the greater community of Minnesota, to deny that anonymity when it sought to bring Jacob home. In asserting itself as a community of neighbors, those who devoted themselves to seeking Jacob overcame the conditions within which he was lost.

In many ways the efforts on behalf of missing children generally have lost sight of this emotional reality. The campaign for missing children has been based on numbers, on convincing the public about the urgency of the issue by dwelling on the scope of the problem. In so doing, the campaign too often rendered the children anonymous, changing faces on a changing billboard. In fact, communities and individuals respond to the specific stories, to the loss of Etan or Kevin or Jacob. When their identities are lost or they become stand-ins for faceless others, the pain and the reality subsides, and we are left instead with faceless fear. At the height of the missing children's furor in the mid 1980s, the NCMEC and other missing children's organizations as well as children's advocates went beyond the numbers abducted by strangers to merge all the missing into a single pool. In so doing, these organizations lost their most effective means to rally emotional support. Confusing numbers for children, they encouraged anxiety for one's own children, not assistance for others. Of course, these organization were intent not on finding a particular child or on creating community solidarity; most were eager to spotlight a social problem. In emphasizing the problem of numbers, the organizations bureaucratized the missing children's problem, and they sacrificed emotional commitment to achieve community alarm. One is left to wonder why organizations committed to children's welfare should choose only the missing to make their claims on children's behalf. American children generally need assistance, and certainly the poor or those emotionally, educationally, or otherwise deprived need attention and social commitment. That very broad social problem requires a broad-based (and, yes, bureaucratic) response. But for those child advocates, why choose missing children to make this point? Historically, Americans have substituted fears for their missing children for a variety of social dilemmas, but this helps neither children in general nor the missing in particular.

Indeed, even from the point of view of the needs of missing children, this campaign is probably strategically a mistake. In confusing numbers with emotional significance, it obscures the specificity of each child and erodes the pain that accompanies a deep sense of loss for a particular child. In order to elevate consciousness, it numbs sensibility and denies the kind of community mobilization that was activated in the Patz, Collins, and especially the Wetterling cases, creating instead the category of missing children. And the emphasis on numbers quite logically leads to insurance, to a betting on the numbers game.

The fixation on numbers has also obscured the problem in a different way. If we focus only on the most extreme cases, what the NISMART study called "stereotypical kidnappings" and put aside the American proclivity to fan hysteria with statistics, what do the figures on stranger abductions mean? What kind of solace can it give to know that each year "only" 200 to 300 children disappear into the worst horror imaginable, beyond mere taboo, into the land of the lost? The figures only seem small when compared to the initial inflation used to fan the campaign in the 1980s. We need to cut away the inflation to be properly stunned by the real numbers. In 1874, even one child lost to a stranger was an outrage. If the children disappear forever, as many of them do, if they lose their identities, their pasts, or their lives (and probably half fall into this last category), then the cumulative numbers over a decade become a terrible chart of social pain and personal loss. Americans love huge numbers because they are a portend of a plague, but once we think of these children as individuals, as Charley Ross or Charles Lindbergh rather than just the changing faces on Advo cards, then each child is a serious wound. The numbers are a cheat; only the children are real. To each parent, the loss is incalculable. To each community, it is a danger that cannot be extinguished by a recitation of the how rare the occurrence is *statistically*. For American culture, where pictures of missing children have become as visible as McDonalds signs, it is a mark of Cain. The campaign of numbers may well obscure the most important meaning of "missing," the one that brings people out to volunteer: a profound sense of personal loss for a particular child.

But "missing" says something about the larger culture, too. The intense sense of loss conveyed by the term may well be related to a social sense of wounded innocence, a wound best expressed in the sexual molestation presumed to be the fate of so many of the missing. That loss of innocence suggests the wounding of a social ideal of childhood nurture and care. It is surely not accidental that so much of the most recent fear of kidnapping has come at a time when women have left their children in larger and larger numbers to the care of others. The lurking (often sexual) suspicion of child-care centers and child-care providers is part of this same deep sense of missing one's own children, of fear for their identities and their safety over which parents seem to have less and less control.

In the last quarter of the twentieth century, kidnapping also confronts us with our own illusions about childhood, illusions that since the mid nineteenth century have swaddled children in dreams of a limitless future. When a child is abducted, not only is the future we envisage for the child gone (whatever his fate), but so is the very dream of our own future with and through the child. For many parents of kidnapped children, in fact, their own futures become rerouted, as David Collins or Patty Wetterling or Christian Ross before them find themselves compelled to learn the fate of their own child and discover the fate of others. Indeed, Christian Ross's image of Charley as a redeemer is not that far-fetched. Just as Christianity's image of resurrection, offered through the birth of God's child, provides a victory over death, our modern attachments to our children have given us similar illusions of immortality, an immortality nurtured by nineteenth-century romanticism and twentieth-century biologism. That dream of a personal secular resurrection—to live once more through our children—has made them dearer to us, while their loss has become all the more unbearable, to outlive them, a modern curse. How much worse, therefore, to have them vanish from our lives, a loss without end. That is, as has been repeated from Charley Ross's day to our own, a "fate worse than death."

Conclusion

Protecting Our Children

Since 1874, child kidnappings, repeatedly publicized, have provided the occasion for Americans to discuss an array of social issues: family and parenting, sexuality and gender, policing and law enforcement, criminality and insanity, community norms, and the role of the state. As each compelling and dramatic story was embedded in a range of issues, the wildly painful and inexplicable loss of a child was given some coherence and meaning. Often, too, political objectives, like changes in the law, were attached to the stories, giving them social momentum as well as a cultural form. Indeed, well-publicized child abductions often become a means for defining the critical social issues of a particular time, and changes in how these crimes have been portrayed provide us with an important measure of who we are and of how we have changed. Since that first, widely publicized loss in 1874, we have been taught to respond to child abduction as an assault on the family above all, but also as an assault on the community and on the self. Our institutional responses to abductions have mobilized, sometimes created, and often altered, among others: neighbors, the police, the FBI, private detective agencies, private associations dedicated to recovering children, psychiatry and social science, newspapers and other media, state and federal laws, the bureaucratic state, and the courts. Indeed, a tour through the history of child abduction brings us through a remarkable array of social, cultural, and political institutions. It also confronts us with the ambiguous results of how we view and treat children and how we use them for our personal pleasures and public purposes.

A quick summary here can hardly do justice to the complex ways in which what had hardly existed in public consciousness before 1874 was transformed first into a crime and then repeatedly into social trauma. But it is well to remember that the issues that brought Charley Ross to public attention in 1874, a new sense of family vulnerability and a heightened sensitivity to child endangerment, have become even more intense in the twentieth century. Our alarm has grown because both our means for understanding and the instruments of publicity—the various psychological and social sciences and the communications media—have grown tremendously and because the social complexity that made strangers into trespassers in the late nineteenth century has been many times compounded in the past hundred and twenty years. At first the danger seemed to lie in the dark dens of the city and was associated with the threat of material depredation as the stranger crossed over to steal the middle class's most valued possession. In the twentieth century, those dangers were no longer so clearly definable geographically. Instead, the fact that an abducted child could be killed, and later that it would likely be sexually mutilated, focused on marauders closer to home, marauders who harbored deep emotional disturbances, strangers who could be found in neighbors' bushes. The vulnerability of all our children, poor and rich, male and female, white and nonwhite, has been brought home (literally) in the pictures of the many missing. In their loss, our society has become poorer not only because of the absence of these children, but because we have often come to regard even our neighbor as the threatening stranger.

Child kidnapping also haunts us because over time it became an unequivocally fascinating crime. As a cultural form, child abduction became an irresistible story, much as narratives of Indian abductions had been for the preceding two centuries. Once developed and widely broadcast, the painful and unforgettable story of Charley Ross made it likely that future stories of child kidnapping—stories that threatened, illuminated, and entertained—would become regular features of the culture. From 1874 to the present, these stories have edified us, told us about our many problems, confirmed our basic commitments to family life and feeling, and emphasized the need for law and order. They have also drawn upon and recharged our sentimental portraits of children, exploited our tenderest feelings, and given us a partial (very partial) understanding of the problems facing our children.

By 1874 when Charley Ross was stolen, childhood had been sufficiently sacralized in the context of the sentimentalization of the Victorian family that the theft of a respectable, middle-class child could be *horrifying*. And ever since Charley disappeared, Americans have been dependably horrified by child abduction. The sentimental attachment to children required that children be sweet, attractive, and innocent. Indeed, the requirements of publicity have exaggerated these basic ingredients, and ever since Charley's time, these have remained essential for eliciting the dependable public response to child kidnapping. The assumptions about children that underlay these responses help us to understand why certain children have become far more visible in public representations of the problem than others. It explains the public response to pretty children like Etan Patz, to young children, to white children, and to male children. Today, as has been true for some time past, it is older female children (between eleven and seventeen years of age and often nonwhite) rather than young boys who are the most common victims of abduction. While these girls, like Stephanie Bryan or more recently Polly Klaas, have also been featured in our representations of child abduction, their position has been more problematic. It was precisely somewhat older girls whose innocence was questioned in the psychological studies of the 1950s. These supposedly complicit victims often came from poor, non-middle-class homes. Thus, while teenage girls are sociologically at the heart of the problem of sexual abduction, both the longer history of child abductions (with its strong focus on boys) and the dominant images of childhood innocence have centered the public image elsewhere. In part, of course, this has been because as teenaged females, their burgeoning sexuality has made it difficult to represent them as wholly innocent; in part, their growing independence has made it difficult to portray them as entirely vulnerable.

Child kidnapping as a crime that outrages public sensibilities has depended on childhood innocence. When Charley Ross's kidnappers proposed to exchange him for money, Americans were horrified by the commodification of childhood that this implied. That horror can be more fully appreciated once we remember that Charley was taken a mere nine years after the conclusion of the Civil War. Before then, human children were torn from their homes and sold regularly. Although those children were not white, even they had been sufficiently sentimentalized to serve as the subject of heart-wrenching tales like *Uncle Tom's Cabin*. The abduction of slave children never openly figured in Charley's story, but it resonated with other horrors, especially those related to the city and beliefs about the corruption to be found in the dens and hovels of the criminal classes. The horror was related to the presumed contact between innocence and corruption that the crime implied and the possible contamination that white children suddenly exposed to the commercialization associated with slavery (both black slavery and the so-called white slave traffic of prostitution) would experience. From the beginning, then, ransomings had a thrilling dimension that resulted from the associations they evoked, associations with groups and experiences understood to be the opposite of innocent.

This association between innocence and corruption, and the danger posed to innocence by its exposure to corrupting influences, have remained essential parts of child kidnapping stories, although over time these associations have become much more explicitly sexual. In the 1920s, the blunt fascination with the opposite of innocence was manifest in the portrayal of Leopold and Loeb (themselves still "children"), whose perversity-immorality-abnormality were all somehow related to the terrible crime they had committed. And the new discipline of psychiatry was prepared to see the boys as not only abnormal, but somehow sexually disturbed. In the 1930s, the corruption was of the state itself and its instruments of justice and control, as the Lindbergh case initially represented the very unhinging of social and political order and the emergence of organized crime and disorder. The crime itself was so unsettling that it has over time acquired images of the foulest corruption, not only of the instruments of justice but of heroism and fatherhood.

By the 1950s, the theme of sexual corruption became manifest in the Stephanie Bryan case. But the hesitations and uncertainties, even the double vision in 1950s America about sexuality and gender, could hardly have been better represented than by the two cases that competed for attention in the San Francisco Bay Area. On the one hand, the Marcus infant elicited a kind of deranged nurturing instinct from a "blowsy, blond" woman and from the public generally; on the other, sweet, shy Stephanie turned a quiet tubercular man into a raging sex maniac and aroused the public's sexual curiosity. In these two cases, the two sides of childhood innocence were conspicuously juxtaposed: the newborn baby, the incipient woman; the one requiring nurture, the other ripe for exploitation. Certainly by the 1950s, American culture broadly—in the movies, advertisements, literature, and fashion—was well on its way to an exploitation of that tension.

By the 1980s, the discourse in social science turned to rape and incest. Within the context of a presumably liberated sexuality and a blatantly sexualized popular culture, sexual satisfaction primarily with children emerged as the dominant motive for child kidnapping. Despite the widespread victimization of young girls, as publicized the crime most often took as its victim the innocent boy rather than the pubescent girl. That choice made the crime more shocking *and* more thrilling because it skirted thoughts of complicity and seduction and breached not one, but two, sexual boundaries. In the enormous outcry against sex crimes aimed at children and the kidnappings presumed to result from these, Americans vocally erected firm limits to the sexual revolution of the time. The defense of those limits created a new social science monitor, the child advocate, and new institutions whose purpose was not only to find missing children, but to warn us of the dangers all around.

It was just a slightly further step beyond pedophilia to incorporate even parental abductions into a portrayal of innocence corrupted. In the 1920s and 1930s, when parental kidnappings were almost exclusively imagined among the promiscuous rich, the kidnappings were a window on a corrupt or at least immoral world. By the 1980s, when the numbers of family kidnappings made them a democratic indulgence, they were strongly connected by child advocates and child-find organizations with stranger abductions, then subtly associated in the public mind with the sexual exploitation of one's own children. Here was perhaps the final implosion of innocence, when nurture breeds exploitation.

Childhood innocence had always had this potential. The vulnerability of children and their dependence on nurture made them appear to be passive objects of private affection and public regard, and these same characteristics made them ripe for exploitation. To this degree, we have become the willing victims of our images of childhood enshrined in kidnap stories, images whose very appeal to our emotions and senses can confuse our best intentions. And, under the tutelage of a media well versed in the exploitation of sensibilities and sensations, we have indulged our deepest fantasies and fears. But our children are the real victims of these representations. For in creating the crime of child kidnapping, we have created not an illusion, but a real crime, one that draws on these representations of childhood. The titillation built into stories about stolen children (endangered by criminal corruption or sexual perversion) have also made these crimes more enticing. Criminals like Leopold and Loeb could always capitalize on the thrill built into such crimes. But other, less grandiose, appetites could also draw on the public images, especially when these became ever more enticing in media representations that have more and more in the second half of the twentieth century shadowed childhood innocence with a ripe sensuality.

In this context, we need to do several things. The first is to recognize, contextualize, and situate the stories as I have tried to do in this book; to understand the purposes they serve, what they tell us socially, culturally, and politically and how they are related to each other as stories. We may thereby at least partially escape from the limitations they impose on our vision. For to see our children and their very real vulnerabilities requires that we understand how they have been used as a cultural construct and as a form of entertainment. This does not mean that they are not exposed to real dangers. American children (and as we are learning daily, children elsewhere in the world) *are* exploited and abused. Some are kidnapped, raped, killed, and mutilated. The desire to inflict pain on children, to get pleasure from their bodies, or to exploit them materially is not a product of our imaginations. Each story of a child lost to a predator (however that is defined) is a true horror story. But our concerns for children must not stop as they too often do with the small, the white, the pretty, and the pure child or be satisfied by a commercialized pity. Nor should the most extreme crimes against children cheat them of the attention they deserve in a much fuller and broader dedication to their welfare. In a sense, the attention to the most extreme dangers to which our children are exposed—dangers we have learned to emplot in stories of abduction—deflect our attention from more common and less dramatic dangers and wound our ability to respond to the horrors that are more banal.

In cautioning our children against strangers, we may have moved toward exposing them to intense alarm without offering them real protection. According to a Roper poll, American children now fear being kidnapped as their "number one concern." Actress Wynona Rider, who is on the board of the Polly Klaas Foundation, observes, "From the time I was really little, I knew what kidnapping was and it was always my worst fear." Similarly, an ad for *Stranger Danger* a special program on television says, "Kids tell us that today, few things are quite as scary as their fear of abduction." What exactly do our children learn from the stories of child kidnapping that they would not learn from ordinary stories about being cautious and knowledgeable? Perhaps only that we seem to value them most conspicuously when they are missing.[1]

Beyond being cautious not to scare them, we must be careful not to scare ourselves and each other away. As a society, we seem to be alarmed for our children and our neighbors' children only when the danger is of the most extreme kind. But the dangers are much more pervasive—bad health, bad schools, unsafe streets, unsafe environments of all kinds threaten all our children. When we protect our own children amidst the alarm created by stories of kidnappings, do we turn our backs on the welfare of other children or even on knowledge of their condition? Kidnap stories have always haunted middle-class families, whose obsessive concern for their children's future were illuminated by the stories of loss and endangerment. In a society in which we are supposed to love our children, does it really require that we feel threatened with their abduction to attend to their needs and the needs of their schoolmates? Ever since Charley Ross disappeared, the stories of child abduction have confirmed our warmest sentiments toward our own children and to neighbors and strangers in a community. Those positive, nurturing emotions are the source of our fascination for the abused. Can we sustain that energy and devotion beyond the most obviously threatening stimulus? If the movements, institutions, laws, and foundations we have built to the children of whom we have been brutally deprived is any indication, Americans have an enormous reserve of real feeling for their children. That affection and concern does not need to be manipulated through representations of loss and exploitation. It can be mobilized for the children we have.

Afterword

Like a never-ending story, child kidnapping confronts us daily on the front pages of newspapers, the covers of news magazines, and the television screen. In the year since I thought to have finished this history, Americans have learned about the immense demonstration staged by more than 300,000 Belgian parents in the streets of Brussels on October 20, 1996. In silence, these parents expressed their outrage at the disappearance of several young girls, the gruesome discovery of their bodies, and the exposure of the detention center where they had been held. That case was entwined with concerns about official corruption and conscious police cover-up, but the anger was about children who had been abducted, abused, and murdered. In fact, the matter spread well beyond Belgium to other European locations.

Meanwhile, thousands of miles away, the police uncovered a computer listing of children from rural and small-town Minnesota, painstakingly gathered from newspaper coverage of boys' amateur sports events and compiled in a Minnesota prison. Available to pedophiles over the Internet, together with physical and other descriptions of the boys that exposed their vulnerabilities and specially pleasing features, the listing of 3,000 children shredded whatever facade of safety still existed around rural America and one of its heartland states. Also making the news was the state of Kansas's Sexually Violent Predator Act, recently judged to be constitutional by the Supreme Court, which permits repeat sexual predators to be confined in mental institutions after the expiration of their prison sentences; President Bill Clinton's announcement of his support for a national sex crime registry; and the decision by the state of California to go ahead with legislation that would allow repeat child sex offenders to be chemically castrated.

Then came the ghastly discovery of the body of six-year-old JonBenét Ramsey, sexually violated and murdered at her wealthy home in beautiful Boulder, Colorado. Somewhere amidst the chaos of her discovery, the police found a note demanding ransom money, whether as cover or as motive it is too early to say. That story tore through the news like a hurricane as preposterously alluring JonBenét strutted her stuff on CNN video clips on an hourly basis, twenty-four hours a day. Every news medium from Public Television's proper *NewsHour* with Jim Lehrer, the *New York Times, Newsweek*, and on down through the supermarket tabliods were obsessed with the little beauty queen and compelled to "expose" the exploitation of the junior beauty contest world of which her life and death seemed to be part. Each, in turn, paraded JonBenét before us again, while brimming with indignation at her exploitation. In crossing the constructed boundary between the child and the woman, the little beauty provided a confusing entertainment to our senses, while exposing us to the terrors of our delight. Just as many inviting photographs and home movies of beautiful Polly Klaas were shown repeatedly long after her body had been found and identified and throughout the long trial of her killer, so enchanting little Jon-Benét's audience has grown with her death. Our children, it seems, always manage to show us up.

None of this is new, as I hope this book has shown. Since Charley Ross was kidnapped, the American public has been repeatedly and regularly outraged and excited to discover how vulnerable our children are to the sundry desires of the human heart, desires for money, sex, power, and death. And Leopold and Loeb made clear that even our own best children are capable of perverse crimes against children. Neither wealth nor geography is a reliable protection, as the Lindberghs discovered in their deserted mountain retreat. Children can be taken from schools, hospitals, street corners, playing fields, and homes. Minnesota's computer listing has merely simplified the search process by using the latest technology. Although the ease through which children can be classified and accessed has grown, it has not changed the goals, the motives, or the desires. The parents in Brussels have found a cooperative means to demonstrate fears that have gripped American parents in the 1870s, 1920s, 1930s, 1950s, 1980s, and today. Parents had earlier formed discussion groups, search alliances, and foundations. And like Americans over the last 120 years, the parents in Belgium have condemned the police's ineffectuality while calling for more police action. The desire to seek means of repression and vengence has followed each serious abduction like a shadow, though the recent activity in Kansas and California suggests the almost unlimited breadth of human resourcefulness in this area. The problem that Europeans had assumed to be peculiarly American when the parents of Charley Ross and Charles Lindbergh appealed to the world to help find their sons clearly has no known boundaries in the Western world. Our children are always at the crossroads of our desires. Anthropologists have long known that in purity lies danger, but our commercial culture has made children's purity an object of available exchange to a new and growing degree. We have surely seen lovely JonBenét's face many times before in the endless advertisements of American desires, while United Nations peacekeepers have been implicated in the trafficking in child prostitution worldwide.

The events of the past year are products of the history I have recounted in this book. Disgust, pity, fear, and lust have become ineluctably part of the modern portraits of children and part of the ways in which tenderness is, ever more rapidly, commercially processed. We have grown accustomed to the face of outraged innocence and familiar with the emotions this affords. Still, there may well be something new besides the worldwide increase in the availability of publicity about the occurrence of harms done to children. We seem to be less shocked; not, I think, because we are less upset, but because familiarity, in this case, may well breed understanding. I say this with some reluctance, because few of us want to delve too deeply into our own very complex forms of child love. As a nation of amateur psychologists invited to think about how JonBenét makes us feel, we have become familiar with predators all around and within. This may well lead us to understand how often we have made children work for us emotionally and culturally, and that it is not just their innocence and dependence that we treasure. With that recognition, we may yet arrive at the point where we can begin to offer our children better care and protection.

NOTES

INTRODUCTION

1. See John L. Diamond, "Kidnapping: A Modern Definition," *American Journal of Criminal Law*, 13 (Fall 1985), 17–18.

2. Stephen Kanter, "Kidnapping," *Encyclopedia of Crime and Justice*, vol. 3, edited by Sanford H. Kadish (New York: Free Press, 1983), 993; Rex A. Collings, "Offenses of Violence Against the Person,"*Annals of the American Academy of Political and Social Science,* 339 (January 1962), 53, 52; Robert Louis Stevenson, *Kidnapped* (New York: Grosset & Dunlop, 1948), 60.

3. I owe this specific reference to Sissela Bok. I would also like to thank Susanna Elm for helping me with the etymology of the word.

4. "Captives, Ransoming of," *Encyclopedia Judaica*, vol. 5 (Jerusalem: Macmillan, 1971), 154–55; Salo Baron, *The Jewish Community*, vol. II (Philadelphia: Jewish Publication Society, 1942), 333–39.

5. Bernard Bailyn, *Voyagers to the West: A Passage in the Peopling of America on the Eve of the Revolution* (New York: Knopf, 1986), 302–12; Richard Hofstadter,*America at 1750: A Social Portrait* (New York: Knopf, 1971), 34–37.

6. For the new humanitarian sensibilities, see Thomas Haskell, "Capitalism and the Origins of the Humanitarian Sensibility," *American Historical Review* (two parts), 90 (April 1985), 339–61, and 90 (June 1985), 547–66.

7. George Bataille, *The Trial of Gilles de Rais*, trans. Richard Robinson (Los Angeles: AMOK, 1991), 190. I would like to thank Peter Sahlins for bringing Gilles de Rais to my attention.

8. Arlette Farge and Jacque Revel, *The Vanishing Children of Paris: Rumor and Politics before the French Revolution*, trans. Claudia Meuille (Cambridge, Mass.: Harvard University Press, 1991). For the blood libel against the Jews, see Gavin I. Langmuir, *Toward a Definition of Antisemitism* (Berkeley: University of California Press, 1990), and *History, Religion and Antisemitism* (Berkeley: University of California Press, 1990); R. Po-Chia Hsia, *The Myth of Ritual Murder: Jews and Magic in Reforma-

tion Germany (New Haven: Yale University Press, 1988). For contemporary Satanism, see James T. Richardson, Joel Best, and David G. Bromley, eds., *The Satanism Scare* (New York: Aldine de Gruyter, 1991).

9. For example, Richard VanDerBeets, introduction, to VanDerBeets, ed., *Held Captive by Indians: Selected Narratives, 1642–1836* (Knoxville: University of Tennessee Press, 1973).

10. "Narrative of the Capture and Subsequent Sufferings of Mrs. Rachel Plummer, Written by Herself," in VanDerBeets, *Held Captive by Indians*, 340–41; Lavinia Eastlock's narrative appears in *Captured by the Indians: 15 Firsthand Accounts, 1750–1870*, ed. Frederick Drimmer (New York: Dover, 1985), 322.

11. "The Soveraignty and Goodness of God, Together with the Faithfulness of His Promises Displayed; Being a Narrative of the Captivity and Restauration of Mrs. Mary Rowlandson," in VanDerBeets, *Held Captive by Indians,* 49, 53, 44; "Narrative... of Rachel Plummer," 341–42.

12. John Demos, *The Unredeemed Captive: A Family Story from Early America* (New York: Knopf, 1994). For an instance of the changeling in William Shakespeare, see *A Midsummer Night's Dream*, Act II, Scene 1.

13. June Namias, *White Captives: Gender and Ethnicity on the American Frontier* (Chapel Hill: University of North Carolina Press, 1993).

14. For a history of the crime and its punishment in the United States, see the innovative Ernest Kahler Alix, *Ransom Kidnapping in America/ 1874–1974: The Creation of a Capital Crime* (Carbondale: Southern Illinois University Press, 1978).

CHAPTER ONE

1. Charles R. Krauth, introduction to *The Father's Story of Charley Ross, the Kidnapped Child Containing a Full and Complete Account of the Abduction of Charles Brewster Ross From the Home of His Parents in Germantown, with the Pursuit of the Abductors and Their Tragic Death; The Various Incidents Connected With the Search for the Lost Boy; The Discovery of Other Lost Children, Etc, Etc. With Facsimiles of Letters from the Abductors* by Christian K. Ross (Philadelphia: John E. Potter, 1876), 9–10.

2. "The Trial and Conviction of William H. Westervelt, for the Abduction of Little Charley Ross: The Tragic Death of the Burglers Mosher and Douglass (on Long Island, N. Y.) Who Were Implicated in Abducting the Poor Little Fellow. The Confession. The Whole Case. The Trial in Full," in *American Versus Italian Brigandage* (Philadelphia: Barclay, 1877), 111. In his memoir, Christian Ross recalled that "men stopped on the streets and talked over the outrage, denominating it *the worst offense ever committed in our country*," thereby elevating it even beyond the century mark (*The Father's Story*, 74).

Other kidnap cases were also known as "the crime of the century," especially the kidnap-murder of Robert Franks by Leopold and Loeb. See Hal Higdon, *The Crime of the Century: The Leopold and Loeb Case* (New York: G. P. Putnam, 1975), following the lead of one of Leopold's lawyers, Elmer Gertz (261), who called it that.

For a history of ransom kidnapping, see the comprehensive Ernest Kahler Alix, *Ransom Kidnapping in America* (Carbondale: Southern Illinois University Press, 1978). Most newspaper coverage at the time of Charley's abduction described the Ross case as the first, as does Ross's memoir, *The Father's Story*, 19.

3. Charley was first called the "stolen child," but this was very early transformed to "lost." For an early usage of "lost child," see letter from consul in Ross, *The Father's Story*, 280.

4. Sir James Matthew Barrie, *Peter Pan* (1904); Charles Dickens, *Oliver Twist* (1838).

5. For the lack of information released to the public, see *New York Times*, July 14, 1874, editorial, p. 4; and Ross, *The Father's Story*, 87. For Ross's desire to shield his wife and prevent copycats, see Ross, *The Father's Story*, 64. Questions were early raised about this defense in the infamous Vindex letter, which articulates the suspicions about Ross; see "Vindex" letter, *New York Herald*, July 25, 1874, p. 4.

For more recent places where Charley's story is told, see Norman Zierold, *Little Charley Ross: America's First Kidnapping for Ransom* (Boston: Little, Brown, 1967); Hank Messick and Burt Goldblatt, *Kidnapping: The Illustrated History* (New York: Dial Press, 1974), 16–22; Edward Dean Sullivan, *The Snatch Racket* (New York: Vanguard Press, 1932), 113–34; Edward H. Smith, *Mysteries of the Missing* (New York: Dial, 1927), 1–22.

6. The press also sometimes emphasized the theme of redemption, but the symbolism is much more secular. See, for example, *New York Times*, February 8, 1878, p. 3.

7. Ross, *The Father's Story*, 53; *Philadelphia Inquirer*, July 17, 1874, p. 8; *New York Herald*, July 28, 1874, p. 10; *New York Times*, September 19, 1875, p. 6. For a rare interview, see *New York Herald*, July 26, 1874, p. 10. See also *New York Times*, February 8, 1878, p. 3, for an interview given more than four years after the abduction. In describing Mrs. Ross, the interviewer for the Herald noted, "There was a mother's grief in every feature of that calm, pale face."

8. Ross, *The Father's Story*, 18.

9. Smith, *Mysteries of the Missing*, xv, 22. We obviously know about these activities from sources other than Christian's memoirs. One of these is a fiftieth anniversary commemoration of the abduction by Clarence Edward Macartney, published by *Ladies' Home Journal* 41 (July 1924), entitled, of course, "Charley Ross, the Unforgotten *Lost* Boy," 7, 75–78 (my emphasis). Zierold, *Little Charley Ross*, is a full account of the case; see 297, 300.

10. Ross, *The Father's Story*, 30, 41, 39.

11. *San Francisco Chronicle*, July 11, 1874, p. 3. Two weeks later, the paper carried

an article, "Another Child Abducted," about a four-year-old abducted by two men, one "colored," who drove off in a wagon (July 20, 1874, p. 3). Since this so closely mimics the Ross scenario, it is unclear whether it is a true abduction or a newspaper exploitation (Ross, *The Father's Story*, 39). For an example of a child runaway, see *New York Times*, "Missing Children," July 14, 1874, p. 2, which reports a thirteen-year-old running from a mother who beat him. Lawrence M. Friedman, *Crime and Punishment in American History* (New York: Basic, 1993), 151; Henry McBride, "The Lost Children of New York," *Harper's Weekly* 39 (January 5, 1895), 16–17; "The Recovery and Care of Lost Children," *Frank Leslie's Illustrated Newspaper* (August 26, 1882), 7; Eric H. Monkkonen, *Police in Urban America: 1860–1920* (Cambridge: Cambridge University Press, 1981), 109–12.

12. Ross, *The Father's Story*, 42; *Philadelphia Inquirer*, February 22, 1875, p. 2. In an unusual sign of tolerance, the *New York Times* attacked the easy assumption that gypsies were involved: "The poor gypsies were seldom guilty of anything worse than poisoning a pig" (August 1, 1874, p. 4). But this tolerance for gypsies did not stop that same newspaper from claiming that the crime of kidnapping was related to increased immigration of that "human vermin" that infested European capitals now come to America (July 14, 1874, p. 4).

13. Ross, *The Father's Story*, 55. Most newspapers seemed to assume that although ransom abductions were new in the United States they had a long history in Europe; for example, *New York Times*, July 26, 1874, p. 5.

14. Ross, *The Father's Story*, 46–47, 48; *New York World*, July 15, 1874, cited in *Philadelphia Inquirer*, July 17, 1874, p. 3.

15. Ross, *The Father's Story*, 97 (emphasis in original), 70, 48. One of the most remarkable of these notes indicates that the kidnappers had been prepared to reduce their ransom demand from $20,000 to $10,000 in light of the fact that Ross's economic "circumstance was not good" (144–45). For John Conway and Eddie Cudahy, see Smith, *Mysteries of the Missing*, 65–81, 133–52.

16. Ross, *The Father's Story*, 84, 96.

17. Ross, *The Father's Story*, 87–88; *Philadelphia Inquirer*, July 27, 1874, p. 2; *New York Herald*, July 25, 1874, p. 4; and "Vindex" letter, July 25, 1874, p. 4. For the libel suit and the public apology, see Ross, *The Father's Story*, 94. *New York Times*, January 12, 1876, p. 4. For the review of the play, see *New York Times*, December 15, 1875, p. 6; and December 24, 1875, p. 4.

18. Ross, *The Father's Story*, 92, 19–20. By late July, the theories about the Ross family were thickest because people could not understand how the police could have spent almost a month and turned up nothing. See, for example, *New York Herald*, July 25, 1874, p. 4, July 26, 1874, p. 10, July 28, 1874, p. 10.

19. Ross, *The Father's Story*, 223. According to the *Philadelphia Inquirer*, Ross had spent $50,000 pursuing his son by February 1875, just one-half year after his abduction. Half of this money had been borrowed (February 19, 1875, p. 2).

20. Ross, *The Father's Story*, 88, 20.

21. Krauth, introduction to *The Father's Story*, 12–13; Ross, *The Father's Story*, 229; *New York Times*, July 14, 1874, p. 4.

22. Ross, *The Father's Story*, 146, 243 (my emphasis).

23. *New York Times*, December 21, 1900, p. 1; and December 20, 1900, p. 1; Messick and Goldblatt, *Kidnapping*, 25.

24. Ross, *The Father's Story*, 132; for the train incident, 126–37. *High and Low*, directed by Akira Kurosawa (1962). For the Coughlin case, see Sullivan, *Snatch Racket*, 107; for Leopold and Loeb, see below, pp. 57–93.

25. For the value of children in the late nineteenth century and the unwillingness to define children in terms of their monetary value, see Viviana Zelizer, *Pricing the Priceless Child: The Changing Social Value of Children* (New York: Basic Books, 1985).

26. *Philadelphia Evening Herald*, cited in *New York Herald*, July 26, 1874, p. 10; *New York Times*, July 16, 1874, p. 2. See also editorial, *Philadelphia Inquirer*, September 14, 1875, p. 4, which cites with approval an article in the *New York World* attacking the police's behavior in the case, and the defense in the Westervelt trial, "The Trial and Conviction," p. 109.

27. *New York Times*, July 28, 1874, p. 8; and September 23, 1874, p. 5. Some parents did not contact the police because they may not have cared. Jacob Riis tells the story of "Harry Quill, aged fifteen," who "disappeared from the tenement No 45 Washington Street, and though he was not heard of again for many weeks, his people never bothered the police. Not until his dead body was fished up from the bottom of the air-shaft at the bottom of which it had lain two whole months, was his disappearance explained." Jacob Riis, *The Children of the Poor* (New York: Arno Press, 1971; originally published 1892), 261–62.

28. *New York Times*, December 15, 1874, p. 1. Ross notes that "The failure to find Charley, or even to learn anything about him after the death of the kidnappers, notwithstanding the extraordinary efforts to that end, has led many to question whether Mosher and Douglass were the abductors. In the minds, however, of those conversant with all the circumstances, there is not a shadow of doubt that they were the projectors and perpetrators of this crime" (*The Father's Story*, 408). I have chosen to adopt Ross's and the authorities' view on this matter.

29. "The Trial and Conviction," 109 (the question of proper jurisdiction was an issue in the trial); Ross, *The Father's Story*, 20, 314–16. Such changes to the laws are very common after major kidnappings.

30. Krauth, introduction to *The Father's Story*, 12.

31. "The Trial and Conviction," 111 (emphasis mine). This complete trial transcript was published in 1877. Clearly the trial was of sufficient interest at the time to warrant publication of the transcript.

The police had sustained criticism from the beginning in the press. By the time of the Westervelt trial, the *Philadelphia Inquirer* was ready to call police action worse than worthless; the lack of action was not a "blunder," but a "crime" (September 14, 1875, p. 4).

32. "The Trial and Conviction," 112; George Washington Walling, *Recollections of a New York Chief of Police* (New York: Caxton Book, 1887), 198.

33. *New York Times*, June 10, 1869, p. 2; and December 28, 1874, p. 5. For the practice of taking lost children to police stations, see Monkkonen, *Urban Police*, 179.

34. *New York Times*, December 28, 1874. This case was first reported in the *New York Times* on December 6, 1873, 2. The editorial comment is from the later date, after Charley's kidnapping; Ross, *The Father's Story*, 90.

35. *New York Times*, July 26, 1874, p. 5; and December 1, 1871, p. 3. Although passing notice was sometimes given to other children held for ransom, I have never come across a documented case of ransom kidnapping before the Ross case. Christian claimed to be frequently asked about this matter and noted that in his own searches he came across none, but that he had encountered two children who had been genuinely "stolen." Most of the others "we have traced, and whose history we could find out, have been those who have been *abandoned* by their parents" (Ross, *The Father's Story*, 387, 388). For discussions of other parental abductions, see *New York Times*, July 22, 1875, p. 2; and August 13, 1873, p. 2; *Philadelphia Inquirer*, February 22, 1875, p. 2; Ross, *The Father's Story*, 275; and below pp. 173–211.

36. *New York Times*, July 26, 1874, p. 5. See also the description of another case of maltreatment, this time of an adopted child in *Philadelphia Inquirer*, February 26, 1875, p. 2. For sexual abductions, *New York Times*, July 26, 1874, pp. 4, 5; August 4, 1874, p. 8; and July 11, 1865, p. 5. For children stolen and put to work, *Philadelphia Inquirer*, July 28, 1874, p. 1; *New York Times*, June 10, 1869, p. 2; Ross, *The Father's Story*, 274; *New York Herald*, July 28, 1874, p. 10. For the opposition to children's street occupations, Zelizer, *Pricing the Priceless Child*, 61–96; David Nasaw, *Children of the City at Work and at Play* (New York: Oxford University Press, 1986).

37. Ross, *The Father's Story*, 388.

38. Miriam Z. Langsam, *Children West: A History of the Placing-Out System of the New York Children's Aid Society*, 1853–1890 (Madison: State Historical Society of Wisconsin, 1964), 12, 25, 26. These figures approximate those offered by Jacob Riis in *The Children of the Poor*. In thirty-nine years of placements in the West, Riis says that 84,318 children were transported; of these something under one-half were true orphans (259).

39. Langsam, *Children West*, 45–46, 51; *New York Times*, May 8, 1860, p. 1. Children adopted from denominational agencies could also suffer terrible abuse as was the case with six-year-old Mary Keating, adopted by William Stuffenberg and Alvina Stuffenberg out of the St. Vincent's Home (a Catholic institution). Teachers at school noticed Mary's wounds and reported the suspicions. The Stuffenbergs were brought to court where Mary described in detail the treatment to which she was subjected. "The artless manner and sweet voice of the little victim affected very deeply

the large crowd that was present at the hearing. . . . There were numerous mothers present who would liked to have taken the case out of the alderman's hands after hearing the sickening complaint made uncomplainingly however, by the little girl." See *Philadelphia Inquirer*, February 26, 1875, p. 2.

40. Jacob Riis, "Lost Children," in "Out of the Book of Humanity," *Atlantic Monthly*, 78 (November 1896), 701 (my emphasis). The story was subsequently republished in Jacob Riis, *Children of the Poor*, 43–44.

41. *New York Times*, March 12, 1881, p. 8; also March 22, 1881, p. 8.

42. *National Police Gazette*, September 21, 1867; p. 4; see also "Beastly Cruelty of a Mother to Her Young Child," November 16, 1867, p. 5; and "Of a Missing and Murdered Girl," June 1, 1878, p. 3. *Philadelphia Inquirer*, July 22, 1874, p. 3. For some of the details of the Pomeroy case, see Negley K. Teeters, with Jack H. Hedblom, ". . . *Hang By The Neck* . . .": *The Legal Use of Scaffold and Noose, Gibbet, Stake, and Firing Squad from Colonial Times to the Present* (Springfield, Ill.: Charles C. Tomas, 1967), 13–15; see also *Philadelphia Inquirer*, July 22, 1874, p. 3; August 3, 1874, p. 4; and February 22, 1875, p. 87; *San Francisco Chronicle*, July 21, 1874, p. 3; and July 24, 1874, p. 3. Ludovic Kennedy, *The Airman and the Carpenter: The Lindbergh Kidnapping and the Framing of Richard Hauptmann* (New York: Penguin, 1985), 122.

43. *Philadelphia Inquirer*, July 22, 1874, p. 3. For the retraction of the confession, see Jesse H. Pomeroy, *Autobiography of Jesse H. Pomeroy Written by Himself* (Boston: J. A. Cummings, 1875).

44. *Philadelphia Inquirer*, February 22, 1875, p. 2.

45. Ross, *The Father's Story*, 160–61, 319–20; Macartney, "The Unforgotten Lost Boy," 7.

46. Ross, *The Father's Story*, 319–20.

47. Ross, *The Father's Story*, 203, 23.

48. *New York Times*, September 19, 1875, p. 6; and October 21, 1874, p. 3. Ross, *The Father's Story*, 334–40.

49. Zierold, *Little Charley Ross*, 276; for the complete story, 275–77. Interview with the *Philadelphia Times*, quoted in Zierold, *Little Charley Ross*, 236. Ross, *The Father's Story*, 151. Other, smaller rewards were offered all through the case, such as the initial $300 offered in the lost and found before Christian received the ransom note; see Ross, *The Father's Story*, 59.

50. Ross, *The Father's Story*, 419, 20, 23, 73; *New York Times*, September 25, 1875, p. 4; and July 14, 1874, p. 1. For a discussion of Victorian crime and its association with the city, see Judith R. Walkowitz, *City of Dreadful Delight* (Chicago: University of Chicago Press, 1993).

51. *Philadelphia Inquirer*, July 28, 1874, p. 4. Ross, *The Father's Story*, 419. *New York Times*, July 14, 1874, p. 4.

52. *New York Times*, July 14, 1874, p. 4.

53. *New York Times*, September 25, 1875, p. 4.

54. Ross, *The Father's Story*, 420–21.

55. Maureen McKernan, *The Amazing Crime and Trial of Leopold and Loeb* (Chicago: Plymouth Court Press, 1924), 317; Ross, *The Father's Story*, 419.

56. Ross, *The Father's Story*, 21, 90 (my emphasis).

57. Ross, *The Father's Story*, 53. On the sanctity of home and privacy of emotions, see Karen Lystra, *Searching the Heart: Women, Men, and Romantic Love in Nineteenth-Century America* (New York: Oxford University Press, 1989). Charley's story was placed in very well prepared soil. Even before he disappeared, a *New York Times* editorial on the mysterious disappearance of adults observed that "such tragic incidents . . . add another to the already numerous good reasons for the cultivation of the domestic virtues" (June 26, 1870, p. 4).

58. Zierold, *Little Charley Ross*, 274.

CHAPTER TWO

Chapter title quotation from *Catholic World*, 119 (July 1924), 550.

1. The story of Leopold and Loeb's plotting is told in many places, including the confessions reprinted by Maureen McKernan, *The Amazing Crime and Trial of Leopold and Loeb* (Chicago: Plymouth Court Press, 1924), 24–52, and most accessibly in the only major historical examination, Hal Higdon, *The Crime of the Century: The Leopold and Loeb Case* (New York: G. P. Putnam, 1975), 95–101. For Loeb's ravenous consumption of detective fiction, see among many others, Clarence Darrow's plea in the defense, reprinted in McKernan, *Amazing Crime*, 260–61. During the hearing, Loeb was described as imagining himself a great criminal (*Chicago Herald and Examiner*, August 2, 1924, p. 3). The day after the kidnap-murder was publicized, well before Loeb's involvement was known, the *Chicago Daily Tribune* reported that the kidnap note resembled a similar note in a recent *Detective Story* magazine (May 24, 1924, p. 2).

2. "Charley Ross Stolen Just Fifty Years Ago," *New York Times,* June 29, 1924, part 8, p. 4; Clarence Edward Macartney, "Charley Ross, the Unforgettable Lost Boy," *Ladies' Home Journal*, 41 (July 1924), 7, 74–78.

3. *Chicago Herald and Examiner*, May 26, 1924, p. 2; "Leopold and Loeb," *New Statesman*, September 20, 1924, p. 669. For an example of how Bobby was depicted, see the pathetic picture on the front page of the *Chicago Herald and Examiner*, May 23, 1924.

The kidnapper as hero had been partially anticipated in the case of Eddie Cudahy. See the story of Pat Crowe in Hank Messick and Burt Goldblatt, *Kidnapping: The Illustrated History* (New York: Dial Press, 1974), 22–27; Edward Dean Smith, *Mysteries of the Missing* (New York: Dial Press, 1927), 133–52. Of course, Pat Crowe was not a murderer.

4. Edward Dean Sullivan, *The Snatch Racket* (New York: Vanguard Press, 1932), 102, the story is told on 96–112. For the ransom notes in the Whitla and Conway cases, see Smith, *Mysteries of the Missing,* 55, 65–66. In the Eddie Cudahy kidnapping, the kidnapper, Pat Crowe, threatened to blind the boy by putting acid in his eyes as a warning to other parents and then immediately kidnap several other children, whose parents would no doubt pay the ransom demands immediately. For the ransom note in the Cudahy case, see Smith, *Mysteries of the Missing,* 137.

5. Leopold article on the Kirkland warbler, previously believed to be extinct in Illinois, was republished after his confession in the *Chicago Herald and Examiner,* June 5, 1924, p. 3; June 7, 1924, p. 4; and June 8, 1924, p. 2.

6. For the Rosenwald connection, see *Chicago Herald and Examiner,* June 3, 1924, p. 1. For Loeb and women, for example, *Chicago Herald and Examiner,* June 4, 1924, p. 3.

7. McKernan, *Amazing Crime,* 11, 8. For the use of this name in the Conway case, see Smith, *Mysteries of the Missing,* 80. Loeb, who was an avid reader of crime stories would have been familiar with this name. Loeb also sent a wreath to Bobby's funeral with the name "George Johnson" on the card.

8. The kidnap note appears in McKernan, *Amazing Crime,* 9, 10; see also in *Chicago Daily Tribune,* May 23, 1924, p. 1.

9. See, for example, "Dangers to the Children of Chicago," *Chicago Herald and Examiner,* May 28, 1924, p. 8. The *Chicago Daily Tribune* early speculated that sexual perversion may have been a motive (May 24, 1924, p. 1). The police rounded up twenty morons in their initial search, see *Chicago Herald and Examiner,* May 30, 1924, p. 2; *Chicago Daily Tribune,* May 27, 1924, p. 2. One schoolteacher at the Harvard School was held for close questioning, see *Chicago Daily Tribune,* May 28, 1924, p. 1. The police also investigated possible narcotics addicts, see *Chicago Daily Tribune,* May 28, 1924, p. 1.

10. McKernan, *Amazing Crime,* called it this as did *Catholic World.* Hal Higdon called his book on the case *The Crime of the Century;* for the role of Goldstein and the confessions, 89–94. George W. Kirchwey described the case as "the *cause célèbre* of the century thus far" in "Old Law and New Understanding," *Survey,* 53 (October 1, 1924), 7.

11. Prosecutor Robert Crowe is quoted in *Chicago Herald and Examiner,* June 1, 1924, p. 1. Prosecutor Crowe would not immediately let the defense attorneys see the two because he did not want to spoil his airtight case (*Chicago Herald and Examiner,* June 2, 1924, p. 2).

For a picture of each pointing an accusing finger at the other, see *Chicago Herald and Examiner,* June 3, 1924, p. 2, under the caption "There's the killer of Robert Franks!" Although we will never know definitively which one killed Robert Franks, the evidence points to Loeb as the killer. Leopold claimed this was the case in his book, although he had obvious motives for making this claim on the eve of his own pending parole. But two defense doctors also asserted that Loeb had admitted the murder to them when they testified at the hearing. See the testimony of Bernard Glueck in the *Chicago Herald and Examiner*, August 7, 1924, pp. 1, 2, 3, 4; and that of H. L. Hulbert, in the same paper on August 9, 1924, pp. 1, 2, 3.

12. See, for example, Meyer Levin, *Compulsion* (New York: Simon & Schuster, 1956), which is a fictionalization that is so close in details to the actual case as to be disorienting. For the importance of *Compulsion*, see Paula S. Fass, "Making and Remaking An Event: The Leopold and Loeb Case in American Culture," *Journal of American History*, 80 (December 1993), 943–45. Another fictionalization, *Nothing But the Night*, by James Jaffe (Boston: Little Brown, 1957), is much more loosely based on the case but also sees the murder as the goal. So does the Alfred Hitchcock movie *Rope* (1948, Warner Brothers).

13. Quoted in *Chicago Herald and Examiner*, August 6, 1924, p. 4 (my emphasis); quoted in Alvin V. Sellers, *The Loeb-Leopold Case, With Excerpts from the Evidence of the Alienists and Including the Arguments to the Court by Counsel for the People and the Defense* (Brunswick, Ga.: Classic Publishing Co., 1926) 164. For the phenomenological and aesthetic possibilities of crimes, see Jack Katz, *Seductions of Crime: Moral and Sensual Attractions in Doing Evil* (New York: Basic Books, 1988).

14. *Chicago Herald and Examiner,* June 1, 1924, part 1, p. 4; and July 30, 1924, p. 2.

15. McKernan, *Amazing Crime*, 6; this introduction was written by two of the defense counselors, Clarence Darrow and Walter Bachrach. *Chicago Herald and Examiner*, August 31, 1924, p. 4. For progressive views, David J. Rothman, *Conscience and Convenience: The Asylum and its Alternatives in Progressive America* (Boston: Little, Brown, 1980). For mental deficiency and delinquency, for example, Henry Herbert Goddard, *Juvenile Delinquency* (New York: Dodd, Mead, 1921).

16. *New York Times*, December 19, 1927, p. 1, was drawing a direct parallel between the kidnap-murderer William Edward Hickman and Leopold and Loeb.

17. Carl Murchison, "Educational Research and Statistics: Criminal and College Students," *School and Society,* 12 (July 3, 1920), 25, 24; and "College Men Behind Prison Walls," *School and Society*, 13 (June 4, 1921), 635.

18. *Chicago Sunday Tribune*, June 1, 1924, p. 1; *Chicago Herald and Examiner*, June 1, 1924, part 1, p. 3. For the thrill killers and the diabolical, see, for example, *Chicago Daily Tribune*, June 1, 1924, pp. 3, 5; *Chicago Daily Tribune*, May 31, 1924, p. 3. On the sensational murders and the press in the 1920s, see John R. Brazil, "Murder Trials, Murder, and Twenties America," *American Quarterly,* 33 (Summer 1981), 163–84; also Charles Merz, "More and Better Murders," *Harper's Monthly Magazine*, 155 (August 1927), 338–43.

19. Leopold quoted in "'Intellectual' Murder in Chicago," *Literary Digest*, 82 (July 15, 1924), 40; *Chicago Daily Tribune,* June 16, 1924, p. 9. In his memoir, Leopold claimed that he was describing how the press was treating him when he spoke about the beetle; see Nathan Leopold, Jr., *Life Plus Ninety-Nine Years* (Garden City, N.Y.: Doubleday, 1958), 48–49. Crowe's description is in *Chicago Daily Tribune*, May 31,

1924, p. 3; for the speculation about Leopold's deliberate experimentation with the glasses, see *Chicago Daily Tribune,* June 1, 1924, p. 1. For Leopold as Svengali, see *Chicago Herald and Examiner,* June 12, 1924, p. 1; for Leopold the mesmerizer, *Chicago Daily Tribune,* June 10, 1924, p. 1; for Loeb's suggestibility, see *Chicago Herald and Examiner,* June 1, 1924, p. 2. For similar contrasts and attributions, see *Chicago Daily Tribune,* June 3, 1924, p. 3; and June 5, 1924, p. 2. See also the comparison of the boys' horoscopes in *Chicago Herald and Examiner,* June 9, 1924, p. 3. For a comparison of Leopold and Loeb to Caligula, see *Chicago Herald and Examiner,* June 9, 1924, p. 3. For pornography, see, for example, *Chicago Daily Tribune,* June 4, 1924, p. 4.

20. James A. Walsh, "Criminal Responsibility and the Medical Experts," *America,* 31 (October 4, 1924), 588. Judge Ben B. Lindsey and Wainwright Evans, *The Revolt of Modern Youth* (New York: Boni & Liveright, 1925), 104. See all of Lindsey's comments in the *Chicago Daily Tribune,* June 8, 1924, sec. 1, p. 2.

21. *Chicago Daily Tribune,* June 5, 1924, p. 3; Billy Sunday is quoted in the *Chicago Herald and Examiner,* June 5, 1924, p. 3, and in the *Chicago Daily Tribune,* June 5, 1924, p. 3. Some ministers blamed "vile movies" as well as "unclean books"; see *Chicago Daily Tribune,* September 15, 1924, p. 4. The need for more religion was a common plaint throughout the decade and used frequently to explain youth's wildness as well as crime; see, for example, Henry Noble Sherwood, "Youth and Crime," *School and Society,* 25 (May 7, 1927), 527–32. See the condemnation of Leopold and Loeb's neglect of Judaism by a rabbi, *Chicago Daily Tribune,* June 2, 1924, p. 3. For other religious views, see, for example, *Chicago Herald and Examiner,* June 9, 1924, p. 4.

For the expansion of education at the university and college level in the 1920s, see Paula S. Fass, *The Damned and the Beautiful: American Youth in the 1920s* (New York: Oxford University Press, 1977). For various comments on too much of the wrong kind of education, see among others the comments of Ben Lindsey in *Chicago Daily Tribune,* June 8, 1924, p. 2; and of Dr. Carleton Simon, in *Chicago Herald and Examiner,* July 25, 1924, p. 3. For the concern with higher education, "Intellectual Murder in Chicago," 41.

22. See, for example, *Chicago Herald and Examiner,* June 4, 1924, p. 2; July 21, 1924, p. 3. See also various techniques suggested by readers to recognize and catch the criminals in response to a $50 contest offer run before the confessions in the *Chicago Herald and Examiner,* May 30, 1924, p. 3; these included dreams, psychic visions, ouija board messages.

23. For Darrow's views, see his *Crime: Its Causes and Treatment* (New York: Thomas Y. Crowell, 1922). For reactions to Darrow, see, for example, C. O. Weber, "Pseudo-Science and the Problem of Criminal Responsibility," *Journal of Criminal Law and Criminology,* 19 (August 1928), 181–95.

24. Thomas W. Salmon, "The Psychiatrist's Day in Court," *Survey,* 74 (October 15, 1925), 74. For an example of the anticipation of the battle of the alienists, see *Chicago Herald and Examiner,* June 7, 1924.

25. *Chicago Herald and Examiner*, June 4, 1924, p. 3; O'Sullivan pieces begin on June 6, p. 6, and continued on June 7, p. 3; June 8, p. 2; and June 9, 1924, p. 2. *Chicago Daily Tribune*, June 19, 1924, p. 1; see also the story of Crowe sending his fellow prosecutors to an "Insanity School" taught by four alienists hired by the state in the *Chicago Daily Tribune*, July 13, 1924, p. 18.

26. S. Sheldon Glueck, *Mental Disorder and the Criminal Law: A Study in Medico-Sociological Jurisprudence* (Boston: Little, Brown, 1925); the quote is from Glueck, "State Legislation Providing for the Mental Examination of Persons Accused of Crime," *Mental Hygiene*, 8 (January 1924), 1. For a century of attempts to accommodate the law to medicine and social science, see Janet Ann Tighe, "A Question of Responsibility: The Development of American Forensic Psychiatry, 1838–1930" (Ph. D. diss., University of Pennsylvania, 1983).

27. William Alanson White, "The Need for Cooperation Between the Legal Profession and the Psychiatrist in Dealing with the Crime Problem," *American Journal of Psychiatry*, 7 (1927), 493, 494.

28. A. Moresby White, "Legal Insanity in Criminal Cases: Past, Present, Future," *Journal of Criminal Law and Criminology,* 18 (1927), 168. William A. White quoted in *Chicago Herald and Examiner*, August 3, 1924, part 1, p. 2. William Healy agreed to this, see *Chicago Herald and Examiner*, August 4, 1924, p. 1. For the history of the insanity plea, see A. Moresby White, "Legal Insanity in Criminal Cases," 165–74; Winfred Overholser, "The Role of Psychiatry in the Administration of Criminal Justice," *Journal of the American Medical Association,* 93 (1929), 830–34.

For a relevant early twentieth-century discussion of the concept of personal responsibility as it was applied before the 1920s, in this instance to the Jesse Pomeroy case, see Charles Follen Folsom, *Studies in Criminal Responsibility and Limited Responsibility* (privately printed, 1909), 1–19. President Garfield's assassin was already tried by the M'Naughton rules; see the discussion of the case in Charles E. Rosenberg, *The Trial of the Assassin Guiteau: Psychiatry and Law in the Gilded Age* (Chicago: University of Chicago Press, 1968).

29. *New York Times,* December 23, 1927, p. 1; and December 20, 1927, p. 1. The Hickman story is told most fully in Richard Cantillon, *In Defense of the Fox: The Trial of William Edward Hickman* (Atlanta: Droke House/Hallus, 1972), 37. See 15 for the ransom note quoted here. See also Milton Mackaye, *Dramatic Crimes of 1927: A Study of Mystery and Detection* (Garden City, N.Y.: Crime Club, 1928), 268–88.

30. Cantillon, *The Fox*, 293.

31. Cantillon, *The Fox*, 295.

32. *Catholic World*, 547; Walsh, "Criminal Responsibility," 588; "Crime and the Expert," *Outlook*, 137 (August 27, 1924), 626; Weber, "Pseudo-Science," 186.

33. Miriam Van Waters, "Why Hickman Hangs," *Survey*, 61 (October 1929).

34. "Unleashed Maniacs Constant Menace to Society," *The World*, September 18, 1925, p. 3S.

35. Loeb was similarly diagnosed. See, for example, Maurice Urstein, *Leopold and Loeb: A Psychiatric-Psychological Study* (New York: Leconver Press, 1924). *Dementia praecox* was the term used by Emil Kraepelin to describe illnesses that are today normally denominated "schizophrenia." The term derives from the observation that the onset of the disease was usually during adolescence. See Ming T. Tsuang, *Schizophrenia: The Facts* (Oxford: Oxford University Press, 1982), 11–13.

36. *New York Times*, September 8, 1925, p. 2. *The World*, September 25, 1925, p. 1. This was somewhat differently reported in the *New York Times,* September 25, 1925, p. 6. *The World*, October 15, 1925, p. 12. For Noel's father's responsibility, see, for example, *The World*, September 8, 1925, p. 1.

37. William Alanson White, "The Need for Cooperation," 501; *New York Times*, May 18, 1926, p. 27; June 17, 1926, p. 21; and May 19, 1926, p. 24. Lindsay quoted in Clara R. Cushman, "Do Alienists Disagree?" *Mental Hygiene*, 13 (July 1929), 449.

38. *The World*, September 18, 1925, p. 3S. For comparisons, see *The World*, September 7, 1925, p. 1; and September 8, 1925, p. 2. For Hickman, see Cantillon, *The Fox*, 266; *New York Times*, December 19, 1927, p. 1. For the precedents set by Robert Crowe, see, *The World*, September 11, 1925, p. 1.

39. Quoted in Sellers, *Loeb-Leopold Case*, 90–91.

40. *Chicago Herald and Examiner,* June 14, 1924, p. 1. "The Loeb-Leopold Murder of Franks in Chicago, May 21, 1924," *Journal of the American Institute of Criminal Law and Criminology*, 15 (November 1924), 347; William Healy, *The Practical Value of Scientific Study of Juvenile Delinquents*, monograph prepared for the Children's Bureau, no. 96 (Washington, D.C., 1922); and, published soon after the case, *Delinquents and Criminals: Their Making and Unmaking* (New York: Macmillan, 1926). Bernard Glueck, *Studies in Forensic Psychiatry* (Boston: Little Brown, 1916). Bernard Glueck was also the brother of S. Sheldon Glueck. Sheldon, a sociologist, would become one of the century's best-known experts on juvenile delinquency, although he, too, was initially concerned with and famous for his study of psychiatry and law (*Mental Disorder and the Criminal Law*).

41. "All is referred back to the glands. They are the Alpha and Omega of personality" (*Chicago Herald and Examiner,* June 18, 1924, p. 3). See also the pictures of the two with their various endocrine glands marked and circled, *Chicago Herald and Examiner,* July 28, 1924, p. 2. Hulbert concluded about Leopold that "his endocrine disorder is responsible for the following mental findings: His precocious mental development, his rapid advance through school, his ease of learning, are of endocrine origins. The fact that the cruel instincts show but little inhibition is of endocrine origin." *In the Criminal Court of Cook County. People of the State of Illinois v. Nathan F. Leopold Jr. and Richard Loeb*, vol. II, pp. 2069–70, Gertz Collection, Northwestern University. The complete Hulbert-Bowman report, plus the psychiatric profiles of each of the boys (written by White) are available in the Gertz Collection at the Northwestern University Library, together with the trial transcript. I have used the news-

paper and published accounts, which were all but complete, whenever possible to get a sense of the public portrait created.

42. *Chicago Daily Tribune,* July 28, 1924, p. 1. For examples of unprintable materials, see *People of the State of Illinois*, vol. II, pp. 1447–57, 1562–64. The report was carried, for example, in the *Chicago Daily Tribune*, July 28, 1924, pp. 1, 2, 3. McKernan, *Amazing Crime*, 83–163.

43. Darrow quoted in Sellers, *Loeb-Leopold Case*, 173; "Psychiatrists' Report for the Defense (Joint Summary)" in *Journal of the American Institute of Criminal Law and Criminology,* 15 (November 1924), 341. *Chicago Daily Tribune*, July 28, 1924, p. 2.

44. The Hulbert-Bowman report noted about Loeb: "There is no reason to feel that the patient's condition is of a hereditary nature or that it will be transmitted to future generations by any of his siblings or relatives. Neither is there any reason to feel that the family were responsible in any way for this boy's condition." Of Leopold, the report concluded: "There is nothing in the family training, either of omission or commission, which is responsible for his present condition. Nor is this condition to be regarded as hereditary" (McKernan, *Amazing Crime*, 108, 140). In the Hickman case, however, heredity played a critical role; see, for example, *New York Times*, January 31, 1928, p. 27.

For Dickie and his teddy bear, see, for example, *Chicago Herald and Examiner*, August 2, 1924, p. 2; and August 4, 1924, p. 3, with picture.

45. *Chicago Herald and Examiner*, June 15, 1924, p. 3; and June 16, 1924, pp. 1, 4. For the mob threat, see *Chicago Sunday Tribune*, August 31, 1924, part 1, p. 8.

46. *Chicago Herald and Examiner*, August 4, 1924, p. 3; and June 9, 1924, p. 4.

47. *Chicago Daily Tribune*, June 5, 1924, p. 3 (my emphasis); Darrow and Bachrach in Sellers, *Loeb-Leopold Case*, 157, 117. For the concepts, see "Psychiatrists' Report for the Defense," 370.

48. Quoted in "Psychiatrists' Report for the Defense," 361, 362, 374.

49. Quoted in "Psychiatrists' Report for the Defense," 366. For Loeb's aggression, see "Psychiatrists' Report for the Defense," 374. See also the photograph in *Chicago Herald and Examiner,* August 6, 1924, p. 3. For criticism, see editorial "The Crime and Trial of Loeb and Leopold," *Journal of Abnormal Psychology and Social Psychology,* 19 (October–December 1924), 221–29, and the response by S. Sheldon Glueck, "Some Implications of the Leopold and Loeb Hearing In Mitigation," *Mental Hygiene*, 9 (July 1925), 448–68. The newspapers frequently called on psychiatric experts to comment; see, for example, *Chicago Herald and Examiner,* June 3, 1924, p. 3; June 5, 1924, p. 2; and July 25, 1924, p. 3; many of these provided similar lessons.

50. In *Chicago Herald and Examiner*, June 9, 1924, p. 2; Darrow is quoted in McKernan, *Amazing Crime*, 233.

51. In Sellers, *Loeb-Leopold Case,* 251; *Chicago Herald and Examiner,* June 6, 1924, p. 2.

52. Joint Medical Report by Doctors White, Glueck, and Hamill, reprinted in McKernan, *Amazing Crime,* 142.

53. *Chicago Herald and Examiner*, July 30, 1924, p. 2; see also Arthur Brisbane's column on the same day p. 2. For a contrasting view, see the interview with people in the street, *Chicago Herald and Examiner*, July 31, 1924, p. 1.

54. *Chicago Herald and Examiner*, June 7, 1924, p. 1. Darrow made a special point of the difficulty the families' wealth presented: "If we fail in this defense it will not be for lack of money. It will be on account of money. Money has been the most serious handicap that we have met" (Sellers, *Loeb-Leopold Case*, 119). See also the *Chicago Daily Tribune*, September 11, 1924, p. 3, which says that most people credited the wealth of the families for the outcome, and the scathing denunciation by Josephus Daniels in a syndicated column published in the *Chicago Herald and Examiner*, August 3, 1924, part I, p. 3: "Are there any criminals in the country . . . whose parents have money in plenty to retain lawyers—who do not seek to escape punishment by trying to prove . . . they are insane. . . . The Chicago horror of horrors has emphasized the need to end the defeat of justice by the insanity plea." Daniels had misunderstood the nature of the defense, but he read public opinion well enough.

55. *Chicago Herald and Examiner,* June 1, pp. 4, 5; and June 3, 1924, p. 2. For Darrow's plea and its effect, *Chicago Daily Tribune*, August 23, 1924, p. 1; and August 24, pp. 1, 8, 9.

56. *Chicago Herald and Examiner,* July 30, 1924, p. 2; July 24, 1924, p. 2; and August 23, 1924, p. 2. Sometimes, Mrs. Franks was cast in a tragic role as well. At the time of her testimony, she was described by the *Chicago Daily Tribune*, "Like an Old Testament figure, tragic and valiant." But usually the descriptions of Mrs. Franks moved into other areas. Thus this article proceeded to describe her further, "Like a statue, caught in a climax of exquisite agony" (July 24, 1924, pp. 1, 2). For the Loebs' absence from the courtroom, see *Chicago Daily Tribune,* July 27, 1924, p. 2. The newspapers faulted no one for their absence and the *Chicago Herald and Examiner,* for example, assured readers that brother Allan had to work hard to persuade the sick parents to stay away (July 29, 1924, p. 3). Allan was also the one described as guarding the parents against interviews (*Chicago Daily Tribune*, June 11, 1924, p. 1).

57. *Chicago Herald and Examiner*, August 12, 1924, p. 3.

58. *Chicago Herald and Examiner*, June 9, 1924, p. 4; June 11, 1924, p. 6; September 11, 1924, p. 8 (emphasis in original). For the tendency to blame governesses in this period for youthful misbehavior, see Arthur Calhoun, *Social History of the American Family,* vol. III (Cleveland: Arthur H. Clark, 1919), 134–36. See also Darrow's statement, "Can I find what was wrong? . . . Here was a boy at a tender age, placed in the hands of a governess" (Sellers, *Loeb-Leopold Case,* 162).

59. Quoted in Sellers, *Loeb-Leopold Case,* 136.

60. Arthur Brisbane in *Chicago Herald and Examiner,* July 30, 1924, p. 2. For parents and youthful misbehavior in the 1920s, see Fass, *The Damned and the Beautiful*, 13–52.

61. Caverly's sentence in Sellers, *Loeb-Leopold Case*, 319, 320–21 (my emphasis). Bachrach's argument is on ibid., 95. In his sentence Caverly announced that Leopold and Loeb should never be released from jail, but the specific terms of the sentence suggested that he believed otherwise. See the view that the verdict meant the boys could be eligible for parole in twenty years, *Chicago Daily Tribune*, September 11, 1924, p. 1. For Leopold's parole hearings and opinions at the time of the parole, see Elmer Gertz, *A Handful of Clients* (Chicago: Follett, 1965), 6–110. For Loeb and Leopold after 1924, see Fass, "Making and Remaking an Event."

The case was such a hot news story that previews of the sentence were much sought after. In *Madhouse on Madison Street* (Chicago: Follett, 1965), 339–43, George Murray tells the story of how Caverly was wined and dined by the editor of the *Herald and Examiner* so that the latter could learn about the verdict before other papers did. As a result, a newspaper extra was on the streets almost instantaneously with the oral verdict.

62. In Sellers, *Loeb-Leopold Case*, 321.

63. Rev. Charles Parsons, "The Influence of War on Crime," in American Correctional Association, *Proceedings of the Annual Congress of Corrections*, 1917, p. 266.

64. Darrow in Sellers, *Loeb-Leopold Case*, 207–8. Meyer Levin brilliantly used war propaganda to titillate Leopold's fantasies in his fictionalization of the case, *Compulsion*, see, for example, 78, 139–40.

There is a very large literature on crime and war, and the picture is quite confused. Among the factors reducing crime during wartime are high employment and the movement of young men out of the civilian population. But others argue that crime goes up because social stability and structures break down and that the highly charged atmosphere increases the restlessness of youth and the appeal of violence. See, among many others: Dane Archer and Rosemary Gartner, "Violent Acts and Violent Times: A Comparative Approach to Postwar Homicide Rates," *American Sociological Review*, 41 (December 1976), 937–63; Dixon Wecter, *When Johnny Comes Marching Home* (Cambridge, Mass.: Houghton Mifflin, 1944), passim; Walter Bromberg, "The Effects of War on Crime," *American Sociological Review*, 8 (December 1943), 685–91; Eleanor T. Glueck, "Wartime Delinquency," *Journal of Criminal Law and Criminology,* 33 (July–August 1942), 119–35; Walter C. Reckless, "The Impact of War on Crime, Delinquency and Prostitution," *American Journal of Sociology,* 48 (November 1942), 378–86; Thorsten Sellin, "Is Murder Increasing in Europe?," *Annals of the American Academy of Political and Social Science*, 125 (May 1926), 29–34; Walter A. Lunden, *War and Delinquency: An Analysis of Juvenile Delinquency in Thirteen Nations in World War I and World War II* (Ames, Iowa: Art Press, 1963); Edith Abbott, "Crime and War," *Journal of Criminal Law and Criminology,* 9 (May 1918), 32–45.

65. Frank Orman Beck, a professor at the Garrett Bible Institute, for example, called them "unnatural" (*Chicago Herald and Examiner*, August 31, 1924, part I, p. 4).

66. Caverly in Sellers, *Loeb-Leopold Case*, 320; Crowe in ibid., 246; Leopold, *Life*

Plus 99 Years, 76. For the police roundup of sex offenders, see, for example, *Chicago Herald and Examiner,* May 30, 1924, p. 2; Judge Caverly cleared the courtroom of women, *Chicago Herald and Examiner,* August 27, 1924, p. 2; for Healy's testimony as not fit for newspapers, *Chicago Herald and Examiner,* August 5, 1924, p. 3.

67. "Comments on the Interrelationship of Loeb and Leopold," Hulbert-Bowman Report, p. 42, Gertz Collection, Northwestern University Library. Ben Lindsey quoted in Higdon, *The Crime of the Century,* 168. For youth and sex in the 1920s see Fass, *The Damned and the Beautiful,* 21–25, 260–90. As soon as the pair confessed, one columnist had at the ready an explanation for the crime: "Erotic Age of Depraved Books is Blamed by Edwin Balmer in Franks Brutal Murder Case," *Chicago Herald and Examiner,* June 1, 1924, part I, p. 4.

68. V. C. Branham, "The Reconciliation of the Legal and Psychiatric Viewpoints of Delinquency,"*Journal of Criminal Law and Criminology,* 17 (1926), 173. For interviews with "experts" about the Noel case and how it was influenced by the Leopold and Loeb case, see *New York World,* October 14, 1925, p. 3. One minister explicitly argued that the Leopold and Loeb case "brought the [insanity] law into disrepute."

CHAPTER THREE

Chapter title quotation from *New York Evening Journal,* May 13, 1932, p. 21.

1. *St. Louis Post-Dispatch,* March 3, 1932, p. 2B.

2. *New Republic,* 70 (March 16, 1932), 110. See also *New York Evening Journal,* March 2, 1932, p. 3, "Lindy Baby Kidnap Recalls Historic Abduction"; *New York World Telegram,* March 3, 1932, p. 21; and *New York Evening Journal,* March 17, 1932, p. 22. See also the *New York Times,* May 13, 1932, p. 4, in an article that remembered not only Charley Ross (whose name is in the headline), but Bobby Franks, Marion Parker (killed by William Hickman), and Mary Daly (killed by Harrison Noel).

3. Walter S. Ross, *The Last Hero: Charles A. Lindbergh* (New York: Harper & Row, 1964). Another biographer, Kenneth S. Davis, called him simply *The Hero* (Garden City, N. Y.: Doubleday, 1959).

4. *New York Evening Journal,* March 3, 1932, p. 25; March 4, 1932, pp. 5, 23; and March 2, 1932, p. 14; *New York Times,* March 4, 1932, pp. 8, 9. For how the press got in to see the baby's body, Joyce Milton, *Loss of Eden: A Biography of Charles and Anne Lindbergh* (New York, 1993), 251.

5. See Anne Morrow Lindbergh, *Hour of Gold, Hour of Lead: Diaries and Letters of Anne Morrow Lindbergh, 1929–32* (New York: Harcourt, Brace, Jovanovitch, 1973), 226–97.

6. The story of the kidnapping is told in many places. Among the best are Jim Fisher, *The Lindbergh Case* (New Brunswick, N. J.: Rutgers University Press, 1987); George Waller, *Kidnap* (New York: Dial, 1961); Sidney Whipple, *The Lindbergh*

Crime (New York: Blue Ribbon Books, 1935); and Milton, *Loss of Eden*.

7. The more recent reexaminations, which cast doubt on Hauptmann's guilt, include Anthony Scaduto, *Scapegoat: The Lonesome Death of Bruno Richard Hauptmann* (New York: G. P. Putnam, 1976), Ludovic Kennedy, *The Airman and the Carpenter: The Lindbergh Kidnapping and the Framing of Richard Hauptmann* (New York: Penguin, 1985); Noel Behn, *Lindbergh: The Crime* (New York: Atlantic Monthly Press, 1993).

The Lindbergh case still remains very much in the news. One example is the segment on NBC's news program, *Dateline*, for December 7, 1993, which featured Noel Behn and his theory about the case.

8. For the airplane rides over the Lindbergh house, *New York Times*, March 7, 1932, p. 11.

9. *New York Evening Journal*, March 12, 1932, p. 2.

10. *New York Times*, March 3, 1932, p. 10.

11. P. W. Wilson, "The Lindbergh Case," *North American Review*, 237 (January 1934), 51, 58 (my emphasis); *Literary Digest*, 113 (May 28, 1932), 6; "Behind the Empty Crib," *Christian Century*, 49 (March 16, 1932), 344.

12. The best and most rounded discussion of Anne and her family is in Milton, *Loss of Eden*.

13. *New York Evening Journal*, March 2, 1932, pp. 1, 2, 3, 4, 16, 17, 18.

14. *New York Evening Journal*, March 3, 1932, p. 14.

15. *New York Evening Journal*, March 4, 1932, pp. 3, 17. For Anne's reactions, Lindbergh, *Hour of Gold, Hour of Lead*, 226–97.

16. *New York Evening Journal*, March 4, 1932, pp. 3, 17; March 7, 1932, p. 3; and March 8, 1932, p. 1.

17. *New York Evening Journal*, March 8, 1932, p. 1; March 10, 1932, pp. 1, 3; and May 13, 1932, p. 3, from two different articles; *New York Times*, January 4, 1935, p. 6.

18. *New York Times*, March 3, 1932, p. 11; and March 5, 1932, p. 2; "When the Kidnapper Comes!" *Delineator*, 123 (November 1933), 56. Compare the description of Jimmy de Jute's mother with that of Anne Lindbergh in the *New York Times*: Mrs. de Jute is hysterical, Anne is brave and "has no breakdown," *New York Times*, March 5, 1932, p. 1.

19. *New York Evening Journal*, March 7, 1932, p. 14; and March 12, 1932, p. 10; *New York Times*, March 2, 1932, p. 1.

20. For some examinations of the problem on the eve of the Lindbergh kidnapping, see *Literary Digest*, 109 (May 23, 1931), 11; *New York Times*, January 25, 1932, p. 10; January 30, 1932, p. 36; and February 27, 1932, p. 3; Albert Bushnell Hart, "The Modern Mafia," *Current History*, 34 (June 1931), 411–13. The only examination of the crime of kidnapping locates the 1930s as the period of its greatest frequency. See Ernest Kahler Alix, *Ransom Kidnapping in America/1874–1974: The Creation of a Capital Crime* (Carbondale, Ill.: Southern Illinois University Press, 1978), 38–124.

21. See map, *Literary Digest*, 113 (May 28, 1932), 7; *New York Times*, March 4, 1932, p. 7. On the rackets, see *New York Times*, May 14, 1933, sec. 8, p. 2; and an article by Robert Isham Randolph, head of the Chicago "Secret Six," April 17, 1932, sec. 9, p. 3; *Literary Digest*, 113 (March 26, 1932), 38, 42. For a possible connection between the Detroit Purple Gang and the Lindbergh case, see *New York Times*, March 4, 1932, p. 8.

22. Summers's remarks appear in *New York Times*, March 3, 1932, p. 8. For one example of the 2,000 figure, among many, see *New York Times*, March 3, 1932, p. 9. For the 285 figure, *Literary Digest*, 113 (May 28, 1932), 7; the *New York Times* used a similar number when it observed that the Lindbergh baby was the two hundred eighty-fourth kidnap victim (March 3, 1932, p. 3). For the sense of kidnapping as a major and growing menace, see *Literary Digest*, 109 (May 23, 1931), 11. See also *New York Times*, "Kidnapping Wave Sweeps the Nation. Lindbergh Crime is Climax of Development of Abductions Into a Major Racket," March 3, 1932, p. 9. For the rapid response, see *New York Times*, March 2, 1932, p. 4.

23. *Editor and Publisher*, 64 (March 12, 1932), 28; Albert Edward Ullman, *The Kidnappers* (New York: Amour Press, 1932).

24. Ullman, *Kidnappers*, 41, 246; *Literary Digest*, 113 (May 28, 1932), 7.

25. *New York Evening Journal*, March 3, 1932, p. 2; *New York Evening Journal, Home Magazine Supplement,* May 14, 1932, pp. 6–7; May 21, 1932, pp. 8–9; and May 28, 1932, pp. 6–7; *New York Times*, March 3, 1932, p. 9; *Minneapolis Journal*, in *Literary Digest*, 113 (May 28, 1932), 6; "Behind the Empty Crib," 343; *Brooklyn Eagle*, in *Literary Digest*, 113 (April 23, 1932), 7 (my emphasis).

26. *Arkansas Gazette*, in *Literary Digest*, 113 (May 28, 1932), 6; *New York Evening Journal*, March 2, 1932, pp. 3–4; and March 7, 1932, p. 26. See also *Literary Digest*, 113 (March 12, 1932), 6; an article by Jack Lait in *New York Evening Journal*, March 3, 1932, p. 4.

27. "Behind the Empty Crib," 343; Harry Elmer Barnes, "The Deeper Lessons of the Lindbergh Kidnapping," *Survey*, 68 (April 1, 1932), 12. For discussions of secret anticrime commissions and groups, see, for example, Frank J. Loesch's articles in *New York Times*, July 30, 1933, sec. 8, p. 3; and April 17, 1932, sec. 9, p. 3. Loesch was the five-term head of the Chicago Crime Commission. "When the Kidnapper Comes!" 56.

28. *Literary Digest*, 113 (March 26, 1932), 38; *New York Evening Journal*, March 3, 1932, p. 34; *New York Times*, May 18, 1932, p. 20; Will Rogers was quoted in *New York Times*, March 7, 1932, p. 11. For the kidnap-murder of Brooke Hart and the lynching of his suspected abductors, see Harry Farrell, *Swift Justice: Murder and Vengeance in a California Town* (New York: St. Martin's Press, 1992).

29. The de Jute case is reported in *New York Times*, March 4, 1932, p. 10; for Byrnes's statement, see *New York Evening Journal*, March 4, 1932, p. 2; for Governor Moore's statement, *New York Times*, March 4, 1932, p. 8.

30. *New York World Telegram*, March 4, 1932, p. 25; *New York Evening Journal*,

March 4, 1932, editorial (no page number); see also March 3, 1932, p. 34; and March 5, 1932, p. 26.

31. For the many unofficially involved in searching for the child, see *New York Evening Journal*, March 3, 1932, p. 3; for the figure on officials involved, see *New York Times*, March 3, 1932, p. 8. The quote is from *Daily News*, as cited in *Literary Digest*, 113 (March 26, 1932), 4, 2.

32. *New York World Telegram*, March 7, 1932, p. 20; "The World Against the Lindberghs," *Nation*, 134 (March 16, 1932), 301.

33. For McMath, see *Boston Evening Transcript*, May 3, 1933, p. 1; *New York Times*, May 6, 1933, p. 3. For crowd at ransom drop-site, see Marcet Haldemann-Julius, *The Lindbergh-Hauptmann Kidnap-Murder Case* (Girard, Kansas: Haldemann-Julius Publications, 1937), 31.

34. The quote is from *New York Evening Journal*, March 9, 1932, p. 3; *New York Times*, March 7, 1932, p. 1.

35. *Literary Digest*, 116 (August 12, 1933), 6; *New York Times*, June 24, 1938, p. 40. See also *Commonweal*, 18 (August 11, 1933), 357. For Canadian case of John S. Labatt, a businessman, see *Literary Digest*, 118 (August 25, 1934), 7.

36. *New York Times*, March 7, 1932, p. 10; for false information released about child's imminent return, see p. 1. As serious as the fact that he misled the press was the possibility that Rosner may have muddied the trail to the kidnapper when he was given access to the original kidnap note, which he showed to various New York connections. Indeed, several of the defenses of Hauptmann have taken for granted that the access to the note and its secret signature were the source of Hauptmann's (inadvertent) involvement in the case.

37. *New York Evening Journal*, March 11, 1932, pp. 1–2.

38. *New York Evening Journal*, March 24, 1932, pp. 3, 12.

39. *Editor and Publisher*, March 12, 1932, p. 28; *New York Times*, April 11, 1932, p. 13.

40. *New York Times*, March 2, 1932, p. 3; *New York Evening Journal*, March 9, 1932, p. 3; *Editor and Publisher*, 64 (March 5, 1932) 5; *New York Evening Journal*, March 14, 1932, p. 7.

41. Laura Vitray, *The Great Lindbergh Hullabaloo: An Unorthodox Account* (New York: Willliam Faro, Inc., 1932), 150–51.

42. Vitray, *The Great Lindbergh Hullabaloo*, 189–90 (my emphasis).

43. See the press defenses of his flight in *Literary Digest*, 121 (January 4, 1936), 27–28. From the beginning, there were those who believed Lindbergh to be personally implicated in the crime. One such individual managed to get inside the Lindbergh house during the early days of the search. For this incident, see Milton, *Loss of Eden*, 244.

44. Scaduto, *Scapegoat*; Kennedy, *Airman and the Carpenter*; Behn, *The Lindbergh Crime*; Gregory Ahlgren and Stephen Monier, *Crime of the Century: The Lindbergh*

Kidnapping Hoax (Boston: Brandon Books, 1993). Many of these books draw inspiration from a breezy article by Alan Hynd, who tried to expose some of the loose threads of the case in "Everybody Wanted in the Act," in *A Treasury of True*, ed. Charles N. Barnard (New York: A. S. Barnes & Co., 1956), 17–45.

45. *New York Evening Journal*, May 15, 1932, pp. 3, 4; May 17, 1932, pp. 3, 6; and May 18, 1932, p. 11.

46. Wilson, "The Lindbergh Case," 51.

47. *Publishers' Weekly*, 127 (February 16, 1935), 788; *New Republic*, 70 (March 16, 1932), 110.

48. *Editor and Publisher*, 64 (March 5, 1932), 5; (March 12, 1932), 5; Silas Bent, "Lindbergh and the Press," *Outlook*, 160 (April 1932), 212; *Editor and Publisher*, 64 (March 19, 1932), 9; the quotes are from *Editor and Publisher*, 64 (March 5, 1932), 5.

49. *Editor and Publisher*, 64 (March 19, 1932), 9; (March 5, 1932), 6; (March 12, 1932), 6, 9; (March 26, 1932) 26.

50. *Editor and Publisher*, 64 (March 26, 1932), 24; Bent, "Lindbergh and the Press," 212; Walter Lippmann is quoted in *Editor and Publisher*, 64 (April 16, 1932), 7. For the defensiveness of *Editor and Publisher*, see for example, editorial, 64 (April 16, 1932), 28, 5–8, 46; and 64 (May 14, 1932), 14. Helen M. Hughes, "The Lindbergh Case: A Study of Human Interest and Politics," *American Journal of Sociology*, 42 (July 1936), 32–54.

51. *Editor and Publisher*, 65 (May 21, 1932), 6, 40, 42 (my emphasis).

52. *New York Times*, May 15, 1932, part 3, p. 11; *St. Louis Post-Dispatch*, March 13, 1932, p. 3E; *New York Daily News* is discussed in Hughes, "Study of Human Interest and Politics," 36; *New York Evening Journal*, May 14, 1932, p. 8.

53. *New York Evening Journal*, May 20, 1932, p. 24; *Editor and Publisher*, 64 (April 16, 1932), 28.

54. *Orlando Morning Sentinel*, in *Editor and Publisher*, 65 (May 12, 1932), 42. The paper devoted the entire front page to the event. *St. Louis Post-Dispatch*, May 13, 1932, p. 1.

55. *St. Louis Post-Dispatch*, March 5, 1932, p. 2.

56. The story is widely reported; the best source is Condon's own memoir, John F. Condon, *Jafsie Tells All: Revealing the Inside Story of the Lindbergh-Hauptmann Case* (New York: Jonathan Lee Publishing Corp., 1936), 145–91.

57. For the early leaks, see *Editor and Publisher*, 64 (March 11, 1932), 5; and 64 (March 15, 1932), 2; *New York Times*, April 11, 1932, pp. 10–11.

58. *New York Times*, September 21, 1934, pp. 1–4; and September 22, 1934, pp. 1–4.

59. David Davidson, "The Story of the Century," *American Heritage*, 27 (February 1976), 23–29, 93; *Editor and Publisher*, 67 (January 12, 1935), 5; and (January 19, 1935), 41. Edna Ferber's piece appeared in the *New York Times* and caused a stir at the time (January 28, 1935, p. 4); see also *Times* letters to the editor, January 30, 1935, p. 18; and February 1, 1935, p. 20. Kathleen Norris's article appeared in the *New York Times*,

January 8, 1935, p. 10. For Jack Franks's reaction, *Chicago Herald and Examiner,* June 11, 1924, p. 5.

60. *New York Times,* February 23, 1935, p. 1; Haldemann-Julius, *Lindbergh-Hauptmann Kidnap-Murder Case,* 94; Thomas D. Thacher, "Trial by Newspaper," *Vital Speeches of the Day,* 2 (September 15, 1936), 778; "Both Guilty," *New Republic,* 82 (February 27, 1935), 62; *Editor and Publisher,* 68 (July 20, 1935), 3.

61. "Both Guilty," 62. For the Weyerhaeuser case, see *New York Times,* May 26, 1935, p. 1; and May 27, 1935, p. 3; *News of the Week at Home,* 5 (June 15, 1935), 5.

62. "Child Murder as Entertainment," *Catholic World,* 140 (March 1935), 641.

63. For Crowe, see *New York World Telegram,* March 4, 1932, p. 23; Edward H. Smith, *Mysteries of the Missing* (New York: Dial, 1927), 133–52; and Pat Crowe's strange autobiography, *Spreading Evil: Pat Crowe's Autobiography* (New York: The Branwell Company, 1927).

64. For Leibowitz's role, see Fisher, *The Lindbergh Case,* 403–8; for Leibowitz's role in the Scottsboro case, see James Goodman, *Stories of Scottsboro* (New York: Pantheon, 1994), 102–5 and passim. For the most important early arguments against the legitimacy of the verdict, see the series by former Governor Harold G. Hoffman, who was involved in the various attempts to pardon, retry, or otherwise overturn the Lindbergh verdict in "What Was Wrong with the Lindbergh Case: The Crime—the Case, the Challenge," *Liberty,* 15 (January 29, 1938), 6–11; (February 5, 1938), 16–20; (February 15, 1938), 20–25; (February 19, 1938), 46–53; (February 26, 1938), 24–31; (March 5, 1938), 48–56; (March 12, 1938), 55–59; (March 19, 1938), 51–58; (March 26, 1932), 55–62; (April 2, 1938), 44–49; (April 9, 1938), 47–50; (April 16, 1938), 55–59; (April 23, 1938), 55–59; (April 30, 1938), 51–55; (July 2, 1938), 26–27; and (July 9, 1938), 13–14. *World Tomorrow,* 17 (March 15, 1934), 126.

65. *Editor and Publisher,* 67 (February 2, 1935), 5. The Highland Park kidnapping is reported in Haldemann-Julius, *Lindbergh-Hauptmann Kidnap-Murder Case,* 35.

66. *New York Evening Journal,* March 4, 1932, p. 25; *New York World Telegram,* March 4, 1932, p. 24; *Literary Digest,* 112 (March 26, 1932), 38; *New York Times,* June 8, 1935, p. 14. For anxiety, *Literary Digest,* 121 (January 4, 1936), 27; the *St. Louis Post-Dispatch* reported that members of the Columbia University football team were serving as escort-bodyguards to wealthy New York children (March 11, 1932, p. 1F). In Central Park, extra police were assigned to guard children of rich New Yorkers (*New York Evening Journal,* March 28, 1932, p. 7). For reports about various celebrities like Gene Tunney who hired guards for their children, see *New York Evening Journal,* March 8, 1932, p. 2. For Lloyd's of London, *New York Evening Journal,* March 3, 1932, p. 4.

67. "When the Kidnapper Comes!" 56; no author "Front Page Stuff," *Saturday Evening Post,* 206 (March 17, 1934), 16–17, 71, 74, 75.

68. *New York Evening Journal,* March 26, 1932, p. 28; see also *New York Evening Journal,* March 4, 1932, p. 9.

69. The first federal law (1932), often called the Lindbergh Law (18 U.S.C. 1201–2 [1976 & Supp. IV 1980]), made it a federal crime to transport a kidnap victim across state lines. It also made the FBI available to assist with the case and with a search when a victim was not returned within twenty-four hours. In 1934, the law was amended to include the death penalty where the kidnap victim was harmed. The second law also stated that after seven days there would be a presumption that some state line had been crossed and the FBI could enter the picture. See Lawrence Freedman, *Crime and Punishment in American History* (New York: Basic Books, 1993), 266.

At the time of the Lindbergh kidnapping, eight states already had the death penalty as a punishment. The penalty in other states ranged from seven years in Colorado and Georgia to life in eleven states and ninety-nine years in one, New Mexico (*New York Times*, March 4, 1932, p. 8). By May 1936, 146 people had been convicted in accordance with the new federal kidnapping law (*New York Times*, May 13, 1936, p. 3). The *New York Times*, March 3, 1932, p. 10, reported that, according to the British press, "Gangdom is virtually in control in the U. S." On Hoover, see the inspirational discussion of the bureau, its chief, and its effective use of the latest scientific techniques in Edwin Teale, "Scientific Detectives Smash Kidnap Gangs," *Popular Science Monthly*, 124 (May 1934), 15–17, 111–12.

70. *Editor and Publisher*, 69 (January 4, 1936), 11.

71. The baby look-alike story is reported in Haldemann-Julius, *The Lindbergh-Hauptmann Kidnap-Murder Case*, 35, and *New York Evening Journal*, May 13, 1932, p. 1; May 14, 1932, p. 1.

72. It was fitting and ironic that when the Lindberghs got rid of their house, they turned it into a child welfare center; Haldemann-Julius, *The Lindbergh-Hauptmann Kidnap-Murder Case*, 54.

CHAPTER FOUR

1. See *Newsweek*, 48 (July 16, 1956), 81; and 48 (September 3, 1956), 81; *Time*, 68 (July 16, 1956), 70; *Nation*, 183 (July 21, 1956), 1; quotes are from *Time*, and *Nation*. For the hoaxes that plagued the case, see *Life*, 41 (July 23, 1956), 30–31.

2. *San Francisco Examiner*, September 20, 1955, p. 1.

3. *San Francisco Examiner*, September 20, 1955, p. 9.

4. *San Francisco Examiner*, September 21, 1955, p. 16; *San Francisco Chronicle*, September 29, 1955, p. 1.

5. *San Francisco Chronicle*, September 21, 1955, p. 1; and September 20, 1955, pp. 1, 2.

6. *San Francisco Chronicle*, September 21, 1955, p. 3; and September 22, 1955, p. 2.

7. *San Francisco Chronicle*, September 23, 1955, p. 1; September 25, 1955, p. 8; and September 27, 1955, p. 1; *San Francisco Examiner*, September 21, 1955, p. 16.

8. *San Francisco Examiner*, September 21, 1955, p. 1, 16; for sketch, *San Francisco Chronicle*, September 21, 1955, p. 1.

9. *New York Times*, August 26, 1923, sec. VII, p. 2; *Newsweek*, 48 (September 17, 1956), 37–38; Faye Kellerman, *Grievous Sin* (New York: Fawcett Gold Medal, 1993); see the diagnosis on page 348: "She fit the profile of a baby kidnapper—an unbalanced person who longed for a child." Television programs have used the idea, but not the psychological or physical profile, for example, *The Baby Snatcher*, with Veronica Hamel, first broadcast on May 3, 1992, on CBS.

The National Center for Missing and Exploited Children in Washington has a separate division for this kind of crime, and the profile they use, based on FBI material, is just the same as the one in the 1950s. See John C. Rabun, *For Healthcare Professionals: Guidelines on Preventing Infant Abductions* (Washington, D.C.: National Center for Missing and Exploited Children, 1993), 3–4. For the FBI category, see also "Stolen Children," *Newsweek*, 103 (March 19, 1984), 85.

10. *San Francisco Examiner*, September 26, 1955, p. 26; *San Francisco Chronicle*, September 25, 1955, p. 1; *Los Angeles Times*, September 29, 1955, p. 3; *San Francisco Examiner*, September 25, 1955, p. 26.

11. *San Francisco Chronicle*, September 26, 1955, p. 11.

12. *San Francisco Examiner*, September 29, 1955, p. 1; *San Francisco Chronicle*, September 28, 1955, p. 1; *Los Angeles Times*, September 29, 1955, part 1, pp. 1, 3; *New York Times,* September 29, 1955, p. 37; *San Francisco Chronicle*, September 29, 1955, p. 1.

13. According to Benedicto's mother, Betty Jean was actually thirty-one (*San Francisco Examiner*, October 2, 1955, p. 24). *San Francisco Examiner*, September 29, 1955, pp. A, 2.

14. *San Francisco Chronicle*, September 29, 1955, p. 1; *San Francisco Examiner*, September 29, 1955, pp. 1, 8. Sanford Marcus had very early made this association by noting that the kidnapper was evidently hungry for a baby (*San Francisco Chronicle*, September 20, 1955, p. 2).

15. *Los Angeles Times*, September 29, 1955, p. 10; *San Francisco Examiner*, September 29, 1955, pp. 1, A.

16. *San Francisco Examiner*, September 29, 1955, p. 2; and October 4, 1955, pp. 4, 17.

17. *San Francisco Chronicle,* September 30, 1955, p. 10; *San Francisco Examiner*, September 29, 1955, pp. A, 6; October 2, 1955, p. 24; and October 7, 1955, sec. II, p. 2.

18. *San Francisco Examiner*, September 30, 1955, p. 1.

19. Herb Caen's observations were in the *San Francisco Examiner*, September 30, 1955, p. 29, 1955; and October 26, 1955, sec. II, p. 1. *San Francisco Examiner*, October 1, 1955, pp. 1–2; October 2, 1955, p. 24; October 3, 1955, p. 3; October 14, 1955, p. 8; and October 21, 1955, p. 9.

20. *San Francisco Examiner,* November 10, 1955, p. 9; and November 11, 1955, pp. 1, 7.

21. *San Francisco Chronicle,* January 27, 1956, p. 4; *San Francisco Examiner,* November 11, 1955, p. 10. A recent book on Abbott was published too late to be considered in my discussion of the case; see Keith Walker, *Trail of Corn: A True Mystery* (Santa Rosa, Ca.: Golden Door Press, 1995).

22. *San Francisco Chronicle,* April 30, 1955, p. 1; *San Francisco Examiner,* July 24, 1955, p. 11.

23. The chronology was recounted during Mary Bryan's testimony; see *San Francisco Chronicle*, November 23, 1955, p. 1.

24. *San Francisco Chronicle*, April 30, 1955, p. 1; May 2, 1955, p. 1; May 1, 1955, p. 1; and July 18, 1955, p. 1.

25. *San Francisco Chronicle*, May 5, 1955, p. 5; May 4, 1955, p. 3; May 9, 1955, p. 1; May 8, 1955, p. 1; May 11, 1955, p. 1; May 12, 1955, p. 1; May 19, 1955, p. 1; and May 20, 1955, p. 5. For examples of sightings, see May 29, 1955, p. 4; and May 17, 1955, p. 3.

26. *San Francisco Chronicle,* December 5, 1955, p. 5.

27. *San Francisco Chronicle*, July 17, 1955, pp. 1, 2.

28. *San Francisco Chronicle*, July 18, 1955, p. 3; and July 17, 1955, pp. 1, 2.

29. *San Francisco Chronicle*, July 19, 1955, p. 1; and July 20, 1955, p. 2. The quote is from July 19, 1955, p. 1. For Reidel, see Erle Stanley Gardner, in *San Francisco Examiner*, November 6, 1955, p. 23; November 7, 1955, p. 14.

30. *San Francisco Examiner*, July 18, 1955, p. 6; *San Francisco Chronicle,* July 19, 1955, p. 3; for Chessman, see *San Francisco Chronicle*, July 15, 1955, p. 55; *San Francisco Examiner*, July 25, 1955, p. 32.

31. *San Francisco Examiner*, July 21, 1955, p. 1.

32. *San Francisco Examiner*, July 27, 1955, p. 24; and July 21, 1955, sec. III, p. 2. For the fears of sex crimes in the 1950s, see Estelle B. Freedman, "'Uncontrolled Desires': The Response to the Sexual Psychopath, 1920–1960," *Journal of American History*, 74 (June 1987), 83–106.

33. *San Francisco Examiner*, July 22, 1955, p. 1; and July 22, 1955, p. 2; *San Francisco Chronicle*, July 27, 1955, p. 2; January 18, 1956, p. 6; January 20, 1956, pp. 2, 1; July 22, 1955, p. A; and January 27, 1956, pp. 1, 4; for Gardner, *San Francisco Examiner*, November 19, 1955, p. 4.

34. *San Francisco Chronicle,* January 26, 1956, p. 9.

35. *San Francisco Chronicle,* July 20, 1955, p. 2; July 22, 1955, p. A; March 16, 1957, p. 4; January 19, 1955, p. 2; January 26, 1955, p. 9; and January 6, 1956, p. 1.

36. Albert Ellis and Ralph Brancale, with Ruth R. Doorbar, *The Psychology of Sex Offenders* (Springfield, Ill.: Charles C. Thomas, 1956), 95–96; Freedman, "Uncontrolled Desires."

37. *San Francisco Examiner*, October 10, 1955, p. 5; and January 26, 1956, pp. B, 1. For Mary Bryan, see, for example, *San Francisco Chronicle*, July 29, 1955, p. 4; November 23, 1955, p. 5; December 5, 1955, pp. 1, 11; and December 7, 1955, pp. 14, 15. For Elsie Abbott, *San Francisco Chronicle*, July 29, 1955, p. 1; August 5, 1955, p. 1; and

January 23, 1956, p. 1; for her outbursts in court, *San Francisco Chronicle*, January 23, 1956, pp. 1, 5; and January 26, 1955, p. 3; *San Francisco Examiner*, January 26, 1956, p. A.

38. *San Francisco Examiner*, July 22, 1955, p. 2 (my emphasis); *San Francisco Chronicle*, January 26, 1956, p. 1; January 27, 1956, p. 1. For Leopold and Loeb, see Paula S. Fass, "Making and Remaking an Event: The Leopold and Loeb Case in American Culture," *Journal of American History*, 80 (December 1993), 919–51; Meyer Levin, *Compulsion* (New York: Simon & Schuster, 1956).

39. *San Francisco Examiner*, July 27, 1955, p. 5; October 8, 1955, p. 14; and October 4, 1955, sec. II, p. 2.

40. *San Francisco Chronicle,* January 26, 1956, p. B; *San Francisco Examiner*, December 8, 1955, p. 18; see also Gardner, *San Francisco Examiner*, November 7, 1955, p. 1, 14, where Gardner specifically defends Berkeley police tactics.

41. *San Francisco Chronicle*, March 7, 1956, p. 3; and April 13, 1956, p. 10; *San Francisco Examiner*, April 13, 1956, p. 14.

42. *San Francisco Chronicle*, December 12, 1955, p. 13; Freedman, "Uncontrolled Desires," discusses how expectations about sexual delinquency were reversed in the 1940s and 1950s.

43. *San Francisco Chronicle*, October 1, 1955, pp. 1, 5; *San Francisco Examiner*, October 1, 1955, pp. 1, 3; *San Francisco Chronicle,* February 4, 1959, p. 16.

44. *San Francisco Examiner*, November 18, 1955, p. 20.

45. *San Francisco Examiner*, January 30, 1956, sec. II, p. 2; Grace Holden Curtis, "The Abbott Case: A Fair Trial and a Free Press" (master's thesis, journalism, University of California at Berkeley, 1957), 126, 117, 64, 62–63, 66.

46. *San Francisco Examiner*, November 6, 1955, p. 23; *San Francisco Chronicle*, January 15, 1956, p. 1. For the intense popular involvement and the possible sympathies for Abbott that resulted, see G. Marine, "The Jury Said 'Death,'" *Nation*, 182 (May 19, 1956), 424–26. On reader's role in fiction, see, for example, Wolfgang Iser, "Interaction between Text and Reader," in *The Reader in the Text: Essays on Audience and Interpretation*, Susan R. Suleiman and Inge Crosman, eds. (Princeton: Princeton University Press, 1980), 106–19; Iser, "The Reading Process: A Phenomenological Approach," in *Reader-Response Criticism: From Formalism to Post-Structuralism*, ed. Jane P. Tompkins (Baltimore: Johns Hopkins University Press, 1980), 50–69, and the volume in general.

47. *San Francisco Chronicle*, November 12, 1955, p. 12; December 13, 1955, p. 1; March 7, 1956, p. 3; March 6, 1956, p. 3; and April 13, 1956, pp. 1, 10.

48. *San Francisco Chronicle,* May 1, 1956, p. 3; July 4, 1956, p. 5; and December 25, 1956, p. 5.

49. *San Francisco Chronicle,* March 8, 1957, p. 30; September 24, 1957, p. 16; and January 5, 1959, p. 1. For a description of the typical female infant abductor, see Rabun, *For Healthcare Professionals*, 3.

50. *San Francisco Chronicle,* September 13, 1961; and March 1, 1962, p. 38.

51. *San Francisco Chronicle*, January 13, 1956, p. 1.

52. *Oakland Tribune*, January 26, 1956, p. 1; *San Francisco Chronicle*, January 27, 1956, p. 1; also *San Francisco Examiner*, January 27, 1927, p. 2; *Oakland Tribune*, January 26, 1956, p. 2.

53. *San Francisco Chronicle*, January 26, 1956, p. B.

54. *San Francisco Chronicle*, January 26, 1956, p. 4; December 6, 1955, p. 1; February 10, 1956, p. 2; and April 2, 1956, p. 1.

55. *San Francisco Chronicle*, July 17, 1956, pp. 1, 13; July 18, 1956, p. 1; and August 8, 1956, pp. 1, 13.

56. *San Francisco Chronicle,* November 24, 1956, p. 1; December 10, 1956, p. 4; and December 20, 1956, p. 24.

57. *San Francisco Chronicle*, January 23, 1957, p. 10.

58. *San Francisco Chronicle*, January 28, 1957, pp. 1, 12; January 29, 1957, p. 1; and January 30, 1957, pp. 1, 2.

59. *San Francisco Chronicle*, January 29, 1957, p. 8; January 30, 1957, p. 2; February 1, 1957, p. 14; and February 2, 1957, p. 1.

60. *San Francisco Chronicle*, September 25, 1961, pp. 1, 6. See also September 22, 1961, pp. 1, 10.

61. Albert Camus, "Reflection on the Guillotine," *Resistance, Rebellion and Death,* trans. Justin O'Brien (New York: Knopf, 1961), 175–234. I owe this reference to Ted Hamm. For the general psychological orientation of the period, see Ellen Herman, *The Romance of American Psychology: Political Culture in the Age of Experts* (Berkeley: University of California Press, 1995).

62. *San Francisco Chronicle,* March 5, 1957, p. 1; March 9, 1957, p. 1; and March 14, 1957, p. 1. A *writ of certiorari* allows a superior court to intervene in a case because it was judged as not tried impartially in the lower court.

63. Quoted in Miriam Allen DeFord, *Murderers Sane and Mad: Case Histories in the Motivation and Rationale of Murder* (London: Abelard-Schuman, 1965), 40; *San Francisco Examiner*, March 16, 1957, p. A. Knight's argument was also published in *Time*, 69 (March 25, 1957), 25.

64. Among many, see the letters in *San Francisco Examiner*, March 30, 1957, p. 57; March 29, 1957, sec. II, p. 2; March 25, 1957, sec. III, p. 2; March 23, 1957, p. 12; March 22, 1957, sec. II, p. 2; and March 20, 1957, sec. II, p. 2; and in *San Francisco Chronicle*, March 20, 1957, p. 22; and March 25, 1957, p. 26. For the national coverage, see *Newsweek*, 49 (May 20, 1957), 43; 49 (April 11, 1957), 11, 14; Marine, "The Jury Said 'Death'"; *New York Times,* March 16, 1957, p. 21; *Christian Century*, 74 (April 3, 1957), 412–13. For the rally, see *San Francisco Examiner*, March 27, 1957, p. 24.

65. *San Francisco Chronicle*, March 16,1957, p. 3. For the obituaries, see *San Francisco Chronicle*, October 29, 1958, p. 2; *San Francisco Examiner*, October 29, 1958, p. 10.

CHAPTER FIVE

Chapter title quotation from Margaret Strickland, "Child Snatched: The Danny Strickland Case," in *How To Deal With a Parental Kidnapping*, compiled by Margaret Strickland (Moorehaven, Fla.: Rainbow Books, 1983), 187.

1. *New York Times*, August 13, 1873, p. 2.

2. Mary Ann Mason, *From Father's Property to Children's Rights* (New York: Columbia University Press, 1994), 59.

3. For Blackstone, see *New York Times*, October 24, 1878, p. 1; and October 26, 1878, p. 5; see also October 25, 1878, p. 1. For Coolidge, see *New York Times*, December 10, 1879, p. 3.

4. *New York Times*, April 3, 1879, p. 8.

5. Ibid.

6. For other late-nineteenth-century abductions, see *New York Times*, October 29, 1877, p. 1; November 2, 1878, p. 3; May 19, 1881, p. 10; May 25, 1881, p. 2; June 5, 1881, p. 5; October 13, 1893, p. 9; September 23, 1891, p. 3; and October 6, 1896, p. 5.

7. *New York Times*, April 2, 1993, p. 11; for earlier examples of such abductions, see, for example, August 13, 1893, p. 5; April 13, 1916, p. 9; and January 28, 1908, p. 7.

8. E. G. Ewaschuk, "Abduction of Children by Parents," *Criminal Law Quarterly*, 21 (1978–79), 176–77; Margaret R. De Haas, *Domestic Injunctions* (London: Seet & Maxwell, 1987), 52–53.

9. *Commonwealth v. Nickerson*, 87 Mass. 5 (Allen) 518; *State v. Farrar*, 41 N. H. 53; *Hunt v. Hunt*, 94 Ga. 257, 21 S.E. 515; *State v. Angel*, 42 Kan. 216, 21 Pac. 1075. The cases are summarized in *Century Edition of the American Digest*, vol. 31 (St. Paul: West Publishing, 1902).

10. For Iowa, *New York Times*, December 26, 1900, p. 1; for New York, *New York Times*, July 9, 1911, p. 4, and April 14, 1911, p. 10; see also April 16, 1911, p. 10.

11. See William O'Neill, *Divorce in the Progressive Era* (New Haven: Yale University Press, 1967); Elaine Tyler May, *Great Expectations: Marriage and Divorce in Post-Victorian America* (Chicago: University of Chicago Press, 1980).

12. *New York Times*, June 11, 1927, p. 24; and June 28, 1910, p. 7; for other auto abductions, see *New York Times*, August 22, 1916, p. 9; May 23, 1916, p. 22; and December 26, 1914, p. 3.

13. *New York Times*, November 11, 1910, p. 9; *Chicago Tribune*, August 28, 1916, p. 1; *New York Times*, August 28, 1916, p. 9.

14. *New York Times*, November 8, 1913, p. 7; and November 11, 1913, p. 8.

15. *San Francisco Chronicle*, July 18, 1966, p. 24; and July 10, 1935, p. 15; *San Francisco Examiner*, April 11, 1925, p. 1; December 5, 1923, p. 1; and April 11, 1925, p. 1; *San Francisco Chronicle*, October 30, 1928, p. 5.

16. *San Francisco Chronicle*, July 10, 1935, p. 15; *San Francisco Examiner,* April 12,

1925, p. 7; *San Francisco Chronicle*, May 23, 1925, p. 17; *San Francisco Examiner*, January 6, 1926, p. 3; *San Francisco Chronicle*, July 10, 1929, p. 1; October 26, 1929, p. 1; and July 30, 1929, p. 3.

17. *San Francisco Chronicle*, January 7, 1926, p. 13; and October 26, 1929, p. 1; Dan Kurzman, *Left to Die: The Tragedy of the USS* Juneau (New York: Pocket Books, 1994), 7–8.

18. *San Francisco Chronicle*, March 23, 1930, pp. 1, 2; January 19, 1935, p. 1; and July 10, 1935, p. 15.

19. *New York Times*, July 12, 1921, p. 17; and July 11, 1921, p. 1.

20. *Chicago Tribune*, September 14, 1924, p. 1; and September 17, 1924, p. 2; *Tulsa Daily World*, September 17, 1924, p. 3.

21. Gloria Morgan Vanderbilt, with Palma Wayne, *Without Prejudice* (New York: E. P. Dutton, 1936), 80, 119; see also the Knickerbocker defense of Gloria at the time of the trial, *San Francisco Examiner*, October 15, 1934, p. 5.

22. The details are available in Barbara Goldsmith, *Little Gloria, Happy at Last* (New York: Knopf, 1980), 246–305; Vanderbilt, *Without Prejudice*; and Gloria (Morgan) Vanderbilt and Thelma Lady Furness, *Double Exposure: A Twin Autobiography* (New York: D. McKay, 1958). The younger Gloria told her story in Gloria Vanderbilt, *Black Knight, White Knight* (New York: Knopf, 1987), and *Once Upon A Time: A True Story* (New York: Knopf, 1985).

23. Gloria Vanderbilt, *Woman to Woman* (New York: Doubleday, 1979), 172. For Gertrude Whitney, see B. H. Friedman, *Gertrude Vanderbilt Whitney* (New York: Doubleday, 1978).

24. For Gloria's difficulty getting to see her daughter, see, for example, *New York World Telegram*, October 23, 1934, p. 17.

25. For testimony about immoral influences, see, for example, *New York Times*, October 3, 1934, p. 22; and October 4, 1934, p. 24; *New York World Telegram*, October 2, 1934, p. 1. For the testimony of Gloria's mother and her daughter, see *New York Times*, September 29, 1934, p. 34; October 10, 1934, p. 4; and December 19, 1934, p. 1; *New York World Telegram*, September 28, 1934, p. 1. For burden of proof of Gloria's unfitness as a mother, see *New York Times*, October 20, 1934, p. 16. For the court ruling, *New York Times*, November 22, 1934, pp. 1, 6. Gloria's quote is from Vanderbilt, *Without Prejudice*, 291.

26. *New York Times,* November 23, 1934, p. 1. For the mother's petition, see *New York Times*, November 10, 1934, p. 3; *New York World Telegram*, November 9, 1934, p. 3. For Seelye's article, *New York World Telegram*, November 17, 1934, p. 6. For kidnap threats, *New York Times*, November 24, 1934, p. 1; for Gloria's kidnap fears, Goldsmith, *Little Gloria*, x–xiii, 140–41, 194–202, 268–69.

27. *New York Times*, November 22, 1934, pp. 1, 6.

28. For side-by-side reports, see, for example, *New York World Telegram,* October

2, 1934, p. 1; Goldsmith, *Little Gloria*, x; Vanderbilt, *Without Prejudice*, chapter 4.

29. *USA Today*, 112 (July 15, 1983), 4d. For the language of epidemic, see, for example, *U.S. News and World Report*, 87 (September 3, 1979), 57; Bruce W. Most, "The Child Stealing Epidemic," *Nation*, 224 (May 7, 1977), 559. For the Mellon case, see *Newsweek*, 87 (March 29, 1976), 30; *New York Times,* March 20, 1976, p. A1; March 21, 1976, p. A24; March 22, 1976, p. 42; and March 24, 1976, p. A40; *Wall Street Journal*, March 24, 1976, p. 1.

30. Sanford N. Katz, *Child Snatching: The Legal Response to the Abduction of Children*, Section of Family Law (American Bar Association Press, 1981), 3, 11–12.

31. Katz, *Child Snatching*, 15.

32. David Finkelhor, Gerald Hotaling, and Andrea Sedlak, *Missing, Abducted, Runaway, and Thrownaway Children in America: First Report: Numbers and Characteristics National Incidence Studies, Executive Summary*, U.S. Department of Justice, Office of Juvenile Justice and Delinquency Prevention (Washington, D.C., 1990), 40; Katz, *Child Snatching*, 123.

33. United States Department of State, Bureau of Consular Affairs, *International Parental Abduction*, 3d ed. (Washington, D.C., 1989), 21. See also *National Law Journal*, 12 (October 9, 1989), 3, 34.

34. The *Denver Post* featured a scathing analysis of the numbers and the hype, see Louis Kitzer and Diana Griego, "The Truth About Missing Kids," *Sunday Denver Post*, May 12, 1985, pp. 1A, 13A; the follow-up, *Denver Post*, May 13, 1985, pp. 1A, 10A; and the editorial, *Denver Post*, May 19, 1985, p. 6H. Probably the most influential social science critique is Joel Best, *Threatened Children: Rhetoric and Concern about Child Victims* (Chicago: University of Chicago Press, 1990).

35. "Child Custody Disputes and Parental Kidnapping: A Conference Report," *Children Today*, 12 (January–February 1983), 32–33. For an excellent discussion of how issues of this kind are created and disseminated, see Cynthia Gentry, "The Social Construction of Abducted Children as a Social Problem," *Sociological Inquiry*, 58 (1988), 413–25.

36. Mason, *From Father's Property to Children's Rights*, 130; U.S. Department of Justice, Office of Juvenile Justice and Delinquency Prevention, U.S. Attorney General's Advisory Board on Missing Children, *Missing and Exploited Children: The Challenge Continues* (Washington, D.C., 1988), 42.

37. *Missing and Exploited Children*, 49.

38. It was ironic that one mother received information about and eventually found her child when her abducting husband appeared on the *Donahue* show on child snatching. When Donahue refused to disclose vital information about her husband, she sued and won a $5.9 million court settlement; see *Newsweek*, 101 (May 30, 1983), 101.

39. Sally Abrahms and Joseph N. Bell, "Have You Seen These Children? Child

Snatching: The Cruelest Crime," *Ladies' Home Journal*, 98 (April 1981), 77; Abrahms and Bell, *Children in the Crossfire: The Tragedy of Parental Kidnapping* (New York: Atheneum, 1983). For the Cain tragedy, see *Newsweek*, 88 (October 18, 1976), 24.

According to the *Oklahoman and Times*, Steven Cain was granted temporary custody of his son in 1976, when his wife, who had previously been granted custody at the time of the divorce in 1973, fled to avoid a bench warrant. Steven brought three others with him to gain possession of his son, while the mother and her brother used guns as they chased Steven, Cody, and the others. For the story, see *Oklahoman and Times*, July 24, 1976, p. 1; July 25, 1976, pp. 1, 2; July 26, 1976, p. 6; and July 27, 1976, p. 18.

40. Eileen Crowley, as told to Karen Freifeld, "I Found My Kidnapped Daughter," *Good Housekeeping*, 197 (August 1983), 117, 180, 182. See also "I Always Knew You'd Find Me, Mom," *Ladies' Home Journal*, 98 (August 1981), 86–87, 151–52.

41. Bonnie Black, *Somewhere Child* (New York: Viking, 1981); Anna Demeter, *Legal Kidnapping: What Happens to a Family When the Father Kidnaps Two Children* (Boston: Beacon, 1977); Thomas Froncek, *Take Away One* (New York: St. Martin's Press, 1985); Joy Fielding, *Kiss Mommy Goodbye* (New York: New American Library, 1981).

42. Lindsy Van Gelder, "Beyond Custody: When Parents Steal Their Own Children," *Ms.*, 5 (May 1978), 52, 94 (emphasis in original); Adrienne Rich, introduction to Demeter, *Legal Kidnapping*, xiv–xv.

43. Margaret Strickland, "Child Snatched: The Danny Strickland Case," in *How to Deal With a Parental Kidnapping*, compiled by Margaret Strickland (Moorehaven, Fla.: Rainbow Books, 1983, originally published 1979), 188, 192.

44. Strickland, *Child Snatched*, 193, 194–95.

45. Strickland, *Child Snatched*, 202–3, 204, 207.

46. Strickland, *Child Snatched*, 210.

47. Strickland, *Child Snatched*, 212 (emphasis in original).

48. Strickland, *Child Snatched*, 224.

49. Strickland, *Child Snatched*, 232–33, 234.

50. Strickland, *Child Snatched*, 237, 248.

51. Strickland, *Child Snatched*, 187, 250, 248–49.

52. *Sunday Denver Post*, May 13, 1985, p. A1. For other studies that question the statistics and the exaggerated alarm, see Best, *Threatened Children*; and Martin L. Forst and Martha-Elin Blomquist, *Missing Children: Rhetoric and Reality* (New York: Lexington Books, 1991).

53. Finkelhor, Hotaling, and Sedlak, *Missing, Abducted, Runaway, and Thrownaway Children in America, Executive Summary*, 5.

54. David Finkelhor, Gerald Hotaling, and Andrea Sedlak, *Missing, Abducted, Runaway, and Thrownaway Children in America, First Report: Number and Characteristics National Incidence Studies* (Washington, D.C.: U.S. Department of Justice; Of-

fice of Justice Programs; Juvenile Justice and Delinquency Prevention, 1990), 45; Finkelhor, Hotaling, and Sedlak, *Missing, Abducted, Runaway, and Thrownaway Children in America, Executive Summary,* 6.

55. Finkelhor, Hotaling, and Sedlak, *Missing, Abducted, Runaway, and Thrownaway Children in America, Executive Summary,* 6.

56. Ernie Allen, "The Crisis of Family Abductions in America," *FBI Law Enforcement Bulletin,* 61 (August 1992), 18–19; Finkelhor, Hotaling, and Sedlak, *Missing, Abducted, Runaway, and Thrownaway Children in America, Executive Summary,* 8; Ernie Allen, "The Kid Is with a Parent, How Bad Can it Be?" National Center for Missing and Exploited Children (n.p., n.d.), 2–3.

57. For clinical studies, Diane H. Sehetky and Lee H. Haller, "Child Psychiatry and Law: Parental Kidnapping," *Journal of the American Academy of Child Psychiatry,* 22 (1983), 279–85; Neil Senior, Toba Gladstone, and Barry Nurcombe, "Child Snatching: A Case Report," *Journal of the American Academy of Child Psychiatry,* 21 (1982), 578–83. Finkelhor, Hotaling, and Sedlak, *Missing, Abducted, Runaway, and Thrownaway Children in America, First Report,* 60.

58. Geoffrey L. Greif and Rebecca L. Hegar, *When Parents Kidnap: The Families Behind the Headlines* (New York: Free Press, 1993), vii, 34, 32, and passim.

59. Greif and Hegar, *When Parents Kidnap,* 179–95; United States Department of State, Bureau of Consular Affairs, *International Parental Abduction,* 3d ed., (Washington, D.C., 1989); and "Child Custody Unit Helps Parents Keep Track," *U.S. Department of State, Dispatch,* 2 (January 21, 1991), 49; *San Francisco Chronicle,* October 11, 1996, p. 11.

60. *New York Times,* September 5, 1994, p. 1; *Los Angeles Times,* November 13, 1994, p. A1. For the Feeneys, see *Newsweek,* 118 (July 8, 1993), 31; *New York Times,* September 5, 1994, p. 1; *Los Angeles Times,* November 13, 1994, pp. A1, A30; "The Search for Lauren," *Readers' Digest,* 135 (August 1987), 77–84. The movie, *Desperate Rescue: The Cathy Mahone Story,* was first broadcast on NBC on January 28, 1993, and starred Mariel Hemingway.

61. *The Elizabeth Morgan Story* was aired on ABC, November 29, 1992. For Paula Oldham, see *New York Times,* December 10, 1994, p. 15; *SF Weekly,* 13 (June 22, 1994), 7. For a very sympathetic portrayal of Oldham see, the appropriately titled "Kidnap or Rescue?" *SF Weekly,* 13 (April 6, 1994), 11–14.

62. Tom Junod, "The Last Angry Woman," *Life* 14 (April 1991), 65.

63. *New York Times,* April 27, 1992, p. A1; and May 16, 1992, p. A6; *Atlanta Constitution,* May 16, 1992, p. B5; *New York Times,* April 27, 1992, p. B10 (my emphasis). See also *New York Times,* May 15, 1992, p. A14; *National Law Journal,* 14 (May 11, 1992), 8. The *Law and Order* segment was aired on NBC, January 6, 1993.

64. "Position Statement of the National Center for Missing and Exploited Children on the 'Underground Railroad'," (n.p., n.d.) (boldface in original).

CHAPTER SIX

1. Stephen E. Steidel, ed., *Missing and Abducted Children: A Law Enforcement Guide* (Arlington, Va.: National Center for Missing and Exploited Children, 1994), 27.

2. Patty Wetterling, in *New York Times*, October 30, 1989, p. A10.

3. *New York Times,* May 30, 1979, p. B3.

4. Phyllis Battelle, "Help Find Etan Patz," *Good Housekeeping*, 190 (February 1980), 66.

5. Battelle, "Help Find Etan Patz," 68.

6. Mary Cantwell, "The Long Year of the Patz Family," *New York Times Magazine* (June 8, 1980), 117; Battelle, "Help Find Etan Patz," 71; Richard K. Rein, "A Little Boy Vanishes, Leading to a Book, A Movie and a Family's Four Years of Pain," *People*, 19 (April 4, 1983), 80.

The fact that some parents murder their own children while claiming that they were kidnapped has recently been brought to sensational attention in the case of Susan Smith in Union, South Carolina; see *New York Times*, November 6, 1994, pp. 1, 12. For another similar case, see *New York Times*, April 12, 1995, p. A16. A much earlier case with a similar theme was that of Eleanor Ruotolo, see *Newsweek*, 48 (September 17, 1956), 37–38. In the most recent Justice Department manual on child abduction, local police departments are urged to quickly ask parents to submit to a lie detector test; see *Los Angeles Times*, November 7, 1994, pp. A1, 10.

7. *New York Times*, June 25, 1979, p. B5; and October 9, 1979, p. B1.

Among the best statistics available are those concerning infant abductions. According to NCMEC, the total number of infant abductions between 1983 and 1995 was 146. Of these, 87 were taken from health-care facilities. The NCMEC has excellent and exact figures for when and from where in the hospital these abductions occur. See Memorandum, Updated March 27, 1995, from John B. Rabun, Re Newborn/Infant Abduction; and Memorandum, March 22, 1995, from Cathy Nahirny, Subject: Infant Abductions from Health Care Facilities, all at the NCMEC. See also National Center for Missing and Exploited Children publication, "For Health Care Professionals: Guidelines in Preventing Infant Abductions" (n.p., June 1993).

8. *New York Times*, May 22, 1981, p. B2; and June 8, 1980, p. 18.

For the Hearst case, see Patricia Campbell Hearst with Alvin Moscow, *Every Secret Thing* (Garden City, N.Y.: Doubleday, 1982). For ransom cases immediately after Hearst, see Thomas Plate, "Kidnapping: The Growing Threat," *Good Housekeeping*, 181 (November, 1975), 60, 62, 64, 66, 70, 72, 74, 77. For the Getty case, see *New York Times*, December 16, 1973, p. A19. For kidnapping in Italy in the 1970s, see *New York Times*, December 17, 1973, pp. A1, A18.

9. *New York Times*, May 2, 1980, p. B1; May 31, 1979, p. B3; May 30, 1979, p. B3; and May 31, 1979, p. B3.

10. *New York Times*, October 9, 1979, p. B1; May 28, 1979, p. B1; and June 1, 1979,

p. B3; Battelle, "Help Find Etan Patz," 68; *New York Times*, June 11, 1979, p. B6; June 16, 1979, p. A19; and June 25, 1979, p. A1.

11. *New York Times*, May 20, 1980, p. B1; and July 26, 1979, p. B1; Rein, "A Little Boy Vanishes," 80; Edward Klein, "The Long Search for Etan Patz," *Vanity Fair*, 54 (June 1991), 137; *New York Times*, July 26, 1979, p. B1.

12. *New York Times*, May 8, 1980, p. B4; Richard K. Rein, "Five Families Recount the Horror All Parents Fear—A Child Who Vanishes," *People*, 66 (October 5, 1981), 31; Cantwell, "The Long Year of the Patz Family," 119.

13. Cantwell, "The Long Year of the Patz Family," 118; *New York Times*, December 28, 1982, p. A23.

14. *New York Times*, October 25, 1979, p. B5; May 2, 1980, p. B1; and May 18, 1982, p. 3. Rein, "Five Families Recount the Horror All Parents Fear," 30; *New York Times*, May 20, 1985, p. B1; and May 25, 1985, p. B3. For National Missing Children Day, Ronald Reagan, "National Children Day, 1983," Proclamation By the President of the United States of America, May 25, 1983. A facsimile copy is available at the National Center for Missing and Exploited Children, Arlington, Va.

15. *New York Times*, October 22, 1979, p. B1; and May 2, 1980, p. B1; *Los Angeles Times*, September 22, 1989, pp. V 1, 10, 11 (discusses the case after Stayner's death in a motorcycle accident).

16. Cantwell, "The Long Year of the Patz Family," passim.

17. Beth Gutcheon, *Still Missing* (New York: G. P. Putnam, 1981); Rein, "A Little Boy Vanishes," 76; *New York Times*, July 26, 1982, p. A13; and about the film, February 7, 1983, p. C13. For the NAMBLA connection, *New York Times*, December 22, 1982, p. B3; December 23, 1982, p. B3; December 28, 1982, p. A23; December 29, 1982, p. B3; and December 30, 1982, p. B2. For the new police attention to the case, see *New York Times*, December 28, 1982, p. B1.

18. *New York Times*, January 4, 1983, p. C1; January 4, 1983, p. C2. For Ramos, see Klein, "The Long Search for Etan Patz," *New York Times*, November 4, 1989, p. 30; August 17, 1990, p. B3; August 18, 1990, p. 29; August 31, 1990, p. B2; October 20, 1990, p. 27; November 30, 1990, p. B3.

19. For the Patzes' reluctance to stay in the limelight of publicity, see Klein, "The Long Search for Etan Patz," 140, 141.

20. *Tammy and the Bachelor*, directed by Joseph Pevney, 1957; *Gigi*, directed by Vincente Minnelli, 1958; *Splendor in the Grass*, directed by Elia Kazan, 1961; *Baby Doll*, directed by Elia Kazan, 1956. *Lolita* was first published in 1955 but was not available in the United States until 1958 (New York: Putnam, 1958). The movie was directed by Stanley Kubrick and released in 1962.

21. J. Paul de River, *The Sexual Criminal: A Psychoanalytic Study* (Springfield, Ill.: Charles C. Thomas, 1949). Alfred C. Kinsey et al., *Sexual Behavior in the Human Female* (New York: Pocket Edition, 1970; originally published, 1953), 116–22.

22. Karl M. Bowman and Bernice Engle, "Review of Scientific Literature on Sex-

ual Deviation," *California Sexual Deviation Research* (January 1953), 105; Sheldon Glueck, "Sex Crimes and the Law," *Nation*, 145 (September 25, 1937), 318; Edwin H. Sutherland, "The Diffusion of Sexual Psychopath Laws," *American Journal of Sociology*, 56 (September 1950), 143. See also "The Sex Rampage," *Newsweek*, 35 (February 13, 1950), 22; A. R. Mangus, "Sex Crimes in California," *California Sexual Deviation Research* (January 1953), 9–22; Estelle B. Freedman, "'Uncontrolled Desires': The Response to the Sexual Psychopath, 1920–1960," *Journal of American History*, 74 (June 1987), 83–106. *M* was directed by Fritz Lang, 1931.

23. J. Edgar Hoover, "How Safe is Your Youngster?" *American Magazine*, 159 (March 1955), 9, 99–103; Edith M. Stern, "The Facts On Sex Offenses," *Parents Magazine*, 29 (October 1954), 43, 140.

24. Bowman and Engle, "Review of the Scientific Literature," 116, 121. For an excellent review of the literature, see J. W. Mohr, R. E. Turner, and M. B. Jerry, *Pedophilia and Exhibitionism: A Handbook* (Toronto: University of Toronto Press, 1964).

25. Bowman and Engle, "Review of the Scientific Literature," 121.

26. A. R. Mangus, "Part A. Sex Crimes in San Francisco," *California Sexual Deviation Research* (March 1952), 51. These conclusions had been anticipated in the pioneer psychoanalytic research of Laurette Bender and Abram Blau, "The Reaction of Children to Sexual Relations with Adults," *American Journal of Orthopsychiatry*, 7 (1937), 500–518.

27. Mangus, "Sex Crimes in San Francisco," 50; "The Sex Rampage," 22.

28. Judson T. Landis, "Experiences of 500 Children with Adult Sexual Deviation," *Psychiatric Quarterly Supplement*, 30 (1956), 107.

29. Patricia Y. Miller, *Blaming the Victim of Child Molestation: An Empirical Analysis* (Ph.D. diss., sociology, Northwestern University, 1976), 142. For an example of the expression of outrage at the extent to which children were abused in America, see Vincent de Francis, *Protecting the Child Victim of Sex Crimes Committed by Adults* (Denver: American Humane Association, 1969). De Francis was a pioneer in this area.

30. For an early example of the new attention to sexual molestation as a widespread social problem, see Susan Sgroi, "Sexual Molestation of Children: The Last Frontier," *Children Today*, 4 (May-June 1975), 18–21, 44.

31. De River, *The Sexual Criminal*, 75–86; A. Nicholas Groth, "Patterns of Sexual Assault against Children and Adolescents," in *Sexual Assault of Children and Adolescents*, ed. Ann Wolbert Burgess et al. (Lexington, Mass.: Lexington Books, 1978), 14. Indeed the Groth work as a whole gives a sense of a new direction in the research, a direction that is also clear earlier in Murray L. Cohen and Richard J. Boucher, "Misunderstandings About Sex Criminals," *Sexual Behavior*, 2 (1972), 56–62.

32. Sgroi, "Sexual Molestation of Children," 19. For the importance of these laws, see the valuable discussion in Vern L. Bullough, "History of Adult Human Sexual Behavior with Children and Adolescents in Western Societies," in Jay R. Feierman,

ed., *Pedophilia: Biosocial Dimensions* (New York: Springer-Verlag, 1990), 79–82.

33. For the Atlanta murders, see *Newsweek*, 97 (March 23, 1981), 18–19; *Time*, 119 (January 18, 1982), 25. For an earlier serial killing in Houston, see Arthur Bell, "The Fate of the Boys Next Door," *Esquire*, 81 (March, 1974), 96–99, 174, 176. The Houston youths were still viewed as runaways and the parents were seen as, at least partly, responsible.

34. David Finkelhor, *Sexually Victimized Children* (New York: Free Press, 1979), 53–54, 131, 147.

35. Miller, *Blaming the Victim of Child Molestation*, 31; Finkelhor, *Sexually Victimized Children,* 13.

36. Ann W. Burgess, "Overview of Child Sexual Abuse," in *Children Traumatized in Sex Rings* (Arlington, Va.: National Center for Missing and Exploited Children, n.d.), 1–2; David Finkelhor, *Child Sexual Abuse: New Theory and Research* (New York: Free Press, 1984), 3, 8. For Russell's research, see Diana E. H. Russell, *Sexual Exploitation: Rape, Child Sexual Abuse and Workplace Harassment* (Beverly Hills: Sage Publications, 1984). Excellent examples of the response to the perceived inflation of advocacy statistics are Joel Best, *Threatened Children: Rhetoric and Concern About Child Victims* (Chicago: University of Chicago Press, 1990); and Neil Gilbert, "Miscounting Social Ills," *Society,* 31 (March/April 1994), 18–26.

37. This relationship between taboo and titillation can be gleaned from Mary Douglas, *Purity and Danger: An Analysis of the Concepts of Pollution and Taboo* (London: Ark Paperbacks, 1989); and Paul Ricoeur, *The Symbolism of Evil* (Boston: Beacon, 1967).

38. Kenneth V. Lanning, *Child Molesters: A Behavioral Analysis* (Arlington, Va.: National Center for Missing and Exploited Children, in cooperation with the FBI, 1992), 6–7. For an example of the earlier, much more benign perspective on the child molester, see Charles H. McCaghy, "Child Molesters: A Study of Their Careers As Deviants," in *Criminal Behavior System: A Typology*, ed. Marshall B. Cunard and Richard Quinney (New York: Holt, Rinehart & Winston, 1967), 75–88. An intermediate position can be found in Cohen and Boucher, "Misunderstandings About Sex Criminals."

For new sexual psychopath laws, see *New York Times*, February 27, 1995, p. 1. For growing public concern about disclosure to local communities, see *New York Times*, March 27, 1994, p. E4; and August 6, 1994, p. A11; *San Francisco Examiner*, March 6, 1994, p. A14. The issue has become extremely prominent in the past two years.

For examples of haunting public fear of sex molesters in the 1990s, see, for example, *New York Times*, January 19, 1992, pp. A1, 15; *New York Times Magazine* (November 2, 1993), 44, 56; Ross M. Nelson, with Ruth Miller Fitzgibbons, "Why I'm Every Mother's Worst Fear," *Redbook* (April 1992), 85–87, 116; Margery D. Rosen, "'Don't Talk to Strangers,'" *Ladies' Home Journal*, 111 (August 1994), 108–9, 153–54. In California, the problem of child molestation was brought to prominent attention when, in open court, Ellie Nesler killed the man who had sexually abused her son.

The case garnered national attention (*San Francisco Chronicle*, April 5, 1993, p. A11).

39. "Stolen Children," *Newsweek*, 103 (March 19, 1984), 78–81, 85–86. The police perspective on Kevin's disappearance was made clear to me by David Collins in an interview on April 27, 1995.

40. David Collins, interview; *San Francisco Examiner,* February 15, 1984, p. A1; *San Francisco Chronicle,* February 14, 1984, p. 4; *San Francisco Examiner,* February 16, 1984, p. B1.

41. *San Francisco Examiner*, February 15, 1984, p. A4; and February 16, 1984, p. B1.

42. "Stolen Children," *Newsweek*, 79; *San Francisco Chronicle*, February 18, 1984, p. 5; *San Francisco Sunday Examiner and Chronicle*, February 19, 1984, p. A1; Collins interview.

43. *San Francisco Examiner*, February 16, 1984, p. B1; and February 20, 1984, p. B7.

44. *San Francisco Examiner*, February 21, 1984, p. 5; *San Francisco Sunday Examiner and Chronicle*, February 26, 1984, p. B1; *San Francisco Examiner*, February 21, 1984, p. B5. For Collins's and Deasy's developing skills in organizing the search, see *San Francisco Examiner*, February 19, 1984, p. A1; February 17, 1984, p. B11; and February 20, 1984, p. B7; *San Francisco Chronicle*, February 20, 1984, p. A4.

45. *San Francisco Sunday Examiner and Chronicle*, February 26, 1984, pp. B1, 2; and March 18, 1984, p. B1.

46. *San Francisco Sunday Examiner and Chronicle*, February 26, 1984, p. B2.

47. *San Francisco Chronicle,* March 13, 1984, p. 1. For a novel in which the ultimate disguise is used on a kidnapped child (her skin is tinted to make her appear African American), see Thomas M. Disch and John Sladek, *Black Alice* (New York: Carroll & Graf, 1968).

48. *New York Times*, February 7, 1988, p. 33. For Walsh's role in congressional testimony and the significance of the broadcast of *Adam*, see Martin L. Forst and Martha-Elin Blomquist, *Missing Children: Rhetoric and Reality* (New York: Lexington Books, 1991), 65–67, 86, 94–95, 101, and passim.

49. In his interview with me, David Collins made clear his views on the inadequacy of the local police.

50. *San Francisco Examiner*, March 25, 1984, p. B8. A good example of the tendency for aggrieved parents to become involved in larger issues of law and crime was the initial involvement of Polly Klaas's father, Marc, in the three-strikes-you're-out initiative in California. Marc Klaas eventually changed his mind about the law but has remained in the public eye, lobbying for legislation; see *San Francisco Chronicle*, February 5, 1994, p. A17.

51. All quotations are from literature provided by the Kevin Collins Foundation for Missing Children, and the information has been supplied to me by David Collins in an interview. For the foundation, see *San Francisco Chronicle*, January 2, 1992, p. C3. Soon after our talk the foundation closed for lack of funds; *San Francisco Chronicle*, April 2, 1996, p. A11.

Polly Klaas's kidnapping received extensive local and national attention. For the initial disappearance, see *San Francisco Sunday Examiner and Chronicle*, October 3, 1993, pp. A1, 14. For a sense of the extraordinary national resonance the case created, see Noelle Oxenhandler, "Polly's Face," *The New Yorker,* 69 (November 29, 1993), 94–96. For the confession, see *San Francisco Chronicle*, April 24, 1996, p. A1.

52. *Los Angeles Times*, January 10, 1994, pp. E1, 2.

53. Steidel, *Missing and Abducted Children,* viii; interview with Julia Caughey Cartwright at the NCMEC, March 28, 1995.

54. Steidel, *Missing and Abducted Children*, viii; interviews with Horace J. Heafner and Ben J. Ermani at NCMEC, March 28, 1995; *Los Angeles Times*, February 26, 1989, pp. I3, 26.

55. Burgess, *Children Traumatized in Sex Rings*; Lanning, *Child Molesters;* Daniel D. Broughton and Ernest E. Allen, *A Lesson for Life: An Examination of the Accuracy and Adequacy of Traditional Child Protection Messages* (Arlington, Va.: National Center for Missing and Exploited Children, 1992). Lanning, *Child Molesters*, v, 9, 11.

56. National Center for Missing and Exploited Children, list of approved non-profit organizations, dated April 1995; Steidel, *Missing and Abducted Children*, 57; an example of reference to NCMEC information, see *Minneapolis Star Tribune*, October 25, 1989, p. 18A.

57. Interview with Barbara Johnson, National Center for Missing and Exploited Children, March 28, 1995.

58. Steidel, *Missing and Abducted Children*, 9; David Finkelhor, Gerald Hotaling, and Andrea Sedlak, *Missing, Abducted, Runaway, and Thrownaway Children in America: First Report: Numbers and Characteristics National Incidence Studies* (Washington, D.C.: U.S. Department of Justice, Office of Juvenile Justice and Prevention, 1990); and David Finkelhor, Gerald Hotaling, and Andrea Sedlak, *Missing, Abducted, Runaway, and Thrownaway Children in America: First Report: Numbers and Characteristics National Incidence Studies, Executive Summary* (Washington, D.C.: U.S. Department of Justice, Office of Juvenile Justice and Prevention, 1990).

59. Finkelhor, Hotaling, and Sedlak, *Executive Summary*, 8; Finkelhor, Hotaling, and Sedlak, *First Report,* 66 (my emphasis).

60. Finkelhor, Hotaling, and Sedlak, *Executive Summary*, 8.

61. Kevin Collins Foundation for Missing Children, "The Fight Goes On," 3; interview with David Collins. For examples of how NISMART has been used by the popular media, see Stephanie Maier and M. C. Blakeman, "Protect Your Child From Abduction," *Consumer's Research*, 77 (February 1994), 33–37; "Robbing the Innocents," *Time*, 142 (December 27, 1993), 31–32.

62. Ernie Allen, "Missing Children: A Fearful Epidemic," *USA Today*, 123 (July 1994), 46–48; the articles in the *Denver Post* appeared on May 12, 1985, pp. 1A, 12A, 13A, 1G; and May 13, 1985, pp. 1A, 10A. The *Denver Post* also had an editorial on the

subject on May 19, 1985, p. 6H. For Sara Wood, *New York Times*, November 11, 1993, p. B9; January 12, 1994, p. B12; and June 21, 1994, p. B6.

63. For the first kidnap insurance, see *New York Times*, September 25, 1920, p. 2. For the new venture, see *San Francisco Chronicle*, April 19, 1995, p. A20; and May 5, 1995, p. A1.

64. *San Francisco Chronicle*, May 5, 1995, p. A1. For other criticisms, see *Boston Globe*, May 13, 1995, pp. A1, 8.

65. *Minneapolis Star Tribune*, October 28, 1989, p. 18A; and October 24, 1989, p. 1A; Patty Wetterling, "Have You Seen My Son?" *Ladies' Home Journal*, 107 (March 1990), 28.

66. *Minneapolis Star Tribune*, October 25, 1989, p. 1A; and October 26, 1989, p. 4B; interview with David Collins.

67. *Minneapolis Star Tribune*, October 24, 1989, p. 8A; Lanning, *Child Molesters*, 18.

68. Wetterling, "Have You Seen My Son?" 22.

69. *Minneapolis Star Tribune*, October 27, 1989, p. 8B; and October 29, 1989, pp. 1, 7B; Wetterling, "Have You Seen My Son?" 32.

70. *Minneapolis Star Tribune*, October 30, 1989, p. 1B; November 1, 1989, p. 1A; and November 7, 1989, pp. 1A, 10A.

71. *Minneapolis Star Tribune*, November 3, 1989, p. 14A; and November 1, 1989, p. 4B.

72. *Minneapolis Star Tribune*, November 5, 1989, p. 5B; and November 16, 1989, p. 26A.

73. *Minneapolis Star Tribune*, January 1, 1989, p. 4B; November 4, 1989, pp. 1A, 11A; and November 6, 1989, p. 1B.

74. The case very quickly appeared on television, first on *A Current Affair* and shortly afterward on *Geraldo*; see *Minneapolis Star Tribune*, October 27, 1989, p. 8B; and November 17, 1989, p. 2B. It was also featured in *People*, 32 (November 20, 1989), 62–65.

75. *Minneapolis Star Tribune*, November 19, 1989, p. 14A; October 14, 1990, pp. 1A, 7A; February 17, 1990, pp. 1A, 12A; and November 24, 1989, p. 2B; Wetterling, "Have You Seen My Son?" 32. The quotes are from November 4, 1989, p. 10B; and February 17, 1990, p. 12A.

76. *Minneapolis Star Tribune*, December 23, 1989, pp. 1A, 12A; December 26, 1989, p. 3Bw; and October 14, 1990, p. 1A.

77. Lanning, *Child Molesters*, 7; Gerald Hotaling and David Finkelhor, "Estimating the Number of Stranger-Abduction Homicides of Children: A Review of Available Evidence," *Journal of Criminal Justice*, 18 (1990), 392. Of 146 infants stolen between 1983 and 1995, only 9 are still missing; see Memorandum, March 27, 1995, from John R. Rabun, In re "Newborn/Infant Abductions," NCMEC, *Minneapolis Star Tribune*, October 14, 1990, p. 7A.

78. *Minneapolis Star Tribune*, October 23, 1992, p. 1B.

79. Steidel, *Missing and Abducted Children*, 7.

CONCLUSION

1. Ernie Allen, "Missing Children: A Fearful Epidemic," *USA Today*, 123 (July 1994), 47; "The Reel Thing," *San Francisco Examiner Magazine*, (March 6, 1994), p. 20; *New York Times*, May 16, 1994, p. A7.

INDEX